# WITHDRAWN
## UTSA LIBRARIES

RENEWALS 458-4574

# FAMILY
# ASSESSMENT

WILEY SERIES IN COUPLES AND FAMILY
DYNAMICS AND TREATMENT
Florence W. Kaslow, Series Editor

Handbook of Relational Diagnosis and Dysfunctional Family Patterns
*Florence W. Kaslow, Editor*

Treating the Changing Family: Handling Normative and Unusual Events
*Michele Harway, Editor*

In-Laws: A Guide to Extended-Family Therapy
*by Gloria Call Horsley*

Strange Attractors: Chaos, Complexity, and the Art of Family Therapy
*by Michael R. Bütz, Linda L. Chamberlain, and William G. McCown*

Child-Centered Family Therapy
*by Lucille L. Andreozzi*

Infertility: Psychological Issues and Counseling Strategies
*Sandra R. Leiblum, Editor*

The Self in the Family: A Classification of Personality, Criminality,
and Psychopathology
*by Luciano L'Abate (with the collaboration of Margaret S. Baggett)*

Painful Partings: Divorce and Its Aftermath
*by Lita Linzer Schwartz and Florence W. Kaslow*

Relationship Enhancement Family Therapy
*by Barry G. Ginsberg*

Ethical and Legal Issues in Professional Practice with Families
*by Diane T. Marsh and Richard D. Magee*

The Art of the Question: A Guide to Short-Term Question-Centered Therapy
*by Marilee C. Goldberg*

Family Assessment: Effective Uses of Personality Tests with Couples
and Families
*A. Rodney Nurse, Editor*

# FAMILY
# ASSESSMENT

## Effective Uses of Personality Tests with Couples and Families

A. RODNEY NURSE

John Wiley & Sons, Inc.

New York • Chichester • Weinheim • Brisbane • Singapore • Toronto

University of Texas
at San Antonio

MCMI-III, MACI, and Millon are trademarks of Dicandrien, Inc. MMPI is a trademark of the Minnesota Multiphasic Personality Inventory, the University of Minnesota.

This book is printed on acid-free paper. ♾

Copyright © 1999 by John Wiley & Sons, Inc. All rights reserved.

Published simultaneously in Canada.

No part of this publication may be reproduced, stored in a retrieval system or transmitted in any form or by any means, electronic, mechanical, photocopying, recording, scanning or otherwise, except as permitted under Section 107 or 108 of the 1976 United States Copyright Act, without either the prior written permission of the Publisher, or authorization through payment of the appropriate per-copy fee to the Copyright Clearance Center, 222 Rosewood Drive, Danvers, MA 01923, (978) 750-8400, fax (978) 750-4744. Requests to the Publisher for permission should be addressed to the Permissions Department, John Wiley & Sons, Inc., 605 Third Avenue, New York, NY 10158-0012, (212) 850-6011, fax (212) 850-6008, E-Mail: PERMREQ@WILEY.COM.

This publication is designed to provide accurate and authoritative information in regard to the subject matter covered. It is sold with the understanding that the publisher is not engaged in rendering professional services. If legal, accounting, medical, psychological or any other expert assistance is required, the services of a competent professional person should be sought.

Designations used by companies to distinguish their products are often claimed as trademarks. In all instances where John Wiley & Sons, Inc. is aware of a claim, the product names appear in initial capital or all capital letters. Readers, however, should contact the appropriate companies for more complete information regarding trademarks and registration.

**Note about Photocopy Rights**

The publisher grants purchasers permission to reproduce handouts from this book for professional use with their clients.

*Library of Congress Cataloging-in-Publication Data:*

Nurse, A. Rodney.
    Family assessment: effective uses of personality tests with couples and families / by A. Rodney Nurse.
        p.      cm. — (Wiley series in couples and family dynamics and treatment)
    Includes bibliographical references and index.
    ISBN 0-471-15397-4 (cloth : alk. paper)
    1. Family assessment.   I. Title.   II. Series.
RC488.53.N87      1999
616.89′ 156—dc21                                    98-37415

**Library
University of Texas
at San Antonio**

In loving memory of my parents,
Helen Alexander Nurse and Weir Cecil Nurse.

# Series Preface

Our ability to form strong interpersonal bonds with romantic partners, children, parents, siblings, and other relations is one of the key characteristics that define our humanity. These coevolving relationships shape who we are, and what we become—they can be a source of great gratification, or tremendous pain. Yet, only in the mid-twentieth century did behavioral and social scientists really begin focusing on couples and family dynamics, and only in the past several decades have the theory and findings that emerged from those studies been used to develop effective therapeutic interventions for troubled couples and families.

We have made great progress in understanding the dynamics, structure, function, and interactional patterns of couples and families—and made tremendous strides in treatment. However, as we stand poised on the beginning of a new millennium, it seems quite clear that both intimate partnerships and family relationships are in a period of tremendous flux. Economic and sociopolitical factors are changing work patterns, parenting responsibilities, and relational dynamics. Modern medicine has helped lengthen the life span, giving rise to the need for transgenerational caretaking. Cohabitation, divorce, and remarriage are quite commonplace, and these social changes make it necessary for us to rethink and broaden our definition of what constitutes a family.

Thus, it is no longer enough simply to embrace the concept of the family as a system. To understand and effectively treat the evolving family, we must incorporate into our theoretical formulations, and therapeutic armamentarium, information derived from research and clinical practice on important emerging issues such as ethnicity, culture, religion, gender, sexual preference, family life cycle, socioeconomic status, education, physical and mental health, values, and belief systems.

The purpose of the Wiley Series in Couples and Family Dynamics and Treatment is to provide a forum for cutting-edge relational and family theory, practice, and research. Its scope is intended to be broad, diverse, and international. All books published in this series share a common mission: to reflect on the past, offer state-of-the-art information on the present, and speculate on, as well as attempt to shape, the future of the field.

FLORENCE W. KASLOW
*Florida Couples and Family Institute*
*Duke University*

# Preface

*F*amily Assessment is designed to help clinicians working with couples and families by demonstrating how to apply findings from traditional individual personality assessment instruments to contribute to the understanding of couple and family relationships and to form a solid base for developing therapeutic approaches. This book will also aid diagnosticians who want to predict couple and family behavior from individual assessments. While there have been many excellent books on family therapy and personality assessment, this is the first book dedicated solely to suggesting ways that the results from traditional individual personality assessments can inform couple and family therapy.

This book has had a long gestation period. Early in my career in counseling and clinical psychology I worked to polish my assessment skills. This was followed by training in the evolving field of family therapy. At that time, the fields of personality assessment and family therapy were so far apart that, while I remember having friends in one area *or* the other, I can recall none in both. By the early 1980s, my identity as a family psychologist had "morphed." At that time, Martin Kirschenbaum, founding president of the California Graduate School of Family Psychology, asked me to join with him to build a doctoral program in family clinical psychology. A primary faculty responsibility of mine was teaching psychological assessment to doctoral students. For the better part of a decade (even as I became dean, and subsequently president of the graduate school), I made time to develop ways for integrating assessment findings with family therapy.

I am appreciative of my students for our learning together as I brought in couple and family cases from my practice for analysis. I also warmly recall the impact of exciting, highly competent, family-oriented faculty members. Most important was Dr. Kirschenbaum who had workshop wizardry and endless creative thinking. I strongly value contributions of dissertation director/clinician Harry Overline, Ed.D. in particular, as well as the contact with Robert Green, Ph.D., Karen Sager, Ph.D. Karen Mashkin, Ph.D., and Felix Polk, Ph.D.

I wish to acknowledge my debt to Erna Olafson, Ph.D., Psy.D., originally a student, subsequently a psychological assistant for me, then a colleague. With her background in history and psychology, she served as a stimulus and joined in my early attempt to organize in writing what I was putting together from teaching, literature, and my own practice, adding important ideas and perspectives of her own. She subsequently left the San Francisco area and is now assistant professor of clinical psychiatry and pediatrics at Children's Hospital Medical Center and the University of Cincinnati School of Medicine. She is also on the Women's Studies faculty at the University of Cincinnati. I'm especially pleased that she was willing to contribute the chapter in this volume, titled "Using Testing When Family Violence and Child Abuse Are Issues," which is a landmark in summarizing the recent explosion of literature in violence and abuse.

Another contributed chapter in this volume, "The 16PF: Assessing Normal Personality Dimensions of Marital Partners," is by Carol Philpot, Psy.D. Dr. Philpot is a professor at the Dean School of Psychology, and director of Community Services, Florida Institute of Technology. She has been a valued colleague working in the American Psychological Association Division of Family Psychology. I am indebted to her for this chapter that fills a very special place due to her focus on the more normal dimensions within the couple relationship, a healthy contrast to the major space in this book devoted to identifying psychopathology and planning treatment.

The third contributor (and also my wife), jointly responsible for the chapter "The KFD: Clues to Family Relationships," is Peggy Thompson, Ph.D. Her dissertation was on the KFD, and I have learned from her about drawing interpretation. We have practiced family psychology together for about 25 years. We have embarked on a new journey, developing Collaborative Divorce, an interdisciplinary, non-adversarial, humane divorce process, for which she serves as director.

Without Peggy's love and support, and that of our children, Eric and Sonya, this book would never have been written. I deeply appreciate their patience while I wrote.

A special acknowledgment is due to Florence Kaslow, Ph.D., ABPP, Editor of this series, and international leader in family psychology. Her encouragement in writing and positive, supportive attitude, coupled with her high professional standards and concern for people, are very much appreciated. I was also fortunate to learn from her directly when she conducted workshops as visiting professor at the California Graduate School of Family Psychology.

I wish to thank Kelly Franklin, publisher, and Alex Mummery, editorial assistant, at John Wiley & Sons, and the staff at Publications Development Company for their help in producing this book. I more than welcome any contact or feedback regarding this book.

A. RODNEY NURSE, Ph.D., ABPP

P.O. Box 175, Orinda, CA 94563
Phone: (925) 254-3606
E-mail: drrnurse@AOL.COM

# Contents

# CONTENTS

## PART II

### INTEGRATED TEST USAGE WITH COUPLES AND FAMILIES

# CHAPTER 1

## Introduction and Overview

People seeking psychotherapeutic help frequently complain about difficulties with their couple/marital and family relationships. This crisis in relationships between men and women comes about in the wake of the changing roles of men and women during the past quarter of a century. That the divorce rate now reaches an estimated 50% reflects often problematic couple relationships (Schwartz & Kaslow, 1997, p. 87). The large number of divorces affects, of course, large numbers of children, perhaps 40% of children in the United States (Hodges, 1991, p. 1). Any procedure or process that can help us better understand troubled couples and families needs attention. This book is about empirically based psychological procedures—psychological tests—that can better inform dedicated professionals striving to serve the needs of these couples and families.

### The Development of Family Therapy and Family Psychology

In response, at least in part, to the evolving crisis of couple and family interrelationships, a new professional field has evolved, that of family therapy, with its systemic emphasis adopted from general systems theory (Goldenberg & Goldenberg, 1998). The development of family therapy has been spurred by the need to improve professional clinical assistance to those increasing numbers of dysfunctional couples and families who seek help as psychotherapy has become more mainstream.

As the upstart field of family therapy emerged from the 1960s, it constructed principles for intervention based on the primacy of the interpersonal and the family system. It was probably initially necessary for the establishment of the new field to push to an extreme the rejection of the importance of the individual as a prime therapeutic target. Instead, the focus was on intervening in the family system. This provided family therapy with the freedom to explore and establish the importance of the family system, as well as to discover the boundaries of the usefulness of the systemic family therapy approaches. The long-standing

1

therapeutic emphasis on the individual was not only downplayed, but sometimes shoved out of the picture entirely.

This systemic approach appeared to be in theoretical conflict with the central focus of traditional psychology, which, during its past century of development, had been that of the individual. Psychology in its applied activities had focused on the study of individual characteristics, including measurement of individual variables deemed clinically relevant for direct professional helping activities. As psychology grew and differentiated into applied specialties, the initial clinical specialty area that evolved became identified as clinical psychology, which defined itself consistently with reference to psychology's scientific base and its emphasis on seeking to understand the individual.

After World War II, clinical psychologists were a scientist-practitioners whose main contributions to mental health were testing and research, with secondary interest in psychotherapy (Korchin, 1975, p. 46). The focus of psychology remained on the individual well past mid–twentieth century. The emphasis of clinical psychology and its psychological testing continued there as well, even as psychotherapy became an increasingly attractive function for the psychologist.

Although seemingly quite separate from clinical psychology, as family therapy evolved it was increasingly informed not only by family-oriented clinical theory and more pinpointed clinical intervention strategies, but also by a body of emerging research findings on the family itself, as well as studies on the degree of effectiveness of therapeutic interventions with the family. Psychologists moved more into studying and treating of the family. Then, in the late 1970s a new subspecialty, family psychology, emerged (Kaslow, 1990; Philpot, 1994).

Family psychology overlaps the field of family therapy, coalescing with it in significant part, and at the same time extending beyond family therapy while drawing on roots in the scientific base of psychology. With the founding in 1984 of the Division of Family Psychology of the American Psychological Association, a new level of integration of clinically developed family therapy and research-based psychology became possible. The new specialty of family psychology working through the structure of the Division of Family Psychology established its own scientific journal and its professional diplomate for practitioners (now under the American Board of Professional Psychology), and began to more regularly utilize the insights and clinical approaches of family therapy within the mainstream of psychology's emphasis on research. This amalgamation resulted in enlarging understanding and furthering the development of a scientifically based practice designed to help families and couples.

As with many new movements, having gone to an extreme and sometimes all but ignoring the individual, with the solid acceptance of the importance of the family system, family therapy came to soften its rigid anti-intrapersonal stance. Models of therapy began to appear in the literature that attempted an integration of the intrapersonal with the family systems approach (e.g., Feldman, 1992; Nichols, 1987; Slipp, 1984; Wachtel & Wachtel, 1986). This integration was expanded by the development of family psychology to clearly include the ecosystemic along with the here and now of the interpersonal and the intergenerational aspects of family therapy (Mikesell, Lusterman, & McDaniel, 1995).

## Changes in Psychological Testing and Clinical Psychology

Meanwhile, psychological testing in clinical psychology, which by midcentury had been at the pinnacle of professional clinical status, was losing its luster and it status. In particular, studies of the Rorschach, a prime assessment instrument, appeared to demonstrate that it had no validity and should not be used by psychologists for that reason (e.g., Jensen, 1958). Simultaneously, psychotherapy with an increasing number of variants (e.g., psychodynamic, client-centered, behavioral) was becoming accepted as a major function of clinical psychology practice for the drastically increasing number of clinical psychologists trained through government-funded programs. This raised the status of psychologists to that of independent practitioners from "handmaidens of psychiatrists," a (gender-biased) term often used at the time. Testing took a second place to the glamour and status of psychotherapy.

By the decade of the 1990s, however, psychological testing had experienced a renaissance. This resurgence was spurred by research in testing of the past quarter of a century. John Exner had developed the Rorschach into an empirically based system featuring consistency of administration and scoring, which led to a significant reliability of scoring, together with an organized start on validity studies (Exner, 1991, 1993; Exner & Weiner, 1995). At the same time, research continued apace with the Minnesota Multiphasic Personality Inventory (MMPI), which resulted in a revised MMPI, the MMPI-2, with an adequate normative base, biased and out-of-date items eliminated, and additional scores developed (Butcher, Dahlstrom, Graham, Tellegen, & Kaemmer, 1989).

A new inventory, the Millon Clinical Multiaxial Inventory (MCMI), appeared on the clinical scene in 1977. In contrast with the empirically developed MMPI, the MCMI had a strong theoretical base in Theodore Millon's (1981, 1996) theory of personality disorders with its specific interpersonal implications. The MCMI provided an inventory that paralleled increasing theoretical developments in the area of personality disorder, including Millon's major contributions, and the increasingly precise revisions of the *Diagnostic and Statistical Manual of Mental Disorders (DSM)* of the American Psychiatric Association (1994). The MCMI is now in its third iteration, labeled MCMI-III (Millon, 1994a).

Special inventories for adolescents were devised, including, very importantly, the Millon Adolescent Personality Inventory (MAPI), which was superseded by the Millon Adolescent Clinical Inventory (MACI; Millon, 1993). Like the MCMI, these inventories emphasized the more enduring traits of personality. In response to the shortcomings of using the MMPI with adolescents, an MMPI just for adolescents was developed, the MMPI-A (Butcher et al., 1992).

Other clinical assessment methods became increasingly popular, such as the Kinetic Family Drawing (KFD; Burns & Kaufman, 1970, 1972), and syndrome-specific measures such as the Trauma Symptom Inventory (Briere, 1995). During these recent decades, psychologists have also created inventories focused primarily on normal dimensions of personality. Particularly prominent among these is the 16 Personality Factors Questionnaire (16 PF; Cattell, Cattell, & Cattell, 1993).

More recent child and adolescent measurement research has resulted in the publication of the Parent-Child Relationship Inventory (PCRI; Gerard, 1994). The Behavior Assessment System for Children (BASC), with its separate forms for children (8 and older), parents, and teachers, provides a basis for reasoning from various perceptual viewpoints about the personality and behavior of children (Reynolds & Kamphaus, 1992).

Still, despite the developments in psychological testing and the increasing receptivity of family therapy and family psychology to an integration of the inter- and intrapersonal, classical psychological testing has not been systematically, practically applied to the family therapy/family psychology fields. This book is designed to begin to address this deficiency.

## The Purpose and Scope of This Book

The assumption underlying the development of this book is that the effectiveness of therapeutic interventions for assisting couples and families can be enhanced by the use of timely, accurate clinical planning made possible by the easy availability of pinpointed descriptive material derived from psychological testing results, providing the testing outcomes are integrated into a family systems framework. Given the trends in family therapy and its move toward developing a more rigorous scientific base and taking account of both intrapersonal and interpersonal systemic aspects, and given psychology's movement toward the interpersonal in both theory and psychological testing, the time seems right for more integration of psychological testing usage with everyday family psychological treatment.

This book is intended to provide clinical (and other practicing) psychologists with useful results from individually focused psychological tests that can be applied to couples and families and interpreted within a systemic family framework. The book also aims to show the family therapist how psychological testing can enhance understanding of and intervention with couples and families. The family psychologist already working within a synthesis of family systemic thinking while mindful of the importance of the intrapersonal may find in this book some new observations that provide a stimulus for carrying the integration process further than the present initial proposals. For the student planning to become a professional psychologist, this book may prove a helpful accompaniment to the various specialized texts focused intensively on teaching about individual tests and inventories. Hopefully, this writing will also stimulate research into addressing the various integrative hypotheses posed in every chapter.

## The Organization of This Book

The initial section of this book describes the practical assessment and therapeutic use with families of the major individual standardized instruments designed to measure personality. Three principal inventory methods are appraised. The first is the Minnesota Multiphasic Inventory (MMPI/MMPI-2), focused especially on assessing the symptoms and problem mood states of the adult partners. The second inventory is the Millon Clinical Multiaxial Inventory (MCMI-III), selected because of its particular usefulness in measuring personality styles or disorders of the partners. Appraisal of an additional inventory, the 16PF, provides for measuring of nonpathological dimensions of personality, a normalizing approach to personality measure particularly compatible with couple systems work.

Because the Rorschach Inkblot method is the most widely used psychological test utilizing more ambiguous stimuli, aspects of the test with implications for relationships between parents and children are described. A second, less structured method, the Kinetic Family Drawing (KFD), is discussed because it provides clues for understanding an individual's view of his or her family system.

The recently developed instrument for appraising adolescents' emotional difficulties is the Millon Adolescent Clinical Inventory (MACI) (the successor to the Millon Adolescent Personality Inventory, MAPI). The use of the MACI is proposed because its brevity lends itself to adolescent cooperation, yet it surveys personality patterns, expressed concerns of the adolescent, plus clinical syndromes. For these reasons, it is especially useful in family situations requiring immediate screening or as a useful self-administered personality inventory serving as one test in a battery of tests.

In concluding Part 1, several individual instruments are considered because of their strategic usefulness in assessing special aspects of family relationships: the Parent-Child Relationship Inventory (PCRI), the BASC, and the State-Trait Anger Expression Inventory (STAXI). Although other potentially useful tests could have been included, the decision was made to select these three measures because of positive experience with their applicability to family problems.

Integrated use of various combinations of tests discussed in Part 1 is the focus of Part 2. The initial chapter in Part 2 presents overall principles and practices in testing couples and using results actively in therapy with couples, regardless of which inventory is used. Then the integrated use of a full battery of tests with family members is described in the following chapter.

Part 2 continues with two substantive chapters on specialized family problem areas. One chapter addresses testing in circumstances of family violence and child abuse. The other considers the use of psychological tests and the understanding they may provide for the process of helping divorcing families.

The concluding chapter in Part 2 addresses the issue of whether to test or not, the cost, and the education and training needed to utilize tests in a practice. Limitations of the book are considered, together with some thoughts on the future directions of psychological assessment with couples and families.

## PART 1

# THE USE OF SPECIFIC TESTS WITH COUPLES AND FAMILIES

# CHAPTER 2

---

# MMPI/MMPI-2:
## Assessing Symptoms, Moods,
## and Couple Types

---

The MMPI is the most widely used clinical testing instrument in the United States (Strupp, in Butcher, 1990). With its half century of development, the MMPI has amassed a literature remarkable in quantity, including over 8,000 published research references (Groth-Marnat, 1990). The first revision in 50 years became available in 1989 (Butcher et al., 1989), making possible a new level of development resting on the shoulders of the originators of the MMPI. This chapter focuses on the use of the MMPI/MMPI-2 with couples. The reader who is already familiar with the MMPI/MMPI-2 may skip the "Capsule Summary of the MMPI/MMPI-2" and begin with the section "Why Use the MMPI-2 with Couples?"

## CAPSULE SUMMARY OF THE MMPI/MMPI-2

The MMPI, first published in 1943, was developed through the joint efforts of psychologist Starke Hathaway and psychiatrist J. Charnley McKinley (1943). The inventory calls for the patient or client to respond "true" or "false" to 566 statements (567 for the MMPI-2) pertaining primarily to psychological/psychiatric symptoms or mood states. The inventory's responses are scored on 10 scales measuring various clinical or personality dimensions and 4 scales that relate to validity and test taking attitude. A number of supplementary and content scales are now scored routinely as well. Several scoring and interpretive computer programs are available, including the version generated by the developers of the MMPI-2, which is distributed by National Computer Systems (NCS). The MMPI/MMPI-2 may be taken in paper-and-pencil format or on computer; audiotapes are available.

The original development of the scales was undertaken by administering the MMPI to a number of patients suffering from depression, hysteria,

9

schizophrenia, and other independently diagnosed psychiatric problems, attempting to identify which items differentiated among these original groups of patients, then cross-validating the resulting scales by administering the MMPI to other similar patient groups. Although it turned out that the MMPI scales did not sufficiently differentiate patients by various psychiatric groupings, the scales did provide a basis for describing various psychological and behavioral patterns observed independently, clinically, and through research studies. Because of continuing clinical experience and research through the years, many useful descriptions of personality and behavioral characteristics associated with each scale and selected frequently occurring patterns of elevated scales have accrued.

During the 1980s, the MMPI-2 was developed based on a better normative sample than the original version, the omission of some problem items and substitution of others, the generation of some new scales, and some other improvements (Butcher et al., 1989). From the MMPI-2 the original clinical and validity scale scores can be derived, thus providing a significant degree of apparent applicability of much of the prior research, plus providing the basis for the development of new scales.

The traditional validity scales are Cannot Say (?), Lie (L), Infrequency (F), and (K). Brief definitions are as follows:

Cannot Say (?) is simply the number of items left unanswered.

Lie (L) is not a measure of lying; it reflects the extent to which an individual puts himself or herself in an overly positive light, but rather naïvely so.

Infrequency (F) measures the extent to which a person answers in a statistically deviant manner.

K assesses the extent to which more sophisticated persons respond in a positive way, seen as defensiveness at the upper end.

Two validity scores developed for the MMPI-2 are of importance (Greene, 1991, pp. 68–69, 74–76). Variable Response Inconsistency (VRIN) consists of 67 pairs of items that have similar meanings. If a client scores in opposite directions with reference to content, that pair is scored as inconsistent. Thus, low scores indicate consistency, whereas high scores point toward inconsistency of response.

Another score, True Response Inconsistency (TRIN), consists of 23 pairs of items wherein the scored pair is either true or false. Despite the word inconsistency in the title, a high score relates to a response set to answer yes to items on the MMPI-2, regardless of content. Conversely, a low score indicates a tendency to respond no to items, despite item content.

Caldwell (1997b) has recently incisively pointed out that MMPI-2 literature indicates that social status can affect certain scores. Overall, higher social status is associated with higher K score and lower L score, with lower status impacting in reverse fashion. Furthermore, lower status correlates with high F and Sc-Scale 8. Nelson (1952) developed a scale, Sc, that Caldwell (1988, pp. 94–96) indicates measures current, "earned" status. He recommends use of this scale.

The clinical scales are 1 Hypochondriasis (Hs); 2 Depression (D); 3 Hysteria (Hy); 4 Psychopathic Deviate (Pd); 5 Masculinity-Femininity (Mf); 6 Paranoia (Pa); 7 Psychasthenia (Pt); 8 Schizophrenia (Sc); 9 Hypomania (Ma); and 0 Social Introversion (Si). The user is cautioned not to take the scale names literally diagnostically, even though the names provide suggestions for dynamic areas. A most important useful trend has been the identification of what are termed "high-point codes" and their relation to specific dynamic patterns (see examples later in this chapter of these combinations of two high-point scale scores).

In addition to the validity and clinical scales, other useful scales frequently used in interpretation are Anxiety (A), Repression (R), Ego Strength (Es), MacAndrew Alcoholism Scale–Revised (MAC-R), Overcontrolled Hostility (O H), Social Responsibility (Re), College Maladjustment (Mt), Gender Role (GM & GF), and Posttraumatic Stress Disorder (PK & PS). The MMPI-2 has specific content scores: Anxiety (ANX), Fears (FRS), Obsessiveness (OSBS), Depression (DEP), Health Concerns (HEA), Bizarre Mentation (BIZ), Anger (ANG), Cynicism (CYN), Antisocial Practices (ASP), Type A (TPA), Low Self-Esteem (LSE), Social Discomfort (SOD), Family Problems (FAM), Work Interference (WRK), and Negative Treatment Indicators (TRT).

Content groupings by Harris and Lingoes (1955) continue to be used by MMPI/MMPI-2 interpreters. These are 28 subgroupings by content for scales 2, 3, 4, 6, 8, and 9. Although they are all useful, subgroupings for scales 4 and 6 are particularly useful for understanding couple MMPIs. Scale 4s(Pd) is broken into subscales for Family Discord, Authority Problems, Social Imperturbability, Social Alienation, and Self-Alienation. Scale 6 (Pa) has subscales for Persecutory Ideas, Poignancy, and Naïveté.

The *Manual for Administration and Scoring* (Butcher et al., 1989, p. 11) states that a user of this inventory should, at a minimum, have graduate-level courses in psychological testing and psychopathology. The service that sells the MMPI/MMPI-2 requires that a purchaser be at Level A, "either a licensure to practice psychology independently or a graduate degree in psychology or a closely related field and either a graduate-level course in Tests and Measurements or participation in an NCS-approved workshop" (National Computer Systems, 1997, p. 94).

For further understanding of the MMPI/MMPI-2 as applied to individuals, the reader is referred to an overview chapter on the MMPI/MMPI-2 in the *Handbook of Psychological Assessment* by Groth-Marnat (1990, pp. 179–234) and the text by Greene (1991), as well as texts by Butcher (1990) and Graham (1990).

## Why Use the MMPI-2 with Couples?

The MMPI was created at a time when the primary concerns of psychiatrists, psychologists, and other mental health professionals were the symptoms and mood states of people with psychiatric or psychological problems. Professionals focused then on understanding patterns of the more seriously disturbed, such as those identified as schizophrenics, and the more flagrantly neurotic, such as the hysterics. This original emphasis on symptoms and mood states has continued through many years of clinical usage and thousands of research studies, culminating in development of the recent revision, the MMPI-2, and the adolescent version, the MMPI-A. Because work with couples usually focuses first on a dysfunctional relationship, an inventory such as the MMPI-2, measuring particularly behavioral symptoms and mood states that may impact a partner and/or stem from a partner's impact, has considerable usefulness.

Although this emphasis on identifying problematic mood states and psychological symptoms is still a major attribute of the MMPI-2, results do provide in addition some hypotheses about ongoing, traitlike personality characteristics. Also of importance is that extensive clinical experience and research has come to allow for use of the inventory with almost anyone, not only the most disturbed. Thus, it can serve as the basis for generating hypotheses about partners who have relationship difficulties, even though both partners may not demonstrate distinct psychological problems apart from their relationship.

Many new scales have been developed, a number of which are routinely used in complex, sophisticated interpretations of the MMPI-2. Reflecting the growing interest in the family area, two of these in the MMPI-2 are the Family Problems Scale and the Marital Distress Scale.

### FAMILY AND MARITAL SCALES USEFUL WITH
### COUPLE INTERPRETATION

The Family Problems Scale (FAM) is one of the MMPI-2 content scales. Butcher (1989) defines this scale as follows: "Considerable family discord is reported by high scores on FAM. Their families are described as lacking in love, quarrelsome, and unpleasant. They may even report hating members of their families. Their childhoods may be portrayed as abusive, and marriages seen as unhappy and lacking in affection" (p. 16). This scale may be useful in initial screening to ascertain the degree of seriousness of family problems, even though it is not designed to measure a psychological dynamic. The FAM is a broad measure reflecting problems, past and present, in the family as a whole, not only marital difficulties.

The Marital Distress Scale (MDS) has the advantage of focusing on measuring distress or discord in close relationships, rather than measuring family problems more generally (Hjemboe, 1991). Thus, it appears to have more usefulness with couples. Hjemboe states that the MDS appears to be an efficient discriminator of maladjustment in marriage at a *T*-score of 60, rather than the *T*-score of 65 delineated for psychopathologic significance on the clinical scales. Although this may seem an unusually low level, estimates of a 30% to 50% marital problem prevalence rate in adult outpatient clinics mean that setting the critical level higher would result in misidentifying as adequate a large number of actually troubled relationships (i.e., too many false positives). A comparison of the MDS results with the FAM may help sort out past from present and general family from specific marital distress. In the practical use of MMPI-2 profiles with couples, however, there remains, the question of finding models or standards for interpreting the MMPI/MMPI-2 clinical profile. Research reported in subsequent sections provides an approach toward satisfying this need for a guide.

## Use the MMPI or the MMPI-2?

There has been controversy over the degree to which clinical descriptions of MMPI scales and, particularly, profile configurations can be generalized to the MMPI-2 (Ben-Porath, & Tellegen, 1995; Graham, Timbrook, Ben-Porath, & Butcher, 1991; Humphrey & Dahlstrom, 1995; Tellegen & Ben-Porath, 1993). A review of this controversy and developing literature suggests that generalizations may be made with a reasonable degree of assurance from MMPI-based research and clinical experience to MMPI-2 configural pattern interpretation of spike and high-point scores on two or three scales (Greene, 1991, pp. 245–250). Generalizing from the earlier to the later form may be appropriate, particularly when the high points stand at least five *T*-score points above the remainder of the profile for these clinical scales. However, persuasive reasoning to the contrary is presented by Caldwell (1997b). He points out that among clinical cases, one-third of the clients belonging to one MMPI-2 profile code type belong to a different MMPI code type (p. 51). With MMPI-2 profiles in the normal range, more than half belong to a different code pattern. Caldwell suggests that double plotting the profiles is the solution. The policy of National Computer Systems (NCS) (1997), the major processor of MMPI/MMPI-2 data, is consistent with this position in that it can provide from the MMPI-2 administration both MMPI and MMPI-2 profiles in their scoring system printouts. Siding with Caldwell, the recommendation is to use both profiles, thus taking advantage of the new MMPI-2 normative data and scores while retaining the benefits of 50 years of research behind the MMPI patterns. When sufficient research information provides adequate pictures of correlates of all the frequent two-point codes and spikes on the MMPI-2, then sole reliance on the MMPI-2 will be justified. A beginning is being made in developing correlative behavioral data based directly on research with the MMPI-2 (e.g., Archer, Griffin, & Aiduk, 1995).

## MMPIs of Distressed Couples Seeking Therapy

Five major MMPI patterns of couples seeking marital therapy are discussed in this section based on thorough, significant research conducted by William Fals-Stewart, Gary R. Birchler, John Schafer, and Steve Lucente (1994). They studied 102 couples via cluster analysis methodology, and successfully replicated the resulting groupings with a different but similar sample of troubled couples. The clinical descriptions of these groups and their probable interpersonal dynamics are based on the findings of Fals-Stewart et al. as augmented by reference to interpretations reported in major MMPI/MMPI-2 texts by Greene (1991), in particular, and Butcher (1990) and Graham (1990). Literature on couple interaction (e.g., Carlson & Sperry, 1998) and this writer's observations of the interactions of distressed couples constitute a basis for proposing hypotheses about couple interactions in each cluster. The mean male and female partner MMPI patterns for these groups are displayed in Figures 2.1 through 2.10.

### OPENLY WARRING COUPLES

Identified as "conflicted" couples by Fals-Stewart et al. (1994, p. 234), these openly warring couples present with a pattern of expressing active anger with each other. Whereas validity scales are satisfactory and unremarkable, the spousal patterns of expression are rather different, appearing consistent with gender stereotypes (see Figures 2.1 and 2.2).

Warring wives present with poorly controlled anger and hostility that is expressed in a cyclical fashion, as reflected in their 4-3 high-point code. Following a submissive, tractable phase, a loss of control can result in angry, aggressive acting-out. This may be generated as much by internal stimuli as by externally based stress. Between stormy bouts of anger expression, these wives appear as cultural stereotypes of, if not caricatures of, "femininity," displaying passive, submissive, and yielding behavior, although periodically complaining. At those times, they are likely to defer easily to their husbands, reinforcing their traditional "feminine" role in relation to the man's "masculine," dominant behavior. This submissive behavior, not surprisingly, builds resentment, which is, however, suppressed or repressed. A bursting forth of anger follows the buildup of resentment.

It is theorized that the relative balance between the repressive, submissive Scale 3 behaviors and the action-oriented, rebellious Scale 4 behaviors continues with first one aspect of the personality dominant, then another. It may be that when they are in their more submissive, "feminine" stereotyped mode, the wives feel attraction for a man who appears very stereotypically "masculine" because of his action-oriented characteristics.

Warring husbands act on their impulses and are frequently rebellious, at least in attitude, against the restraints of authority and usual socially accepted standards. Note their Scale 4 at $T$ 78. To the extent that their wives represent authority and attempt to constrain these husbands' behavior, these males are resentful and rebellious in their marital relationship. Accompanying these Scale 4 dynamics is a high level of energy reflected in Scale 9, which serves to provide fuel to the acting-out. These rebellious attitudes and action-oriented behaviors might have made for success on the Wild West frontier many decades ago, but make for problems now, particularly in ventures requiring cooperation. Thus, considering both the Scale 4 dynamics and thinking about these men from the standpoint of a 4–9 high-point code is a useful approach.

Because of their freedom from anxiety, worry, and guilt, these husbands often make a comfortable, smooth, and socially facile appearance initially. At the same time, warring husbands are ordinarily impatient with anything beyond a superficial relationship; they crave excitement.

Having a seemingly highly submissive mate who follows the husband's lead unquestioningly and uncritically at least for significant periods of time and having satisfied needs for attention and sex fit the husband's need for a relationship that caters to his impulses and general action-orientation. His action-oriented, even acting-out behavior may be vicariously satisfying to her when she feels constrained by her stereotypic submissive role, even though she may complain about his behavior.

Therapy with this couple is going to be volatile, especially when changes are likely. One danger is that when the therapist promotes more change, stirring up even a little anxiety, the partners may collude against the therapist in one of their times of "peace" when the wife is behaving in a submissive fashion; then they may believe that their problems are solved and the therapist's services are no longer needed. If, on the other hand, this couple continues with their periodic

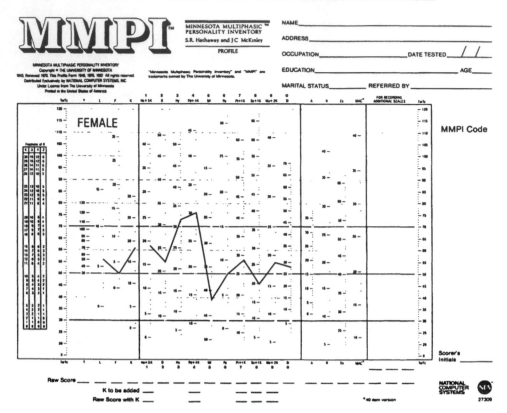

Figure 2.1
Cluster 1, Openly Warring Females
Reprinted with permission of the publisher from *Minnesota Multiphasic Personality Inventory*. Copyright © by the Regents of the University of Minnesota 1942, 1943 (renewed 1970), 1982. This form 1948, 1970, 1982.

fighting style, the therapist can join with this style and help them learn to fight fairly. It is important for the therapist to remember that this may not be a couple that will communicate ideally verbally or reason well with problems. Instead, this is an action-oriented couple that, if they can fight fairly to resolve conflicts, may prove to be like one of Gottman's (1994, p. 28) "volatile" marriages filled with verbal altercations, but where the couple reaches solutions to problems nevertheless and stays together satisfactorily.

## UNHAPPY, PROBLEM-FOCUSED COUPLES

With these couples, the validity scores fall within normal limits, but elevated F scores are higher than L and K scores. Butcher (1990) describes this validity

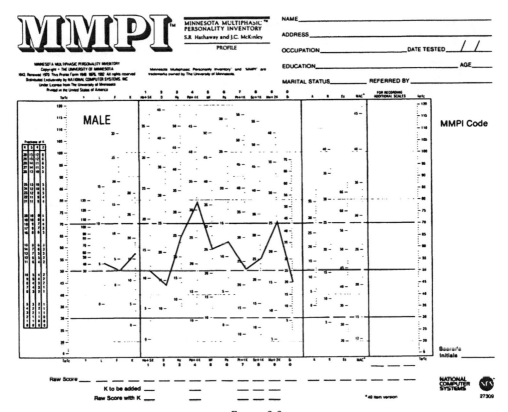

Figure 2.2
Cluster 1, Openly Warring Males

Reprinted with permission of the publisher from Minnesota Multiphasic Personality Inventory Copyright © by the Regents of the University of Minnesota 1942, 1943 (renewed 1970), 1982. This form 1948, 1970, 1982.

pattern as indicative of "open, frank problem expression" (p. 52). The therapist is likely to find a problem-oriented approach on the part of the couple, with openness to self-appraisal. Specific symptoms can be targeted for couple (and/or individual) work. Fals-Stewart et al. (1994) refer to this group as their Depressed cluster. Because of their problem-solving orientation and because their unhappiness does not differentiate them from some other clusters, they are referred to here as "unhappy, problem-focused couples." Their MMPI profiles are provided in Figures 2.3 and 2.4.

The common motivation toward therapy for these partners is unhappiness. Both are depressed, possibly even clinically depressed. They do not like their present existence. They report high levels of marital dissatisfaction that can serve as a motivator for undergoing couples therapy.

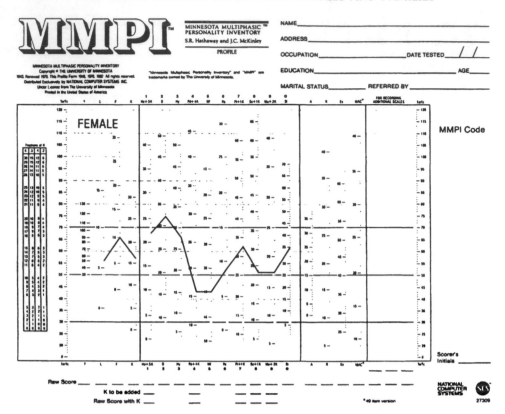

Figure 2.3
Cluster 2, Unhappy, Problem-Focused Females
Reprinted with permission of the publisher from *Minnesota Multiphasic Personality Inventory*. Copyright © by the Regents of the University of Minnesota 1942, 1943 (renewed 1970), 1982. This form 1948, 1970, 1982.

Unhappy, problem-focused husbands have 2–7 codes, common in psychiatric/psychological settings (Greene, 1991, p. 267). Along with their pronounced symptoms of unhappiness and depression go worry, anxiety, and tension. At an extreme, they are susceptible to cardiovascular symptoms, insomnia, and decreased appetite—all in response to their chronic level of tension. At an extreme, screening for suicidal ideation and plans is recommended. Abuse of alcohol is possible, with alcohol overused as a tension reducer. These husbands take things to heart, blaming themselves easily, being, in short, intrapunitive. They feel inadequate, despite often being achievers. They are turned in on themselves, rather than having a reasonable amount of energy available for focusing on their partners and despite having the ability to make reasonable interpersonal relationships. They seek advice and help from the therapist and are likely to follow suggestions of the therapist. By all accounts, they are open to psychodynamic exploration and focused problem solving.

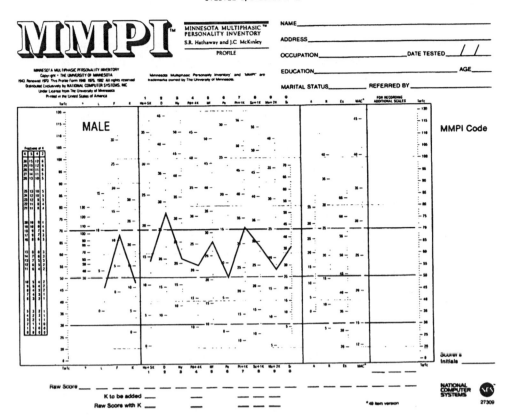

Figure 2.4
Cluster 2, Unhappy, Problem-Focused Males
Reprinted with permission of the publisher from *Minnesota Multiphasic Personality Inventory*. Copyright © by the Regents of the University of Minnesota 1942, 1943 (renewed 1970), 1982. This form 1948, 1970, 1982.

The unhappy, problem-focused wives are at least somewhat open to problem solving, as noted above, and have a major symptom of depression. However, their overall MMPI pattern, a 2-1-3, has been described as one of the "neurotic triad configurations" (Greene, 1991, p. 149–150). In this configuration, with Scale 2 higher than Scales 1 and 3 but with all three scales elevated, at least a mildly chronic neurotic pattern with mixed symptoms presents itself. Hysteroid indications together with some physical concerns are present. Like their husbands, they are anxious and self-doubting. They may prove rather dependent and immature. They seem capable of maintaining in a long-suffering, unhappy role over an extended period of time, almost as if they have some investment in the role. As such, motivation may be less than optimal. Screening for suicidal thoughts and planning is suggested with these wives. Not only could a worsening of the relationship present a crisis, but so could positive change upset the couple or family homeostatic balance (Goldenberg & Goldenberg, 1998, p. 32).

The therapist may face several problems with this couple. First, the couple is likely handling their problems of intimacy through maintaining some level of disengagement. Therefore, as the therapist attempts to help them gain more personal contact, interaction, and intimacy, conflict may increase. They may then see therapy as having "made things worse." At this point, seeing that the husband is more introspective and open to observing himself and his behavior, the therapist might be tempted to undertake individual psychodynamic therapy with him. Meanwhile, the wife might be seen individually by this therapist or another; she may receive medication for her depression or a flare-up may occur of whatever physical ills are present. Although some aspects of their individual problems may be ameliorated by taking these steps, the fundamental couple problem of disengagement may remain unsolved. Whether or not any treatment adjunctive to the couple work is undertaken, a useful strategy is to continue couples therapy but focus gently on the dynamics of interaction, without blaming, and concentrate on the couple's ability to work on practical solutions to identified problems, such as aspects of communication, working together, parenting, and so on. (If ongoing, long-term individual therapy is undertaken, it is best handled by someone other than the couple's therapist, lest the couple system become unbalanced by the therapist's aligning with the spouse seen in individual therapy.) Finding active ways to increase the proportion of positive-to-negative experiences daily for this depressed couple would be especially important (Gottman, 1994, p. 57). To this end, and to help ameliorate their intrapunitive style, a couples group might be a help (Framo, 1982).

It is likely that this problem of intimacy is a core problem, and for that reason, possibly the final problem to be directly managed in therapy. It is important for the therapist to remain respectful during the therapy process of what may appear to be an indirect, avoidant style of relating. Some couples do maintain long-standing marriages, solving problems somehow by seeming avoidance but yet resolving their problems. This may not be the ideal model from the standpoint of mental health practitioners, but it is a workable model nevertheless, according to Gottman's (1994, p. 28) research. If therapy goes even reasonably well, this couple has the potential to move past the avoidant pattern, interact more directly, and evolve into enjoying a positive, growing marriage relationship.

## HUSBAND-BLAMING COUPLES

These couples are quite different from the self-punitive unhappy problem-focused ones and different from the openly warring couples. These cluster 3 couples focus on husband-blaming by the wives, linked to apologetic, although sometimes resentful, acceptance of blame by the husbands. They are similar in mood to the unhappy problem-focused couples. However, in the husband-blaming couples, wives express their unhappiness in a more dissatisfied, complaining way, and husbands demonstrate their unhappiness through a more distinct depressive mood with accompanying symptoms. Figures 2.5 and 2.6 show their MMPI profiles.

The husband-blaming wives attempt to present themselves as psychologically healthy (Fals-Stewart et al., 1994, p. 235), yet are guarded, as reflected in the L and K scores being elevated above the F score. They tend to see the world in right-wrong, black-white terms and are reluctant to engage in self-criticism (Graham, 1990, p. 48). Their somewhat elevated Scale 1 ($T$ 70) indicates that they are likely to be rather whining somatizers (Greene, 1991, p. 262). Tying this scale with their moderately elevated Scales 4 and 6 (both $T$ 69) means these outgoing (0, $T$ 45) women are likely to focus their anger on others. These angry spouses are resentful to the point of rage at times. They blame others, in particular their spouses. Butcher (1990) states, "Clinicians using the MMPI-2 in evaluating clients in marital therapy might find that their clients' Pd Scale elevations (a frequent finding among marital therapy clients) can result from situationally based marital or family problems" (p. 91).

These blaming women are wary and suspicious. If there is verified reason for this suspiciousness, no delinquent history or past major difficulty in interpersonal relations in general, and if the scores just reach the significant level, the hypothesis is that this person is reacting to the present couple dispute and the 4–6 does not represent a characterologic problem.

Sometimes, application of the Harris and Lingoes (1955) subscales on Scale 4 will prove a useful way to clarify the meaning of the 4–6 pattern. Using these subscales may indicate a particularly high score on the Family Discord Subscale, with a nonsignificant score (less than $T$ 70) on the Authority Conflict Subscale. Applying the Harris and Lingoes subscales to Scale 6 may reveal a high Persecutory Score, indicating marked blaming, including blaming of a spouse for good, verified reasons as confirmed in an interview. When these conditions have been met, the 4–6 or 6–4 pattern may truly be a state condition relative to the couple conflict and not a trait reflection, as it is often considered.

Although women with this 4–6 pattern registered a mean $T$-score of 54 on Scale 5, in applying this cluster as a guide, it is useful to see if Scale 5 is low, below $T$ 35. If this is the case, coupled with the high 4–6 or 6–4, a particularly demanding, manipulating, and hostile quality to their relatedness is expected. They provoke others (including therapists) into aggressing against them, at least verbally, then feel hurt and put upon. Greene (1991) reports that "marital difficulties, family problems, and sexual dysfunctions are common" with these women (p. 163).

Although the husbands in this husband-blaming group tend toward a problem-solving interactional approach, as suggested by a slightly elevated Scale F with lower Scales L and K (Butcher, 1990, p. 52), the striking feature of the

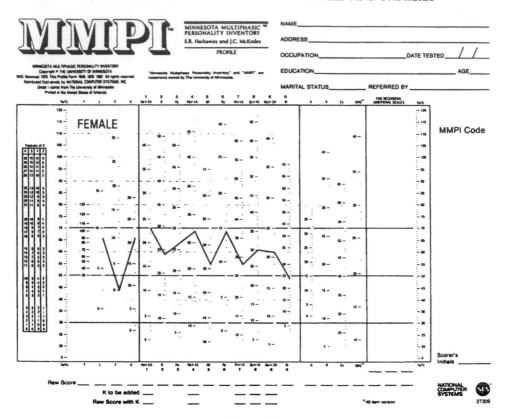

Figure 2.5
Cluster 3, Husband-Blaming Females

Reprinted with permission of the publisher from *Minnesota Multiphasic Personality Inventory*. Copyright © by the Regents of the University of Minnesota 1942, 1943 (renewed 1970), 1982. This form 1948, 1970, 1982.

husbands' average profile is depression, evidenced by Scale 2 at $T$ 75 and reinforced by Scale 9 at $T$ 45. They are suffering from a generally unhappy, dysphoric mood state accompanied by feelings of inadequacy, lack of self-confidence, self-depreciation, and strong guilt feelings (Greene, 1991, p. 264); this pattern is likely at the level of a clinical depression. Because Scale 4 reaches $T$ 70, it is hypothesized that they are also experiencing some resentment and anger, although perhaps expressing it indirectly (Greene, p. 264). As with their spouses, it is useful to apply the Harris and Lingoes (1955) subscales to Scale 4 to help determine whether this elevation is determined primarily by family discord. It is also worthwhile to refer to the literature on code type 2–4. Various interpretive possibilities are cited by Greene (1991, p. 204), including this depressed, maritally resentful profile and the profile reflecting caught psychopaths or alcoholics. Scores on additional scales unreported in the Fals-Stewart et al. (1994) research, such as alcoholism and dominance, can provide clarification.

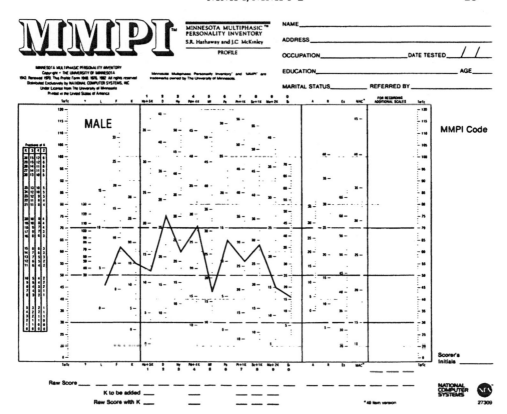

Figure 2.6
Cluster 3, Self-Blaming Males

Reprinted with permission of the publisher from *Minnesota Multiphasic Personality Inventory*. Copyright © by the Regents of the University of Minnesota 1942, 1943 (renewed 1970), 1982. This form 1948, 1970, 1982.

Alcohol abuse and suicidal ideation are areas with which to be concerned in treating these couples. Identifying these features is important in that the symptoms accompanying these patterns may make them more amenable to psychotherapy (which must address these issues); missing these markers may result in vitiated therapy or death. This identification is especially likely to be the case because these husbands are apparently action-oriented, although depressed, and are not particularly sensitive, fitting a masculine stereotype to a considerable extent; they have lower Scale 5 scores than males in the other clusters.

It is hypothesized that inept, insensitive, or self-destructive behavior on the part of these husbands makes it easy for the wives to blame them, and with some justification. For the husbands, the blaming and perceived nagging may provide justification for these males' resentfulness and for their self-destructive behavior. The definers of "reality" in these couples would appear to be the wives, inasmuch as their pattern (as noted above) is that of seeing the world in black-white, right-wrong ways, blaming others, and absorbing psychological tensions physiologically rather than being self-aware. Thus, it is important to recognize that neither the husbands nor the wives are psychologically sensitive in their relationship.

Therapy needs to focus on both partners learning to take responsibility for themselves, avoiding blaming, and understanding more of their own psychological makeup. The therapist can help them learn to be more empathetic with their partners. To this end, a couples group could prove useful (Framo, 1982). In fact, a general adult group designed to increase sensitivity and empathetic behavior often would be very helpful for husbands with this profile. If the husbands' depression continues, evaluation for psychoactive medication should be considered. For the wives, a group separate from their husbands could provide a place to learn to modify the extreme black-and-white thinking and to learn how to shoulder more responsibility for themselves without blaming.

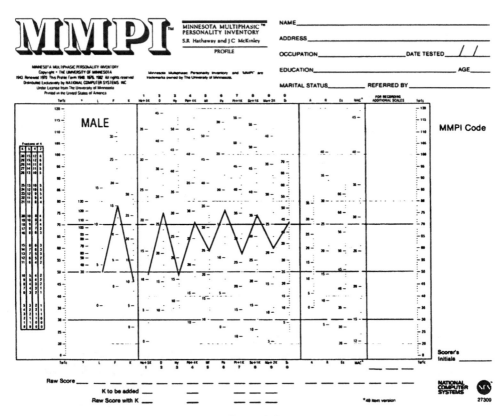

Figure 2.7
Cluster 4, Psychologically Disordered Males

Reprinted with permission of the publisher from *Minnesota Multiphasic Personality Inventory*. Copyright © by the Regents of the University of Minnesota 1942, 1943 (renewed 1970), 1982. This form 1948, 1970, 1982.

PSYCHOLOGICALLY DISORDERED COUPLES

In the data of Fals-Stewart et al. (1994, p. 235), these couples had the greatest number of scale elevations, and on other research measures had severe dyadic distress. Data indicated that couples in this cluster had greater conflict potential than those in all other clusters. Calling them "dysphoric couples," as did Fals-Stewart, does not help differentiate them sufficiently from couples in some other groupings. Instead, the marked disturbance suggested by the profiles of both husbands and wives indicates that a useful title is that of "psychologically disordered couples" (see Figures 2.7 and 2.8).

Psychologically disordered husbands are clearly seeking help (Greene, 1991, p. 116) and may even be exaggerating symptoms to attract attention (Butcher, 1990, p. 51). However, they appear to be seeking help for good psychological reasons. Their clinical scale profile is a sawtoothed pattern in which

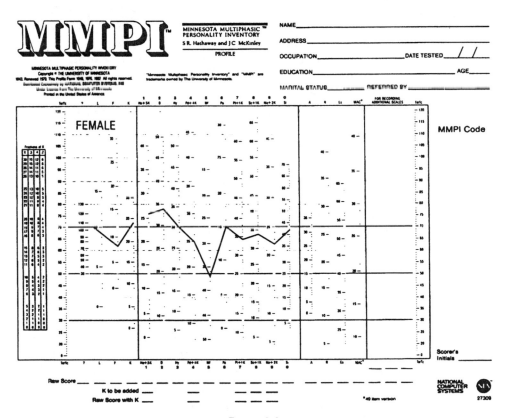

Figure 2.8
Cluster 4, Psychologically Disordered Females
Reprinted with permission of the publisher from *Minnesota Multiphasic Personality Inventory*. Copyright © by the Regents of the University of Minnesota 1942, 1943 (renewed 1970), 1982. This form 1948, 1970, 1982.

Scales 2, 4, 6, and 8 are clinically significantly elevated above other scales. Greene (1991) states that this is "a particularly malignant pattern" that may be indicative of a psychotic condition (p. 294). Sometimes, this pattern is reflective of a borderline personality disorder. Fals-Stewart et al. (1994, p. 235) describe these husbands as "depressed, angry, distrustful" and that they "feel alienated from others." Others see them as moody and unpredictable. They are likely ruminative, preoccupied, and inflexible in problem solving.

Another way to look at these husbands' profile is to consider Scale 2 reflective of depression, but with Scales 6–8 as a high-point code. With the 6–8 code type, these husbands are likely to evidence "a thought disorder with paranoid features" (Greene, 1991, p. 280); at an extreme, they may evidence paranoid schizophrenia. In contrast to the overtly acute nature of their husband's presentation, the psychologically disordered wives are attempting to avoid, deny, and generally not deal with unacceptable feelings and impulses (p. 119). Despite this effort, however, they appear to have "a chronic neurotic condition" (p. 150). With their Scales 1–3 significant and within five points of each other, symptomatology is mixed, but these wives are usually diagnosed with somatoform disorders, anxiety disorders, or depressive disorders (Graham, 1990, p. 103). With their Scale 6 at 70, these are also sensitive if not hypersensitive women who are wary and suspicious of others. They are unsure, rather inept females who may have grown accustomed to a high level of unhappiness and considerable discomfort.

Because of these wives' melancholy adjustment to a chronic condition and their attempts at denial, they are not likely to be highly motivated for psychological treatment for themselves. This contrasts with their husbands, as noted above, who are actively seeking help; the husbands' difficulty is, however, that they may be so unstable that they have problems in persevering. Therefore, of all clusters, these husbands and wives appear to need extensive individual psychological evaluation and probably collateral psychiatric evaluation to plan treatment effectively. Both spouses may need psychoactive medication. Wives' probable somatization may also call for specific medical evaluation. Only with attention to the individual needs accompanying the couple problems will an appropriate, thorough treatment plan be developed. Fals-Stewart et al. (1994) note that these are the youngest in age of the couples studied and have the shortest marriages, "factors that may add further stress on these marriages and the partners involved" (p. 236). It is at least equally likely that deeply rooted individual psychopathology based in flawed personality development contributed to the earlier appearance of more marked marital conflict. Assuming this later hypothesis is correct provides a basis for the proposition that individual treatment interventions must be carefully crafted, whether or not the interventions include couple therapy per se.

When couple therapy is undertaken, the therapeutic plan, including goals, objectives, and immediate tactics, must be thoughtfully delineated with as much collateral help as appropriate, such as medication, support groups, and availability for emergencies. If the couple makes changes, these will be even more threatening than for some couples. If the disordered husband behaves in a more sane way, he must take more responsibility for his actions. At the same time, the disordered wife must tolerate the anxiety of looking at herself psychologically and assuming more responsibility for herself without focusing as much on her husband; psychophysiological stress reactions are to be expected.

DISTANT, CALM COUPLES

The average MMPI profile for these husbands and wives falls within normal limits (WNL). Fals-Stewart et al. (1994) term this cluster "Domestic Calm." Marital measures suggest they are relatively satisfied with their marriages, especially in contrast to other clusters. These couples are older on the average than other clusters, especially older than the psychologically disordered couples. Given that their marriages are longer, distant, calm couples may have ways of resolving conflict. This would be consistent with Gottman's (1994, pp. 28–29) findings that longevity of marriage is associated with having developed ways of resolving conflict more than being associated with any particular marital interactional style.

The MMPI profile in Figure 2.9 shows that, although for the distant, calm husbands all scores are within normal limits, Scale 8 is a T of 63, a score not at the pathologically significant level but slightly elevated. This score is, however, 10 T-score points above a contemporary normative sample Scale 8 average of T 53 (Colligan, Osborne, Swenson, & Offord, 1993); thus, this would appear to be a clearly elevated score, although within normal range. Greene (1991, p. 172) identifies scores as moderately elevated if they fall between T 60 and 69. He interprets these scores as reflecting clients who think differently from others, "though this may reflect creativity, an avant-garde attitude, or actual schizoid-like process. These clients tend to avoid reality through fantasy and daydreams" (p. 172).

Distant, calm wives' Scale 8 score is also their highest, although only at a T of 61 (see Figure 2.10). This suggests that these women may be somewhat similar to their husbands in that they may have some sense of differentness and distance. They also have another mildly elevated score, Scale 4 at 60. Greene (1991) describes people with Scale 4 scores from T 60 to 69 as follows: "These clients may be genuinely concerned about social problems and issues; they may be responding to situational conflicts, or they may have adjusted to an habitual level of interpersonal and social conflict" (p. 155).

It is clear from these Fals-Stewart et al. (1994) MMPI profiles and accompanying research data that these couples are "not suffering from a significant amount of distress" (p. 236). In comparison with the other clusters, they are in domestic calm, as the researchers label them. However, the lack of significant

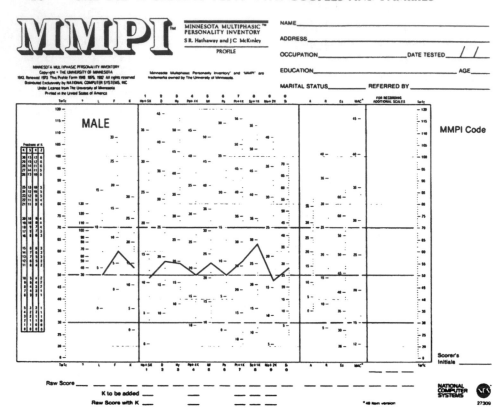

Figure 2.9
Cluster 5, Distant, Calm Males
Reprinted with permission of the publisher from *Minnesota Multiphasic Personality
Inventory*. Copyright © by the Regents of the University of Minnesota 1942, 1943
(renewed 1970), 1982. This form 1948, 1970, 1982.

psychological/psychiatric symptoms does not mean that there is not the angst of
emptiness, separation, depravation, and lack of meaning that might be reflected
in their elevated Scale 8 scores. Additionally, some relationships may be troubled
because the partners' personality styles or disorders make living together difficult. Some personality styles and disorders may make living together possible
without symptoms, but also without much satisfaction.

An important tactic for interpreting these WNL profiles is to attenuate
the more extreme psychopathological descriptions of the scales. Excellent atten-
uated descriptions are available, particularly in Greene (1991). The meaning of
WNL profiles might be clarified with the application of other measurement approaches, such as the MCMI-III because of its explicit measurement of personality disorders. Or perhaps the focus should be on more normal dimensions

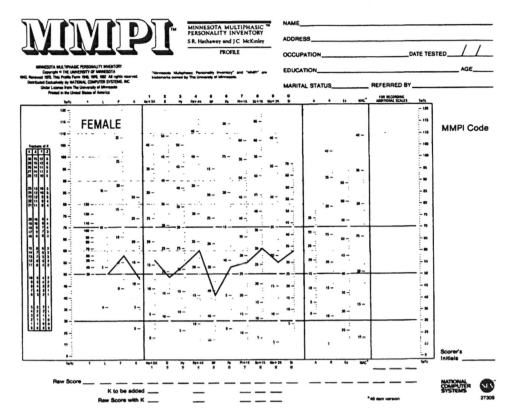

Figure 2.10
Cluster 5, Distant, Calm Females

Reprinted with permission of the publisher from *Minnesota Multiphasic Personality Inventory*. Copyright © by the Regents of the University of Minnesota 1942, 1943 (renewed 1970), 1982. This form 1948, 1970, 1982.

of personality, as are measured by the 16PF or the new Millon Index of Personality Styles.

Of course, two people without symptoms, no obvious psychopathology, no personality disorders, and even theoretically compatible personality styles might not fit well together. One may have "outgrown" the other, or changed circumstances in the individual or family life cycle may make for a significantly less fulfilling marital existence. These are the seemingly less complicated couples' counseling cases, however, for which inventories and tests are often of relatively lesser importance. The MMPI interpreter should be forewarned, however, that in psychiatric settings, the WNL profile can mean patients' "problems tend to be chronically ingrained and they have become adjusted to them. They frequently are psychotic or manifest a severe characterological disorder" (Greene,

1991, p. 259). Thus, it is very important not to take the WNL MMPI profile at face value; information from other sources is especially important.


HOW MANY COUPLES FIT THE FIVE-CLUSTER CLASSIFICATION?

Of course, a number of couples do not have MMPIs that fit the five identified couple patterns. To gain some sense of the frequency with which the above descriptions might serve as useful interpretive guides, a review was undertaken of the most frequently found MMPI-2 code types in large samples of male and female psychiatric inpatients and outpatients (Greene, 1991, pp. 241–242; Hedlund & Won Cho, 1991). Using 2.5% or more frequency as a cutoff for inclusion in the individual code type frequency count, all of the high-point codes in the first four marital conflict types were included within the analysis. In other words, there were no frequently found individual code types missing from among these four marital conflict types. For males, 40% of the high-point code types were covered by the first four code types; for females, the comparable figure was 35%. If the figures are comparable to similar MMPI samples, approximately 16% additional for the MMPI-2 samples are WNL cases. Thus, at least the total of the five marital conflict pairs identified probably represent more than 50% of the patterns found individually. The data are not available to provide the percentage of individuals lining up in the specific pair descriptions developed. With the available data, however, it is estimated that approximately half of the MMPI-2 protocols found will be covered by at least the description of one partner in the five pairs. It seems reasonable to assume that a significant number of these individuals will be paired as they were in the original research, particularly given the cluster and cross-validation pattern of that research. Thus, clinicians working with couples and families should find some usefulness in keeping these patterns available as prototypes when evaluating and doing therapy with couples and families. But what about those 50% or more of couples not falling within the five classifications?


# Interpreting Couple MMPI/MMPI-2s Not in the Five Clusters

Some of the MMPI couple patterns falling outside the five groupings will have one partner that does fit a pattern in one of the five groupings. A reading of the pertinent descriptive section above may prove useful, followed by attempting to construct the potential interaction with the other partner by reference to code types in Greene (1991) and other sources (Butcher, 1990; Graham, 1990). These resources would also prove useful for assisting in interpreting the patterns for instances where neither partner's MMPI falls with the couple grouping description above. The evaluating clinician needs also to be cognizant of certain high-point codes or single spikes that are red flags warning about potentially dangerous conditions. These will be considered below, followed by a consideration of specific gender-related scales and pertinent content scales.

RED FLAGS

There are several scales and high-point codes that, when clearly above a $T$ of 65 for the MMPI-2 or a $T$ of 70 for the MMPI and distinctly higher than other clinical scales (usually much more than five $T$-score points), are of serious concern. These red flags warn of suspected psychologically serious problems (see Table 2.1).

A Scale 9 spike meeting the above criteria points toward an affective disorder, with potentially out-of-control behavior. Narcissistic, grandiose, and overly active hypomanic behavior is anticipated that calls for individual attention; the immediate "cause" of the marital disruption may be a general personality disruption, perhaps partially biologically based, of one spouse. Sometimes, this disordered type of patient is capable of a reasonable, controlled appearance in a quiet one-on-one interview with a therapist, so the therapist can be easily fooled into thinking he or she has seen a typical sample of client behavior. Then, with the stimulus of an angry marital dispute with or without the therapist present, the

Table 2.1
*Red Flag MMPI/MMPI-2 Indicators, Predicted Symptoms, and Contrast with Interview*

| Red Flag MMPI/MMPI-2 Indicators | Test-Predicted Symptoms | Interview Suggestions |
| --- | --- | --- |
| High Scale 9—Mania | Narcissistic, grandiose, and overly active hypomanic behavior | A typical quiet individual interview does not indicate manic behavior |
| High Scale 6—Paranoid | Suspicious hostility, blaming, projecting of negative feeling onto others | Seems organized, calmly logical, and sensitive |
| High-Point 89/98 | Overly energized, confused, hostile potential sudden emergence of psychotic state | Seems only scattered and energized, often very enthusiastic |
| High-Point 68/86 | Confused, disordered thinking with paranoid features | Seems scattered, disorganized, with blaming |
| High MAC-R | Alcoholism involving impulse problems, rebelliousness, and control problems | Seems psychologically intact, but may minimize, deny, or otherwise rationalize drinking |

hypomanic spouse can become overwhelmed with energizing feelings and lose control.

Another problematic scale score is the high 6, suggesting a paranoid stance possibly accompanied by a thought disorder. This falls in the category of needing special consideration by the therapist. The spouse with the high Scale 6 may seem quite organized, calmly logical, and individually sensitive, but with a part-ner or other source of information the therapist may discover a picture of general suspicious hostility, a consistent blaming of others, and even a projection onto others of the spouse's own negative qualities.

In addition to these single scale red flags, there are two particularly problem high-point codes: 8–9 and 6–8. The 8–9s are potentially dangerous because of the combined energized aspect of Scale 9 and the confused, distorted thinking of the high Scale 8. Greene (1991, p. 283) states that these psychotic states come on suddenly. With the 6–8s, a thought disorder with paranoid features, possible paranoid schizophrenia is a major consideration.

Another red flag is a high score on the MAC-R, which predicts at a high level of accuracy (probabilistically for a group) the sort of alcoholism problem in-volving impulsivity, action orientation, rebelliousness, and overall problems in control. This appears to be a personality dimension akin to Scale 4. A high score here may pick up a recovering alcoholic as well. But it should be noted that a low score can point to an obsessive, worried, anxious individual who, in self-medicating for anxiety, abuses alcohol. Thus, this is a true red flag pointing to investigation, not a precipitous conclusion that alcoholism is or is not present.


GENDER ISSUES

Two scales are worth appraising in evaluating gender issues: Gender Role–Masculine (GM) and Gender Role–Feminine (GF). Each gender scale consists of items that are consistent with masculine and feminine stereotypes. Spouses scoring high on a same-gender scale may be caught in rigid role-conforming be-havior, which may be impeding the marriage or, alternatively, may provide a framework within which the therapist may need to work.


SPOUSAL DOMINANCE/SUBMISSION ISSUES

Those high (above T 65 on the MMPI-2) on Dominance (Do) are confident and take responsibility for themselves. If Do is very high, they may tend to take responsibility for others; this may prove a valuable style if they are in an occupa-tion that requires very active leadership (e.g., military officer), but may be sti-fling to the spouse if the spouse seeks an egalitarian relationship. A Do that is significantly high accompanied by elevated clinical scales such as Scales 4 and 9 may point toward even more dominating behavior that is highly energized and resists limitations.

High scorers on Dependance (Dy) tend to be submissive and passive and to lean on others. Research indicates that such scores may be contaminated by a depressive quality (Greene, 1991, p. 213). However, they may provide a clue to a general psychological orientation to interpersonal relationships, including with a spouse.

Because the Do and Dy are framed as normal characteristics, they provide a base for feedback for a couple. The content scores also meet this criteria for beginning interpretation.

CONTENT SCALES

MMPI-2 content scales include scales of what the test developers refer to as Internal Symptomatic Behavior, such as Anxiety, Depression, and Health Concerns; External Aggressive Tendencies, such as Anger and Antisocial Practices; and General Problem areas, such as Family Problems (mentioned earlier) and Social Discomfort. When scores in these areas reach a significant level, they reflect the consciously perceived problems of partners, and so, as noted above, provide a good basis for beginning test interpretations to the spouses. The process of feedback to couples using the MMPI/MMPI-2 and other inventories is addressed in Chapter 9.

## Summary

This chapter presents an approach toward interpreting couple MMPI/MMPI-2s based on an elaboration of probable interactional dynamics of an MMPI typology of five types of couples as identified in previous research: openly warring couples, unhappy problem-focused couples, husband-blaming couples, psychologically disordered couples, and distant, calm couples. Possibly as many as 50% of couples with marital problems fall into this typology. Suggestions are made for considering other patterns and further understanding couple patterns by use of various specialized and content scores.

# CHAPTER 3

## The MCMI:
### Assessing Personality Styles
### or Disorders of Marital Partners

This chapter addresses the most recent iteration of the 20-year-old MCMI™, the MCMI-III™. Developed in the 1970s by personality theorist Theodore Millon and colleagues, the MCMI has relatively rapidly reached an established place with clinicians concerned with identifying and describing personality disorder and/or personality style. The place of what might be termed the Millon approach is evident in recent literature. For example, in a recent text, *Integrative Assessment of Adult Personality* (Beutler & Berren, 1995) the MCMI is one of three methods discussed for assessing personality, along with the MMPI-2 and the Rorschach. A recent issue of the *Journal of Personality Assessment* placed as its lead research article a comparison of the diagnostic efficiency of these three instruments (Ganellen, 1996).

The reader experienced with the MCMI may wish to skip the "Capsule Summary" and go straight to the section "Why Use the MCMI-III with Couples?"

### CAPSULE SUMMARY OF THE MCMI-III

The MCMI-III consists of 175 statements about personality and behavior to which the client responds "true" or "false" as applied to himself or herself. An eighth-grade reading level is required. The MCMI-III is user-friendly in that it can usually be completed within 20 to 30 minutes and may be taken directly on a computer or in paper format. For the clinician, the inventory is efficient in that computer scoring on 28 scales and a computer-based interpretive report can be produced within a few minutes.

The MCMI-III is the product of extensive and exhaustive research strategies, which include a theoretical base, sophisticated item development (including utilization of items from earlier inventory versions along with

34

newly selected items), submission to about 1,000 clients, and ratings by several hundred clinicians.

Of the 28 scales, 4 concern reliability and validity; 11 measure clinical personality patterns (including disorders); 3 indicate severe personality patterns (disorders); 7 measure clinical syndromes; and 3 reflect serious clinical syndromes.

## VALIDITY AND RELIABILITY INDICES

*Validity Index (Scale V)*. This scale consists of three items that are highly improbable. When two of these are endorsed, the profile is considered invalid.

*Disclosure Index (Scale X)*. This scale measures the degree to which the client is inclined to be frank and self-revealing (a high score) or reticent and secretive (a low score). The MCMI-III should be considered invalid when the raw score drops below 34 or rises above 178. This is the only MCMI-III scale with a low score that is interpretable.

*Desirability Index (Y)*. The higher the BR (base rate) score on Index Y, the more the client is presenting in a positive light, maximizing virtues, and appearing emotionally composed.

*Debasement Index (Scale Z)*. This scale reflects tendencies to present with more troublesome emotional and personal difficulties, especially when the Scale Z BR score is above 75.

## CLINICAL PERSONALITY PATTERNS

These scales parallel the categories of personality disorders in *DSM-IV* (APA, 1994). Truncated descriptions below are adapted from the *MCMI-III Manual* (Millon, 1994a, pp. 11–14). Each description represents a cardinal category designed to provide a guide for reasoning about actual profiles, which are frequently combinations of categories having various degrees of seriousness ranging from features of personality to traits to disorders.

Scale 1, Schizoid. People with this personality disorder are demarcated by a lack of desire and the incapacity to experience pleasure or pain. Distant and asocial, their emotional needs are minimal.

*Scale 2B, Avoidant*. Though they may appear as withdrawn as the schizoid, these persons long for contact with others but have developed a solitary lifestyle to protect themselves from experiencing potential pain and anguish.

*Scale 2B, Depressive.* Although similar to the schizoid and the avoidant in many ways, including the inability to experience pleasure, lack of joy, and glumness, the depressives have a significant sense of loss and a loss of hope that joy can be retrieved.

*Scale 3, Dependent.* These persons turn to others for nurturance, security, and guidance, waiting passively for others to show them the way.

*Scale 4, Histrionic.* Though similar to dependents in turning to others, histrionics are active, manipulative, and usually socially clever in order to feed an insatiable need for tribute and affection from others while hiding a fear of genuine autonomy.

*Scale 5, Narcissistic.* Overvaluing themselves, these persons appear arrogant, express unthinking entitlement, are egotistically self-involved, and may be sublimely confident that things will work out well even if they do not deign to engage in social give-and-take.

*Scale 6A, Antisocial.* These persons behave in enterprising ways but with little regard for rules of society, thus engaging in duplicitous, exploitive, or even illegal behavior in a world where they assume others will cause them pain, for which they seek revenge.

*Scale 6B, Aggressive (Sadistic).* These persons aggress against others in ways that provide satisfaction as they humiliate others and violate their rights and feelings during malicious, power-oriented behaviors.

*Scale 7, Compulsive.* Controlling and perfectionistic, compulsives place high demands on themselves and others; although they appear to conform, underneath they are angry and resentful.

*Scale 8A, Passive-Aggressive (Negativistic).* These persons vacillate between deference to and defiance of others, paralleling their inner struggles, sometimes erratically exploding in anger and stubbornness intermingled with periods of guilt and shame.

*Scale 8B, Self-Defeating.* Obsequious and self-sacrificing in manner, these persons place themselves in a position to be exploited; they recount past shames and anguish that may seem to be deserved, pessimistically anticipating a continuation of degradation in the future.

SEVERE PERSONALITY PATHOLOGY: THREE VARIATIONS

*Scale S, Schizotypal.* Cognitively dysfunctional and interpersonally detached, schizotypals think in peculiar ways, are isolative and ruminative, with an emotionally flattened affect.

*Scale C, Borderline.* Labile in emotions, intense, moody, angry, anxious, and depressed in varying proportions and with some seeming contradictory feelings appearing side by side, borderlines have difficulty maintaining a clear sense of identity and are preoccupied with securing affection, yet with their emotional expressions push others away.

*Scale P, Paranoid.* Remarkably set in their feelings and in thought patterns, paranoids appear defensively edgy, highly mistrustful, suspicious, and abrasively irritable as they overwork to maintain their own personal space against anticipated personal intrusions.

CLINICAL SYNDROMES

These are patterns that arise predominantly from the interaction of personality patterns with the environment. They often take the exaggerated form of some aspect of the fundamental personality pattern, and thus are transient, waxing and waning with stressors impinging on them personally. The syndromes parallel Axis I diagnoses in the *DSM-IV*.

*Scale A, Anxiety.* Apprehensive or specifically phobic, fearful, with somatic discomfort and a worrisomeness regarding and hyperalertness to the environment.

*Scale H, Somatoform.* Expression of psychological difficulties through somatic channels, which typically appear designed to gain attention.

*Scale N, Bipolar: Manic.* Superficial elation, restless overactivity, pressured speech, irritability, demanding, and dominating; when scores are marked, may be psychotic.

*Scale D, Dysthymia.* Poor self-esteem, discouragement, sadness, pessimism, a sense of futility, although to some extent still involved in life.

*Scale B, Alcohol Dependence.* Probable and continuing history of alcohol-related problems.

*Scale T, Drug Dependence.* Recurrent or recent history of drug abuse.

*Scale R, Posttraumatic Stress Disorder.* Anxious arousal, attempts to avoid distressing recollections or stimuli for possible recollections, along with possible nightmares and flashbacks that follow a fearful incident(s) perceived as life-threatening.

## SEVERE SYNDROMES

*Scale SS, Thought Disorder.* Possibly schizophrenic, schizophreniform, or brief reactive psychosis; may appear withdrawn, incongruous, disorganized, confused with inappropriate affect, thought disturbance, possibly scattered hallucinations, and unsystematic delusions.

*Scale CC, Major Depression.* Severely depressed, incapable of functioning, marked sense of dread, hopeless, suicidal potential, and general somatic problems.

*Scale PP, Delusional Disorder.* Feelings of being picked on, mistreated; harboring suspicions, highly paranoid, irrational, and belligerent, with interconnected delusions.

In developing measures for the 24 clinical dimensions, Millon utilized the prevalence and severity of a given disorder in the populations studied. The resulting BRs establish anchoring points for interpretations. BR 60 corresponds to the median average raw score. BR 75 indicates the "presence" of a "trait," and BR 85 indicates the "prominence" of a personality disorder, when considering the personality disorder scales. For the clinical syndrome scales, BR 75 indicates presence and BR 85 prominence of a syndrome.

The user is cautioned that the MCMI-III results are based on people coming for clinical assessments and therapeutic help. Therefore, ordinarily it should not be used beyond the clinical assessment situation (e.g., using the MCMI-III for employment screening is not appropriate). The problem is that it tends to overpathologize if used in a nonclinical setting.

At the same time, the MCMI-III is likely to understate pathology with the truly severely disturbed. Therefore, it is best applied to the vast majority of patients who are mildly to markedly (but not truly severely) disturbed. It should be underlined that the printout obtained on a given patient provides databased hypotheses to be investigated and interpreted by the trained clinician.

The MCMI-III scale results and the computerized report are linked with Theodore Millon's (1981; Millon & Klerman, 1986, 1994, 1996) personality theory and with the accepted standard for diagnosing mental disorders, the

*DSM-IV* (American Psychiatric Association, 1994). As to the first link, the MCMI-III was developed by Millon based on his comprehensive clinical theory. Although it provides useful information relative to the presence of Axis I syndromes, the MCMI-III's unique contribution to assessment is in its identification and description of personality disorders, Axis II in the *DSM-IV.*

Along with the important database on which the inventory rests, equally solid and particularly elegant is its tightly woven theoretical structure. Millon's theory, developed over many years and making thorough use of previous theorists, posits at its core that personality may be structured according to the balance of three polarities: pleasure-pain, self-other, and active-passive. He also posits thinking-feeling as a major polarity (1996, p. 191). This conceptualization serves as a basis for describing the clinical personality disorder prototypes that are characterized by an imbalance of one or more of these polarities. They are further delineated by four levels of clinical meaning taking these polarities into account: behavioral, phenomenological, intrapsychic, and biophysical. The concept of imbalance of polarities woven into the levels of clinical description provides a basis for both description and defining targets for therapy and therapeutic methods. The resulting construction is organized in the system of extensive hypotheses presented in the computerized printout on a given client, or can be derived by the clinician with a profile in hand of the 28 scale results and a thorough knowledge of Millon's theoretical approach. Clinicians new to the MCMI-III who wish to obtain an in-depth understanding of the MCMI-III are referred to the MCMI-III's excellent manual (Millon, 1997a). For a thorough understanding of Millon's theory of personality disorders, the reader needs to study Millon's *Disorders of Personality: DSM-IV and Beyond* (1996), a major revision and expansion of his classic book in this area (1981). Also strongly recommended is the *Interpretive Guide to the Millon Clinical Multiaxial Inventory,* published by the American Psychological Association (Choca & Ven Denburg, 1997). This book provides an orientation to interpreting this inventory in terms of personality styles, particularly useful in understanding disturbed couples. The psychotherapist developing treatment plans might wish to consult *Tactical Psychotherapy of the Personality Disorders: An MCMI-III–based Approach* (Retzlaff, 1995). *The Millon Inventories* (1997b) contains recent advances in interpreting the MCMI-III; note particularly the chapter "The MCMI in Treating Couples" (Nurse, 1997b).

Theodore Millon (1993) writes: "Those who use the MCMI-III and its reports should have at least a master's degree in clinical or counseling psychology or psychiatric social work with a graduate-level course in Tests and Measurements or internship or psychiatric residency status" (p. 6). The firm that sells the MCMI-III states that the purchaser must possess "a license to practice psychology independently or a graduate degree in psychology or a closely related field and either a graduate-level course in Tests and Measurements or participation in an NCS-approved workshop" (National Computer Systems, 1997, p. 94).

## Why Use the MCMI-III with Couples?

During the past 25 years, there has been a markedly increasing interest in ongoing personality characteristics, personality styles, and especially in personality disorders (Millon & Klerman, 1986, pp. 640–642). This shift has accompanied an increasing societal and professional interest in relationships, acknowledging their importance, especially familial ones (Kaslow, 1990). The ongoing relationship behaviors are often more important to clinicians in the long run than a transitory condition, such as a reactive depressive state or infrequent, uncharacteristic acting-out. Both are common reactions to major family system changes such as those stimulated by the death of a family member. Because the MCMI-III addresses itself primarily and uniquely to these persistent characteristics of personality style and disorder (along with measuring various clinical syndromes), it has a special usefulness for the contemporary clinician who must differentiate chronic behaviors from situationally related ones. The MCMI-III is at present the only major, widely used inventory that focuses on assessing qualities of personality disorders and their lesser variants—styles, traits, and features—within the context of a well-developed theory consistent with the *DSM-IV*. That fact alone makes it not simply an add-on, but a central instrument for a comprehensive assessment battery. And the MCMI-III's potential for uncovering personality style or disorder also provides a rationale for using the MCMI-III alone with couples. It is ordinarily essential for the therapist to look quickly beneath immediate conflict, overt anxiety, and depression to understand the couple relationship rooted in their personality styles, which form the basis for their symptoms.

## Individual Systems and Couple Systems

Although measuring individual personality characteristics, the MCMI-III is compatible with a systemic way of thinking. Of nine principles that Millon (1996) provides for conceptualizing personality and its disorders, two are particularly pertinent: "Personality pathogenesis is not linear, but sequentially interactive and multiply distributed through the entire system. . . . Personality criteria by which to assess pathology should be logically coordinated with the systems model itself" (p. 7). With these principles in mind, applying a systems approach to a couple or an entire family seems naturally consistent with a systems approach applied to an individual.

For a full understanding of the couple relationship, sufficient attention needs to be paid to the interactions of the systems of the partners and their individual personality systems. For practical therapeutic purposes, a therapist can, however, act effectively primarily on the interaction between the individuals: a couple system approach. Or a therapist can with success chose to intervene to assist each partner in modifying his or her own personality system, whether or not the partners are seen together. In the present therapeutic world, the therapist ordinarily will need to choose one emphasis or another in couple therapy, while taking account of the unemphasized other (perhaps only momentarily) secondarily. In the approach described here, the primary base for understanding focuses first on the personalities of the individuals, then on how their systems interrelate, and finally on developing tactics for intervention. The interventions become based on a solid grasp of intrapersonal systems and some hypotheses about the probable interactions between the two individual systems constituting the partners' personalities. The belief is that newly developed ways of thinking about and measuring individual personality (using the MCMI-III) may lead quickly to fresh, more individually tailored approaches in couple (and family) therapy (Nurse, 1997b). This can come about because of the enrichment provided by a well-organized understanding of the individual that is based firmly in the context of in-depth personality theory, and is an understanding that can occur before or even as the partners are beginning to be understood in their uniqueness individually and the uniqueness of the system of their relationship.

## The Personality Style–Disorder Continuum

Everyone manifests a personality style (or combination of styles). The assumption is made that no sharp line separates the normal from the psychopathological. In fact, the assumption is made that the normal personality style and the pathological personality disorder fall at different ends of a continuum (Millon, 1996, p. 7). The more the personality style is characterized by inflexibility, the fostering of vicious or self-defeating cycles, and either a fragility or a lack of resilience under stress, the more the style is considered to move along the continuum toward becoming classified as a disorder. These classifications are abstractions that serve to guide thinking, not to be misconstrued as diseases that one "catches" or is possessed by. Particularly early on in treatment, the abstractions and the related theory can provide very useful guidance with two clients who are initially unknown to the therapist. As struggling partners become known and their individual psychologies and couple system become understood, the uniqueness of the individuals and their individual system comes to the fore-front for both the therapist and the couple. As the original classification fades into the background, it remains available as a framework to be brought into the light as a guide to be considered when therapeutic problems arise or therapeutic progress is evaluated.

## The Process of Couple MCMI-III Analysis

Having first checked for satisfactory validity and response style scores, overall meanings of all scores need to be considered. The therapist needs to see if the profile of either partner reaches a level of BR that suggests hypotheses indicating a personality disorder (BR 85+), personality trait (BR 75–84), or personality features (scores approaching BR 75).

Next, the significant scores should be compared with other information collected. This would include, for example, discovering consistencies or inconsistencies within data about presenting complaints, socioeconomic level, occupation, and general personal and family history, including paying particular attention to identifying any individual life cycle and family life cycle issues. Family of origin history may not be easily volunteered without appropriate prompting from the interviewer. Adults frequently are not aware or tend to deny connections between family of origin issues and couple and family issues.

As an aspect of this initial assessment of available data, the general functionality of each individual's overall style needs to be considered with reference to his or her occupation outside the home. For example, finding that the Compulsive scale is at least to some degree significant for a successful accountant would be expected, and finding some dramatic, histrionic features on the profile of a good teacher would not be a surprise. It could be a surprise if the reverse were true, especially if a very high single score were obtained on the Histrionic scale by the accountant and for the teacher on the Compulsive scale. One would expect, in this latter case, that their disorders might not be functional in major aspects of their professional existence—a possible problem area.

An overall consideration of a pronounced style or disorder may generate hypotheses about the couple's interrelationship. For example, with the stereotypic histrionic/compulsive couple, her expressive (histrionic) style might have been attractive to him initially and pulled him out of his usual patterns and increased his level of awareness of feeling. For her, his stability and pattern of achievement through hard work might have been attractive and reassuring. With time, however, for him her style might have turned into an annoying series of crises, and his comfortable stability might have boring (compulsive) sameness for her.

Finally, it may be that a change in the family environment needs to be factored into the picture. The arrival of the first baby, which changes the dyadic system to a triadic one, is an adjustment for everyone (Cowan & Cowan, 1992). The family system is rebalanced at that time. This may be especially difficult for those with stereotypically dependent or narcissistic personality aspects. The dependent must become more self-sufficient and the narcissist must learn to function with less general attention and specific adoration centered on him or her.

Having completed this overall analysis, an in-depth analysis of the personalities needs to be undertaken. This can be done with the help of the *Manual* (1997a) and/or, even better, Millon's *Disorders of Personality* (1996). This shift aims to provide a review of the significant personality disorder scale descriptions. These are not simply paragraphs of descriptions, but are focused on a review of the clinical domains of the prototypes of the highest significant personality pattern scores. These clinical domains are categorized by four levels: behavioral, phenomenological, intrapsychic, and biophysical (Millon, 1994a, 1996).

With couple interpretations, it is particularly important to look at the behavioral level, made up of two sections, expressive behavior and interpersonal behavior. This is, as may be obvious, because the behavioral level is immediately available to therapist observation as partners complain about each other and engage in repetitive patterns of behavior. From that level, inferences can be systematically drawn about linkages with features of domains falling at other levels. This analysis permits the development of more detailed descriptions of the interacting personality expressions of the couple and provides a basis for psychotherapeutic planning and intervention.

The different levels call for differential interventions and are drawn from large amounts of theory, clinical experience, and (sometimes) research relative to particular levels. At the immediate behavioral level, interventions based on behavioral marital therapy may be called for. For intervention at the phenomenological level, a humanistic or client-centered approach could be considered, or a cognitive therapy. And for the intrapsychic level, psychodynamic and psychoanalytical approaches may be suggested. However, much, if not all, of the therapy with personality disorders requires an integrative approach.

Millon's (1996) theoretical framework posits that there are three fundamental polarities in understanding personality that can provide overall guides for therapeutic interventions contingent upon the framework described above. As noted earlier, these three polarities are pleasure-pain, self-other, and active-passive. Different personality disorders or permutations of cardinal types have different combinations of strengths or weaknesses in each polarity for each individual. Just as with each partner, it is proposed that each couple develops a compensatory balance of weaknesses and strengths growing with reference to their polarity balances. For years, family therapists have observed the homeostatic function of these balances as the couple or family system tends to make adjustments to maintain itself, thereby preserving the relationships between individuals, which meet some individual needs. Thus, identifying where individuals fall with reference to polarities and their personality styles or disorders and the accompanying reinforcing couple/family system linked to these polarities provides a basis for deciding what level and what therapeutic approach to select and with what timing.

At a practical clinical level, with these basic data available, it is useful to look at the polarities of the major high scores for each partner and simply compare them. Often, at this level, immediate compatibilities will be suggested. Particular attention should be paid to the self-other polarity because of its implications for the couple relationship. For example, a narcissist (self-emphasis) is likely to need a mate who looks up to him or her and continues to reflect his or her superiority (Nurse, 1997a). His or her mate might be a dependent personality (other-emphasis) who needs a strong figure with whom to identify, submit to, and manage their life.

Another "classical" combination is the compulsive and histrionic couple (Sperry & Maniacci, 1998). The compulsive, with a conflict between self-other polarities, an orientation to avoid pain, and a passive attitude, may be stirred up by the histrionic, who has an active attitude focused on the other of the self-other polarity. The histrionic in turn may be reassured with the stirred-up feelings focused on the compulsive that he or she is able to generate.

Practical cases will now be considered, which take into account the polarity relationships along with the behavioral, phenomenolgical, intrapsychic, and biophysical levels of clinical meaning. These cases are also considered from the standpoint that symptoms may have developed for one or both partners based on a change of circumstance for the couple/family system, such as the arrival of a child, the insatiable quality of some need structures for persons with certain personality disorders, the reality of being together and knowing each other more deeply, maturing at different rates, gender differences through the life cycle, and so on. The change of circumstance may have disrupted the way their personality styles complemented each other, including how they solved problems. Of course, they might have always had problems and things might have deteriorated even more. And a major disruption may have been the arrival of a child; given their personality styles, one spouse or both may have taken this change personally and feel unduly deprived of nurturance and/or support from the other. These and related ideas may help therapists think through to what degree the MCMI-III inventory results reflect situational versus long-term manifestations of personality characteristics.

## Some Examples of Prototypic Couples

These examples focus on the couple relationships and their personality styles or disorders. Millon's theoretical and interpretive information and the author's experience with couples are used as a background for proposing interpretations. Data are derived from actual cases of couples, but represent no specific unaltered case.

NARCISSISTIC MALE/HISTRIONIC FEMALE, EARL AND DOROTHY

Earl, 49, and Dorothy, 44, came to the therapist's office to work on their relationship, which had been tumultuous from its beginning 10 years before. They
had their ups and downs, punctuated by threats of leaving their relationship.
They also had some concerns about how their relationship might be affecting
their 8-year-old son. Earl, a wholesale salesman, was on the road a fair amount of
time, and Dorothy worked part-time as a receptionist in a professional office,
taking pride in homemaking as well. Earl believed that Dorothy was too easy on
their son, Edward, lavishing too much affection on him. Dorothy believed she
needed to be protective of her son and that Earl was too hard on him. Dorothy
had a concern that Earl might be "having a midlife crisis," resulting in his stray-
ing into relationships when on his selling trips. This fear was compounded by a
sense that her own looks were beginning to reflect her age, and that she could
no longer pass for being in her twenties.

*Dorothy's MCMI-III Profile*

As may be seen in Figure 3.1, Dorothy's MCMI-III profile is valid, although suggesting she lacks openness (Disclosure, Scale X, low). She shows a clear peak on
the Histrionic Scale, Scale 4, almost reaching the level of a personality disorder.
Thus, one might expect a general histrionic style but not the entrenched level of
a disorder; there may be some flexibility for change. There also appears to be
present some compensating characteristics in the form of a mildly elevated Compulsive score, Scale 7. Her general emotional style is likely to be balanced by
some ability to be organized, thorough, and conscientious. Characteristics of immediately engaging affect coupled with some need for organization and order
stand her in good stead in her work out of the home. These are positive characteristics that were conveyed to her in interpreting the results of her MCMI.

At a behavioral level, Dorothy conveys an *engaging* and sometimes *dramatic*
attitude. She can manipulate others, paying attention to them in a somewhat se-
ductive way. This interpersonal style, in fact, was one that had intrigued Earl
from the start of their relationship. He interpreted her behavior as reflecting
real interest in him, rather than that she needs to be constantly seeking reassurance as to her value.

She has appeared like an "airhead" to him, which reflects the fact that, at
a phenomenological level, she is *cognitively flighty.* She perceives herself as *gregarious;* others may sense her as shallow. Given the lack of any symptoms evident in
the MCMI-III (very low clinical syndrome scores), she may *dissociate* effectively
and avoid reflecting on even fleeting unpleasant emotions. Alternatively, she may
be denying different feelings, either in her life in general or on this test in particular. Whatever the case may be, her internal process reinforces the idea that
Earl needs to change; he has the "problem." She is probably only vaguely aware
that her rapidly shifting moods, including both happy and angry expressions, may

MCMI-III™

## MILLON CLINICAL MULTIAXIAL INVENTORY - III
### CONFIDENTIAL INFORMATION FOR PROFESSIONAL USE ONLY

Valid Profile

PERSONALITY CODE:  - ** 4 * 7 5 + - " 2A 3 8A 6A 6B 1 2B 8B ' ' // - ** - * //
SYNDROME CODE:  - ** - * // - ** - * //

| CATEGORY | | SCORE | | PROFILE OF BR SCORES | | | | | DIAGNOSTIC SCALES |
|---|---|---|---|---|---|---|---|---|---|
| | | RAW | BR | 0 | 60 | 75 | 85 | 115 | |
| MODIFYING INDICES | X | 45 | 10 | | | | | | DISCLOSURE |
| | Y | 13 | 59 | | | | | | DESIRABILITY |
| | Z | 1 | 34 | | | | | | DEBASEMENT |
| CLINICAL PERSONALITY PATTERNS | 1 | 1 | 23 | | | | | | SCHIZOID |
| | 2A | 2 | 30 | | | | | | AVOIDANT |
| | 2B | 0 | 13 | | | | | | DEPRESSIVE |
| | 3 | 2 | 26 | | | | | | DEPENDENT |
| | 4 | 14 | 83 | | | | | | HISTRIONIC |
| | 5 | 10 | 68 | | | | | | NARCISSISTIC |
| | 6A | 1 | 25 | | | | | | ANTISOCIAL |
| | 6B | 1 | 25 | | | | | | AGGRESSIVE (SADISTIC) |
| | 7 | 15 | 73 | | | | | | COMPULSIVE |
| | 8A | 2 | 26 | | | | | | PASSIVE-AGGRESSIVE |
| | 8B | 0 | 13 | | | | | | SELF-DEFEATING |
| SEVERE PERSONALITY PATHOLOGY | S | 0 | 7 | | | | | | SCHIZOTYPAL |
| | C | 0 | 7 | | | | | | BORDERLINE |
| | P | 0 | 7 | | | | | | PARANOID |
| CLINICAL SYNDROMES | A | 0 | 7 | | | | | | ANXIETY DISORDER |
| | H | 0 | 7 | | | | | | SOMATOFORM DISORDER |
| | N | 0 | 7 | | | | | | BIPOLAR: MANIC DISORDER |
| | D | 2 | 20 | | | | | | DYSTHYMIC DISORDER |
| | B | 0 | 7 | | | | | | ALCOHOL DEPENDENCE |
| | T | 0 | 7 | | | | | | DRUG DEPENDENCE |
| | R | 0 | 7 | | | | | | POST-TRAUMATIC STRESS |
| SEVERE SYNDROMES | SS | 1 | 16 | | | | | | THOUGHT DISORDER |
| | CC | 0 | 7 | | | | | | MAJOR DEPRESSION |
| | PP | 0 | 7 | | | | | | DELUSIONAL DISORDER |

Figure 3.1
Dorothy, Histrionic

Copyright © 1994 DICANDRIEN, INC. All rights reserved
Published and distributed exclusively by National Computer Systems, Inc.,
Minneapolis, MN 55440. Reprinted with permission by NCS.

be disconcerting to others. At first, they were entertaining to Earl, but he grew tired of them. This, coupled with her somewhat superficial interest in him, tended to cool his interest in her. However, whenever she sensed this decline in mutual interest occurring, she put on a show of showering him with special attention (as she read that she needed to do, according to some popular magazine articles).

## Earl's MCMI-III Profile

Figure 3.2 presents Earl's MCMI-III profile. His moderately high score for Narcissism suggests a style or a trait but not a disorder. As with Dorothy, this is a positive indication because it does not point to the entrenchment of a personality disorder. His positive self-regard was pointed out to him in discussing the inventory results, as was his expectation that he will do well and that he probably expends considerable energy to live up to his high standards.

Unfortunately, at a behavioral level, he may act in an arrogant fashion with a tendency to irresponsibly ignore social norms and standards. He may fail to be empathetic and be *interpersonally exploitive*, seemingly unaware of the negative impact on others. Phenomenologically, he may imagine in immature and self-glorifying fantasies how successful he is or may become. Not surprisingly, he does not stay with any one job for more than three years, always looking for a position that more meets how he thinks he should be treated. He has the unfortunate ability to lie to himself or distort the truth and then, worse, believe himself. He is maintained in this proclivity at the intrapsychic level by his *rationalization mechanism*. At a biophysical level, he maintains a cool aura, seemingly not shaken by anything. One of the attractions for Dorothy was that he had this cool aura and accompanying self-confidence.

Earl was initially taken by Dorothy because she seemed to be so taken by him, and because of his sense of how people may think of his being able to attract beautiful, vivacious Dorothy. He was flattered by the fact that she seemed to be focused on him, which he interpreted as being attracted to him because of his superior presentation and development. To his chagrin, as they moved through the early stages of their marriage, he began to understand her need to gain attention at parties. This conflicted with his need to be viewed by others as superior to them.

When they had a male child, Earl began to have feelings of jealousy, which he pushed away, believing that having this feeling was beneath him. But he found himself feeling deprived of much-needed adulation as Dorothy doted on their child, and also experienced being overly critical of his growing son, who was getting lots of attention from Dorothy.

In sum, Dorothy had been originally attracted to Earl because of his sureness, command, and interest in her. He had been attracted to her because of her apparent attraction to him and his own images of how enhanced his life would be, how people would see him, with her on his arm. They both became disillusioned, periodically fought, and then triangulated their growing son in a struggle to gain

MCMI-III™

## MILLON CLINICAL MULTIAXIAL INVENTORY - III
### CONFIDENTIAL INFORMATION FOR PROFESSIONAL USE ONLY

Valid Profile

PERSONALITY CODE:   - ** 5 * 6A 8B 6B 2B + 4 7 8A " 3 2A 1 ' ' // - ** - * //
SYNDROME CODE:   - ** - * // - ** - * //

| CATEGORY | | SCORE | | PROFILE OF BR SCORES | | | | | DIAGNOSTIC SCALES |
|---|---|---|---|---|---|---|---|---|---|
| | | RAW | BR | 0 | 60 | 75 | 85 | 115 | |
| MODIFYING INDICES | X | 75 | 49 | | | | | | DISCLOSURE |
| | Y | 14 | 65 | | | | | | DESIRABILITY |
| | Z | 1 | 34 | | | | | | DEBASEMENT |
| CLINICAL PERSONALITY PATTERNS | 1 | 0 | 0 | | | | | | SCHIZOID |
| | 2A | 1 | 12 | | | | | | AVOIDANT |
| | 2B | 3 | 60 | | | | | | DEPRESSIVE |
| | 3 | 3 | 30 | | | | | | DEPENDENT |
| | 4 | 17 | 52 | | | | | | HISTRIONIC |
| | 5 | 18 | 81 | | | | | | NARCISSISTIC |
| | 6A | 10 | 72 | | | | | | ANTISOCIAL |
| | 6B | 10 | 63 | | | | | | AGGRESSIVE (SADISTIC) |
| | 7 | 10 | 39 | | | | | | COMPULSIVE |
| | 8A | 5 | 38 | | | | | | PASSIVE-AGGRESSIVE |
| | 8B | 4 | 68 | | | | | | SELF-DEFEATING |
| SEVERE PERSONALITY PATHOLOGY | S | 4 | 62 | | | | | | SCHIZOTYPAL |
| | C | 5 | 50 | | | | | | BORDERLINE |
| | P | 2 | 24 | | | | | | PARANOID |
| CLINICAL SYNDROMES | A | 1 | 20 | | | | | | ANXIETY DISORDER |
| | H | 0 | 0 | | | | | | SOMATOFORM DISORDER |
| | N | 10 | 69 | | | | | | BIPOLAR: MANIC DISORDER |
| | D | 3 | 60 | | | | | | DYSTHYMIC DISORDER |
| | B | 5 | 65 | | | | | | ALCOHOL DEPENDENCE |
| | T | 4 | 60 | | | | | | DRUG DEPENDENCE |
| | R | 0 | 0 | | | | | | POST-TRAUMATIC STRESS |
| SEVERE SYNDROMES | SS | 4 | 60 | | | | | | THOUGHT DISORDER |
| | CC | 0 | 0 | | | | | | MAJOR DEPRESSION |
| | PP | 1 | 25 | | | | | | DELUSIONAL DISORDER |

Figure 3.2
Earl, Narcissistic

Copyright © 1994 DICANDRIEN, INC. All rights reserved.
Published and distributed exclusively by National Computer Systems, Inc.,
Minneapolis, MN 55440. Reprinted with permission by NCS.

a relationship with him to help make up for what they did not have with each other.

*Planning for Treatment*

Each spouse was initially seen individually by a same-gender psychologist. In individual sessions, each seemed rather reasonable. Dorothy was only somewhat emotional, and Earl was a little self-aggrandizing, but when they were seen by the therapists in a four-way meeting, their complementary histrionic and narcissistic styles became exacerbated. She became very emotional and he very haughty in their relationship disorder. They blew up and declared they were divorcing. However, they called a week later for another appointment. They had made up, seducing each other, literally and figuratively.

On returning to therapy, the goals for Dorothy were to learn to put restraints on her emotionality by capitalizing on the strength of her more factual, organizing side; moving in this direction would help her be less cognitively flighty and help her develop a more solid cognitive structure. She needed to be helped to find out more of what she wanted for herself in her family relationships, which would result in strengthening the self (as opposed to the other) in the polarity and put less emphasis on her habitual pattern of focusing on others.

At the same time, it was necessary to work actively to help Earl begin to be more in touch with his own feelings and better understand Dorothy's feelings. Actively challenging him to guess, then checking out feelings that she might be having, was helpful in his learning to be more empathetic. Also, family sessions including their son were prescribed; at these sessions, the therapist would work to help Earl get in contact with his son's experience, thereby fostering Earl's empathetic responses. This also might enable the therapist to intervene to block any inadvertent disdainful, discounting comments by father aimed at son or wife.

It was anticipated that in the ongoing couples sessions, they would be repeating in various forms the enticer-enticed patterns that cyclically led to the marital/family disruption. Despite the seeming fury of their periodic explosions, because their patterns were not markedly entrenched and because they seemed to have interpersonal difficulties particularly in their family relationship, it seemed that couple and family therapy would be ideal interventions for improving their family relationships and also for positively modifying their general coping styles.

## COMPULSIVE FEMALE/ DEPENDENT-AVOIDANT MALE, LILA AND PAUL

Lila, 32, and Paul, 36, had two children under 6 and a baby 10 months old. In talking with same-gender cotherapists separately, each complained that the other no longer was interested in or cared about the partner. Paul believed Lila made decisions unilaterally; he thought that she did not want him at home very much. Lila complained that Paul was not home enough and neglected his parenting. Paul worked for a high-tech firm that employed an equal number of young men and women, many of whom were single. The work environment required Paul to be heavily involved on task forces that demanded intense interpersonal cooperative discussions aimed at developing new products. In this environment, Paul became emotionally engaged in a relationship with one of his female coworkers. When Lila found out that Paul frequently spend many hours per week with the coworker, not only working but during lunch and after work, Lila became resentful and jealous. Her feelings escalated when work team trips out of town were being planned. Paul believed she was making a mountain out of a molehill; after all, they were not going to bed together. He didn't mind if she talked much to her male cohorts at work, as long as it didn't become physical. Lila's position was that she cared for three small children, kept the house immaculate, and was going back to work part time; she felt overwhelmed with responsibility.

Given what had happened, Lila saw no other choice but to have Paul move out. Paul was going along with this, experiencing being cut out of home life significantly already. They came to couples therapy as a last resort. Lila wanted to make sure she gave the marriage every opportunity, and Paul privately wished that it didn't have to be this choice, feeling rejected but going along with Lila as usual.

### Lila's MCMI-III Profile

Although the profile (see Figure 3.3) is valid, Lila clearly was presenting herself in the best possible light (Desirability, Scale Y). Lila scores just at a level to be considered a compulsive personality disorder. At a behavioral level, the profile reveals Lila is *excessively disciplined*, maintaining a highly structured, organized life. She appears very conscientious about taking care of job and home responsibilities, including her mothering activities. *Interpersonally respectful*, she is valued at work and organizes her children as much as a 3- and a 6-year-old can be organized.

Phenomenologically, consistent with her behavior, she sees herself as *conscientious*, devoted to thoroughness, and thus fearful of not getting things done in the best possible way. For example, she works long hours to ensure that her house is spotless, despite the realities of the normal behavior of her preschool children. She maintains an inner world, *cognitively constricted*, that is narrow and rule-bound, anticipating that others will behave similarly. Using *reaction formation* as a major defense, she appears superreasonable, not dealing with sometimes contrary feelings, being fearful of underlying feelings, especially anger. Thus, her underlying state is one of tension, grimness, and tight control of emotions; a *solemn mood* characterizes her psychological state.

MCMI-III™

## MILLON CLINICAL MULTIAXIAL INVENTORY - III
### CONFIDENTIAL INFORMATION FOR PROFESSIONAL USE ONLY

Valid Profile

PERSONALITY CODE:   7 ** - * 4 + 5 " 3 2A 6B 1 2B 8A 6A 8B ' ' // - ** - * //
SYNDROME CODE:   - ** - * // - ** - * //

| CATEGORY | | SCORE | | PROFILE OF BR SCORES | | | | | DIAGNOSTIC SCALES |
|---|---|---|---|---|---|---|---|---|---|
| | | RAW | BR | 0 | 60 | 75 | 85 | 115 | |
| MODIFYING INDICES | X | 59 | 33 | | | | | | DISCLOSURE |
| | Y | 18 | 84 | | | | | | DESIRABILITY |
| | Z | 1 | 34 | | | | | | DEBASEMENT |
| CLINICAL PERSONALITY PATTERNS | 1 | 2 | 21 | | | | | | SCHIZOID |
| | 2A | 3 | 27 | | | | | | AVOIDANT |
| | 2B | 2 | 14 | | | | | | DEPRESSIVE |
| | 3 | 5 | 34 | | | | | | DEPENDENT |
| | 4 | 16 | 71 | | | | | | HISTRIONIC |
| | 5 | 10 | 56 | | | | | | NARCISSISTIC |
| | 6A | 0 | 1 | | | | | | ANTISOCIAL |
| | 6B | 2 | 25 | | | | | | AGGRESSIVE (SADISTIC) |
| | 7 | 21 | 85 | | | | | | COMPULSIVE |
| | 8A | 1 | 8 | | | | | | PASSIVE-AGGRESSIVE |
| | 8B | 0 | 1 | | | | | | SELF-DEFEATING |
| SEVERE PERSONALITY PATHOLOGY | S | 1 | 16 | | | | | | SCHIZOTYPAL |
| | C | 0 | 1 | | | | | | BORDERLINE |
| | P | 2 | 31 | | | | | | PARANOID |
| CLINICAL SYNDROMES | A | 0 | 1 | | | | | | ANXIETY DISORDER |
| | H | 0 | 1 | | | | | | SOMATOFORM DISORDER |
| | N | 2 | 25 | | | | | | BIPOLAR: MANIC DISORDER |
| | D | 0 | 1 | | | | | | DYSTHYMIC DISORDER |
| | B | 2 | 61 | | | | | | ALCOHOL DEPENDENCE |
| | T | 0 | 1 | | | | | | DRUG DEPENDENCE |
| | R | 0 | 1 | | | | | | POST-TRAUMATIC STRESS |
| SEVERE SYNDROMES | SS | 0 | 1 | | | | | | THOUGHT DISORDER |
| | CC | 0 | 1 | | | | | | MAJOR DEPRESSION |
| | PP | 0 | 1 | | | | | | DELUSIONAL DISORDER |

Figure 3.3
Lila, Compulsive

Copyright © 1994 DICANDRIEN, INC. All rights reserved.
Published and distributed exclusively by National Computer Systems, Inc.,
Minneapolis, MN 55440. Reprinted with permission by NCS.

One question regarding her MCMI profile is whether this compulsive pattern has existed as a style that—under pressure of caring for three small children, a good-sized home, part-time work, and her marriage relationship—has escalated to the level of personality disorder, or whether her compulsivity has always been at essentially the level of disorder.

### Paul's MCMI-III

As may be seen in Figure 3.4, Paul does not score at the level of personality disorder. However, he reaches the threshold for dependent-avoidant personality traits. This profile suggests that he has need for close relationships but has a hesitancy about approaching others for fear of rejection. At a behavioral level, Paul is *interpersonally submissive* and not expressive. His style is to protectfully distance himself, but as has been indicated, he is needful of relationships, requiring some sort of reassurance so that he does not constantly have to warily scan for problems or potential difficulties. Phenomenologically, he may be seen as *cognitively naïve*, avoiding confrontations, sometimes experiencing himself as weak and alienated. Thus, Paul believes that if he were to express himself more directly with Lila, he might be subject to criticism; this would spell rejection to him.

Intrapsychically, he feels a need to involve, if not devote, himself with others, *introjecting* their views and maintaining relationships through the use of considerable *fantasy*, avoiding significant anxiety. At a fundamental level, he experiences alternation between a *pacific mood* and, when he cannot manage things, a moderately *anguished mood.*

His pattern is one of trait or style. This makes it easier than if it were a disorder to appeal to him for reasonable collaboration, which might involve his modifying his style of interaction to reach his goal of increased closeness.

### Planning for Treatment

When Paul and Lila came in for help, they were first dealt with together to assist in stabilizing their living arrangements and set a contract so that there would be a time during which any major actions involving divorce would take place. Lila, who was headed for an attorney's office, agreed to hold off, conforming to what the cotherapists thought best. Paul arranged to live with relatives rather than take an apartment. He was pleased that the therapists strongly suggested at least temporary stabilization of their situation without taking active legal steps toward divorce.

Individually with the male cotherapist, Paul revealed that, although he had continued in his submissive pattern at home, he was cautiously becoming much more active at work, suggesting that he might be open to being more disclosing at home. He acknowledged his need for others, his dependency, and his pattern of avoiding conflict, but indicated that under the controlled conditions of therapy, just as with the controlled conditions at work, he would be more willing to

MCMI-III™

# MILLON CLINICAL MULTIAXIAL INVENTORY - III
## CONFIDENTIAL INFORMATION FOR PROFESSIONAL USE ONLY

Valid Profile

PERSONALITY CODE:  - ** 3 2A * 2B + 7 1 8A 5 4 6A " 6B 8B ' ' // - ** - * //
SYNDROME CODE:  - ** - * // - ** - * //

| CATEGORY | | SCORE RAW | BR | PROFILE OF BR SCORES 0 · 60 · 75 · 85 · 115 | DIAGNOSTIC SCALES |
|---|---|---|---|---|---|
| MODIFYING INDICES | X | 73 | 47 | | DISCLOSURE |
| | Y | 13 | 59 | | DESIRABILITY |
| | Z | 4 | 45 | | DEBASEMENT |
| CLINICAL PERSONALITY PATTERNS | 1 | 4 | 48 | | SCHIZOID |
| | 2A | 7 | 75 | | AVOIDANT |
| | 2B | 5 | 68 | | DEPRESSIVE |
| | 3 | 10 | 78 | | DEPENDENT |
| | 4 | 11 | 40 | | HISTRIONIC |
| | 5 | 9 | 42 | | NARCISSISTIC |
| | 6A | 5 | 38 | | ANTISOCIAL |
| | 6B | 3 | 26 | | AGGRESSIVE (SADISTIC) |
| | 7 | 15 | 49 | | COMPULSIVE |
| | 8A | 6 | 45 | | PASSIVE-AGGRESSIVE |
| | 8B | 1 | 20 | | SELF-DEFEATING |
| SEVERE PERSONALITY PATHOLOGY | S | 2 | 40 | | SCHIZOTYPAL |
| | C | 3 | 30 | | BORDERLINE |
| | P | 4 | 48 | | PARANOID |
| CLINICAL SYNDROMES | A | 2 | 40 | | ANXIETY DISORDER |
| | H | 1 | 30 | | SOMATOFORM DISORDER |
| | N | 3 | 36 | | BIPOLAR: MANIC DISORDER |
| | D | 2 | 40 | | DYSTHYMIC DISORDER |
| | B | 3 | 45 | | ALCOHOL DEPENDENCE |
| | T | 3 | 45 | | DRUG DEPENDENCE |
| | R | 1 | 15 | | POST-TRAUMATIC STRESS |
| SEVERE SYNDROMES | SS | 1 | 15 | | THOUGHT DISORDER |
| | CC | 0 | 0 | | MAJOR DEPRESSION |
| | PP | 0 | 0 | | DELUSIONAL DISORDER |

Figure 3.4
Paul, Dependent-Avoidant

Copyright © 1994 DICANDRIEN, INC. All rights reserved.
Published and distributed exlcusively by National Computer Systems, Inc.,
Minneapolis, MN 55440. Reprinted with permission by NCS.

open up. This verified to his male cotherapist that he was not rigidly caught in his style, as would be someone with a true disorder.

Lila appeared to have in fact a very structured existence. The female cotherapist was unable to discern exactly how strong her compulsive pattern had been prior to the stress of the recently evolving family crisis. Once she began trusting the therapist, Lila revealed that she sometimes experienced being overwhelmed. She could not imagine letting anything go. Though she saw no alternative to divorce, she was willing to explore how they had gotten to this point in their family life and why her husband had become emotionally unfaithful. She was initially ambivalent about how much of her feelings she would be able to expose in the four-way sessions.

Couples therapy proceeded, paced carefully by the cotherapists, being mindful of the need to move slowly with this couple. These couple sessions were accompanied by individual sessions with the same-gender cotherapist. The individual sessions were needed for Lila to get in contact with her anger and hurt so that she might look more broadly at alternatives. Paul needed the individual sessions to bring up feelings and wishes to test if the male cotherapist would reject or support him, and to practice how he might bring things up in joint sessions.

When they did finally open up, each of the clients was amazed that their beliefs about the other frequently did not fit reality. Paul felt Lila rejected him and only wanted his paycheck. Lila believed Paul no longer had an interest in the children, which (righteously) angered her. In straightening our their communication, they were able to reach an agreement to work on their marriage while living under one roof, so Paul moved back. With therapeutic help, Lila was able to be less concerned about having a spotless house, freeing her to concentrate on mothering directly. Paul was able to do more of the housework and spend more time with their children. Both, being loving parents whose children were their top priority, were able to develop a new practical and emotional contract for their relationship.

In this instance, the MCMI-III profile had alerted the cotherapists to insist on a time for couples therapy to be tried, appealing to Lila's need to do the right thing and Paul's need for a close relationship. Because of her distancing by a compulsive work pattern and his avoidance of conflict by distancing through stonewalling, both retreating maneuvers, they had not realized that the potential existed for reestablishing a closeness in their relationship and toward their children.

It was made safe for Paul to be more self-assertive and capitalize on an ability, developed outside the home, to be more active in the home. Paul moved from a passive polarity at home to being closer to the active end of the polarity. This movement allowed him to be more balanced in taking care of his needs as well as others'.

Lila became less overtly accommodating. She, too, moved from the passive end of the passive-active polarity toward the more active polarity. She also moved from only nurturing others to paying increased attention to her polarity of individual needs. She was enabled to modify her compulsive pattern so that she was more in control of it, turning it to positive use in her life pattern and lessening being driven by it. With a more supportive relationship, her underlying anger lessened, and while staying disciplined in her life, she no longer felt out of control.

## NARCISSISTIC MALE/NARCISSITIC FEMALE, GEORGE AND GEORGIA

George, 36, and Georgia, 30, had a 1-year-old child. These new parents were up in arms at each other. Each stated that if their relationship did not return to something like its earlier idyllic, passionate, and beautiful state, each was determined to take the child and raise him by himself or herself. Each one felt deprived. However, George came across in a smooth, nonanxious way, stating that he was ready to devote himself to his son if the couple did divorce. Georgia, on the other hand, seemed highly agitated and fearful, despite her assumption that she was the best parent for their son.

### George's MCMI-III Profile

A look at Figure 3.5 shows that George's Disclosure score is low (below 34). This suggests that he is busy putting up a socially acceptable front and minimizing self-revalation; the profile has been modified to compensate.

His Narcissistic score, Scale 5, is clearly at the level of predicting a personality disorder (BR 96). This scale needs to be interpreted in relation to his Histrionic score, Scale 4, which falls at the trait level.

At a behavioral level, George conveys a subtly *condescending* manner, while appearing smooth and interested in the other person. And he is interested in the other person, but in significant part for what he can get from that other person. A sense of *entitlement* may show in *exploitive* behavior. An *amorous interest* in another focuses on a relationship that primarily bolsters his own sense of self-esteem.

Phenomenologically, he thinks of himself as *special*; fantasies of love and success are crucial, driving his behavior. He may *repress* and/or reshape affect and *distort facts* to maintain self-illusions.

Intrapsychically, he tends to *rationalize* as he suffers from a *flimsily organized inner world*. Unless his confidence is suddenly shaken, he appears "cool," self-possessed, and optimistic at a basic biosocial level.

### Georgia's MCMI-III Profile

Characterologically, Georgia's profile is essentially like George's, as may be seen in Figure 3.6. She, too, has a high Narcissistic score, Scale 5, with Histrionic traits, Scale 4. She does seem a bit more open and less defensive than George.

MCMI-III™

---

## MILLON CLINICAL MULTIAXIAL INVENTORY - III
### CONFIDENTIAL INFORMATION FOR PROFESSIONAL USE ONLY

Valid Profile

PERSONALITY CODE:  5 ** 4 * - + 7 " 3 6B 6A 1 2A 2B 8A 8B ' ' // - ** - * //
SYNDROME CODE:   - ** - * // - ** - * //

| CATEGORY | | SCORE | | PROFILE OF BR SCORES | | | | | DIAGNOSTIC SCALES |
|---|---|---|---|---|---|---|---|---|---|
| | | RAW | BR | 0 | 60 | 75 | 85 | 115 | |
| MODIFYING INDICES | X | 57 | 31 | | | | | | DISCLOSURE |
| | Y | 18 | 84 | | | | | | DESIRABILITY |
| | Z | 0 | 0 | | | | | | DEBASEMENT |
| CLINICAL PERSONALITY PATTERNS | 1 | 0 | 3 | | | | | | SCHIZOID |
| | 2A | 0 | 3 | | | | | | AVOIDANT |
| | 2B | 0 | 3 | | | | | | DEPRESSIVE |
| | 3 | 2 | 23 | | | | | | DEPENDENT |
| | 4 | 22 | 76 | | | | | | HISTRIONIC |
| | 5 | 21 | 96 | | | | | | NARCISSISTIC |
| | 6A | 2 | 18 | | | | | | ANTISOCIAL |
| | 6B | 2 | 20 | | | | | | AGGRESSIVE (SADISTIC) |
| | 7 | 15 | 52 | | | | | | COMPULSIVE |
| | 8A | 0 | 3 | | | | | | PASSIVE-AGGRESSIVE |
| | 8B | 0 | 3 | | | | | | SELF-DEFEATING |
| SEVERE PERSONALITY PATHOLOGY | S | 2 | 42 | | | | | | SCHIZOTYPAL |
| | C | 0 | 2 | | | | | | BORDERLINE |
| | P | 0 | 2 | | | | | | PARANOID |
| CLINICAL SYNDROMES | A | 1 | 22 | | | | | | ANXIETY DISORDER |
| | H | 0 | 2 | | | | | | SOMATOFORM DISORDER |
| | N | 3 | 38 | | | | | | BIPOLAR: MANIC DISORDER |
| | D | 0 | 2 | | | | | | DYSTHYMIC DISORDER |
| | B | 0 | 2 | | | | | | ALCOHOL DEPENDENCE |
| | T | 1 | 17 | | | | | | DRUG DEPENDENCE |
| | R | 0 | 2 | | | | | | POST-TRAUMATIC STRESS |
| SEVERE SYNDROMES | SS | 3 | 47 | | | | | | THOUGHT DISORDER |
| | CC | 0 | 2 | | | | | | MAJOR DEPRESSION |
| | PP | 1 | 27 | | | | | | DELUSIONAL DISORDER |

Figure 3.5
George, Narcissistic

Copyright © 1994 DICANDRIEN, INC. All rights reservd.
Published and distributed exclusively by National Computer Systems, Inc.,
Minneapolis, MN 55440. Reprinted with permission by NCS.

MCMI-III™

---

## MILLON CLINICAL MULTIAXIAL INVENTORY - III
### CONFIDENTIAL INFORMATION FOR PROFESSIONAL USE ONLY

Valid Profile

PERSONALITY CODE:   5 ** 4 * 7 + 2B " 8A <u>6A</u> <u>6B</u> 3 2A 1 8B ' ' // - ** - * //
SYNDROME CODE:   - ** A * // - ** - * //

| CATEGORY | | SCORE | | PROFILE OF BR SCORES | | | | | DIAGNOSTIC SCALES |
|---|---|---|---|---|---|---|---|---|---|
| | | RAW | BR | 0 | 60 | 75 | 85 | 115 | |
| MODIFYING INDICES | X | 70 | 44 | | | | | | DISCLOSURE |
| | Y | 14 | 65 | | | | | | DESIRABILITY |
| | Z | 10 | 63 | | | | | | DEBASEMENT |
| CLINICAL PERSONALITY PATTERNS | 1 | 1 | 10 | | | | | | SCHIZOID |
| | 2A | 2 | 16 | | | | | | AVOIDANT |
| | 2B | 9 | 59 | | | | | | DEPRESSIVE |
| | 3 | 3 | 20 | | | | | | DEPENDENT |
| | 4 | 19 | 76 | | | | | | HISTRIONIC |
| | 5 | 17 | 85 | | | | | | NARCISSISTIC |
| | 6A | 2 | 24 | | | | | | ANTISOCIAL |
| | 6B | 2 | 24 | | | | | | AGGRESSIVE (SADISTIC) |
| | 7 | 16 | 63 | | | | | | COMPULSIVE |
| | 8A | 5 | 33 | | | | | | PASSIVE-AGGRESSIVE |
| | 8B | 0 | 0 | | | | | | SELF-DEFEATING |
| SEVERE PERSONALITY PATHOLOGY | S | 0 | 0 | | | | | | SCHIZOTYPAL |
| | C | 2 | 14 | | | | | | BORDERLINE |
| | P | 3 | 45 | | | | | | PARANOID |
| CLINICAL SYNDROMES | A | 10 | 82 | | | | | | ANXIETY DISORDER |
| | H | 5 | 43 | | | | | | SOMATOFORM DISORDER |
| | N | 3 | 36 | | | | | | BIPOLAR: MANIC DISORDER |
| | D | 4 | 27 | | | | | | DYSTHYMIC DISORDER |
| | B | 1 | 25 | | | | | | ALCOHOL DEPENDENCE |
| | T | 2 | 60 | | | | | | DRUG DEPENDENCE |
| | R | 14 | 72 | | | | | | POST-TRAUMATIC STRESS |
| SEVERE SYNDROMES | SS | 4 | 34 | | | | | | THOUGHT DISORDER |
| | CC | 6 | 45 | | | | | | MAJOR DEPRESSION |
| | PP | 1 | 25 | | | | | | DELUSIONAL DISORDER |

Figure 3.6
Georgia, Narcissistic
Copyright © 1994 DICANDRIEN, INC. All rights reserved.
Published and distributed exclusively by National Computer Systems, Inc.,
Minneapolis, MN 55440. Reprinted with permission by NCS.

Much that was said about George may be said about Georgia. She is *behaviorally amorous*, buoying up her *inflated self-image* by collecting positive experiences with others. She, too, seems interested in others, but in large part for what she can gain from them in terms of her self-esteem. She is *self-deceptive, self-centered*, and *rationalizes* with a *flimsy internal structure*. Except when her confidence is shaken, she presents with a *"cool," imperturbable demeanor*.

What is so different from George is that she is now shaken. Her Anxiety score, Scale A, is significant (see below for discussion of clinical syndromes). Her Posttraumatic Stress score is high as well. She is being overwhelmed by *anxiety* and possibly related depressive symptomatology.

In reviewing the past in sessions, it appeared that this was another of those couples made for each other at first glance. They both tuned in to each other's needs and responded to those for their own purposes. Because they had similar blind spots, that is, repressing and denying the same negative aspects of their personalities, neither could confront the other without being aware of similar self-aggrandizing traits in themselves. Because their disorders (or styles) focused on amorously attracting and seducing the opposite sex, they fitted together wonderfully in the early part of the relationship. They were always "up" for each other.

When they began caring for a baby, however, and the focused intensity was off each of them, they became anxious with the lack of reinforcement for their inflated sense of themselves. Then the "flip" occurred: They began to blame each other, pointing out the negative parts of the other's personality, and thereby warding off confronting themselves. So the intense attachment switched from positive to negative. Georgia had less stability emotionally as she faced raising the child. This enabled George to continue to play the role of the competent one, blaming her and saying he would do a better job as primary parent if they split. Neither could face buckling down and moving through the ups and downs of a relationship, and so they did separate and divorce.

## Brief Examples: Three Other Couple Types

Many individuals present with two or three high points, just as with the MMPI-2 profiles. Below are some brief examples of couples wherein at least one partner has a mixed personality disorder. Special features will be noted where appropriate.

### HISTRIONIC-NARCISSISTIC FEMALE/COMPULSIVE MALE

In this profile, the histrionic pattern mixed with narcissistic qualities of superiority and entitlement increases the possibility of irresponsible, acting-out behavior considerably beyond that of the cardinal histrionic personality disorder. This is particularly true, of course, if a disorder is hypothesized. If the pattern is at the level of personality style, the first impression may be of an intriguing, colorful, vivacious person—just the sort to stir up the compulsive, conforming male. She may have seen him as a good "catch," but may have become quickly bored. In seeking other relationships, she may have been wounded, retreating to a safe husband-father to lick her wounds. She entered therapy as a way to mollify her mate, but her enthusiasm for couple therapy is likely to wane if she is unsupported in her display of charm in the therapy.

As a compulsive, he is likely to have been excited and attracted to this affectively dominated woman. She expressed the feelings in the family, and he was the reasoning power. This is an exaggeration of two of the cultural stereotypes of males and females. Without psychological intervention or other corrective experience, neither partner will get beyond his or her role to a broader experiencing of his or her humanity. In this instance, the MCMI-III can establish from the first goals that at least may be modified, even in the most traditional of couples.

## ANTISOCIAL FEMALE/ANTISOCIAL-NARCISSISTIC MALE

On seeing these profiles, clinicians inexperienced with the MCMI-III can make the mistake of coming to the conclusion that they have two truly antisocial (read psychopathic or sociopathic) persons on their hands. Not necessarily so at all! What they likely have are two aggressive, competitive entrepreneurs. Choca, Stanley, and Van Denburg (1992) write that competitiveness is the major trait found in individuals scoring high on this MCMI scale. Millon's Antisocial Personalty scale is in keeping with his dynamic formulation, which he calls the Aggressive Pattern. Of course, taking a careful history coupled with collecting corollary information should disclose whether one or both parties come from the subset of antisocial psychopathic persons.

These MCMI-III profiles actually reflect the competitive, aggressive attitudes and style called for with successful entrepreneurs. These individuals have succeeded where the majority of small businesses fail in the first two years. They take risks, they exploit (usually within the limit of the law), they shade the truth to meet their own needs. But they are for themselves, are law-abiding, and are not opposed to society. However, when they get together, they carry some of these same qualities into the relationship. They are competitive and may see the relationship as a game in which they match wits with each other. They may admire each other's ability to make it in the rat race. As Choca, Stanley, and Van Denburg (1992) indicate, they are tough, argumentative, and may be insensitive to each other's feelings.

With this type of couple, an imbalance will be anticipated sooner or later because of the male's narcissistic characteristic of entitlement. His partner will become incensed because of his assumptions and indicate that the playing field is not level. When she finds ways to puncture his confident front, he may respond with hurt, rage, and vindictiveness. The motivation for coming into couple therapy is likely to be to gain the upper hand, and also to be part of a broader manipulative pattern, such as to get a material or custody edge in the event of a breakup. Therapists need to be aware that this couple therapy could be the first stage in a long divorce battle where neither will give in—although parted, they may struggle to their (metaphorical) death because winning is all.

## DEPENDENT MALE/DEPENDENT FEMALE

These people are so "nice" to each other they must always tread softly in their relationship. Moving around on tiptoes, they never come to grips with their problems. Problem solving occurs when one quickly acquiesces to the suggestions of the other. They avoid criticizing each other, and as previously noted, they thereby avoid being criticized. At some level, they may be looking for a good parent and hence may develop considerable resentment, although they tend to squelch this; if irritation comes out unexpectedly, they may hurriedly apologize. They have the capacity to be kind, loving, and caring with each other. If they grow outside the relationship, through work experiences, for instance, and maintain their same way of couple relating, this dissonance in their lives may bring them to couple therapy.

# Clinical Syndromes as Scored on the MCMI-III

With couples coming for assistance, the complaint is for the most part about the relationship or about the other spouse or oneself in the relationship. Couples come with a relational disorder provoked and/or maintained by their personality style (or disorder). Either they have not developed a way to work out their issues that is compatible with their personality style interaction, or it may be that a change in circumstance has unbalanced the relationship, making the earlier dispute resolution style no longer effective for meeting their needs.

When the symptomatic and mood scales are close to or into the significant area beginning with BR 75, the client is complaining about individual psychological symptoms possibly experienced as separate from the couple system (even though the symptoms may sometimes seem to be in response to system dysfunction). For example, sometimes a modest elevation in the Bipolar Depression Scale can be enough to clue in questioning to turn up a recent manic episode that otherwise might have gone unnoticed. A high Anxiety Scale might be useful in the interpretive session to gain acknowledgment of a state of fear. Other scales may prove of clinical usefulness, but are not dealt with here because they do not necessarily pertain to the couple relationship.

## The MCMI-III and Alcoholism

Substance abuse research, reported by Nerviano and Gross (in Choca, Stanley, & Van Denburg, 1992), identified various alcoholism subtypes. MCMI research supports the existence of at least four of these types. One type used alcohol for self-medicating purposes. An Anxious group demonstrated at least borderline and paranoid trends. Recreational drinkers were defined by elevated scores on Narcissistic and Histrionic scales. For a third group, those with high scores on the Compulsive Scale, alcohol abuse provided a release from the load of responsibilities and/or permitted anger expression. A final group was characterized by schizoid, avoidant, and dependent characteristics, with drinking seeming to alleviate social anxiety. When seeing a couple wherein allegations of alcohol abuse arise, if the alleged abuser fits one of these MCMI-derived groups, planning couple and adjunct treatment around the differential personality functioning would seem wise.

## Summary

The MCMI-III uniquely provides informational, descriptive hypotheses about the personality's core: personality features, personality traits, or personality disorder. The inventory also provides syndromal indications. The MCMI-III profile helps the couples therapist draw understandable hypotheses about the couple relationship to guide planning for interventions. This chapter stressed thinking in terms of domains of personality functioning and the usefulness of planning for balancing the basic polarities of individual personalities with reference to the couple's interactive patterns.

# CHAPTER 4

---

## The 16PF:
## Assessing "Normal" Personality
## Dimensions of Marital Partners

---

CAROL L. PHILPOT, Psy.D.

The beauty of the 16 Personality Factor (16PF) Questionnaire designed and constructed by Raymond Cattell et al. (1993) almost 50 years ago is its focus on *normal* personality variables as opposed to psychopathology. Unlike those instruments designed to highlight areas of dysfunction, the 16PF, as it has come to be known, is a nonthreatening and nonjudgmental personality assessment, which looks at stable personality traits. Due to its descriptive focus on normal variations in personality characteristics, the 16PF is particularly suitable to a nonblaming, systemic approach in therapy. That is, as systems thinkers, family therapists do not focus on "faults" or "virtues" of individual members of the system, but on how satisfying and functional the interaction between them is. The 16PF personality profiles of a couple charted on the same profile sheet provide a marvelous vehicle for looking at areas of conflict, complementarity, and similarity in a nonjudgmental, neutral manner, consistent with the values of systemic thinking.

The reader familiar with the 16PF may wish to proceed to the section "Interpretation of Primary Factor Scales."

## CAPSULE SUMMARY OF THE 16PF

### TEST CONSTRUCTION

The 16PF was first published by IPAT (Institute for Personality and Ability Testing, Inc.) in 1949. The construction of the 16PF is rather unique. The test was designed to measure all of the most fundamental dimensions of normal personality—no easy feat. To determine what these dimensions might be, Cattell (1949) combed the English dictionary for words that described human personality, 4,000 of them to be exact. He grouped these words into 180 categories, which were reduced by correlational methods to 45 categories, which were then factor analyzed and further reduced to 15 factors. These factors were labeled alphabetically A through O, proceeding from those that contribute most to the variance between persons to those that contribute the least. As it turned out, factors D, J, and K were not very replicable in adults and were therefore left out when the test was published. However, Cattell found that there were four factors that showed up on paper-and-pencil inventories that did not seem to emerge from the factor analysis of the English language, which he felt were important enough to include in his measure. These he named Q1 through Q4, commonly called the Q factors, and tacked them onto the bottom of the remaining 12 factors, thus making up the 16 personality factors.

When Cattell (1949) designed the 16PF, he believed that related factors were more likely to reflect real-world personalities, and therefore his factors are correlated or "oblique." As that is the case, it was possible to conduct further factor analysis that produced five broader and more general second order factors, I through V. In the fifth edition of the 16PF (Cattell et al., 1993), these second-order (now called global) factors are named (I) Extroversion, (II) Anxiety, (III) Tough-Mindedness, (IV) Independence, and (V) Self-Control. When interpreting these scales, it must be remembered that the factors loading on them are related, but not perfectly, and that the global factor extracts the dimension they have in common. Therefore, although they may provide a good starting point for assessing a personality, the first-order or primary factors will provide a much richer picture.

As with other personality inventories, the 16PF contains validity scales that allow the clinician to assess the client's test-taking response style. In previous editions of the 16PF, these were known as Fake Good, Fake Bad, and Random scales, and raw scores of six or more were considered suspicious. In the fifth edition of the 16PF (Cattell et al., 1993), the scales are Impression Management (IM), a social desirability scale; Infrequency (INF), which is similar to the F scale on the MMPI; and Acquiescence (ACQ) which indicates random or inconsistent responding or a high need for approval.

Internal consistency coefficient alpha reliabilities on the primary factor scales average .74, with a range from .64 to .85. Test-retest reliabilities average .80 for a two-week interval and .70 for a two-month interval. For clinicians who are interested in complete data on scale reliability scores and construct and criterion validity information, these can be found in the fifth edition of the 16PF *Administrator's Manual* (Russell & Karol, 1994).

## ADMINISTRATION AND SCORING

The 16PF fifth edition consists of 185 items that make up the 16 primary personality factor scales and the IM scale. Each scale contains 10 to 15 items. Except for the Factor B items, the test questions have a three-choice response format, with the middle response choice being a question mark (?). The test is designed to be administered to individuals 16 or older, and normative data are based on an age range of 15 through 92 years. The test has an overall readability at the fifth-grade level; it is self-administerable and untimed. Average test-completion time ranges from 35 to 50 minutes. As with other personality inventories, the client should be encouraged to answer the questions honestly and spontaneously, without agonizing over choices.

The test may be computer-scored through IPAT's mail-in scoring service or OnSite System software or hand-scored using scoring keys. Specific directions for scoring can be found in the *Administrator's Manual*. Essentially, all raw scores are converted to Sten scores with the use of the norm table. Sten scores are based on a 10-point scale with a mean of 5.5 and a standard deviation of 2. These Sten scores can then be graphed on the profile sheet to achieve a pictorial representation, much like the MMPI. When using the 16PF with a couple, it is helpful to score both profiles on the same profile sheet, color coding them for easy identification.

Recently, IPAT has developed a computer-scoring program for couples counseling (Russell, 1995) and will provide the marital therapist with a couple's counseling report that identifies areas of potential conflict and complementarity. Furthermore, the couple's questionnaire gathers additional information such as the relationship history, demographic variables, and marital satisfaction ratings on a variety of broad areas, which is not found on the individual version of the 16PF. This report is intended to be used in helping people who are in a committed, intimate relationship, whether or not they are married, and therefore the report uses language such as "partner" rather than mate. The format and use of this report will be discussed further after a thorough explanation of the primary and secondary factors of the 16PF is provided.

## Interpretation of Primary Factor Scales

The 16PF scales are bipolar in nature, with high and low scores designating opposite poles of the same dimension. For example, a low score on Factor A indicates a more introverted individual, a higher score is typical of an extrovert. Clinicians should not place value judgments of good or bad on high or low scores: These scores are descriptive of normal personality variables among individuals. Sten scores between 4 and 7 are considered to be average, with about 68% of the population falling within this range. Sten scores of 1–3 and 8–10 represent the polar extremes of each dimension, with 16% of the population falling at each end of the normal curve. As with any normed assessment instrument, confidence intervals and standard errors must be remembered, and differences of one Sten score should not be overinterpreted. Although the 16PF was designed to measure normal personality variables, it is sensitive to pathology, particularly when certain configurations of scales are found. Although, for the purposes of this chapter, the focus is on the complementarity and similarity of a couple's profile rather than on individual psychopathology, an example of detecting possible psychopathology from scale configurations will be provided during the description of the primary factors.

A more detailed discussion of the primary factor scales follows. This information is a composite of several sources (Cattell, Eber, & Tatsuoka, 1988; Karson, 1985; Karson & O'Dell, 1976; Russell & Karol, 1994). Remember that the factors are listed in the order of their weight in determining differences between individuals.

## FACTOR A, WARMTH

This scale, like the Extroversion/Introversion Scale on the Myers-Briggs (1962), measures one's comfort with others, or tendency to approach or withdraw from people. It is the factor that contributes most to the variance between people, and Cattell (1949) believed it to have a hereditary component. People with a high A are characterized by an attentiveness to the needs of others, emotional expressivity, friendliness, a desire to be with people, and a tendency to join in group activities. At the extremely high levels, some of the negative aspects of this trait include emotional lability, dependency, and discomfort with being alone. Individuals with low scores on the A scale prefer to be alone, avoid intense interaction or emotional closeness, hide their feelings from others, and present as aloof or reserved. They are likely to be precise and rigid in the way they do things and in their personal standards. They prefer to work alone and with things rather than interact with people. Although, in our culture, extroversion is more socially acceptable, people with low scores on A are likely to be the researchers, inventors, and artists whose self-imposed isolation allows them to make important contributions to society. Extremely low scores may indicate a history of disappointments in relationships and a fear of interpersonal contact, often resulting in a reclusive lifestyle. Due to gender socialization, there are significant differences between men and women on this scale, with women generally scoring higher than men.

FACTOR B, ABSTRACT VS. CONCRETE REASONING

Factor B is a brief measure of reasoning or intelligence, but must be interpreted cautiously due to the low number of items, which provides a very small sample of mental ability. It is not intended to replace full-length measures of intelligence. It is included in the test because intelligence moderates the expression of many personality traits and appears to be a major factor in variance between individuals. High scorers are usually bright, adept at abstract thinking, fast learners, adaptable, and alert. They are more likely to show good judgment and are inclined to have more intellectual interests. Generally, B+ scorers have a high morale and persevere with a project. Lower scores may reflect concrete thinking, literal interpretations, poor judgment, mental dullness, or poor motivation. These individuals are more likely to have low morale and quit easily when faced with a challenge. However, high scores are generally correlated with exposure to cultural and educational advantages, whereas low scores may indicate a lack of these advantages. Additionally, low scores may reflect depression, preoccupation with other problems, or distraction by environmental stimuli. Although there does not appear to be any bias for gender or race, level of education can affect Scale B scores.

SCALE C, EMOTIONAL STABILITY (STABLE VS. REACTIVE)

This scale measures an individual's ability to cope with the daily vicissitudes of life in an adaptable and proactive style. High scorers feel that they have control over life and can deal with events in a mature and calm manner. In psychodynamic terms, high Cs have good ego strength and a good self-concept that is not affected by external events. They do not give up easily when confronted with difficulties, but seem to be able to find options to solve their problems. They do not have difficulty facing reality or managing their emotions in a balanced manner. They show restraint in interpersonal relationships, which helps them avoid getting into altercations. Low scorers, on the other hand, seem to have an external locus of control, reacting to events in an emotionally labile manner and feeling unable to cope when things go wrong. They worry a great deal, are anxious, excitable, easily perturbed, evasive of responsibilities, and give up easily. Their attitudes and interests may change often and quickly in response to external events. They do not seem to have the strong sense of self displayed by high C individuals. They may get into frequent interpersonal arguments due to their emotional reactivity and inability to meet their emotional needs. People with extremely high Cs may be denying problems to present themselves in a favorable light. People with extremely low Cs may not have the ego strength to respond well to treatment.

## FACTOR E, DOMINANCE (SUBMISSIVE VS. DOMINANT)

Factor E is not a measure of simple assertiveness. Rather, high scores on this scale reflect an individual's tendency to try to control others and subjugate their wishes to his or her own. Very high Es are aggressive, competitive, bossy, hostile, and stubborn. They are authoritarian in leadership style, very forceful and vocal in their opinions, and critical of those with whom they disagree. They are willing to manipulate others to control them and, at the extremes, can alienate those who do not wish to be controlled. They tend to be egotistical, independent-minded, and rebellious and often demand admiration. Moderate scores are more likely to be reflective of assertive behavior that serves to protect one's own boundaries. Those with moderately high scores can also command a leadership position without alienating others. Low scores, on the other hand, indicate a willingness to sacrifice one's own wishes to accommodate to the needs of others and, at the extreme end, often to the detriment of oneself. They are considerate of others and diplomatic in their interactions. Low Es will avoid conflict by conforming to the will of other people. They are often easily led and dependent on social approval. They can be characterized as cooperative, self-effacing, docile, and submissive. Like scale A, this scale is also affected by gender socialization. In general, women, who have been taught to put the needs of their families and friends before their own score lower on the dominance scale than do men. On the other hand, dominance, aggression, and competitiveness are stereotypical male values, essentially defining traditional masculinity.

## FACTOR F, LIVELINESS (LIVELY VS. SERIOUS)

Karson and O'Dell (1976) labeled this factor impulsivity, which in some ways is a better descriptor. High F individuals are like the spontaneous, unsocialized child who is active, talkative, enthusiastic, energetic, and enjoys being the center of attention. These individuals are often the life of the party, cheerful, fun, and uninhibited. Because they are attention-seeking and lively, they sometimes behave in inappropriate ways in public gatherings that call for restraint. On the other hand, people with high Fs are often quite popular and frequently chosen as leaders. People with low Fs are serious, somber, introspective, and generally responsible, dependable individuals. They can be pessimistic and overly cautious, totally lacking in spontaneity and enthusiasm, which sets them up to be the wet blanket in a group activity. They usually are not perceived as being a lot of fun.

The F factor becomes part of an equation along with G, H, O, and Q3 in the prediction of acting-out, irresponsible, impulsive behavior and, conversely, obsessive-compulsive, perfectionistic, and possibly depressed personalities. As these factors are discussed, I shall point out how they interact to warn the therapist of the potential for pathology.


## FACTOR G, RULE-CONSCIOUSNESS (RULE-CONSCIOUS VS. EXPEDIENT)

This factor was intended to measure the level to which an individual has internalized the moral ideals of the environment and has been associated with the psychoanalytic concept of superego. However, one must remember that the belief that rule-bound individuals are desirable and those who break the rules are not is based on cultural values connected to the Puritan ethic of North America and Northern Europe. High scores on G indicate that the individual is conscientious, moralistic, and proper, conforming to the dictates of the larger society. The high G is dominated by a sense of duty and is often inflexible and self-righteous. This individual has often been described as the person who would sit at a red traffic light on an empty street at 4 in the morning until it turned green rather than break a rule. High Gs are positively correlated with the IM scale, the validity scale that measures one's attempt to appear socially desirable. On the contrary, the low G disregards the rules and feels little obligation to conform to group norms. These individuals have a high need for autonomy and flexibility and can be unpredictable or antisocial. Because they believe that most rules can be broken, if there is a good reason to do so, they will have a difficult time in any situation where they are expected to follow strict rules and regulations. However, because they think "outside the envelope," they can be effective problem solvers. Although low Gs were once regarded as having poor superego and low internal controls, it is now generally understood that low Gs can also result from following a value system that does not conform to that most often endorsed by North Americans.

As mentioned above, individuals with high impulsivity (F+) and low conformity (G−) can find themselves in trouble with the law, whereas those individuals who are high on conformity (G+) and low on spontaneity (F−) can be identified as obsessive-compulsive individuals who are prone to depression. This is especially true when factors H, O, and Q3 are considered.


## FACTOR H, BOLDNESS (SHY VS. VENTURESOME)

The H factor measures one's comfort in social situations. Unlike the A factor, which is more a measure of one's enjoyment of social interaction, the H factor reflects the individual's comfort in initiating social contacts and being the center of attention. High Hs are very bold in social interaction, finding it easy to meet new people, engage in conversations, fit in with the crowd, and join large groups with ease. They enjoy making speeches in public gatherings and, in fact, are quite exhibitionistic at the extremely high levels. They are risk-takers and adventurous, ready to try new things. At extreme levels, they ignore danger signals and can be careless of details. High Hs fit the stereotype of masculine ideal in our society. Low Hs, on the other hand, are very shy and easily threatened in social situations. They find it hard to strike up conversations, are cautious when meeting others, and are horrified if the spotlight falls on them in a social group. They usually have inferiority feelings and are susceptible to overwhelming anxiety regarding whether they will say or do the right thing. For this reason, low Hs prefer one or two friends to large groups and avoid occupations that require a lot of personal contact.

It becomes easy to understand how a high H (bold, risk-taker), a high F (impulsive), and low G (rule-breaker) can combine to produce a person with antisocial tendencies. Conversely, the individual who is very serious (low F), rule-bound (low G), and afraid of social interaction (low H) is prone to depression in a society where extroversion and spontaneity are highly valued.

## FACTOR I, EMOTIONAL SENSITIVITY (TOUGH-MINDED VS. TENDER-MINDED)

Factor I measures the emotional sensitivity of the individual. High Is are empathic, intuitive, and sensitive to the needs and feelings of others. They base their judgments on subjective tastes and sentimentality. At extreme levels, they can be temperamental, unrealistic, and demanding of attention. Their increased level of sensitivity can lead to their experiencing more pain, discomfort, guilt, and anxiety than moderate or low Is. They tend to daydream and frequently fail to consider the practicality of their plans. They usually have refined interests and dislike crude people or rough occupations. Low Is have a practical, objective, no-nonsense attitude in life. They repress emotional expressivity, are insensitive to the feelings of others, and focus on utilitarian and realistic goals. They tend to be self-reliant and handle stressful jobs well, but at extreme levels, they are perceived as cynical and hard-hearted.

This is the third primary factor related to gender socialization. In our society, men are taught to be low Is; that is, they are expected to shut down emotionally and be tough, self-reliant, realistic people. As a group, they seem to prefer action adventures to poetry and prefer to tinker with mechanical things rather than paint a picture. Women, on the other hand, are taught not only to express themselves emotionally, but to monitor the emotions of significant others as well. Their interest in refined pursuits such as poetry, art, music, and theater is encouraged rather than discouraged. Therefore, there are separate gender norms for men and women on this factor because, as a whole, women tend to score high on factor I and men low. By using separate gendered norms, one can tell whether the male is scoring high as compared to other men rather than to women, and vice versa.

## FACTOR L, VIGILANCE (SUSPICIOUS VS. TRUSTING)

This factor is a measure of one's level of interpersonal trust. High Ls do not trust the motives of others and expect to be taken advantage of. Therefore, they are skeptical, questioning, resentful, hostile, and insecure. Low Ls, on the other hand, are adaptable, free of jealousy, cheerful, open, and tolerant. They expect to be treated with equity and loyalty. In general, low Ls feel good about themselves.

## FACTOR M, ABSTRACTEDNESS (PRACTICAL VS. IMAGINATIVE)

High M individuals are creative, unconventional, absentminded, self-motivated, and inner-directed. Because they focus on the world of ideas and fantasy, they are not always grounded in reality, showing a carelessness regarding everyday matters. One is reminded here of the absentminded professor who can explain the theory of relativity but wears one black sock and one white sock to work. They invariably engage in intellectual and aesthetic pursuits, but may well forget to pay the bills. On the other hand, low Ms are intensely concerned with the practical details of daily life. They are perceived as sensible, conventional, and grounded. They tend to be unimaginative and concrete and lack intellectual or aesthetic interests. Although they may indeed pay the bills, they will be unlikely to invent the product that produces the money to pay the bills. In fact, at extremely low levels, they may be so concrete as to be unable to find solutions to their problems.

## FACTOR N, SHREWDNESS (FORTHRIGHT VS. PRIVATE)

High Ns are generally closed individuals. That is, they value privacy and do not indulge in self-disclosure. They may indeed be insightful and socially alert, but like the polished and shrewd politician, their interactions with others are likely to be more calculating than genuine. At the extreme level, high Ns may fail to form close, intimate relationships that require honest and open self-disclosure. Low Ns are open and genuine, exhibiting a great deal of natural warmth and genuine liking for people. They spontaneously share information about themselves without much concern regarding the consequences. In our culture, low Ns are more socially desirable. At the extreme, low Ns are forthright when it would be to their advantage to hold back.


## FACTOR O, APPREHENSION (GUILT-PRONE VS. SELF-ASSURED)

High Os are chronic worriers. They feel apprehensive and insecure and often suffer overwhelming guilt. They have high expectations of themselves, are self-critical, and continually reproach themselves if they feel they fall short of obligations. They are intropunitive and frequently prone to depression. They are perceived as worried, anxious, and troubled individuals. Low Os, in contrast, are self-assured, confident, and self-satisfied. Generally, they demonstrate a mature, unanxious sense of adequacy and are confident in their capacity to deal with things. They are resilient and secure, but at extremely low levels, they may deny inadequacies that *do* exist, thus blocking an opportunity for self-improvement.

When one considers the O factor in relationship to the previously discussed formula of F+ (impulsive), G− (disregards rules), and H+ (risk-taker), one can easily see that a low O (self-assured, no guilt) contributes to a tendency to act out in antisocial ways, and a high O tends to put the brakes on such activity. Likewise, a high O (chronic worrier) in combination with a low F (serious), high G (rule-bound), and low H (shy) can be indicative of even higher levels of anxiety and depression.


## Q1, OPENNESS TO CHANGE (CONSERVATIVE VS. EXPERIMENTING)

It is of sociological and historical interest to know that this scale was at one time considered the radicalism scale. Because our society now values change and endorses the questioning of authority, this scale is more positively entitled the Openness to Change scale. This fact merely highlights the importance of the clinician's sensitivity to the power of cultural variables in forming and judging personality characteristics. Regardless of its valence, this scale measures one's tendency to experiment with the new versus one's need for predictable structures and rules. High scorers do not function well as a subordinate, challenge authority, look for new ways of doing things, like innovation, are interested in intellectual matters (particularly varying viewpoints), like to experiment in life generally, and tolerate change well. Indeed, high scorers are usually bored by routine and predictability. Low scorers are confident in what they have been taught to believe and prefer the structure of traditional ways. They tend to oppose and postpone change, demonstrating caution in regard to new ideas. They prefer routine, they don't like to consider varying viewpoints, and they prefer the status quo to the danger of change, no matter how unsatisfactory it might be.

## Q2, SELF-RELIANCE (SELF-RELIANT VS. GROUP-ORIENTED)

High Q2 scores are indicative of individuals who are independent, accustomed to making decisions, and taking action on their own. They do not dislike people, but simply do not need their agreement or support in making a decision or accomplishing a task. In fact, they prefer to work by themselves and often are hesitant to ask others for help, even when they could use it. People with extremely high scores on self-reliance may fail to see the interpersonal consequences of their decisions. Although it is not as socially desirable in our society to endorse this attitude, it is nevertheless a healthy, creative sort of introversion, resulting in high self-sufficiency and good work habits. It is more consistent with the traditional male value system than with stereotypically female behavior. On the other hand, low scores on Q2 indicate an extroverted work style. Low Q2s are joiners and committee members and prefer to work with others. They depend on social approval and often will go along with the group rather than pursue their own solution to problems. Low Q2s run the risk of being easily influenced by bad companions or bad ideas endorsed by the group.

## Q3, PERFECTIONISM (PERFECTIONISTIC VS. TOLERATES DISORDER)

High Q3 individuals are concerned with organization and planning. They take good care of their possessions, put everything in its place, keep an organized calendar, do not miss appointments, and have high standards of performance. Their habits are compulsive enough for them to realize their potential. They can be rigid and inflexible and are most comfortable in predictable situations. Low scorers are unconcerned about disorganization and clutter. They leave things to chance, are more spontaneous and less planful. They fail to think ahead and therefore are often less efficient at accomplishing a task. They are often labeled lackadaisical, chaotic, and disorganized by others. They are prone to be careless of protocol, basically following their own urges.

Q3— is the final ingredient of the F+ (impulsivity), G— (breaks rules), H+ (risk-taker), and O— (self-assured, no guilt) configuration that may indicate a tendency toward antisocial or, at the very least, irresponsible behavior. When an individual is not concerned with doing the job right and fails to think ahead, he or she is more likely to behave in ways that will get him or her in trouble with the authorities. On the other hand, a high Q3 is frequently found with G+

(rule-bound), O+ (worrying, guilt-ridden), F– (serious), and H– (shy, timid), indicative of a shy, obsessive-compulsive, guilt-prone, rule-bound, and anxiety-ridden individual. By looking at these scales in combination, the therapist can determine how they interact with one another either by enhancing or correcting for pathological tendencies. This particular configuration is only one of many possibilities, but serves as an illustration of how the therapist can use the primary scales in a more complex manner to predict behavior.

### Q4, TENSION (RELAXED VS. TENSE)

The items of this scale are face-valid; therefore, this scale is easily faked to reflect the socially desirable relaxed end of the scale or, conversely, to call for help by endorsing the anxiety items. High scorers admit to feeling frustrated, impatient, tense, irritable, anxious, and driven. This level of tension interferes with self-control and makes them less effective than they would like to be. This tension is likely a result of a present life situation and should be investigated to discover the source. On the other hand, low scores on Q4 usually indicate a relaxed, composed, satisfied individual. These people are patient and comfortable with themselves and their life situation. Occasionally, this comfort can lead to complacency and a lack of motivation, but generally, a low Q4 is a positive indicator for mental health.

## Global Factors

The primary scales cluster on five global factors that will give the clinician an opportunity to look at broad personality variables. These second-order factors are (I) Extroversion, (II) Anxiety, (III) Tough-Mindedness, (IV) Independence, and (V) Self-Control. A brief discussion on the global factors follows.

### (1) EXTROVERSION/INTROVERSION

Primary factors A, F, H, N, and Q2 load on the Extroversion/Introversion second-order factor. A+ (warm), F+ (lively), H+ (bold), N– (forthright), and Q2– (group-oriented) contribute to the Extroverted polarity, A– (reserved), F– (serious), H– (shy), N+ (private), and Q2+ (self-reliant) are correlated with an introverted personality style. When interpreting the second-order factors, it is informative to look at the direction and magnitude of Sten scores on each of the primary factors, rather than merely considering the total extroversion score. For example, an individual with a Sten score of 5 on A, 8 on F, 8 on H, 4 on N, and 6 on Q2 will have a different sort of extroverted personality than one who has a Sten score of 8 on A, 6 on F, 6 on H, 2 on N, and 2 on Q2. The first individual, although very comfortable with people and enjoying the role of life of the party, will be less dependent on approval of others and more self-reliant. The second individual may not be the center of attention as much, but may feel a need to be with people and to have their approval. There is a strong relationship between the IM scale and the extroverted factors, a fact that reflects our society's preference for extroverted personality types.

## (2) HIGH ANXIETY/LOW ANXIETY

Primary factors that contribute to the Anxiety polarity include C− (emotionally reactive), L+ (distrustful), O+ (apprehensive), and Q4+ (tense). On the contrary, the emotionally calm (C+), trusting (L−), self-assured (O−), and relaxed (Q4−) individual reflects the low anxiety. The anxiety factor is a good indicator of the level of emotional health of an individual.

## (3) TOUGH-MINDEDNESS/RECEPTIVITY

Tough-minded individuals tend to be A− (reserved), I− (practical), M− (grounded), and Q1− (traditional). Receptive individuals, on the contrary, are A+ (warm), I+ (sensitive), M+ (abstracted), and Q1+ (open to change). This second-order factor divides along gender lines, the tough-minded individuals reflecting the masculine gender stereotype and the receptive a more feminine gender stereotype.

## (4) INDEPENDENCE/ACCOMMODATION

Although it has been changing in the past several decades, this is another second-order factor that has a relationship to traditional gender socialization. Independent individuals score E+ (dominant), H+ (bold), L+ (vigilant), and Q1+ (open to change); accommodating people score E− (deferential), H− (timid), L− (trusting), and Q1− (traditional). Thus, independent types are self-determined, persuasive, assertive, socially bold, willing to challenge the status quo, and suspicious of the input of other individuals. More accommodating types, on the other hand, value affiliation more than self-determination and are more likely to compromise. They tend to be unassertive and easily influenced by others. They are trusting and accepting of the status quo. Traditional gender messages endorsed high independence for men and high accommodation for women. Today, those messages have become blurred, although old values do not die easily.

## (5) SELF-CONTROL/UNRESTRAINT

This second-order factor is a measure of one's tendency to curb one's impulses and maintain control of oneself. High Fs (lively), low Gs (expedient), high Ms (creative), and low Q3s (tolerant of disorder) combine to produce an unrestrained personality, characterized by self-indulgence, disorganization, impulsivity, and irresponsibility. Low Fs (serious), high Gs (rule-conscious), low Ms (practical), and high Q3s (perfectionistic) contribute to a more self-controlled individual. Self-control is related to social desirability in our society, although self-control often comes at the expense of flexibility and spontaneity. The primary factors can combine in any number of ways to produce a more balanced interaction between the polarities. For example, a lively, enthusiastic (F+), and creative (M+) person can have a moderate respect for rules (G+) and an organized approach to tasks (Q3+), which counterbalances the negative aspects of both poles.

# Relationship Adjustment and the 16PF

When using the 16PF in couples work, the clinician should be alerted to certain predictors of successful marital therapy and marital satisfaction. Below, I discuss briefly the most relevant primary scale and global factor scores, as well as significant research results.

## FACTOR A, WARMTH

Extreme differences between spouses on the interpersonal warmth scale will often be reflected by conflict around how much time they each wish to spend with others, both with extended family and in social activities involving people. Although individuals who are basically shy and withdrawn are initially attracted to outgoing people who make them feel comfortable, as the relationship matures, each partner becomes dissatisfied with the other's need or lack of desire for interpersonal contact. As previously mentioned, extremely high scores on Factor A indicate emotional lability, dependency, discomfort with being alone, and a tendency to be very demanding in relationships—in other words, high-maintenance spouses. On the other hand, extremely low scores may indicate a history of disappointments in relationships and a fear of interpersonal contact—not a good candidate for marriage.

FACTOR B, ABSTRACT VS. CONCRETE REASONING

High scores on B are positively correlated with better problem-solving skills in a marital relationship and thus predict positive outcomes from marital therapy. Interestingly, Karol and Russell (1995) found that for men, significant differences in scores on Factor B created numerous problems in a marriage, including difficulties with affectional expression; dissatisfaction with division of responsibilities, sex, and financial matters; and ineffective problem solving. The implication is that the man who marries for beauty without concern for intellectual compatibility soon finds he has made a mistake, as he is unable to communicate with his spouse on many matters of importance.

FACTOR C, EMOTIONAL STABILITY

A high score on C for both partners is a major contributor to a functional, satisfying relationship. In fact, this scale, more than any other primary factor scale, can predict positive or negative outcomes in couples work. When either partner has a low score on C, thus admitting to high emotional reactivity, it may be necessary to do individual work to bring that partner to a level of emotional maturity necessary for successful marital work.

FACTOR E, DOMINANCE

Large differences on Factor E are found in the dominant/submissive relationship pattern identified in the early days of marital therapy. In this marital pattern, the submissive partner, unable to assert his or her needs and get them met, is frequently the identified patient. Dysfunction may take the form of depression, alcohol or drug abuse, psychosomatic complaints, mental illness, passive-aggressive behavior, and so on. The dominant partner, though appearing healthy, is actually controlled by the dysfunction of the submissive spouse. Two high Es are likely to be locked in a power struggle for control of the relationship. In this case, the solution to a problem is not as important as is who makes the decision. On the other hand, two low Es may suffer from decision paralysis.

FACTOR F, LIVELINESS

Frequently, just as mentioned in our discussion of Factor A, individuals who are quite different in their level of enthusiasm and inhibition are initially attracted to one another. However, high F partners can be a source of embarrassment and anxiety to low F individuals, and low Fs seem to be boring spoilsports to their high F partners. This can be a significant source of conflict.

## FACTOR G, RULE-CONSCIOUSNESS

Likewise, large differences on Factor G can lead to arguments over what one should or should not do. Low Gs will behave in ways that offend and anger high Gs, who are convinced that one should conform to society's norms. The interaction between the two approaches can lead to long lectures from the high G partner falling on deaf ears, while the low G continues to regard societal rules as something to be "gotten around."

## FACTOR H, BOLDNESS

Although the high H and low H can complement one another, large differences in scores on this scale will result in extreme frustration for the high H, who begins to see his or her spouse as a wimp, needing to be pushed and prodded. The low H usually responds to such prodding with anxiety and withdrawal, and the two become locked in a schismogenetic pattern.

## FACTOR I, EMOTIONAL SENSITIVITY

Although, as mentioned previously, Factor I is related to traditional gender socialization (i.e., in general, women are more sensitive than men), it is important to note that in Cattell and Nesselroade's (1967) original research on marital stability as predicted by 16PF factors, higher I in husbands was significantly more favorable to marital stability. That is, the husband who does not fit the stoic, insensitive, tough masculine stereotype is more likely to be found in a stable, happy marriage than is his low I counterpart.

## FACTOR L, VIGILANCE

Because this factor is a measure of one's level of interpersonal trust, it is of major importance in marital therapy. Clearly, the high L partner will be very suspicious of the spouse's actions and motives, which sets up an accuse-and-defend communication pattern. High L individuals also tend to project their angry feelings onto their spouses. They are not capable of lowering their guard in an intimate relationship even though it might bring much greater satisfaction. Thus, they are very difficult to get along with. Individuals with low trust level are poor candidates for marital therapy until the original cause of the lack of trust has been dealt with in individual therapy. Although it is possible that low Ls could be fooled in a relationship because they are not vigilant regarding the motives of their spouse, generally an individual with a low L is a much better relationship risk. Satisfactory relationships are highly correlated with low Ls.

## FACTOR M, ABSTRACTEDNESS

Large differences in Factor M can be a source of extreme irritation or can be affectionately appreciated and accepted, as in a complementary relationship. The low M individual often serves as organizer and helpmate to the creative but impractical high M partner, who may make noteworthy contributions to society while forgetting to put on his or her shoes. On the other hand, high and low Ms are on different developmental levels of cognitive reasoning, which can result in communication difficulties and sexual dissatisfaction (Karol & Russell, 1995).

## FACTOR N, SHREWDNESS

Very high Ns may not be able to form intimate relationships because they will never allow themselves to be vulnerable and exposed, which is an important component of emotional intimacy. Low Ns, on the other hand, are a better relationship risk, although they may be too forthright in their communications without appreciating the impact their comments will have on their partner.

## FACTOR O, APPREHENSION

High scores on Factor O are indicative of a spouse who will need constant reassurance, encouragement, and bolstering, which can become a real drain on the partner. Low Os usually make better marital partners, but they may fail to see their own faults in a partnership and need confrontation from the therapist.

## Q1, OPENNESS TO CHANGE

It would seem obvious that individuals who present for marital therapy with high scores on Q1 are more likely to try new patterns of interaction and follow through on homework or experiential tasks, which may lead to a more functional marriage. Low scorers will be resistant to those same interventions, which will slow therapy down. High scores on Q1 are positively correlated to marital satisfaction.

## Q2, SELF-RELIANCE

Although large differences in Q2 scores may be a source of confusion and misunderstanding between partners who do not understand or appreciate the style of the other, this factor is not generally a significant source of marital conflict. As previously mentioned, traditional gender socialization trains men to be more self-reliant and women to depend on the opinions of others more frequently.

## Q3, PERFECTIONISM

Large differences in scores on Q3 can lead to severe and chronic conflict between spouses. The spouse who wants a spotless home and organized closets, who carefully keeps a daily calendar, and who develops a long-range plan is driven crazy by the low Q3, who could care less about scheduling and organization. Likewise, the low Q3 is subjected to constant admonishment and criticism by the high Q3, who has a tendency to be rigid and inflexible. When both spouses have very low Q3s, a chaotic and disorganized family structure can be expected. Two high Q3s may have a very organized lifestyle but lack spontaneity and flexibility.

## Q4, TENSION

In marital therapy, a high score on Q4 is frequently a result of an unsatisfying, conflictual marital relationship. When the issues of conflict and dissatisfaction in the relationship are addressed, this score may go down. Occasionally, the comfort of a low Q4 can lead to complacency and a lack of motivation, but generally, a low Q4 is a positive indicator of the potential for a satisfying marital relationship.

## (1) EXTROVERSION/INTROVERSION

As previously mentioned when discussing Factor A, large differences on the Extroversion/Introversion scale can be a source of major dissatisfaction in a couple. The partner who wishes to entertain large groups of people in the home will run into great resistance from the "loner" spouse who prefers to spend time alone. The partner who spends much time in solitary activities will not meet the interpersonal needs of the spouse who must be surrounded by people. This factor will be discussed in more complexity when I illustrate the use of the 16PF in couples work in a later section.

## (2) ANXIETY/COMFORT

People with high anxiety have difficulty in marital relationships as should be intuitively obvious. An individual who tends to overreact to every potentially negative event, has low trust in his or her spouse, anticipates getting hurt, worries constantly, has low self-esteem, and whose tension level makes him or her terribly irritable is not going to be easy to live with. Low anxiety or relaxed people generally make better marital partners. However, they may minimize negative affect and be unmotivated to change because they are more comfortable. Again it is important to look at the individual primary scales in order to understand how the anxiety or lack of anxiety will be manifested. And since anxiety can be internally or externally generated, it will be important to look at the context in which the marital partners are expressing their anxiety. A spouse with a high L who has endured the infidelity of his or her spouse in the past may not be reflecting a generally distrustful outlook on life so much as reacting to past experience in this relationship. The spouse whose work situation is putting a great deal of pressure on him/her may score higher on O and Q4 in response to occupational stress and still be functioning adequately as a marital partner. On the other hand, the individual who comes to the marriage with an internalized anxious approach to life is a poor marital risk.

## (3) TOUGH-MINDEDNESS/RECEPTIVITY

Although tough-minded individuals perform very well in occupations that call for clear thinking and logical decision making, they do not do well in marital relationships unless their partners are also tough-minded. Many of the qualities marital therapists view to be necessary for good marital adjustment load on the receptive polarity of this second-order factor, most importantly, sensitivity to the emotions and needs of one's partner and a willingness to change. On the other hand, an individual with a very high score on this second-order factor may lack the ability to attain objectivity, which is also necessary in marital negotiations. Because so much of what loads on this factor is a result of traditional gender socialization, it is the opinion of this author that it can also be relearned, at least for the purposes of preserving a marital relationship that is of importance to both partners. New skills, both in learning to be sensitive and flexible and in gaining objectivity, can be taught (Philpot, 1991; Philpot & Brooks, 1995; Philpot, Brooks, Lusterman, & Nutt, 1997).

(4) INDEPENDENCE/ACCOMMODATION

At one time, women were encouraged, both by gender socialization and by a lack of power and status, to be more accommodating, whereas one of the hallmarks of the male value system in Western society has been independence. A complementary relationship thus developed between the traditional male and female in which the male "naturally" assumed the leadership position and the female accommodated, often to the detriment of her mental health. Alternatively, the male dominated with regard to factors outside the home, and the woman maintained dominance within the home. Due to the feminist movement and women's greater economic and legal power, these personality traits do not break down along gender lines as much as they once did. However, a new problem has developed. A male who continues to identify with extreme levels of independence and therefore exhibits traits of inflexibility and domination will find himself challenged by the woman who no longer accommodates to his needs. In the present social climate, both partners may exhibit traits of dominance and independence, which can lead to power struggles within the relationship unless negotiation and problem-solving skills are good.

(5) SELF-CONTROL/UNRESTRAINT

Although they may be initially attracted to one another, couples who score at the opposite ends of the self-control/unrestrained second-order factor will experience a great deal of conflict and discomfort with the lifestyle of the other. This will be illustrated in a later section.

## Correlation between 16PF Profiles and Relationship Adjustment

In 1967, Cattell and Nesselroade (1967, 1968) investigated the likeness versus completion theories of marital selection using the 16PF. The likeness hypothesis suggests that partners who are alike in personality are more likely to have stable, satisfactory relationships; the completeness theory postulates that individuals seek mates who can make up for deficits in their own personalities. Cattell and Nesselroade administered the 16PF to 139 couples, 37 of whom were identified as unsatisfactorily married. The results of that study, now three decades old and clearly irrelevant with regard to sex-role assignments, nevertheless are interesting to report because despite major sociological changes in the past 30 years, certain findings continue to play an important role in marital stability today (Russell, 1995).

The 1967 study found that husbands and wives who scored in the same direction on the Extroversion second-order factor were more likely to be in stable marriages. That is, if both husband and wife were either extroverted or introverted, the marriage was more likely to be stable. On the contrary, like scores on the second-order Anxiety factor were indicative of a stable marriage only if the anxiety level was low. High scores on the second-order Anxiety factor, whether of the male, the female, or both, were more likely to be correlated with unstable marriages. As for primary factors, positive correlations between husband and wife scores on B (intelligence), C (emotional stability), F (impulsivity or liveliness), G (rule-boundedness), H (boldness), M (imaginativeness), Q1 (conservatism or openness to change), and Q3 (self-discipline) were found in stable marriages. On the contrary, large differences on A (interpersonal warmth), F (impulsivity), I (sensitivity), and Q4 (tension) contributed to unstable marriages. Differences in E (dominance) and O (guilt-proneness or worrying), on the other hand, were found in stable marriages, which is indicative of some complementarity operating. High scores on B (intelligence) and C (emotional stability) and low scores on E (dominance) and N (forthrightness) were also correlated with stable marriages. Taken together, the 1967 study indicated that intelligent, emotionally stable, accommodating, genuine, and forthright individuals who were alike on the level of extroversion, liveliness, rule-boundedness, social boldness, level of abstractedness, openness to change, and self-discipline were most likely to be in stable marriages. On the contrary, couples with high anxiety, high dominance, low intelligence, low emotional stability, a lack of openness, and large differences on interpersonal warmth, impulsivity, sensitivity, and tension were found to be in unhappy marriages. There were also a number of complex interactions between husband and wife scores that appeared to be correlated with stable versus unstable marriages. However, because many of these were based on role assignments of the 1960s that used firmly entrenched gender stereotypes as the norm, several of these findings may no longer be relevant. The interested reader is referred to Cattell and Nesselroade (1967) for elaboration.

Recently, Karol and Russell (1995) examined the relationship between scores on the 16PF factors and scores obtained on the Marital Satisfaction Inventory (MSI) and Dyadic Adjustment Scale (DAS) for 321 couples. They also reported preliminary findings regarding couples' personality differences and their relationship to marital satisfaction. These more recent findings are in many ways consistent with the work of Cattell and Nesselroade (1968) three decades ago. However, Karol and Russell had the advantage of comparing the subscales on the DAS and the MSI to the 16PF factors rather than merely looking at stable versus unstable marriages. This analysis provides the user of the 16PF with a rich source of information.

At the global or second-order factor level, correlations between low scores on the 16PF Anxiety global scale and high relationship adjustment were significant in the positive direction at the $p < .0001$ level. This is consistent with Cattell and Nesselroade's (1967) earlier findings that high anxiety and happy marriage do not mix. Other second-order factors that correlated with relationship adjustment included the following: Tough-Mindedness was associated with lower Dyadic Cohesion and traditional relationships; Independence was correlated with nontraditional relationships; Self-Control was positively related to Dyadic Consensus, traditional relationships, and less distress in sexual matters.

At the primary-factor level, Emotional Stability (C) was correlated with all adjustment factors except Role Orientation on the MSI. Clearly, emotional stability is a plus in a marital relationship. Likewise, Vigilance (L), Apprehensiveness (O), and Tension (Q4) were highly correlated with adjustment. For example, Vigilance, Apprehensiveness, and Tension were found to be related to problems with affective communication, problem-solving communication, and extended family. In addition, Factor L was also correlated with less dyadic consensus, Factors O and Q4 with more conflict over child rearing, and Factor Q4 with sexual dissatisfaction. It is clear that high scores on C (Emotional Stability) and low scores on L (Vigilance), O (Apprehension), and Q4 (Tension) continue to be important in marital adjustment.

Other interesting correlations that corroborate earlier findings include high scores on N (privateness) correlated with poor problem-solving communication, high scores on Q1 (Openness to Change) correlated with more dyadic cohesion and less traditional relationships, and higher scores on B (reasoning ability) correlated with better problem-solving communication, less distress in financial matters, and nontraditional relationships. Karol and Russell (1995) also found that Factor A (Warmth) was associated with more satisfaction with child rearing; Factor G (Rule-Consciousness) with higher dyadic consensus, less distress in sexual matters, and more traditional marriages; Factor I (Emotional Sensitivity) with less traditional relationships; Factor M (Abstractedness) with less dyadic consensus, poorer problem-solving communication, and problems with extended family, and Q1 (Extroversion) with less traditional relationships.

Personality differences between partners were also examined on the 16PF. Differences between partners on Factor I (Emotional Sensitivity) were related to poorer dyadic consensus, cohesion, and overall adjustment on the DAS and problems with time spent together on the MSI. This finding corroborates earlier findings by Cattell and Nesselroade (1967, 1968). It appears that less traditional, more sensitive men make better husbands for sensitive, more traditional women, and only women who are more tough-minded and less traditional can deal with the traditional male. Differences in Abstractedness (M) were related to overall lower marital adjustment, consensus, and sexual satisfaction, implying that differences in information processing can lead to less understanding of one another and less satisfaction with sex. Differences in Q3 (Perfectionism) were related to less overall satisfaction, less consensus, poor communication, and less satisfying time together. Differences on L (Vigilance) were related to overall distress, less effective problem-solving skills, more conflict around childrearing, and seeing one's partner as having less satisfaction with the relationship. Finally, differences on Q4 (Tension) were related to poor problem-solving communication and seeing one's partner as less satisfied.

There were some differences that seemed to break down along gender lines. For women, differences in the Self-Control, Tough-Mindedness, and Independence global factors were related to global distress and problems in sex, agreement, communication, and problem solving. Although both men and women report problems with finding agreement when there are large differences on Emotional Sensitivity (I), for women these differences also affected the expression of affection and sexual satisfaction. A similar result occurs for women when there are large differences on M (Abstractedness). Women were also more affected by differences on E (Dominance) in obtaining agreement. Differences on L (Vigilance) created more problems for women in demonstrating affection. And finally, couple differences in Perfectionism (Q3) were related to dissatisfaction with the division of roles. The difference score that affected men more so than women was Factor B (reasoning ability). When there were large differences in Factor B, men had difficulty with affectional expression and overall adjustment and less satisfaction with financial matters, role division, sex, and the ability to agree about things, implicating an inability to work on reasonable solutions to problems.

Finally, Karol and Russell (1995) found that more satisfied couples show more Emotional Stability (C+), more Openness to Change (Q1), less Vigilance (L−), and high IM scores. Less satisfied couples show lower scores on reasoning ability (B−) and higher scores on Apprehension (O+) and Tension (Q4+). These findings remain consistent with Cattell and Nesselroade's (1967, 1968) work three decades ago. Clearly, couples must not overreact emotionally, must be adaptable and willing to grow with their partner, and must be trusting in an intimate relationship. In fact, constant worry and self-doubt combined with irritability and tension and an inability to problem solve in a reasonable manner is a formula for unhappy marriages.

## Using the 16PF in Couples Therapy

The above reported research provides clinicians with normative data to guide their use of the 16PF in couples work. Below, I discuss the ways in which I have used the 16PF, diagnostically, prognostically, premaritally, in treatment planning, and therapeutically in my work with couples. Although the 16PF will give clinicians very useful information no matter what systemic orientation they adopt when working with couples, I find this instrument particularly relevant to an object relations approach. A brief explanation of this approach follows for those clinicians not familiar with object relations theory.

## Object Relations Theory (Simplified and Abbreviated)

Klein (1948), Winnicott (1965), Fairbairn (1954), Dicks (1967), Zinner and Shapiro (1972, 1975), and many others have contributed to the formulation and concepts of object relations theory. More modern writers (Scharff & Scharff, 1991; Slipp, 1984, 1991) have incorporated this psychoanalytically based theory into family and couples therapy approaches. Still others (Hendrix, 1988; Scarf, 1987) have popularized concepts emerging from object relations theory by simplifying and clarifying, using less technical language, and providing many examples. The following account of object relations theory is a compilation of terms and ideas from a variety of sources likewise made simple and therefore frequently lacking in technical accuracy. The interested reader is referred to Scharff and Scharff for a more precise history of the development of object relations theory.

Object relations theory postulates that the primary motivation of newborns is to develop a loving, satisfying connection with a nurturing parent. The term *object* is used to designate the object of the individual's love and object relations, the emotional attachment between the one who loves and the *image* of the beloved as it exists in the lover's own mind. An introject is an internalized mental representation of people and relationships about which an individual has felt deeply. Object relations theory suggests that in cases where individuals have good, strong egos due to "good enough" parenting, the marital relationship is between two individuals who are largely conscious of their own assets and failings and who see one another in fairly realistic terms. On the other hand, when, during the course of development, children experience what they perceive to be rejection, they employ repression, introjection, and projection to preserve their own egos. The result is that they perceive the world through introjects, emotionally charged images of early relationships between self and other, and reality becomes distorted. These individuals tend to idealize or reject others. They see themselves and others in terms of all-good or all-bad qualities, sometimes referred to as splitting. They demand idealistic perfection in a marital partner, whose task is to serve as the all-good parent, but expect rejection based on introjects from early childhood. Thus, present marital interactions are distorted by introjects. Both partners are trying to work through early childhood conflicts by marrying the offending parent and making it turn out better this time.

They are drawn to one another by unconscious signals, as they recognize on a deep level how they fit like a lock and key. They make active but unconscious efforts to shape the intimate partner in adulthood to the model of the parent to work out unconscious issues of abandonment, rejection, unavailability, and so on. Each distorts the image of the other to fit with early introjects. To further complicate matters, they make use of projective identification; that is, they deny parts of themselves that they find unacceptable and project them onto their partner, where they attempt to control and change these aspects. They act in collusion to externalize what is intolerable within, a mechanism that alters both the image of self and other and protects the ego.

In plain English, this means that we fall in love with a person because he or she demonstrates the very characteristics with which we have difficulty due to early parenting experiences. Then, through a combination of distorted perceptions and actual instigation, we begin to see our partner as that early parent. We see what is good as being part of ourselves or what we want in an imagined idealized partner. We project onto our partner all that is negative in ourselves and begin to try to change him or her. But we do so only half-heartedly, because we need our partner to express the unwanted parts of ourselves, which our partner will not do if he or she truly changes. So we remain stuck. In reality, we must own the disowned aspects of ourselves and see our partner more realistically to have a satisfying intimate relationship.

Hendrix (1988) has proposed that this marital dilemma can result from the socialization process that all children endure in civilized society. He states that all children are forced to repress aspects of themselves due to the demands of society. These parts he called the "lost self." He then suggested that people create a façade to fill the void created by the repressions and by a lack of adequate nurturing in the socialization process. This he called the "false self." Finally, he theorized that the negative parts of the false self that met with disapproval had to be denied; these he called the "disowned self." Hendrix believes that we choose marital partners who have both the negative and positive qualities of our primary caretakers and who can compensate for the positive parts of our being that make up our lost self. Furthermore, we project our disowned self onto our partner. The goal of the treatment program is the acceptance and integration into our self-concept of our disowned parts and the recognition that when we stretch to change the parts of ourselves that our partners want changed, we are actually reembracing the lost self and becoming whole again. In some ways, the finding of the lost self echoes Cattell and Nesselroad (1968) notions of the completeness theory of marital selection. There appears to be a need for unconscious complementarity; that is, each partner provides some of the qualities for the whole personality (Dicks, 1967).

Some theorists see the autonomy/intimacy issue as lying at the core of object relations theory. Individuals have two major drives: to be self-determined and to be loved and accepted. In the course of socialization, people struggle with these sometimes contradictory needs. Those who are perceived by therapists as most healthy are those who have integrated these two needs most successfully. Johnson (1987) has developed five levels of relational functioning that reflect different levels of integration of autonomy and intimacy. The lowest level is paradox; at this level, autonomy and intimacy are seen as mutually exclusive. Intimacy is seen as a fusion of self to another and total loss of self, whereas autonomy is experienced as abandonment and emptiness. Relationships formed between partners at this level are conflictual and unstable, characterized by cycles of closeness and distance. Level 2 is projective identification: Neither partner is truly differentiated and neither partner can address *internally* the simultaneous need for affiliation and autonomy. Because autonomy and affiliation are not reconcilable, each partner takes half of the polarity and projects the other half onto the spouse. These relationships are characterized by pursuer/distancer dances and polarization on issues. The third level is conscious splitting; at this level, the partners can acknowledge the ambivalence they each feel regarding the autonomy/intimacy issue during periods of calm but revert to projective identification when under stress. The fourth level is tolerating ambivalence; individuals on this level see autonomy and intimacy as existing on a spatial continuum. They believe that greater closeness may mean giving up some autonomy, but that individuals can move back and forth on that continuum. They accept both self and other as complex individuals with both weaknesses and strengths. The fifth and highest level is the integrated level; at this level, autonomy and intimacy are seen by the couple as mutually self-supporting and enhancing. Each individual experiences himself or herself as more fully autonomous, more of who he or she really is, when in the presence of the intimate other. Differences and disagreements are not experienced as a threat to intimacy or disapproval, but are accepted, because each person is fundamentally a different person and appreciated as much for differences as for likenesses. The goal of therapy, then, is to move the couple up the ladder of relational functioning.

## How the 16PF Fits In: An Interpretive Strategy

Information gleaned from the 16PF can guide the clinician's treatment strategy in attaining the above goal. I begin with a general interpretive strategy for individual profiles and then discuss the systemic, interactive interpretation of couples' profiles. The reader will quickly recognize that an object relations theoretical orientation is not a requirement to make good use of the 16PF in couples work.

The general interpretive strategy for the 16PF begins with an examination of the response-style indicators (i.e., Impression Management, Infrequency, and

Acquiescence). High scores on IM can reflect an attempt to present oneself in the best possible light or unconscious denial of negative aspects of self. It can also mean that the examinee really does behave in highly socially desirable ways. It must also be remembered that the IM scale is highly correlated with many of the more prognostically positive scores, such as C+, L–, O–, and Q4–. The high INF score may be due to random responding, reading difficulties, inability to decide, or trying to avoid making the wrong impression. High scores on ACQ may be due to random, inconsistent, or indecisive responding or a high need for approval. As with other personality inventories, such as the MMPI, cutoff scores are recommended to identify invalid profiles.

Second, the clinician should examine the global factors of Extroversion, Anxiety, Tough-Mindedness, Independence, and Self-Control. Although individual primary scales will tell clinicians a great deal more about the interaction between the couple, the global factors can alert them to potential serious problems or strengths. The most important global factor in terms of marital adjustment is the Anxiety scale, where, as previously mentioned, low scores are correlated with marital satisfaction and stability and high scores are prognostic of more severe difficulty. The Tough-Mindedness global factor also appears to be correlated negatively with marital cohesion. On the other hand, the Independence factor is positively correlated with nontraditional relationships, and the Self-Control factor is correlated with positive dyadic consensus and less distress in the area of sexuality. Differences between partners at the global level appear to be less relevant to marital satisfaction and stability than at the level of the primary factors (Karol & Russell, 1995).

The third step in interpreting the 16PF is to examine the primary factors. Here, the clinician can look at areas of similarity and difference in couple profiles by plotting both profiles on the same sheet. I use an absolute difference of 4 Sten scores as well as the existence of extreme scores (1–2 or 9–10) on individual profiles as indication of potential difficulty. IPAT's Couple's Counseling Report provides an overall similarity coefficient and highlights extreme scores (1–3 or 8–10). Either method provides similar information. The Couple's Counseling Report provides the couple with a chart that compares their personalities, putting characteristics that are extreme in boldface print. The report includes many cautionary statements regarding the fact that there is no "right" combination or standard that all marriages should attain. The language of the report is neutral, using such terms as "style," "unique relationship," and "especially strong," to make the material more palatable for clients. The real work of interpretation and utilization is left up to the clinician who is expert at tests and measurements as well as the conceptualization of marital interaction. A detailed explanation of how I interpret a couple's profiles simultaneously is provided below in Step 2.

# Interpreting the 16PF with Couples: Case Examples

I find the 16PF to be useful in many different ways on several levels.

## ASSESSING THE VIABILITY OF COUPLES WORK: CASE EXAMPLE

First, the 16PF can alert the clinician to the potential for individual pathology, approaches to life, and personality variables. For example, we have already seen that certain 16PF profiles are pathological and, furthermore, lead to a poor prognosis in couple relationships. Whenever an individual profile shows low scores on C (Emotional Stability) and Q1 (Openness to Change) and/or high scores on L (Vigilance), O (Apprehension), and Q4 (Tension), we know individual work either within or outside of couples work must be done before the marriage will stabilize. On the other hand, when we see moderate or high scores on C and Q1 and moderate or low scores on L, O, and Q4, we know that we have a good prognosis for this relationship despite conflicts that may be present initially. This is particularly true if partners also have high scores on B (Abstract Reasoning), which has been correlated with more stable marriages. Couples work will be more effective and briefer with these couples because two fairly healthy, bright individuals are presenting for therapy. Their problems are more likely to be resolved with psychoeducation, skills training, and exercises (experiential or cognitive) designed to provide both insight into their dynamics and potential solutions to their issues. Of course, the entire cluster of variables in either the negative or positive direction does not always appear together. Individual scale scores, however, can alert the clinician to potential strengths or shortcomings that will affect the couple relationship.

The following case may serve as an example. Mrs. Smith requested therapy because she was extremely frustrated with her husband, whom she described as weak, forgetful, and unambitious. She had considered leaving him, but the fact that she had quit her job as a supervisor in a bank when she and her husband had moved a year ago and had a 15-month-old baby to care for kept her in the relationship. She did not want to return home to her domineering mother, with whom she did not get along, yet that seemed to be her only other option. She brought Mr. Smith to couples counseling to be "fixed." Mr. Smith was pleasant and cooperative, but very quiet in the session. His demeanor and body language shouted depression or, at the very least, dysthymia. After the initial sessions, a Couples 16PF was administered to assess the marital interaction (see Figure 4.1, Profile 1). Although it is not recommended that the 16PF be used to diagnose pathology (the MMPI and other instruments that are designed to do so would be

**16PF® Fifth Edition Individual Record Form**
*Profile Sheet*

Instructions: Write the sten score for each factor in the second column. Starting with Factor A, place a mark over the spot representing the appropriate sten score. Repeat for each factor. Connect the marks with straight lines.

IPAT

Profile 1
Name  The Smith's

Date  Mrs. - - - -
      Mr.  _____

## PRIMARY FACTORS

| Factor | Sten | Left Meaning | Standard Ten Score (STEN) | Right Meaning |
|---|---|---|---|---|
| A: Warmth | | Reserved, Impersonal, Distant | | Warm, Outgoing, Attentive to Others |
| B: Reasoning | | Concrete | | Abstract |
| C: Emotional Stability | | Reactive, Emotionally Changeable | | Emotionally Stable, Adaptive, Mature |
| E: Dominance | | Deferential, Cooperative, Avoids Conflict | | Dominant, Forceful, Assertive |
| F: Liveliness | | Serious, Restrained, Careful | | Lively, Animated, Spontaneous |
| G: Rule-Consciousness | | Expedient, Nonconforming | | Rule-Conscious, Dutiful |
| H: Social Boldness | | Shy, Threat-Sensitive, Timid | | Socially Bold, Venturesome, Thick-Skinned |
| I: Sensitivity | | Utilitarian, Objective, Unsentimental | | Sensitive, Aesthetic, Sentimental |
| L: Vigilance | | Trusting, Unsuspecting, Accepting | | Vigilant, Suspicious, Skeptical, Wary |
| M: Abstractedness | | Grounded, Practical, Solution-Oriented | | Abstracted, Imaginative, Idea-Oriented |
| N: Privateness | | Forthright, Genuine, Artless | | Private, Discreet, Non-Disclosing |
| O: Apprehension | | Self-Assured, Unworried, Complacent | | Apprehensive, Self-Doubting, Worried |
| Q₁: Openness to Change | | Traditional, Attached to Familiar | | Open to Change, Experimenting |
| Q₂: Self-Reliance | | Group-Oriented, Affiliative | | Self-Reliant, Solitary, Individualistic |
| Q₃: Perfectionism | | Tolerates Disorder, Unexacting, Flexible | | Perfectionistic, Organized, Self-Disciplined |
| Q₄: Tension | | Relaxed, Placid, Patient | | Tense, High Energy, Impatient, Driven |

## GLOBAL FACTORS

| | | | Average | |
|---|---|---|---|---|
| EX: Extraversion | | Introverted, Socially Inhibited | | Extraverted, Socially Participating |
| AX: Anxiety | | Low Anxiety, Unperturbed | | High Anxiety, Perturbable |
| TM: Tough-Mindedness | | Receptive, Open-Minded, Intuitive | | Tough-Minded, Resolute, Unempathic |
| IN: Independence | | Accommodating, Agreeable, Selfless | | Independent, Persuasive, Willful |
| SC: Self-Control | | Unrestrained, Follows Urges | | Self-Controlled, Inhibits Urges |

Copyright 1993 by the Institute for Personality and Ability Testing, P.O. Box 1188, Champaign, Illinois, U.S.A. 61824-1188. All rights reserved. May not be reproduced in whole or in part, stored in a retrieval system or transmitted in any form or by any means, photocopying, mechanical, electronic, recording or otherwise without prior permission in writing from the publisher. Printed in the U.S.A.

Figure 4.1
Profile 1: The Smith's

Copright © 1993 by the Institute for Personality and Ability Testing,
P.O. Box 1188, Champagn, Illinois, USA, 61824-1188.
All rights reserved. Used with permission.

more appropriate), nevertheless, Mr. Smith's profile confirmed the therapist's impression that depression and anxiety were present at a clinically significant level. The most notable scores of Mr. Smith's profile were:

1. His extremely low score on Factor A, which indicated a very introverted lifestyle, a dislike and avoidance of social interaction;
2. Low ego-strength as indicated by Factor C, which is manifested by high emotional reactivity, a sense of helplessness, and lack of perseverence in the face of difficulty;
3. A submissive, dependent attitude, including a fear of authority, as seen on Factor E (the positive aspect of this score is his tendency to be considerate and diplomatic);
4. Severe shyness, as seen on Factor H, manifested by timidity, lack of confidence, and inhibition in social settings, and resulting in a withdrawn, emotionally cautious approach to others;
5. An extremely low score on Q3, which indicates a total lack of self-discipline, direction, or sense of purpose; in more psychoanalytic terms, lack of clear identity;
6. A very high score on Q4, indicating severe tension and anxiety and, because Q4 is so face-valid, most likely a cry for help;
7. Very low scores on the Extroversion and Independence global scales; and
8. An extremely high score on the Anxiety global scale.

Important patterns that point to clinical problems include low A, E, H, and F and high Q2, which is often an indication of the burnt child syndrome; high O, Q4, and Q2 and low E, F, C, Q3, H, and A, which indicate depression is present; and low C and Q3 present with a high O and Q4, which points to high anxiety (Karson, 1985). The interpretation of Mr. Smith's profile is that he is a man who was possibly abused as a child, at least emotionally, and is consequently very submissive and dependent, shy and lacking in self-confidence, and unable to express anger directly. He suffers severe anxiety, which he defends against by withdrawing from interpersonal interaction, has a poor self-concept, is very depressed, and may even be at risk for suicide. Clearly, his depression and anxiety must be addressed before he is able to effectively participate in marital therapy. Therefore, the clinician would refer for medication, obtain a suicide contract, work on issues of identity and self-esteem, and teach assertiveness skills in preparation for later marital work.

Although Mrs. Smith's profile did not look quite so pathological, she did have a low score on C, indicating high emotional reactivity, and a relatively high score on L, indicating a lack of trust in others. Both of these scores are indicative of poor marital adjustment and risk. Therefore, while the clinician is bolstering

Mr. Smith in preparation for marital work, he or she can be working with Mrs. Smith on developing more ego strength and reducing her level of suspiciousness. Individual work for both partners would very likely involve some family of origin work and could be done in a typical Bowenian fashion, if desired. On the positive side, both of the Smiths are intelligent, a welcome resource in a sea of poor indicators.

UNDERSTANDING THE SYSTEMIC INTERACTION:
CASE EXAMPLES

When both husband's and wife's profiles are plotted on the same profile sheet, both clinician and clients have a graphic representation of areas of similarity and difference in personality style. The interactions between these two personalities can then be interpreted and discussed with the clients, using language that is easily understood by the layperson. Neither differences nor similarities necessarily imply a healthy, satisfying relationship nor a conflictual, unhappy one. It is the interaction between the two that makes the difference. Because most of the descriptors on the 16PF are not colored by positive and negative connotations but are simply normal personality variables, the systemic therapist can easily maintain a neutral stance while pointing out the negatives and positives of the interaction between two "normal" personalities. The language of the 16PF provides an excellent way of reframing conflicts as different ways of looking at life as opposed to the right way versus the wrong way: No one is at fault; the interaction is not good. Alternatively, the differences in personality *are* good because they complement one another. Or yet again, the similarities are a strength because the partners agree on an approach to life and understand one another. In yet other cases, the similarities are problematic because complementarity in interaction is sometimes necessary or preferable. A few examples will serve to demonstrate how this works.

Partners with extreme differences on A (Warmth) and H (Boldness), for example, may have conflict regarding the amount of time they spend with other people. Even though the A–, H– individual may have been made to feel comfortable and accepted by his or her A+, H+ partner and was therefore initially attracted to him or her, the A–, H– partner will not enjoy going out and socializing, whereas the A+, H+ partner will feel bored and deprived if he or she does not interact with others on a regular basis. Partners who are strongly mismatched on G (Rule-Consciousness) and Q1 (Openness to Change) may become frustrated with the other's attitude. The G–, Q1+ individual will see the partner as inflexible, rigid, self-righteous, and dull; the G+, Q1– partner will view the other as irresponsible, rebellious, immoral, and radical. A G+ (rule-bound), O+ (worrying) partner will be embarrassed and horrified by the F+ (impulsive), H+ (socially bold), G– (expedient), O– (guilt-free), and Q1+ (open to change) partner who behaves impulsively with little concern for the opinions of others. The Q2+ (self-sufficient) individual will not understand the need for his or her Q2– (group-oriented) partner to talk over every decision with friends; in fact, the Q2+ partner will see such behavior as a weakness and feel betrayed if the problems Q2– discusses are in regard to the couple relationship. The I+ (emotionally sensitive) partner will find the I– (insensitive) partner to be insensitive and unfeeling, and the I– partner will wonder what all the fuss is about. Partners with large differences on Q3 (Perfectionism) frequently find themselves in conflict over missed appointments, messy closets, and forgotten chores. (See the premarital counseling case example below for an illustration of several of these patterns.)

In the above cases, one can see that if the partners were more similar on certain scales, they would be more comfortable with one another. For example, two Q3+s live in an orderly house and keep a calendar book, two Q3–s live in chaos and disarray, but both couples are comfortable with that lifestyle. However, similarity has it own problems. Imagine two E+s (dominant) vying for control of the relationship, for example, or two C–s (emotionally reactive) trying to resolve a problem. Likewise, two L+s (vigilant) would not be able to trust one another, and two N+s (private) may never reach a point of intimacy because neither will reveal himself or herself to the other. Of course, this last circumstance may not bother either partner and therefore not be a problem to them, although it does not meet the definition of intimacy touted by our society. Therefore, in some cases, complementarity is a better mix. The C+ individual can calm the C–, the E– individual compromises with the E+, and so on.

The couple can also come to view their marriage as a partnership, with each partner supplying the expertise in a particular area. For example, the A+, H+ individual can be the social secretary and plan events, which put his or her A–, H– partner more at ease. The practical M–, Q3+ individual can provide the organization for the M+, Q3– absentminded professor. As long as the couple accepts the differences and respects the contribution of each partner, their relationship can be very satisfying.

When giving feedback to the couple, the therapist can use the information from the 16PF to identify strengths as well as areas of conflict, provide psychoeducation regarding the effects of gender socialization and cultural variables, open up nonblaming dialogue around hot issues, reframe problems in neutral terms, offer suggestions regarding areas of individual change that might enhance marital satisfaction based on normative data, and provide an example of how a partnership might work using the strengths of each. I have found clients to be very receptive when approached in this manner. They each feel validated and understood by the therapist and essentially interpreted to their partner in a positive way. They are then ready to look at potential for self-change and for acceptance of partner differences.

A case example may serve to illustrate. The Hendersons came in to therapy at the request of Mr. Henderson, who had the insight to recognize that his teenage son's acting-out was partially in response to marital strife within the family system. In the usual progression of family therapy, after addressing issues with the three children, the therapist began work with the marital subsystem. As part of the routine interview for couples work, the therapist asked the couple what originally attracted them to one another. Mr. Henderson talked about how Mrs. Henderson had approached him for a date, had made him feel comfortable, safe, and appreciated, and had been a "whole lot of fun." Mrs. Henderson said that she admired Mr. Henderson's intelligence, self-sufficiency, and willingness to compromise. She also admits that she found his quiet manner and shyness endearing, because she really didn't trust "slick" men. A Couples 16PF revealed the following patterns (see Figure 4.2, Profile 2).

Mrs. Henderson was a warm, extroverted (high A), somewhat dominant, aggressive (high E), spontaneous, enthusiastic (high F), and slightly adventurous woman who married a cool and reserved (low A), cooperative (moderate E), serious, careful (low F) low risk-taker (low H). Both of the Hendersons are somewhat suspicious and distrusting of the motives of others (high L). The most salient scores on the global factors are the Extroversion and Independence scales, on which one finds extreme differences between the spouses; that is, Mr. Henderson is quite introverted and accommodating, and Mrs. Henderson is very extroverted and independent. Mrs. Henderson wants to go out and have fun with large groups of people, go to dances, and party at nightclubs. Mr. Henderson is uncomfortable with that level of social activity, preferring family outings and camping trips. Mrs. Henderson is spontaneous; she has an idea and acts on it immediately. Mr. Henderson is very cautious and plodding in his decision making, which irritates Mrs. Henderson, who thinks he'll never get moving. Mrs. Henderson essentially controls the family activities and plans because she asserts her wishes, and generally Mr. Henderson goes along with her wishes to be cooperative and avoid conflict. Nevertheless, he "spoils" the fun, because he is a wet blanket at parties, which embarrasses her. In fact, he too is embarrassed by her behavior when she sings karoake or dances wildly on the dance floor.

During the 16PF feedback session, the therapist was able to point out how the very factors that had originally attracted the Hendersons to one another were the ones they were squabbling about at this point. They quickly became aware that they each had begun to polarize on these traits to correct for the other's behavior, which had resulted in conflict rather than teamwork. It did not take them very long to recognize that as a team they each contributed certain strengths to their relationship, which they had appreciated at one time and could appreciate again. Mrs. Henderson had enough insight to know that if Mr. Henderson were as much of a partier as she was, she would distrust him and be afraid of losing him (high L). She felt safe with her quiet loner. Mr. Henderson realized that his life would be pretty dull and uncomfortably lonely if it weren't for Mrs. Henderson's acting as social secretary for the family. Mrs. Henderson knew that she sometimes got

**16PF® Fifth Edition Individual Record Form**
*Profile Sheet*

Profile 2
Name The Henderson's

**Instructions:** Write the sten score for each factor in the second column. Starting with Factor A, place a mark over the spot representing the appropriate sten score. Repeat for each factor. Connect the marks with straight lines.

IPAT

Date Mrs. – – – –
Mr. _____

## PRIMARY FACTORS

| Factor | Sten | Left Meaning | Standard Ten Score (STEN) | Right Meaning |
|---|---|---|---|---|
| A: Warmth | | Reserved, Impersonal, Distant | | Warm, Outgoing, Attentive to Others |
| B: Reasoning | | Concrete | | Abstract |
| C: Emotional Stability | | Reactive, Emotionally Changeable | | Emotionally Stable, Adaptive, Mature |
| E: Dominance | | Deferential, Cooperative, Avoids Conflict | | Dominant, Forceful, Assertive |
| F: Liveliness | | Serious, Restrained, Careful | | Lively, Animated, Spontaneous |
| G: Rule-Consciousness | | Expedient, Nonconforming | | Rule-Conscious, Dutiful |
| H: Social Boldness | | Shy, Threat-Sensitive, Timid | | Socially Bold, Venturesome Thick-Skinned |
| I: Sensitivity | | Utilitarian, Objective, Unsentimental | | Sensitive, Aesthetic, Sentimental |
| L: Vigilance | | Trusting, Unsuspecting, Accepting | | Vigilant, Suspicious, Skeptical, Wary |
| M: Abstractedness | | Grounded, Practical, Solution-Oriented | | Abstracted, Imaginative, Idea-Oriented |
| N: Privateness | | Forthright, Genuine, Artless | | Private, Discreet, Non-Disclosing |
| O: Apprehension | | Self-Assured, Unworried, Complacent | | Apprehensive, Self-Doubting, Worried |
| Q₁: Openness to Change | | Traditional, Attached to Familiar | | Open to Change, Experimenting |
| Q₂: Self-Reliance | | Group-Oriented, Affiliative | | Self-Reliant, Solitary, Individualistic |
| Q₃: Perfectionism | | Tolerates Disorder, Unexacting, Flexible | | Perfectionistic, Organized, Self-Disciplined |
| Q₄: Tension | | Relaxed, Placid, Patient | | Tense, High Energy, Impatient, Driven |

## GLOBAL FACTORS

| | | Average | |
|---|---|---|---|
| EX: Extraversion | Introverted, Socially Inhibited | | Extraverted, Socially Participating |
| AX: Anxiety | Low Anxiety, Unperturbed | | High Anxiety, Perturbable |
| TM: Tough-Mindedness | Receptive, Open-Minded, Intuitive | | Tough-Minded, Resolute, Unempathic |
| IN: Independence | Accommodating, Agreeable, Selfless | | Independent, Persuasive, Willful |
| SC: Self-Control | Unrestrained, Follows Urges | | Self-Controlled, Inhibits Urges |

Copyright ©1993 by the Institute for Personality and Ability Testing, P.O. Box 1188, Champaign, Illinois U.S.A. 61824-1188. All rights reserved. May not be reproduced in whole or in part, stored in a retrieval system, or transmitted in any form or by any means, photocopying, mechanical, electronic, recording, or otherwise without prior permission in writing from the publisher. Printed in the U.S.A.

Figure 4.2
Profile 2: The Henderson's

Copyright © 1993 by the Institute for Personality and Ability Testing,
P.O. Box 1188, champagn, Illinois, USA, 61824-1188.
All rights reserved. Used with permission.

into trouble because she acted without thinking and needed to consult with Mr. Henderson to avoid mistakes due to her tendency to be impulsive. Meanwhile, Mr. Henderson became more fully aware that Mrs. Henderson's encouragement and enthusiasm pushed him to take moderate risks that paid off in his career, investments, and social life. In these areas, the Hendersons reframed their personality differences as teamwork and accepted each other's contributions. The therapist used Mrs. Henderson's desire for more warmth in her relationship as motivation to become a better listener and less of a dictator in the marriage. Mr. Henderson responded with more enthusiasm and affection when his wishes were considered. Couples communication training and a little assertiveness training for Mr. Henderson made conflict resolution more effective and satisfying. Although some of the dynamics with this couple were similar to those of the Smiths (see above), the lack of extreme scores anywhere in the profile, the presence of average ego strength (C), high intelligence (B), and at least an average willingness to change (Q1) made this case more immediately responsive to systemic intervention.

OBJECT RELATIONS APPROACH: CASE EXAMPLE

At a deeper level, the clinician is alerted to possible unconscious processes in couple interaction. Using the object relations approach as a therapeutic model, the clinician is able to see where one partner may be projecting unwanted or repressed aspects of self onto the other or where the partners have attempted to complete missing aspects of themselves by pairing with someone who has those traits. In either case, one usually finds that the very characteristics that drew the partners to one another are now the traits they wish to change. By clarifying the underlying dynamics for the clinician, the 16PF aids in treatment planning.

Profile 3 (Figure 4.3) provides an example of this. Mr. Lewis, a somewhat aloof (A−), calm and rational (C+, I−), practical (M−), conservative (Q1−), and disciplined (Q3+) accountant married Mrs. Lewis, a slightly emotional (C−), vivacious (F+, H+), warm (A+), and undisciplined (Q3−) artist (M+). He was drawn to her extroverted, vivacious behavior, her fun-loving approach to life, and her creativity. She was drawn to his grounded, calm nature, which made her feel safe and secure. He had suppressed his emotionality and his creativity during the socialization process; instead, he was governed by rules and practical affairs that he handled in a logical, calm manner. She had never developed self-discipline and tended to react more emotionally than logically because such behavior was tolerated in a woman. On the other hand, she had not suppressed her childlike exuberance for life or her ability to see possibilities beyond the daily practicalities of life. Nevertheless, she had no confidence in herself to harness her capabilities and so looked for a more grounded spouse to take care of her.

When the Lewises presented for therapy, he was angry that she seemed unable to keep the checkbook properly, that she spent too much time painting and

**16PF® Fifth Edition Individual Record Form**
*Profile Sheet*

Profile 3
Name  The Lewis'

**Instructions:** Write the sten score for each factor in the second column. Starting with Factor A, place a mark over the spot representing the appropriate sten score. Repeat for each factor. Connect the marks with straight lines

Date  Mrs. - - - -
Mr. _____

IPAT

## PRIMARY FACTORS

| Factor | Sten | Left Meaning | Standard Ten Score (STEN) | Right Meaning |
|---|---|---|---|---|
| A: Warmth | | Reserved, Impersonal, Distant | | Warm, Outgoing, Attentive to Others |
| B: Reasoning | | Concrete | | Abstract |
| C: Emotional Stability | | Reactive, Emotionally Changeable | | Emotionally Stable, Adaptive, Mature |
| E: Dominance | | Deferential, Cooperative, Avoids Conflict | | Dominant, Forceful, Assertive |
| F: Liveliness | | Serious, Restrained, Careful | | Lively, Animated, Spontaneous |
| G: Rule-Consciousness | | Expedient, Nonconforming | | Rule-Conscious, Dutiful |
| H: Social Boldness | | Shy, Threat-Sensitive, Timid | | Socially Bold, Venturesome, Thick-Skinned |
| I: Sensitivity | | Utilitarian, Objective, Unsentimental | | Sensitive, Aesthetic, Sentimental |
| L: Vigilance | | Trusting, Unsuspecting, Accepting | | Vigilant, Suspicious, Skeptical, Wary |
| M: Abstractedness | | Grounded, Practical, Solution-Oriented | | Abstracted, Imaginative, Idea-Oriented |
| N: Privateness | | Forthright, Genuine, Artless | | Private, Discreet, Non-Disclosing |
| O: Apprehension | | Self-Assured, Unworried, Complacent | | Apprehensive, Self-Doubting, Worried |
| Q₁: Openness to Change | | Traditional, Attached to Familiar | | Open to Change, Experimenting |
| Q₂: Self-Reliance | | Group-Oriented, Affiliative | | Self-Reliant, Solitary, Individualistic |
| Q₃: Perfectionism | | Tolerates Disorder, Unexacting, Flexible | | Perfectionistic, Organized, Self-Disciplined |
| Q₄: Tension | | Relaxed, Placid, Patient | | Tense, High Energy, Impatient, Driven |

## GLOBAL FACTORS

| | | | Average | |
|---|---|---|---|---|
| EX: Extraversion | | Introverted, Socially Inhibited | | Extraverted, Socially Participating |
| AX: Anxiety | | Low Anxiety, Unperturbed | | High Anxiety, Perturbable |
| TM: Tough-Mindedness | | Receptive, Open-Minded, Intuitive | | Tough-Minded, Resolute, Unempathic |
| IN: Independence | | Accommodating, Agreeable, Selfless | | Independent, Persuasive, Willful |
| SC: Self-Control | | Unrestrained, Follows Urges | | Self-Controlled, Inhibits Urges |

Copyright ©1993 by the Institute for Personality and Ability Testing, P.O. Box 1188 Champaign, Illinois, U.S.A. 61824-1188. All rights reserved. May not be reproduced in whole or in part, stored in a retrieval system, or transmitted in any form or by any means photocopying, mechanical electronic recording, or otherwise without prior permission in writing from the publisher. Printed in the U.S.A.

Figure 4.3
Profile 3: The Lewis'
Copyright © 1993 by the Institute for Personality and Ability Testing,
P.O. Box 1188, Champagn, Illinois, USA, 61824-1188.
All rights reserved. Used with permission.

doing crafts and not enough time with housework, and that he couldn't discuss things rationally with her because she would cry and get upset. She felt that he had become a scolding parent and no longer appreciated her for what she had to offer. On an unconscious level, this couple had projected intolerable aspects of themselves onto each other and were playing out relationships with parent figures. The 16PF made this clear to the clinician very quickly, which guided her to begin family of origin work within couples therapy relatively soon into the process.

Mr. Lewis had been raised in a family that reinforced responsibility and rule-following as part of the socialization process. As is most often the case, he had identified with his father in an effort to develop his sense of masculinity. His father had been a rational, controlled, organized, hard-working, responsible, independent, and self-sufficient individual, the stereotypical version of the traditional male. Because his father did not approve of the spontaneous, enthusiastic, childlike, imaginative parts of himself, he had suppressed them. Although Mr. Lewis appreciated his mother's affection and emotional support, he rejected the expression of emotion because it was not masculine. His parents' marriage was typical of that period, with the father being the patriarchal head of the house who made the decisions and took responsibility for financial matters. Mr. Lewis had come to believe that his mother, and indeed, women in general, were fiscally irresponsible, if not stupid. His relationship with his mother was a conflicted one: He needed her affection and sense of fun because he did not get it from his father, but he disrespected her abilities in things that "really mattered."

Mrs. Lewis was raised in an environment that rewarded creativity, tolerance of disorder, spontaneity, imagination, experimentation, and flexibility. Her parents were both musicians, who were artistic, creative, and relaxed. These characteristics were reinforced, while responsibility, steadiness, and dependability were not. She never learned to appreciate the benefits of schedules and budgets. Her father, however, was a perfectionist when it came to music, and no matter how hard Mrs. Lewis tried, she was never able to please her father as a musician. When he became critical, she reacted by emotionally withdrawing from him.

As would have been predicted by object relations theory, Mr. Lewis fell in love with the lost part of himself—the lively, fun, creative, spontaneous artist, who filled the voids in his life. Mrs. Lewis fell in love with his responsibility and dependability—the repressed parts of herself. After marriage, they projected the unacceptable parts of themselves onto one another and began to replay child-parent patterns. Mr. Lewis needed his wife's affection but disrespected her abilities. Mrs. Lewis needed her husband's protection and organization to feel safe but felt she could never please him. By treating her like a child, Mr. Lewis produced the very childlike behaviors he projected onto her. By not taking responsibility for the duties to which she had agreed, Mrs. Lewis brought about the overbearing lectures and lack of approval she feared most. She reacted first by crying and then emotionally withdrawing from him, which took away the affection he so dearly craved.

The couple, who were basically healthy individually, gained insight into their dynamics, regained their appreciation for their differences, and found solutions to their current conflicts. The wife, for example, became aware that she could not have it both ways: If she did not wish to discipline herself enough to do the daily things that make life function smoothly, she would have to expect someone else to do them instead and simultaneously lose her adult status (i.e., her husband would handle the checkbook and merely give her an allowance). She opted instead to impose self-discipline and develop that neglected aspect of her personality. The husband recognized that he was very bad at expressing emotion and that his wife's ready access to her emotions frightened him; however, he also was aware that he would feel "dead" without the emotionality she brought into the relationship. He decided to try to get in touch with his own emotions with the help of the therapist and his wife, and she agreed to use cognitive-behavioral techniques to quelch her initial reactions and resolve conflicts more rationally. That is, she moved toward the center on C (Emotional Stability) of the 16PF and he toward the center on I (Emotional Sensitivity). Both partners began to express their appreciation for the desirable characteristics of the other, as they had during courting. He became much more supportive of her artistic career and she showed him gratitude for providing the practical guidance and financial expertise she needed to actually start a gallery. They became a team, using and appreciating each other's strengths rather than focusing on weaknesses.

It should be noted here that, although the object relations approach was used to understand the deeper dynamics between this couple, many of the polarities that created conflict in this couple can also be explained by traditional gender socialization: Men are socialized to repress emotion, be responsible and self-sufficient, control their surroundings, and have all the answers; women are socialized to be dependent, emotional, and childlike in their interactions. Whichever explanation one endorses, the solution remains the same. Each person must become more of a whole individual, incorporating aspects into his or her personality that previously have been rejected. Both must come to respect and appreciate the differences between them.

## PREMARITAL COUNSELING: CASE EXAMPLE

Finally, the 16PF can be used in premarital counseling to identify potential areas of conflict in future years. This intervention frequently catches the couple when they are still enamored with the qualities they will later come to hate in the other. Looking at personality differences as represented on the 16PF profile will afford the clinician an opportunity to point out where they might become

**16PF⁹ Fifth Edition Individual Record Form**
Profile Sheet

**Instructions:** Write the sten score for each factor in the second column. Starting with Factor A, place a mark over the spot representing the appropriate sten score. Repeat for each factor. Connect the marks with straight lines.

IPAT

Profile 4

Name   Pre-marital

Date   Jill   - - - -
       Jack   ————

## PRIMARY FACTORS

| Factor | Sten | Left Meaning | Standard Ten Score (STEN) 1 2 3 4 5 6 7 8 9 10 | Right Meaning |
|---|---|---|---|---|
| A: Warmth | | Reserved, Impersonal, Distant | | Warm, Outgoing, Attentive to Others |
| B: Reasoning | | Concrete | | Abstract |
| C: Emotional Stability | | Reactive, Emotionally Changeable | | Emotionally Stable, Adaptive, Mature |
| E: Dominance | | Deferential, Cooperative, Avoids Conflict | | Dominant, Forceful, Assertive |
| F: Liveliness | | Serious, Restrained, Careful | | Lively, Animated, Spontaneous |
| G: Rule-Consciousness | | Expedient, Nonconforming | | Rule-Conscious, Dutiful |
| H: Social Boldness | | Shy, Threat-Sensitive, Timid | | Socially Bold, Venturesome, Thick-Skinned |
| I: Sensitivity | | Utilitarian, Objective, Unsentimental | | Sensitive, Aesthetic, Sentimental |
| L: Vigilance | | Trusting, Unsuspecting, Accepting | | Vigilant, Suspicious, Skeptical, Wary |
| M: Abstractedness | | Grounded, Practical, Solution-Oriented | | Abstracted, Imaginative, Idea-Oriented |
| N: Privateness | | Forthright, Genuine, Artless | | Private, Discreet, Non-Disclosing |
| O: Apprehension | | Self Assured, Unworried, Complacent | | Apprehensive, Self-Doubting, Worried |
| Q₁: Openness to Change | | Traditional, Attached to Familiar | | Open to Change, Experimenting |
| Q₂: Self-Reliance | | Group-Oriented, Affiliative | | Self-Reliant, Solitary, Individualistic |
| Q₃: Perfectionism | | Tolerates Disorder, Unexacting, Flexible | | Perfectionistic, Organized, Self-Disciplined |
| Q₄: Tension | | Relaxed, Placid, Patient | | Tense, High Energy, Impatient, Driven |

## GLOBAL FACTORS

| Factor | Average 1 2 3 4 5 6 7 8 9 10 | Right Meaning |
|---|---|---|
| EX: Extraversion | Introverted, Socially Inhibited | Extraverted, Socially Participating |
| AX: Anxiety | Low Anxiety, Unperturbed | High Anxiety, Perturbable |
| TM: Tough-Mindedness | Receptive, Open-Minded, Intuitive | Tough-Minded Resolute Unempathic |
| IN: Independence | Accommodating, Agreeable, Selfless | Independent, Persuasive, Willful |
| SC: Self-Control | Unrestrained, Follows Urges | Self-Controlled, Inhibits Urges |

Copyright ©1993 by the Institute for Personality and Ability Testing P.O. Box 1188 Champaign, Illinois, U.S.A. 61824-1188. All rights reserved. May not be reproduced in whole or in part, stored in a retrieval system, or transmitted in any form or by any means, photocopying, mechanical, electronic, recording, or otherwise, without prior permission in writing from the publisher. Printed in the U.S.A.

Figure 4.4
Profile 4: Pre-Marital

Copyright © 1993 by the Institute for Personality and Ability Testing,
P.O. Box 1188, Champagn, Illinois, USA, 61824-1188.
All rights reserved. Used with permission.

annoyed with each other in future years, providing examples of potential negative interactions. The clinician can also use this opportunity to make suggestions of possible solutions to these difficulties. Whether or not the clients begin to tackle these problems premaritally (more likely in second marriages), they often remember the words of the counselor when the actual conflict begins. Instant recognition of a predicted problem based on personality variables leads them to seek help quickly to resolve the difficulty.

For example, a young, unmarried couple took the 16PF as part of an experiment (see Figure 4.4, Profile 4). Jill showed an E+ (dominant), F– (serious), G+ (rule-bound), Q3– (undisciplined), Q4+ (tense) personality. All other scales were within normal range. Jack, on the other hand, had an extremely high F+ (impulsive), I+ (sensitive), M+ (imaginative), moderately high L+ (suspicious), and extremely low G– (expedient), N– (forthright), and Q3– (undisciplined). All of his other scores were within normal range. It would not be difficult to predict that although she sees him as exciting and creative now, his lack of concern for the rules and his impulsive behavior will begin to bother her. At that time, she will attempt to impose her own serious, rule-bound nature on him (E+), but he will be hurt (I+) and suspicious of her motives (L+) and will resist. Because she is tense and irritable (Q4+), she may not find ways to motivate change in his behavior that are productive. Because they both have low Q3, it may even be possible to predict that her attempt to bring him into line will occur only when life is chaotic for both of them and may revolve around the lack of discipline they both demonstrate. This information can be shared with the couple as a possibility that may come to pass, thus sensitizing them to potential difficulties.

## Summary

This chapter provided the reader with a working knowledge of the 16PF, the relevant research that applies to marital interaction and 16PF scores, a recommended interpretive strategy for both individual and couples profiles, and examples of how the 16PF can be used diagnostically, prognostically, in conceptualization and treatment planning, and as a therapeutic intervention. The author highly recommends the 16PF as a tool for understanding the marital subsystem in family work.

# CHAPTER 5

# The Rorschach:
## Applications in the Family
## Assessment Process

The Rorschach, named after the Swiss psychiatrist who developed it over 70 years ago (1921), is one of the most commonly used assessment instruments in the practice of psychology (Groth-Marnot, 1990, p. 275). Considered primarily to be a method for gathering information describing personality functioning (Weiner, 1994), the Rorschach reflects broadly both the perceptual processes of the person and the associational dynamics related to content. These different but complementary aspects may be interpreted from various theoretical vantage points, borrowing on two major traditions in psychology: the nomothetic, which stresses generalizations drawn from research with large numbers of people, and the ideographic, which focuses on the unique aspects of the individual (Allport, 1937).

This chapter is based on the Comprehensive System, with its standardized administration procedure, perceptual process emphasis, and mass of empirical and research data accrued over the past 25 years (Exner, 1991, 1993; Exner & Weiner, 1995). Consistent with the purpose of this book, this chapter considers the place of the Rorschach in family assessments, identifies those Rorschach features that have particularly important implications for understanding family relationships, and presents an illustrative family case study with suggestions for family interventions.

This broader family context contrasts with that of the previous chapters on the MMPI/MMPI-2 and the MCMI-III, which attended to interpretations of couple interaction. As with the chapters on these inventories, the clinician experienced with the Rorschach may wish to skip the "Capsule Summary on the Rorschach" and begin with the section titled "The Place of the Rorschach in Family Assessments."

## CAPSULE SUMMARY OF THE RORSCHACH

Herman Rorschach published his 10 inkblots in 1921 accompanied by a monograph presenting an approach to administering, scoring, and interpreting patients' responses to those blots. During the 1920s and 1930s, the Rorschach rapidly gained popularity with professionals in both Europe and America, furthered particularly in the United States by the development of child guidance clinics. World War II saw the Rorschach used widely in the armed services, particularly to diagnose and plan treatment for traumatized military personnel. Following World War II, programs developed using federal funds to train doctoral clinical psychologists for the Veterans Administration. The psychologist's role as diagnostician, armed particularly with the Rorschach, was a primary area of professional responsibility.

By the late 1950s and into the 1960s, disappointing research findings on the validity of the Rorschach resulted in some prominent psychologists labeling it unscientific, advocating its abandonment (e.g., Jensen, 1958), or, in one instance, scientifically restructuring another series of blots and procedures to create an entirely new inkblot-based instrument (Holtzman, 1968).

Psychologist John Exner (1969) studied the Rorschach's use and, in a landmark publication, demonstrated that the five different approaches to the Rorschach actually had created quite different Rorschach systems with, in some cases, greatly different scoring, administration, and interpretive procedures. Exner set about researching Rorschach scoring and developed the Comprehensive System (Exner, 1974) based on those scores that proved to have a reasonable degree of reliability (or consistency) of scoring.

In the succeeding years, an empirical base has been established by Exner and associates, as well as others, using a variety of clinical and experimental approaches resulting in standardized administration, scoring, and basic approaches to interpretation. The interested reader is referred to the following by Exner: *The Rorschach: A Comprehensive System*, Volume 1: *Basic Foundations*, third edition (1993); and *The Rorschach: A Comprehensive System*, Volume 2: *Interpretation*, second edition (1991). An additional book of importance by Exner and Irving B. Weiner Jr. is *The Rorschach: A Comprehensive System*, Volume 3: *Assessment of Children and Adolescents*, second edition (1995). For an overview of the Rorschach, the reader may wish to turn to the Rorschach chapter in the *Handbook of Psychological Assessment* (Groth-Marnat, 1990). It is important to recognize that learning Rorschach administration, scoring, and basic interpretation requires anywhere from 30 to 50 hours of class time and practicum experience, plus intensive supervision on actual cases through at least a year's internship to adequately use the Rorschach.

In administering the Rorschach using Exner's Comprehensive System, the examiner sits side by side with the examinee, thus avoiding any distractions or unconscious shaping of responses caused by an examiner's inadvertent changes of facial expression or body posture. The examiner shows each blot with the instructions to respond to the question "What might this be?" A follow-up using carefully delimited questioning helps the examiner be clear about the location of the response, what went into making the response, and a sense of the nature of the content of the response.

These data, which consist of the free responses of the client and responses to the inquiry by the assessor, are then categorized by using scoring procedures painstakingly developed to maximize consistency of assessor scoring. These resulting scores, entered into a computer, are combined based on research-derived procedures. A computer program provides not only the combinations of scores but also a lengthy narrative of research and clinically based hypotheses for the assessor to use as an interpretive base (Exner & Ona, 1995). Alternatively, this process may be done in its entirety by the clinician without computer program assistance. Despite the empirically based generation of hypotheses, crafting of a solid clinical report still requires extensive experience with the Rorschach coupled with interview data about the examinee, typically complemented by the results of various additional psychological inventories and tests.

## The Place of the Rorschach in Family Assessments

The Rorschach has a unique, significant, and oftentimes essential place in family situations when a thorough, in-depth understanding of personality is required on which to base decisions having far-reaching effects on the lives of family members, especially children. For example, where an appraisal is sought about the mental state of parents and children in a heated, drawn-out, child custody dispute, the Rorschach can be a crucial source of uniquely salient information. When there is a question of psychosis or clinical depression with any family member, using the Rorschach is the most dependable psychological method. Ganellen (1996a) reviewed studies comparing the diagnostic efficiency of the MCMI-II, the MMPI, and the Rorschach. He found that with very serious mental conditions, the Depression (DEPI) and Schizophrenia (SCZI) indices on the Rorschach were diagnostically superior to the MCMI-II and the MMPI, particularly in comparison with single scales on the inventories.

The Rorschach is also particularly helpful in complicated family situations when a puzzling child problem presents itself. Notably, the Rorschach findings in these situations may uncover processes not readily apparent, such as a thinking disorder, the discovery of depression and its depth, as noted above, and the dynamics of acting-out problem behavior. These processes are covered particularly well in the revision of their volume on the Rorschach with children and adolescents by Exner and Weiner (1995). Their approach also provides a way of identifying and thinking about the youngster with "the faltering personality," often seen as an evolving borderline personality disorder (pp. 231–284).

Rorschach results describe the perceptual and internal dynamic processes of the person. The findings then also provide indirect information about the interpersonal processes within the family. For example, in a study comparing Rorschach scores of marital partners with brief audiotaped problem-solving discussions by the couples, researchers found that greater intrapsychic self-delineation predicted decreased submission and sulky resentment and increased control behaviors toward the partner (Blake, Humphrey, & Feldman, 1994).

## Dominant Rorschach Features Impacting Family Analysis

While Exner's (1993, p. 404) use of the phrase "dominant personality styles" does not coincide with Millon's (1996) description of personality disorders or styles, Exner, nevertheless, has made a major contribution to understanding personality by calling attention particularly to various major, traitlike features of personality measurable with the Rorschach. These response styles have particular relevance for understanding family behavior because they consistently influence or provide direction for various and sometimes diverse personality features manifest in family interaction. As such, they form major anchoring points for the therapist searching for family system patterns. At the same time, the therapist must pay attention to consistent, pervasive behaviors on the part of each individual. These dominant Rorschach features are the Lambda Index, Experience Balance, Reflections, the Passive/Active Relationship, and the Hypervigilance Index. In discussing each feature, specific suggestions are presented providing examples of how the feature may impact the family process and the strategy of the family therapist.

### LAMBDA INDEX

Lambda (L) is a ratio that compares the frequency of pure form (F) responses to all other responses. When the record indicates a high Lambda index (> .99), this reflects a pervasive processing simplification that occurs when some elements of a field are considered of lesser importance when judged "against the needs of the subject plus the perceived demands of the situation" (Exner, 1993,

p. 405). Children under 11, especially those very young, frequently use a tactic of simplification when faced with the complexities of the world. For the adolescent and adult, however, the continuation of this style appears to occur in response to a history of social depravation and concern for need gratification. The interpersonal consequences of this style are that the individual may fail to meet some family and social expectations and may deviate from socially expected patterns.

For example, a high Lambda teen may be expressing a general Lambda coping style that ignores elements of a complex situation, with the resulting behavior becoming inadvertently confrontational. With adolescents particularly, this deviation can be misperceived as primarily an authority conflict or simply being negativistic. This information in the hands of a family therapist could result in a difference in treatment tactics when dealing with a supposedly acting-out teenager who confronts parental authority primarily out of an overly simplistic (high Lambda) style as compared with another youngster's actions that represent the need to challenge authority. An experienced family therapist might intuitively sense the process underneath the overt challenge. But, because all that can be clearly seen overtly in therapy is the challenge itself, even the veteran therapist can be assisted by anticipating and understanding the psychological underpinnings of the seemingly challenging behavior.

In contrast with the high Lambda style of selectively responding to environmental elements, the low Lambda style implies a failure to see simplified solutions, with resulting overinvolvement leading to an experience of being overwhelmed. An intensified family therapy situation where one or more members feel overwhelmed is not one that will facilitate learning new ways of relating within the family. In this case, a therapist may look for ways to strategically simplify and structure a session so as to help a low Lambda family member from becoming overwhelmed by whatever difficult feeling emerges (e.g., anger). The therapist can plan ahead to lessen the complexity of the family process, taking charge, structuring issues, and managing relationship expression, helping family members to contain and constructively express their feelings. Other Rorschach elements can inform the therapist about the reasons for this style and whether it might prove adaptive in some situations but not others.

## EXPERIENCE BALANCE (EB)

The Experience Balance (EB) indicates a relationship between human movement responses (M) and the (weighted) sum of chromatic color responses (C). When the balance is more toward M, a person, labeled *introversive*, is likely to use his or her inner life as a primary source of satisfaction; when the balance is in the direction of C, an individual is described as *extroversive*, placing more emphasis on interactions between self and the world as sources of gratification

(Exner, 1993, p. 410). (The terms introversive and extroversive do *not* mean the same thing as introvert and extrovert.) The introversive more often likes to delay, push feelings aside, look at all possible alternatives, and then make decisions. By contrast, the extroversive merges feeling with thinking while seeking to solve problems and reach decisions by more emphasis on interactive, trial-and-error behaviors. Neither dominant style is superior to the other.

A third category, *ambitent*, has equal or almost equal portions of M and C, seemingly balanced between the extroversive and introversive. Although this might seem ideally flexible, contrary to what Rorschach (1921/1942) originally believed, this ambitent style is in reality apparently the lack of development of either an extroversive or an introversive style. The ambitent's emotions are inconsistent in terms of their impact on thinking, being sometimes strong, sometimes minimal. This seems to leave the ambitent unsure and vulnerable. Ambitents, with therapy, tend to adopt one major style or another as preferred rather than remain ambitent (Exner, 1993, p. 413).

Although effective people tend to be either introversive or extroversive, being rigidly and pervasively one or the other, regardless of circumstance, is a liability. People need to be able to shift to the secondary style in selected circumstances. A target in family therapy can be to assist the person with the rigid, pervasive style to learn in the family session to explore using the infrequently used style as a source of gratification. For example, when the therapist helps the extroversive delay reacting to think through before responding, this can result in more flexible family interactional patterns, modifying a problem family system. Likewise, when the therapist encourages the introversive to experiment with responding more readily to immediate family actions, increased flexibility of family pattern interaction may result. The family therapist, despite his or her own extroversive or introversive style, can bring about more acceptance of these individual family members' differences by being able to normalize both styles as having advantages and disadvantages, depending on the qualities of a situation. One reason for taking the EB into account in therapy is because the EB and the associated extroversive and introversive styles are extremely stable over time, relatively resistant to change, and therefore require acceptance, although sometimes with modifications, within the family relationship attitudes (Exner, Armbruster, & Viglione, 1978).

THE REFLECTION RESPONSE

The presence of any reflection response indicates a major element to be considered in evaluating a person's self-concept and his or her relationships in the family. Persons with Reflection responses tend to overvalue their own personal worth (Exner, 1993, p. 432). What happens in the family appears to be interpreted, albeit sometimes subtly, in terms of themselves. Of course, for children, this is not that inappropriate. But for adolescents and adults, this self-centeredness becomes a problem.

For older adolescents and adults who have one or more Reflection responses, an inflated sense of one's self-worth is indicated. Should this sense of self be reinforced by worldly success and by the family pattern, such as the favored child or the doted-upon only child, the individual is likely to have little discomfort. However, this narcissistic-like feature suggests a restriction of empathy for other family members and a restriction on parenting ability. Also, the narcissistic sense of entitlement is an attitude other family members may come to resent. Having competitive siblings close in age may be helpful in extinguishing a child's narcissistic attitude. Any family interaction that helps the narcissistic person attend more to others than self should be reinforced by the therapist. This stance is consistent with Millon's (1996, p. 191) recommendation that therapeutic interventions may be conceptualized around fundamental polarities, of which one is self/other (the others are active/passive, pleasure/pain, and thinking/feeling). For the narcissistic person overbalanced toward the self, therapy is likely more efficient when the therapist is constantly aware of the need to reinforce any expressions of empathy toward other family members (Millon, 1996, p. 443).

The family therapist encountering a person with the Reflection response(s) in the family may not immediately understand its importance when the manifestations are subtle and, particularly, when an individual's over-self-valuing is almost unconsciously accepted within the family. For example, a father with significant narcissistic features may be complemented by a mother with a dependent style, both these aspects being exaggerations of male and female American cultural stereotypes (Nurse, 1997a). Children growing up in this family structure may naturally model themselves after their parents, particularly the same-sex parent. As the family matures, if the mother seeks more independent expression and development as the children reach older ages, the implicit marriage agreement is broken, and the father feels wounded and angry; the children chose sides, withdraw, or act out; a family crisis ensues. One crucial point for the family therapist is the early identification of the father's narcissistic features so that this can be managed (along with the mother's movement away from dependence) as normal changes brought about by the developing family life cycle with its lessening of constant parental monitoring as children grow.

Of course, it is equally likely that the mother and/or teenager might have the Reflection response. Again, a focus in family therapy would be on assisting in the development of empathy with that family member and the reduction of the family interaction pattern that reinforces the self-centered dynamic.

There is one caution about the Reflection response. Exner (1993, p. 433) indicates that the Reflection response has "considerable temporal stability," suggesting that it is a relatively permanent, traitlike characteristic. However, recent preliminary studies of Rorschachs given before and after Eye Movement Desensitization and Reprocessing (EMDR) interventions for trauma relief suggest that the Reflection response under these conditions at least may be fairly quickly extinguished (Levin, 1996). It may be that the Reflection response is a more malleable characteristic in some cases and conditions than has previously been believed.

## THE ACTIVE/PASSIVE RELATIONSHIP

As noted in the previous section, the active/passive dimension is one of four dimensions in Millon's (1996) polarity model for developing personality theory. The active:passive ratio (a:p), derived from movement responses, ordinarily favors active movement; the ratio is significant when passive responses are equal to passive plus 1. When this is the case, passivity (but not necessarily submissiveness) is to be expected in relationships (Exner, 1993, p. 436). When the ratio is applied only to human movement, passivity emphasis, depending on its severity, suggests excessive reliance on fantasy, a flight into fantasy, and avoidance of responsibility and decision making (Exner, 1991, p. 222). Thus, this measure can be useful in considering the role of particularly a teenager's fantasy life and, despite its simplicity, may reflect generally avoidant behavior within the family system.

Food content suggests marked dependency on others, perhaps appropriate with children but not with functioning adults. When this feature is positive and the adult has a passive style, a passive-dependent quality to a personality is proposed by Exner (1991, p. 184). Armed with this information, the family therapist is alerted to the importance of reinforcing any more active independent behaviors on the part of the person with passive-dependent characteristics.

## THE HYPERVIGILANCE INDEX

The Hypervigilance index (HVI) is positive when no texture-related responses (T) are found and four of seven conditions are present. A positive finding on this index indicates a hyperalert state accompanied by feelings of vulnerability and mistrust. The therapist of a family that includes one or more people significant on HVI needs to be aware that they have major issues around personal space and boundaries: These must be respected. Family members significant for HVI appear overly guarded and almost paranoidlike. Attending to issues around familial trust within the session must initially take priority over other problems. It is of utmost importance to establish a safe atmosphere to reduce family members' feelings of vulnerability. Accomplishing this will permit the encouragement of feelings and thoughts ordinarily withheld from family members; not establishing the family sessions as safe will undermine apparent therapeutic advances.


## Key Rorschach Variables

In considering the interpersonal, family-related implications of Rorschach findings, Exner's (1991) revised volume on interpretation can serve as a primary reference. Research reported in that volume on interpretation has resulted in identifying 11 key variables, or clusters, which provide the most substantial core information on the individual's personality and point the way toward organizing the remaining Rorschach data. These include the variables already discussed as particularly important for family/interpersonal interpretation, that is, Lambda, Experience Balance, Reflections, Passive/Active, and Hypervigilance Index. The additional key variables are:

> Schizophrenia (SCZI) positive, greater than 3 (possible thinking disorder);
>
> Depression (DEPI) greater than 5 (clinical depression);
>
> Adjusted D greater than D (alerting to situational stress);
>
> Coping deficit index (CDI) greater than 3 (predisposition to disorganization under stress or demanding interpersonal situations); and
>
> Adjusted D score minus (developmental problem or deterioration).

The Suicide Constellation (S-CON) is also reviewed for individuals 15 or older. Depending on empirically developed guidelines, any one of these 11 keys, when positive, may be selected as a starting point for a necessarily linear but at the same time integrated, interpretive, hypothesis-generating journey taken a step at a time by the clinician (Exner, 1991), preferably facilitated by a computer program (Exner & Ona, 1995), following paths that branch according to well-defined decision-making rules.


## Self-Perception and Interpersonal Perception

Exner's (1991, pp. 172–190) cluster "Self-perception and interpersonal perception" has particular salience for understanding family interaction. Although self-perception and interpersonal perception appear to be different processes, the data for self-perception and interpersonal perception overlap. How one views oneself influences the view of others, and vice versa. Therefore, these two processes are considered together.

SELF-PERCEPTION

Self-image and self-esteem, which make up self-perception, are represented in the following Rorschach scores: Egocentricity Ratio; Reflection (Fr, rF); Form-Dimension (FD); Vista (FV, VF, V); Human responses (H, Hd, [H], [Hd]), Anatomy + Xray (An + Xy), and Morbid (MOR). Helpful also is to read the content of these responses: MOR, Minus responses, and Movement responses (M, FM, m).

The Egocentricity index provides a core measure of self-concern or self-attending behavior. A high (above .45 for an adult) Egocentricity index suggests considerable self-involvement. A low index (below .33) points to a quite negative estimate of personal worth. An overly self-involved parent is less likely to attend to a child's needs, whereas a parent with a negative sense of self may overly focus on a child.

In evaluating children's Rorschachs, it is necessary to consider the mean Egocentricity index for a given child's age. A younger child should developmentally be more self-involved than an older child. The data indicate that, for example, for age 5, the mean Egocentricity score is .67 with a standard deviation of .15; for age 10, the mean is .54 with a standard deviation of .07; and for age 15, the mean is .44 with a standard deviation of .10 (Exner & Weiner, 1995, pp. 55–78). At least one standard deviation above or below the mean is termed high or low. When a child is less self-involved, this suggests a pseudo-maturity wherein the child may be inappropriately overly involved with others, such as in taking emotional care of a parent. For a child overly self-involved by age norms, that child may be immature, behaving toward self more like younger children do. The next step in looking at attitude toward self is the analysis of the degree and nature of emphasis on self-inspecting behavior. FD (Form Dimension) and Vista responses provide this information. Lack of FD and Vista suggests a less than usual involvement with oneself, implying naïveté. One or two FD responses is likely a positive self-consideration, implying a healthy perspective on oneself. More than two FD responses or any Vista response points to an unusual and probably psychologically painful self-inspecting process. However, Exner (1991, p. 175) points out that this unusual self-inspecting behavior is not necessarily remarkable, especially during puberty and aging. Should this finding be coupled with one or more Reflection responses, a conflict between inflated self-value and emerging self-awareness involving negative self-features is suspected.

It can be helpful to compare the relationship between the presence of a painful, self-inspecting process (two or more FD responses or any Vista) to the Egocentricity index. For example, when the Egocentricity index is low, the painful self-inspection focuses on a negative sense of self. When the Egocentricity index is average, considerable self-rumination is suggested.

In considering self-perception, three other scores need reviewing. For self-image and self-value to be based on experience more than imagination, the majority of human contents must include whole figures. More than two An + Xy present signals some unusual body concern. If two MOR (Morbid) responses are found, negative aspects of the self-image are suggested. With three or more MOR responses, more distinct negative self-characteristics are indicated, with some significant pessimistic moods assumed. A careful reading through the content of MOR, minus responses, and movement responses can frequently enrich the evolving hypotheses about self-perception.

## INTERPERSONAL PERCEPTION AND RELATIONS

Interpersonal perception is inferred from variables representing some needs, attitudes, sets, and coping styles, writes Exner (1991, p. 182). This cluster comprises a number of variables. The first of these, and one of the most important, is the Coping Deficit Index (CDI).

Individuals who reach a significantly high level (4 or 5) on the Coping Deficit Index (CDI) are generally people with impoverished or unrewarding social relationships. Their histories are "marked by limited interpersonal effectiveness or success, frequent social ineptness, or even instances of social chaos " (Exner, 1993, p. 363). They have difficulty coping with the natural demands of the social world, including, of course, their families. Yet, difficulty in coping can easily be mislabeled by other family members, or even therapists, as indications of negativism, obstructionism, and/or primary conflicts with authority. As to the last, although CDI-significant people may have authority conflicts, such conflicts, because they affect only one aspect of relationships, are secondary to the overall style, which potentially impacts all relationships. High CDI people may even appear almost psychotic as they behave at times in a confused, inept fashion. But the problem is that they lack the internal psychological resources and appropriate interpersonal, social skills. The good news is that, once identified, people with high CDIs unaccompanied by a high DEPI score are very amenable to carefully planned treatment, as judged by at least two treatment effectiveness studies of brief and short-term therapy (Exner & Sanglade, 1992; Weiner & Exner, 1991). Inept behavior on the part of a family member diagnosed as CDI-generated can signal the therapist to shift consciously to include within family therapy structured therapeutic approaches for this member and/or to refer for adjunctive, structured, social learning therapy apart from family therapy.

Texture (FT, TF, T) indicates how closeness may influence perceptions of others. Above one (for age 9 and older) points to strong needs for closeness, such as might be expected with a recent emotional loss or a chronic state of neediness. If a recent loss, such as a death in the family, has not occurred, high T may reflect a more chronic condition, suggesting the potential usefulness of reasonably long-term individual psychotherapy.

Human content suggests the degree of interest in people. Five to seven human contents of any sort appears average. This may not hold, however, for children 8 and under. For a parent with no or few human contents, the family therapist needs to somehow reward or set the family interaction so that the parent learns that he or she can gain something in family relationships.

One Personal (PER) content may be expected. Higher than two suggests intellectual authoritarianism to ward off interpersonal challenges. A parent "getting on his or her high horse," making demands of a child with a "because I say so" attitude, may be manifesting this dynamic. The family therapist needs to lessen the apparent challenges to head off the defensive response or help the parent reinterpret the seeming challenge as posing less of a threat. The parent's behavior may respond to direct dyadic communications work, but if the underlying dynamic of intellectual authoritarianism is there rather than being a learned style, it would be helpful to know it.

Cooperative Movement (COP) suggests a cooperative attitude and behavior, and Aggressive (AG) content suggests aggression, but the meaning of these is in part clouded. It does appear that family members who have three or more COP scores with no AG are viewed by others as outgoing and likeable (Exner, 1991, p. 187). People with no COP are seen as not gregarious. A family therapist aware of the COPs in a family can utilize this attitude, even during conflict, to have family members help each other change their behaviors. On the other hand, assuming a cooperative pattern in a family that has no individuals with cooperative attitudes may lead the family therapist into a blind alley of persuasion, attempting to use a nonexistent attitude rather than seeking a behavior modification approach.

Exner (1991, p. 186) indicates that people with two or more AGs view interpersonal relationships as marked by aggression. Recent research by Gacomo and Meloy (1994), however, suggests that the presence of AG indicates the ability to hold in aggressive tension rather than acting it out. For example, in their research, only 38% of conduct disordered 9-year-olds presented with AG responses, in contrast to 91% of normals (p. 25). Gacomo and Meloy suggest, however, that until the implication of AG is clearer, predictions of interpersonal relationships based on AG should be undertaken cautiously (p. 261).

The Isolation Index (An + Xy) at 25% or higher points to a lack of interest in social/family relationships. When the index reaches one-third of the total responses, social isolation is anticipated. There are ordinarily obvious behaviors and attitudes supporting this finding.

A final step in individual score analysis is to review movement responses with a coding for pair (2) and all responses with human content. Considering the content directly may help enrich the psychometrically based interpretation.

Reflecting on the intricate and detailed nature of the various elements contributing directly to likely interpersonal processes leads to the conclusion that it is preferable to have the computer compile and sort through these to raise tentative hypotheses. The experienced Rorschach interpreter can then blend these into hypotheses about how the overall personality functions and postulate the existence of certain interpersonal family dynamics.


AN ADDITIONAL NOTE: AFFECT AND COLOR

Though it is beyond the scope and focus of this chapter to review the extensive literature on color responses on the Rorschach, it is important to note the con-nection between these variables and family climate. More form emphasis over color (FC > CF + C) in responses is associated with more emotional constraint and modulation of emotional expression. Relatively more stress on color over form (FC < CF + C) is correlated with less restraint and more affective reactiv-ity. It is theoretically conceivable that a family style reflected in the adult's FC:CF + C could include either style or a mixed style.

Children typically have more unmodulated expression than adults and therefore tend to produce fewer FCs than CFs + Cs. For instance, the average ratio at age 5 (rounded) is 1 FC to 4 CF + C. By 10, the ratio is 3 FC to 4 CF + C. At 15, the ratio is 3 FC to 3 CF + C. For nonpatient adults, the ratio is 4 FC to 2 CF + C.

The family therapist, forearmed with knowledge of the general level of emotional maturity of various family members and aware that some family mem-bers have the potential for unmodulated emotional eruption and some may be overly constrained, has an edge in planning tactics ahead of time to take these aspects into account, particularly with short-term therapy, where there are few chances for learning by trial and error. Without this knowledge, the therapist may be surprised and have to take undue time to repair damage inflicted by the acting-out or acting-in within the family.


# Interpretation and Treatment Planning for a Problem Family

As a way to convey a pattern of thinking about the Rorschach as used with fam-ilies, this section considers the Rorschachs of one problem family. Discussion of the Rorschachs of an 8-year-old girl and her separated parents is designed to demonstrate a process for interpreting Rorschachs in terms of family relation-ships and for establishing treatment targets. In clinical practice, Rorschachs are ordinarily interpreted with awareness of Rorschach content, including review of minus responses and movement responses and consideration of general behavior, history, and other test information. But for purposes of focusing on major, sturdy features of the Rorschach that pertain to the family context, only the

Rorschach Structural Summaries, Ratios, Percentages, and Derivations are presented. To clarify exposition, the *principal* anchoring referent scores are ordinarily indicated in parentheses.

DAWN

In 8-year-old Dawn's Rorschach summary data (Figure 5.1), significant DEPI (Depression) and CDI (Coping Deficit Index) indicate that she is suffering from a depression that is linked to some problems in coping effectively, possibly with

========================= STRUCTURAL SUMMARY =========================

| LOCATION FEATURES | DETERMINANTS BLENDS | SINGLE | CONTENTS | S-CONSTELLATION |
|---|---|---|---|---|
| | | | H = 0, 0 | ..FV+VF+V+FD>2 |
| | | | | ..Col-Shd Bl>0 |
| Zf = 10 | C.C' | M = 0 | (H) = 2, 0 | ..Ego<.31,>.44 |
| ZSum = 39.0 | M.FD | FM = 3 | Hd = 0, 0 | ..MOR > 3 |
| ZEst = 31.0 | | m = 1 | (Hd)= 0, 0 | ..Zd > +- 3.5 |
| | | FC = 1 | Hx = 0, 0 | ..es > EA |
| W = 11 | | CF = 0 | A = 5, 0 | ..CF+C > FC |
| (Wv = 2) | | C = 1 | (A) = 0, 0 | ..X+% < .70 |
| D = 4 | | Cn = 0 | Ad = 1, 0 | ..S > 3 |
| Dd = 0 | | FC'= 0 | (Ad)= 0, 0 | ..P < 3 or > 8 |
| S = 4 | | C'F= 0 | An = 0, 0 | ..Pure H < 2 |
| | | C' = 0 | Art = 0, 0 | ..R < 17 |
| DQ | | FT = 0 | Ay = 0, 0 | x.....TOTAL |
| .........(FQ-) | | TF = 0 | Bl = 0, 0 | |
| + = 0 ( 0) | | T = 0 | Bt = 0, 1 | SPECIAL SCORINGS |
| o = 13 ( 4) | | FV = 1 | Cg = 0, 0 | Lv1 Lv2 |
| v/+ = 0 ( 0) | | VF = 0 | Cl = 0, 0 | DV = 0x1 0x2 |
| v = 2 ( 0) | | V = 0 | Ex = 0, 0 | INC = 3x2 0x4 |
| | | FY = 0 | Fd = 1, 0 | DR = 0x3 0x6 |
| | | YF = 0 | Fi = 2, 0 | FAB = 0x4 0x7 |
| | | Y = 0 | Ge = 0, 0 | ALOG = 0x5 |
| FORM QUALITY | | Fr = 0 | Hh = 0, 0 | CON = 0x7 |
| | | rF = 0 | Ls = 2, 0 | Raw Sum6 = 3 |
| FQx FQf MQual SQx | | FD = 0 | Na = 1, 0 | Wgtd Sum6 = 6 |
| + = 0 0 0 0 | | F = 6 | Sc = 0, 0 | |
| o = 6 1 1 2 | | | Sx = 0, 0 | AB = 0 CP = 0 |
| u = 3 2 0 1 | | | Xy = 0, 0 | AG = 0 MOR = 0 |
| - = 4 3 0 1 | | | Id = 1, 0 | CFB = 0 PER = 1 |
| none= 2 -- 0 0 | | (2) = 0 | | COP = 0 PSV = 0 |

====================== RATIOS, PERCENTAGES, AND DERIVATIONS ======================

| | | | |
|---|---|---|---|
| R = 15 | L = 0.67 | FC:CF+C = 1: 2 | COP = 0 AG = 0 |
| | | Pure C = 2 | Food = 1 |
| EB = 1: 3.5 | EA = 4.5 EBPer= 3.5 | SumC':WSumC= 1:3.5 | Isolate/R =0.33 |
| eb = 4: 2 | es = 6 D = 0 | Afr =0.36 | H:(H)Hd(Hd)= 0: 2 |
| | Adj es = 6 Adj D = 0 | S = 4 | (HHd):(AAd)= 2: 0 |
| | | Blends:R= 2:15 | H+A:Hd+Ad = 7: 1 |
| FM = 3 : C'= 1 T = 0 | | CP = 0 | |
| m = 1 : V = 1 Y = 0 | | | |
| | | P = 2 | Zf =10 3r+(2)/R=0.00 |
| a:p = 2: 3 | Sum6 = 3 | X+% =0.40 | Zd = +8.0 Fr+rF = 0 |
| Ma:Mp = 0: 1 | Lv2 = 0 | F+% =0.17 | W:D:Dd =11: 4: 0 FD = 1 |
| 2AB+Art+Ay= 0 | WSum6 = 6 | X-% =0.27 | W:M =11: 1 An+Xy = 0 |
| M- = 0 | Mnone = 0 | S-% =0.25 | DQ+ = 0 MOR = 0 |
| | | Xu% =0.20 | DQv = 2 |

| SCZI = 2 | DEPI = 5* | CDI = 5* | S-CON =N/A | HVI = No | OBS = No |
|---|---|---|---|---|---|

Figure 5.1
Rorschach Summary Data: Dawn. Reproduced with permission.

both her family and her general environment. She probably does not have very good social skills and appears to suffer from some impoverishment in her social relationships (CDI). That she is easily overwhelmed and subject to disorganization as reflected in the CDI is underlined by a restriction of her personal resources (EA low). Given this combination of Rorschach indicators, she is not only subject to being easily overwhelmed in the face of stress, but probably the resulting unsatisfying life situation leads to and/or exacerbates her depression.

With her periodic depressive moods causing emotional turmoil, she understandably works hard to avoid feelings (Affective Ratio very low). So that feelings do not arise to overwhelm her, she is more socially constrained than others her age. Thus, the everyday emotional exchanges required for development in a child are dampened or missing. However, when she is engaged, she may respond with the exuberance and lack of modulation typical of younger children (FC < CF + C).

She appears to be oppositional and stubborn, as judged by the 4 white space responses (S). Since 3 Ss appear with the responses on Card I (not shown in the table), this may mean that she was unprepared for the testing. It may also reflect the above-noted characteristic for avoiding or approaching cautiously situations that might stimulate her feelings. Perhaps she is fearful in new situations.

She tends to ruminate negatively about herself (V 1) and has a very poor sense of her own self-worth (3r + (2)/R = .00). She needs a more balanced understanding of herself, and also of other people; like many children, she does not understand them well (H < [H] + Hd + [Hd]). Given her social ineptness (CDI) and her lack of understanding, she backs away from people, tending to be a social isolate (Isolate/R .33). Her social isolation makes it difficult to develop and maintain social relationships. A lack of social relationships means she loses out on some everyday interaction, a vital ingredient in a child's interpersonal and general social learning. She will be seen as socially immature.

In assessing the Rorschach's cognitive implications, her thorough style is very important (Processing Efficiency, Zd + 8). She invests in scanning cautiously at a much higher level than usual for other children, probably to ensure that she makes no mistakes. This feature is an unusual finding for her age and suggests that some less-than-desirable perfectionist trends are developing. A hypothesis that she is a fearful child seems inescapable. A search for data bearing on that hypothesis will point later toward ascertaining if there are any particular characteristics of either or both parents that might be frightening for a child.

There are major problems in her cognitive mediation (X + %, F + %, low). These portend serious difficulties in reality testing, which in turn suggest that she may sometimes behave with others in an inappropriate fashion, which would imply her generating some rejection from others, reinforcing her emotional isolation and her poor sense of self-worth.

In spite of her interpersonal difficulties, she has a trial-and-error approach to problem solving, where her feelings tend to merge with her thinking (EB 1:3.5).

With this style she will get feedback when she is willing to step out of her isolation and become involved with others. Although perhaps too rigidly adhering to this style, at the same time, it is more age-appropriate to use this intuitive process, as seen in the extroversive EB pattern.

In summary, Dawn may be often withdrawn and emotionally isolated within her family and in other settings, probably covering over frequent episodes of depression and internal turmoil. Despite typical 8-year-old outbursts, she appears to be evolving a pattern of avoidance of feelings and, sometimes, emotional relationships. She is in some ways inept interpersonally, contributing to rejection by others, with her consequent withdrawal leaving her in emotional isolation and less available to responses from others to learn new behaviors and correct misperceptions. Her misperceiving situations is both a consequence and cause of problems of probable deficits in learning interpersonally. Not surprisingly, she regards herself less favorably when she compares herself to others; her self-esteem is very low.

In initial family sessions, a therapist would need to be aware of Dawn's poor self-esteem so that any interaction in the therapeutic session that is positive for her can be reinforced. The therapist needs to be sensitive to her fears and attempt to make the therapy safe for her. There may be opportunities in family therapy for the therapist to help her express more of the exuberant child part and be relieved in the interaction of the heavier, self-blaming, depressed attitude. As a corollary treatment, a therapy group for young latency-age children might help improve her social learning.

JOHN

Although no special indices are significant in John's profile (see Figure 5.2), of importance is that Dawn's father age 32, is an ambitent (EB = 3:2.0). His inconsistent emotions impact his cognitions so that his behavior, including parenting behavior, is expected to vary somewhat unpredictably from one situation to another. Not only does he have few personal resources available, represented by his Experience Actual Score (EA 5), but when his feelings become particularly intense (Color Over Form, 2 responses, 2 CF), this lack makes him especially vulnerable to emotional overwhelm, leading him to avoid emotional stimuli as much as possible (Affective Ratio .29). He is inconsistent and unpredictable, making it difficult for others, including his family, to know just where they stand with him.

When emotions are expressed, they are only relatively modulated (CF 2) and are often negative (2 Vista Responses), which could be scary to a small child. Perhaps because of this unstable emotionality, he sometimes substitutes a false pleasant emotion for an irritating one (1 Color Projection), and tends to bend reality to avoid dealing with anticipated negativity from others. These ways

======================= STRUCTURAL SUMMARY =======================

| LOCATION FEATURES | DETERMINANTS BLENDS | SINGLE | CONTENTS | S-CONSTELLATION |
|---|---|---|---|---|
| | | | H = 3, 0 | NO..FV+VF+V+FD>2 |
| Zf = 17 | CF.FM | M = 3 | (H) = 1, 0 | NO..Col-Shd Bl>0 |
| ZSum = 46.5 | | FM = 2 | Hd = 0, 0 | NO..Ego<.31,>.44 |
| ZEst = 56.0 | | m = 0 | (Hd)= 0, 0 | NO..MOR > 3 |
| | | FC = 0 | Hx = 0, 0 | YES..Zd > +- 3.5 |
| W = 14 | | CF = 1 | A = 8, 0 | YES..es > EA |
| (Wv = 0) | | C = 0 | (A) = 1, 0 | YES..CF+C > FC |
| D = 4 | | Cn = 0 | Ad = 2, 0 | YES..X+% < .70 |
| Dd = 0 | | FC'= 0 | (Ad)= 0, 0 | NO..S > 3 |
| S = 2 | | C'F= 0 | An = 0, 0 | NO..P < 3 or > 8 |
| | | C' = 0 | Art = 0, 0 | NO..Pure H < 2 |
| DQ | | FT = 1 | Ay = 2, 0 | NO..R < 17 |
| .........(FQ-) | | TF = 0 | Bl = 0, 0 | 4.....TOTAL |
| + = 5 ( 0) | | T = 0 | Bt = 1, 0 | |
| o = 13 ( 1) | | FV = 0 | Cg = 0, 1 | SPECIAL SCORINGS |
| v/+ = 0 ( 0) | | VF = 0 | Cl = 0, 0 | Lv1   Lv2 |
| v = 0 ( 0) | | V = 0 | Ex = 0, 0 | DV = 1x1   0x2 |
| | | FY = 0 | Fd = 0, 0 | INC = 0x2   0x4 |
| | | YF = 0 | Fi = 0, 0 | DR = 0x3   0x6 |
| | | Y = 0 | Ge = 0, 0 | FAB = 0x4   0x7 |
| FORM QUALITY | | Fr = 0 | Hh = 0, 0 | ALOG = 0x5 |
| | | rF = 0 | Ls = 0, 2 | CON = 0x7 |
| FQx FQf MQual SQx | | FD = 0 | Na = 0, 0 | Raw Sum6 = 1 |
| + = 1  0  0  0 | | F = 8 | Sc = 0, 0 | Wgtd Sum6 = 1 |
| o = 11  5  2  0 | | | Sx = 0, 0 | |
| u = 5  3  1  1 | | | Xy = 0, 0 | AB = 0   CP = 1 |
| - = 1  0  0  1 | | | Id = 0, 0 | AG = 0   MOR = 0 |
| none= 0  --  0  0 | | (2) = 6 | | CFB = 0   PER = 1 |
| | | | | COP = 0   PSV = 0 |

================= RATIOS, PERCENTAGES, AND DERIVATIONS =================

| R = 18 | L = 0.80 | | FC:CF+C = 0: 2 | COP = 0   AG = 0 |
|---|---|---|---|---|
| | | | Pure C = 0 | Food = 0 |
| EB = 3: 2.0 | EA = 5.0 | EBPer= N/A | SumC':WSumC= 0:2.0 | Isolate/R =0.17 |
| eb = 3: 3 | es = 6 | D = 0 | Afr =0.29 | H:(H)Hd(Hd)= 3: 1 |
| | Adj es = 6 | Adj D = 0 | S = 2 | (HHd):(AAd)= 1: 1 |
| | | | Blends:R= 1:18 | H+A:Hd+Ad =13: 2 |
| FM = 3 : C'= 0 | T = 1 | | CP = 1 | |
| m = 0 : V = 2 | Y = 0 | | | |
| | | P = 7 | Zf =17 | 3r+(2)/R=0.33 |
| a:p = 5: 1 | Sum6 = 1 | X+% =0.67 | Zd = -9.5 | Fr+rF = 0 |
| Ma:Mp = 3: 0 | Lv2 = 0 | F+% =0.63 | W:D:Dd =14: 4: 0 | FD = 0 |
| 2AB+Art+Ay= 2 | WSum6 = 1 | X-% =0.06 | W:M =14: 3 | An+Xy = 0 |
| M- = 0 | Mnone = 0 | S-% =1.00 | DQ+ = 5 | MOR = 0 |
| | | Xu% =0.28 | DQv = 0 | |

| SCZI = 0 | DEPI = 3 | CDI = 3 | S-CON = 4 | HVI = No | OBS = No |
|---|---|---|---|---|---|

Figure 5.2
Rorschach Summary Data: John. Reproduced with permission.

of handling feelings would lead to confusion within the family and make it especially difficult for a child to know where she stands with him and unsure of herself.

While he seems to have a reasonable balance between a focus on himself and others (3r + [2]/R + .33), he tends toward ruminating negatively about himself, possibly experiencing guilt, shame, or remorse, as implied above (Sum V = 2). He is likely to anticipate that family and others will also view him negatively, and so he may not anticipate positive interchanges with them (COP 0, AG 0); he may seem distant and aloof.

Cognitively, he is hasty and haphazard in his processing of information, which leads him to overlook or neglect critical cues in a situation (Zd −9.5) This can result in his not perceiving the total context of a family situation. Anticipating this characteristic, a family therapist could help John slow his processing to be more thorough, rather than possibly reacting negatively to John's seeming ignoring or individualistic obliviousness of some significant inputs from family members, including his daughter. John might be taught the value of noting more thoroughly others' feelings, thus opening the way to his learning to cooperate better with others, a present lack (COP 0). The family therapist needs to be aware that getting John adequately interactionally connected with others is an important goal. Being aware of this cognitive style and working with it when it appears is particularly important because John is quite inflexible (a:p 5:1). The therapist needs to assume that John's inflexibility is a general characteristic and make assertive interventions regularly, particularly when family interactions are clearly impeded by John's rigidity and his lack of concern for acceptability of his behaviors.

To sum up, John will stubbornly expect to have his way, not taking in much of the less obvious clues from family members' behaviors. He will respond inappropriately and inconsistently, potentially causing confusion and consternation in others. This behavior, coupled with occasionally relatively unmodulated expression of feeling, likely contributes to others withdrawing from him, particularly his daughter, who already exhibits signs of fear. The therapist may find openings, however, by being persistent and direct and remembering that John is actually worried about some undesirable features of his personality.


ALEXIA


Ordinarily, Dawn's mother, Alexia, has the capacity to exercise adequate control and tolerate stress (Adj D 0, CDI < 4, EA 9; see Figure 5.3). However, situational stress is impinging on her control, resulting in potential for disorganization and impulsiveness with accompanying diffuse negative feelings of anxiety, depression, and inadequacy (Adj D 0, D −1, Y 4, V 3, m 1).

She is an extratensive person (EB 3:6) who is strongly, but not pervasively, influenced by feelings as she problem-solves in a trial-and-error fashion (more than reflecting and thinking things through). She is not rigid about her preferred style. She is likely to respond immediately within family therapy sessions and be willing to try new behaviors. She does remain rather adolescentlike or even childlike in her strong expression of feelings (FC:CF + C 1:5).

A major feeling is anger (S 6). And although anger is expressed outwardly, she may also be feeling angry and upset with herself and her sense of her own self-worth as negative when she compares herself with others (3r + 2)/R .17). In fact,

============================ STRUCTURAL SUMMARY ============================

| LOCATION FEATURES | DETERMINANTS BLENDS | SINGLE | CONTENTS | S-CONSTELLATION |
|---|---|---|---|---|
| | | | H = 2, 0 | YES..FV+VF+V+FD>2 |
| Zf = 21 | FM.Y | M = 3 | (H) = 1, 0 | YES..Col-Shd Bl>0 |
| ZSum = 72.0 | m.YF.CF | FM = 3 | Hd = 0, 0 | YES..Ego<.31,>.44 |
| ZEst = 70.0 | FM.FV | m = 0 | (Hd)= 0, 0 | NO..MOR > 3 |
| | FM.FV | FC = 1 | Hx = 0, 0 | NO..Zd > +- 3.5 |
| W = 13 | | CF = 3 | A =13, 0 | YES..es > EA |
| (Wv = 1) | | C = 1 | (A) = 0, 0 | YES..CF+C > FC |
| D = 11 | | Cn = 0 | Ad = 2, 0 | YES..X+% < .70 |
| Dd = 0 | | FC'= 0 | (Ad)= 0, 0 | YES..S > 3 |
| S = 6 | | C'F= 0 | An = 1, 0 | NO..P < 3 or > 8 |
| | | C' = 0 | Art = 1, 0 | NO..Pure H < 2 |
| DQ | | FT = 0 | Ay = 0, 0 | NO..R < 17 |
| .........(FQ-) | | TF = 0 | Bl = 0, 0 | 7.....TOTAL |
| + = 13 ( 2) | | T = 0 | Bt = 2, 3 | |
| o = 10 ( 1) | | FV = 1 | Cg = 0, 1 | SPECIAL SCORINGS |
| v/+ = 0 ( 0) | | VF = 0 | Cl = 0, 0 | Lv1    Lv2 |
| v = 1 ( 0) | | V = 0 | Ex = 0, 0 | DV = 0x1    0x2 |
| | | FY = 1 | Fd = 1, 1 | INC = 0x2    1x4 |
| | | YF = 1 | Fi = 0, 1 | DR = 0x3    0x6 |
| | | Y = 0 | Ge = 0, 0 | FAB = 1x4    0x7 |
| FORM QUALITY | | Fr = 0 | Hh = 0, 1 | ALOG = 0x5 |
| | | rF = 0 | Ls = 0, 1 | CON = 0x7 |
| FQx FQf MQual SQx | | FD = 1 | Na = 0, 0 | Raw Sum6 = 2 |
| + = 1 0 0 1 | | F = 5 | Sc = 1, 0 | Wgtd Sum6 = 8 |
| o = 13 2 2 4 | | | Sx = 0, 0 | |
| u = 6 2 1 1 | | | Xy = 0, 0 | AB = 0    CP = 0 |
| - = 3 1 0 0 | | | Id = 0, 1 | AG = 0    MOR = 0 |
| none= 1 -- 0 0 | | (2) = 4 | | CFB = 0    PER = 0 |
| | | | | COP = 0    PSV = 0 |

===================== RATIOS, PERCENTAGES, AND DERIVATIONS =====================

R = 24          L = 0.26

FC:CF+C = 1: 5          COP = 0    AG = 0
Pure C = 1             Food = 2

EB = 3: 6.0   EA = 9.0   EBPer= 2.0     SumC':WSumC= 0:6.0    Isolate/R =0.25
eb = 7: 7     es = 14    D = -1          Afr =0.71             H:(H)Hd(Hd)= 2: 1
              Adj es = 11  Adj D = 0      S = 6                 (HHd):(AAd)= 1: 0
                                          Blends:R= 4:24        H+A:Hd+Ad =16: 2
FM = 6 : C'= 0   T = 0                    CP = 0
m = 1 : V = 3   Y = 4

                          P = 8          Zf =21                3r+(2)/R=0.17
a:p = 8: 2   Sum6 = 2    X+% =0.58       Zd = +2.0             Fr+rF = 0
Ma:Mp = 2: 1  Lv2 = 1    F+% =0.40       W:D:Dd =13:11: 0      FD = 1
2AB+Art+Ay= 1  WSum6 = 8  X-% =0.13       W:M =13: 3            An+Xy = 1
M- = 0        Mnone = 0   S-% =0.00       DQ+ =13               MOR = 0
                          Xu% =0.25       DQv = 1

SCZI = 1    DEPI = 4    CDI = 2    S-CON = 7    HVI = No    OBS = No

Figure 5.3
Rorschach Summary Data: Alexia. Reproduced with permission.

some concern for self-destructive behavior exists, with a Suicide Index of 7, only one point below the critical level of 8; an increase of one Popular response, from 8 to 9, or a decrease from 2 to 1 of pure H would shift the balance to a critical level. Her anger toward herself could also set the stage for her to accept blame from John before she considers whether his accusations are realistic. And, in fact, their marriage from its inception, when John and Alexia were both teenagers, was characterized by John's extreme overt control coupled with Alexia's conformance. The present crisis occurred when the maturing Alexia became more independent, upsetting John, ending in her leaving the marriage.

In many ways, she appears to be needy and dependent (FM 6, Fd 2). She is likely to continue to look for support and direction from John or another "strong" person, who she expects will be able to anticipate her needs and demands, an unrealistic vision of a mate.

A cross-current in this picture is that, despite her apparent dependent qualities, she is less interested in social interaction and less interested in people than are others (Human Cont 3, Pure H 2). Furthermore, she is concerned about maintaining her personal space and cautious about building ties with others (T 0). Thus, there is a question about how close she is willing to be with a partner, despite her apparent dependence. This might result in her inadvertently sending mixed signals to John, suggesting both an invitation to and a rejection of relationship, consistent with a hysteroid dynamic, particularly given her marked anger, already noted (S 6)

With her unfilled needs, conflicts, and emotions, under her present situational stress she becomes overly emotionally involved in situations (low Lambda .26). This may well underlie her other needs to be separate and not be easily close, lest she lose a sense of herself because of fluid boundaries. Therefore, the therapist needs to help Alexia establish ways to better maintain her boundaries in her dealing with John and Dawn and simplify her overly complex psychological world. With surer boundaries, she may be able to experience closeness more easily when she chooses. In addition, when her emotions are better channeled and controlled, they will not overshadow her logical thinking process as they do to some extent now.

In summary, Alexia is presently responding situationally with feelings that are getting out of control. These include anger toward others and toward herself with self-criticism, producing an emotional overwhelm, interfering at times with her thinking logically. She is needy and dependent, yet overly cautious about being close. The therapist needs to help her channel her feelings more effectively, especially her angry ones, and develop sureness in maintaining her boundaries so that her experience of overwhelm and becoming engulfed by complexity will recede, resulting in being able to use her adequate personal resources to problem-solve.

THERAPEUTIC INTERVENTION WITH THIS CHANGING FAMILY

Therapeutic intervention with this family would be designed to deal with the immediate crisis of the parents' separation and probable divorce and the child's reaction to her changing family. Knowing about the styles of relating and areas of difficulty of Dawn, John, and Alexia as revealed through the Rorschach makes it possible to begin brief family interventions with some very specific tactics in mind.

In beginning brief family therapy, the therapist needs first to focus on developing emotional conditions within the sessions so that Dawn can experience a reasonable degree of safety, given her depression, fearfulness, and tendency to withdraw. This is a crucial condition for Alexia and even for John (although he might deny this).

The family therapist will need to block the father's stubborn, often insensitive push to control. The therapist has to cushion John's potential angry outbursts; John needs to avoid frightening Dawn and, if he does, to understand how he does frighten his daughter, so that he might modify his behavior. At the same time, the family therapist would do well to help Alexia contain and/or express her feelings, particularly her angry ones, so that they do not overwhelm the family session, also frightening to Dawn. Yet, she needs to be assertive with John. Both parents can be instructed to express their feelings and thoughts about each other in a couples session. The initial family therapy session then can be focused on helping the parents reassure Dawn of their love and caretaking. They need to demonstrate that they can keep her out of the middle, that she is not used as a go-between. They need to be able to listen and reflect back to Dawn to acknowledge whatever feelings and ideas she has, even though the parents might not like some of their child's responses.

If Dawn can begin to feel reassured about a positive connection with both parents, it may be more comfortable to bring up the possibility of Dawn's having her own (play) therapist to discuss what's happening with her, including her present unhappiness. The play therapist would also include her in a therapy group to help her improve her social sensitivity and skills. At the same time Dawn sees her therapist, the parents would be talking over parent/adult problems of coparenting to resolve them with the family/couple therapist. Soon, in family therapy with Dawn, the parents can discuss an actual coparenting plan.

In continuing family therapy, the therapist would need to encourage Dawn to express herself by making the therapy situation as emotionally safe as possible through supporting Dawn in her comments. The family therapist would work to help the parents contain their anger, to be dealt with in couple sessions. The parents would be helped to focus on Dawn, avoiding criticism of her (especially from John).

Specific problems of favoritism could arise. For example, Dawn might well blurt out that she wants to be with her mother (she said this privately), but then acknowledge that she is fearful of losing her father. John would need to be reassured by practical planning for his coparenting time with Dawn and at the same time assisted in understanding his hurt and not being overcome by his feelings at not being "picked" by his daughter. Alexia may need help in maintaining her mothering closeness with Dawn. Dawn may need to be helped to avoid the role of caretaker of her mother and to understand that she will be with her father on a regular basis.

## Summary

The Rorschach is particularly helpful in situations where in-depth personality evaluations are required because a family is facing situations that have far-reaching effects on its members, especially those involving children. These include issues of separation and divorce, abuse, and identifying psychosis and clinical depression.

This chapter focused on the dominant interpersonal styles and key characteristics of the Rorschach and their implications for understanding family interaction and for developing targets for therapeutic change. An analysis was presented of major Rorschach features of a family undergoing separation and divorce, together with suggestions for intervening by the family therapist.

# CHAPTER 6

# The KFD:
## Clues to Family Relationships

PEGGY THOMPSON, PH.D. and A. RODNEY NURSE, PH.D.

For the family therapist or the psychological evaluator with a family systems orientation, the Kinetic Family Drawing (KFD) technique holds promise as a useful clinical method: "holds promise" because the KFD lacks a research base comparable to established psychological instruments such as the MMPI-2, MCMI-III, and the Rorschach. The KFD is, however, included in this volume because it is the only widely used drawing method that attempts to elicit responses pertaining directly to understanding the family system from the perception of the drawer. Another reason for considering the KFD is its present popularity with clinicians, and because of the ease with which the clinician can apply the method, its widespread use is likely to continue.

The clinician familiar with the using the KFD may wish to skip to the section "Development of the KFD."

## CAPSULE SUMMARY OF THE KFD

The instructions for administering the KFD to children are presented by Robert C. Burns and S. Harvard Kaufman (1970) in their original volume: Provide the child with a plain white sheet of paper and a number 2 pencil. Ask the child to "Draw a picture of everyone in your family, including you, doing something. Try to draw whole people, not cartoons or stick people. Remember, make everyone doing something—some kind of action" (pp. 19–20). Though it would not appear to be necessary to repeat these directions word-for-word, it is very important to stress that the child draw everyone in the family doing something. Do not be concerned if children omit someone, unless it is themselves. In that case, encourage them to include themselves. Always stress the family doing something.

The KFD has also been used extensively with adolescents and adults. Instructions are basically the same as for children, including an emphasis on the family doing something.

There is no generally accepted scoring procedure, even though Burns and Kaufman (1972) introduced a formal scoring system focused on actions, styles, and symbols, which followed their initial volume focused on case discussions. Burns (1982) subsequently considered scoring around the categories of actions; distances, barriers, and positions; physical characteristics of the figures; and styles. As will be noted in the body of this chapter, for the most part, scoring of individual signs such as the originators proposed has not proved particularly productive. An integrative, holistic approach holds more potential.

One holistic approach to understanding the meaning of drawings, including the KFD, is for the therapist/evaluator after the drawing session to try to physically duplicate the actual postures and imagine the actions indicated on the KFD. These kinesthetic experiences can trigger feelings and thoughts for the therapist/evaluator that may be akin to the client's. For example, acting out a child's smile with arms out toward family members as compared with duplicating a scowling, hiding child crunched up in a ball would certainly elicit different feelings and thoughts for the clinician.

## Development of the KFD

Handler and Habenicht (1994) authored an excellent summary of the KFD literature, referencing studies published through 1992. Historically, these writers point out, clinicians had been requesting drawings of families for some years, but Burns and Kaufman (1970) made a major advance when they advocated instructions that emphasized drawing in action, drawing the family "doing something," hence establishing a new method emphasizing the kinetic aspect (Handler & Habenicht, 1994, pp. 40–41). It seems that adding the simple feature of drawing family members doing something brought family relationships into play. The importance of this critical instruction probably had a receptive audience because the 1970s saw an accelerated development and acceptance of family therapy, following its gradual start in the 1950s and 1960s. In addition, the late 1970s saw large numbers of professional psychologists beginning to be trained by the newly established graduate schools of professional psychology; these new schools were increasingly open to the clinical advances of the family system concept and family therapy itself. This environment paved the way for adding to the psychological assessment armamentarium the new assessment tool, the KFD. A commonality of the evolving family therapy and the KFD was the emphasis on the here and now, in contrast with the earlier stress on historical, intrapersonal, insight-focused, individual assessment and psychotherapy. The KFD may be considered a pictorial analog to family sculpturing, as described by family therapy pioneer Satir (1967).

Although the KFD is now used worldwide (Handler & Habenicht, 1994, p. 41), there is as yet no generally accepted scoring system. As noted in the "Capsule Summary," Burns and Kaufman (1972) originally proposed a scoring system for individual drawing characteristics classified as actions, styles, and symbols, with an augmented classification later by Burns (1982). Actions refer to content or theme of the KFD, such as energy between people characterized as love, violence, competition, and harmony, reflected concretely in such various actions as cooking, playing ball, reading, mowing the lawn, working, and so on.

Styles were originally viewed as pathological with children by Burns and Kaufman (1970), but at least 3 of their original 11 styles were found to be normative for adolescents by Thompson (1975). One of the three styles seems particularly important, that of compartmentalization. Compartmentalization is the intentional separation of family figures through lining. This probably reflects the importance of boundaries and beginning separation for the adolescent living in the family.

A. Jacobson (1993) found 2 of the original 11 styles to be present in 20% to 25% of the drawings of 6- to 9-year-old boys. Thus, there appear to be some age and sex differences in styles.

Recently, Burns, one of the originators of the KFD, stated to reviewers Handler and Habenicht that styles represent "techniques for coping and for survival" (Handler & Habenicht, 1994, p. 444). Styles include compartmentalization (as noted above, intentional separation of family figures through the use of lining); edging (placement of all family figures on the perimeter of the paper in rectangular style); encapsulation (encapsulating one or more figures by lines or objects); folding compartmentalization (folding the paper into segments and then placing individual figures within each segment); bottom lining (more than one line covering the entire bottom of the drawing); top lining (more than one line extending across the entire top of the drawing); and underlining individual figures (lines immediately below a standing individual or individuals). Examples of symbols, needing to be interpreted in clinical context, as initially proposed include bed (sexual or depressive themes); drums (displaced anger); flowers (beauty, growth process, feminine); kites (attempting to get out of or above a family environment seen as restrictive); ladders (tension and precarious balance); lamps (warmth and love); lawn mowers (cutting and castrating); rain (depressive tendencies); and vacuums (powerful, controlling, sucking up). Under the original scoring system, characteristics of individual figures are noted, for example, elevated figures (striving for dominance); erasures (conflicts); and omission of body parts (conflicts).

Although Burns and Kaufman (1972) suggested specific meanings for these indicators, they actually interpret KFDs somewhat differently depending on the family context. Research has often focused, however, on the single characteristics with an attempt to establish single interpretations for specific signs. This classical research approach focusing on single variables is at variance with the integrated, holistic approach of the clinician. This may be why very little has come of searching for consistent meanings for specific signs or drawing characteristics. Though knowing the suggested possible meanings of the signs may prove useful as guides for the clinician interpreting the KFD, it is well to keep in mind the statement of literature reviewers Handler and Habenicht (1994, p. 447) commenting on research that "the analysis of single signs or variables is to be discouraged." These same reviewers point to more positive findings when multiple variables are employed. At this point, the number of studies is small with as yet no major consistent findings that are particularly helpful for the practicing clinician.

## Suggested Modifications of the KFD

An interesting variation with families is to have everyone in a family session do a KFD by themselves, then have the family discuss the different drawing perceptions of the family members with the guidance of the therapist. Discussion of similarities and differences may stimulate talk about affectionate family bonds and significant differences among family members.

Alternatively, a clinician may have family members work together to draw one KFD. When this is done, we recommend using a large sheet of art paper and crayons rather than a regular sheet of paper and a pencil. The instructions are the same as with the standard KFD, except to ask family members to decide together what each member is to draw and where on the large sheet of paper each member will accomplish the drawing task. This step is particularly important because it gives the observer examples of family interaction. The observer may pay attention to such questions as who leads, who has the final say, and how the actual drawing is executed by those involved. These observations may later be integrated by the therapist/assessor into subsequent discussion with the family to see if these family patterns are representative of family interaction outside the consulting room and, if they are, what might be the implications of these patterns.

In another variation, appropriate when the identified patient is a very young child, 2 to 4, the therapist/assessor can do the drawing for the child, asking the child to say where to put the person, what that person is doing, and what expression to draw on the face. In this procedure, the clinician has an opportunity to observe and comment on family interaction patterns in response to the KFD.

An additional approach, more directly therapeutic, is for the family to act out the actions depicted in the family KFD. And, of course, the KFD can serve as a starting point for a general family discussion, either with the drawer(s) of the picture alone or involving the entire family.

A major advantage of a drawing task is that adults are not ordinarily accomplished artists any more than are their children. Thus, compared with talking, there is more equality and possible playfulness in this task.

## Case Examples

Interpretation of KFDs is so individualized that it is difficult, if not impossible, to make many generalizations about interpretive features. However, several cases are presented to provide the reader with a general pattern for thinking about the KFD in the context of the presenting problem and other test findings.

ELSA

Figure 6.1 presents the KFD for Elsa, age 16. The first thing to notice is that all the figures are drawn in separate activities. This separateness is typical for adolescents (Thompson, 1975). In her picture, others appear to be engaged actively, whereas Elsa seems to be just sitting, perhaps watching her father. Father has an axe and stepmother has an eggbeater, which may be interpreted as aggressive instruments. Does this represent her view of them, or possibly a projection of feelings toward them and/or their feelings?

Given that the erasures are on father and on Elsa, this may suggest some anxiety in their relationship. The axe, a phallic symbol or symbol of aggression, is between them. Although not always the case in all KFDs, that she is closest to her sister in the drawing suggests that she may in reality be closer, or wish to be. And her sister is pregnant. How does she view this? Except for the pregnancy, Elsa's drawing of the women do not indicate sex characteristics. Even the stepmother has no indication of breasts; perhaps she is not nurturant with Elsa. They all seem young, as do the males. This may tie into a denial of these adult differences, relating to the hypothesis of need for further individuation on Elsa's part.

Returning to Elsa, she, as noted above, is sitting. She appears to be an observer. Lack of activity may be an indication of immobility and hence depression. Like all the others in her drawing, she seems to have a phony smile on her face, covering her feelings. This is consistent with the remainder of the personality testing summarized below.

Elsa had improved her relationship with her stepmother through family therapy that included the stepmother, Elsa's father, and Elsa's stepbrother. Elsa,

Figure 6.1
Kinetic Family Drawing: Elsa

however, remained depressed and withdrawn. She was administered a battery of tests, including the KFD, to assist planning to her process of individuation, identified as a core problem through the family therapy process.

Results of the Wechsler Intelligence Scale for Children–Revised (WISC-R) indicated that her ability level was in the average ranges. Rorschach and the MAPI pointed to continued low self-esteem, anxiety, withdrawal, and depression, consistent with the interpretation of her inert, immobilized, picture of herself in the KFD. She remained a very needy teen, seeking nurturance, but so angry that she was likely to drive others away as they sensed or experienced her hostility directly. This indication of anger is consistent with the KFD depiction of parents wielding aggressive tools, possibly a projection of Elsa's anger in her relationship with her parents, as suggested in the analysis of the KFD. She consciously indicated more emphasis on conflicts with other teenagers than with her family.

Elsa received feedback from the assessor about the test findings. Discussing and looking at the drawing pinpointed her isolation, seeming passivity, yet potential underlying anger. She agreed to enter a therapy group for teenagers to work on her relationships and develop herself as an individual apart from her family.

JOHN

In 6-year-old John's KFD (Figure 6.2), his mother is the tall person toward the left. On the extreme left is the new baby. John is to the right of his mother, and on the other side of John is his 3-year-old brother. John's father rounds out the picture on the extreme right. John states that the whole family went to have their picture taken. This would appear to be an active family, as judged by all the arms in the air. If the KFD interpreter raises his or her own arms in the air, he or she might sense that this position could indicate a "hooray" or "touchdown," perhaps reflecting the exuberant side of a 6-year-old, perhaps the exuberance of the whole family.

The mother's arms may suggest to some evaluators openness, acceptance, and perhaps a readiness to embrace. In this family picture, the mother is described by John as "tired," not surprising given the age of the baby (2 months) so the lowered position of her arms might also indicate a droop from her demanding role.

Many writers have considered shading to be an indication of anxiety, which it may be sometimes. In drawing his mother, John has indicated that she is wearing a dress. John has related that he has on long ski gloves. The only

Figure 6.2
Kinetic Family Drawing: John

shading in the KFD is mother's dress, the lower half of John's body, and John's ski gloves. These aspects of the drawing may reflect his trying to understand what has been going on beneath the clothes (i.e., pregnancy) and perhaps anxiety related to the new younger sister. One of the reasons John was brought for evaluation was his parents' therapist's concern about John regularly trying on his mother's clothes as well as his father's. He may have been anxious about his mother and himself, and his seeming cross-dressing may have been an attempt to master the situation. Shading his hands may also have a masturbator connotation. These, of course, are speculations. They might, however, prove useful hypotheses for a play therapist observing what John does in his play, or for the couple therapist, who might expand his role to become a family therapist for this family.

That John draws himself next to his mother may suggest to the therapist either how he feels or how he would wish to feel: close to his mother.

The parents wondered if John might not be a "gifted" child; he seemed verbally precocious to them. Administration of the Wechsler Intelligence Scale for Children-Revised (WISC-R) resulted in a verbal IQ of 122 (93rd percentile). Although this is not considered "gifted," because his vocabulary and comprehension scores fell at the 99th percentile, he might in future testing score in the "gifted" range verbally. However, his performance IQ was significantly lower at 85 (16th percentile). Children develop different aspects of themselves at quite variable rates as preschoolers, so this variability among scores might not continue. However, his visual-spatial abilities as reflected in his block design score were severely low, at the 1st percentile, raising major concern about his ability to manage right brain–oriented tasks involving visual-spatial abilities. John's skill at drawing does not seem advanced at all but is not out of keeping with his nonverbal scores on the WISC-R. He may be excessively verbal through natural variation and/or possibly partially as a compensation for marked visual-spatial deficiencies. Depending on follow-up diagnostic work, remedial therapy around general right brain functioning deficit may be called for as John matures.

These results were presented in a couple session with the parents. The suggestion was made that the parents observe John's play around trying to work out the newly enlarged family system. A family session was planned to include John playing and drawing with his parents. Depending on the family session results, some play therapy sessions were to be considered.

AMY

The KFD of Amy, age 8, is presented in Figure 6.3. She has drawn seemingly static figures. She says, however, in describing her KFD, that she and her 6-year-old brother are playing a game involving skipping a disk. The disk may be observed in

Figure 6.3
Kinetic Family Drawing: Amy

her brother's right hand. Her mother is reading a book, and her father is playing on his computer. Amy states that she is about to go visit her best friend, who lives next door. One implication is that there is not much interesting going on at her house. Actions are depicted as diverse and not interrelated in this family, particularly those of the parents, who are involved in their own individual pursuits. Unlike many family drawings for this age child, the actions do not focus on family relationships, except that of the girl and her younger brother. Even with this relationship, she indicates in her verbalization that she is about to leave the family to visit her best friend The KFD is consistent with other test results, indicating an avoidance of emotion and an intellectual emphasis, even a pseudo-maturity, pushing aside usual feeling interaction, leaving the child feeling somewhat isolated.

At eight and a half, Amy is quiet and withdrawn. She seems not to mix well with her peers and so had been referred for evaluation. Testing results point to a child with a verbal ability level better than 96% of the general population (WISC-R verbal IQ 127) and a performance score in the average range. On the Rorschach, she seems an overcontrolled child who avoids emotions, and thus emotionally did not interact well with others, missing out on much of the give-and-take that she needed for her own development. This Rorschach picture is consistent with the isolated intellectualized actions of her parents as depicted on the KFD, and, except for Amy's game with her brother, the lack of family interaction.

## RENE

The KFD for Rene, age 9, is shown in Figure 6.4. Her father is bringing ice cream to the table from the left side of the picture. Her stepmother is seated at the table looking at a birthday cake on which are lit candles. Rene's brother, Sam, age 11, is seated at the table looking at the cake. Rene is apart from the family group on the right side of the KFD. She is drawn looking at the viewer rather than being involved in the birthday celebration for her brother.

A presumption may be made based on the KFD content that Rene sees her brother as getting nourishment (warmth and love) coupled with special treatment from her father and stepmother. At least in this drawing, Rene is not getting

Figure 6.4
Kinetic Family Drawing: Rene

nourishment, nor is she being treated as special. Rene may be seeking to get attention from the viewer. Although she smiles, the smile appears artificial. These are all clues that can be followed up in play interviews with this child, in testing, and in interviews with her parents.

Rene lives with her father and stepmother, as depicted in her KFD. She visits her mother and stepfather. Her mother has a long history of deficient control over her expression of anger, and, especially when she was younger, Rene was clearly afraid of her. On the Behavior Assessment System for Children (BASC) inventory, (see Chapter 8, this volume) her mother views Rene as depressed, anxious, distractible, hyperactive, and aggressive. In fact, Rene's mother sees her as having significant behavior problems overall, as well as being a child who both internalizes and externalizes her problems; her mother believes Rene is low on resources to adapt successfully to her world. By marked contrast, the father's BASC on Rene indicates that he does not see problems, and even indicates that she has unusually good social skills. (The BASC is discussed in Chapter 8.)

Rene's Rorschach results point to a very angry child whose strong negative feelings may be interfering with her cognitive processing. She maintains a constant level of alertness, characterized as hypervigilance. Her self-esteem is very low.

The contribution of the KFD in this instance is to point out the probable depravation Rene experiences in contrast to the nurturance her brother appears to get. So, in addition to exploring her relationships with her parents, a hypothesis is posed for the family therapist that sibling rivalry may be a problem. Feedback sessions included recommending that the father, stepmother, and two children have a series of family therapy sessions. In addition, a therapist was to include Rene in some therapy sessions with her mother.

## Summary

The KFD is a useful method for the family therapist or family assessor. Although it lacks the extensive empirical and experimental data that would provide it the validity of such clinical instruments as the MMPI/MMPI-2, the MCMI-III, and the Rorschach, the KFD is the only drawing method that seems to consistently tap into the family interrelationships. Because it can provide clues about family relationships, it is particularly helpful as one instrument in a battery of tests, although it can be used by itself. Given its simplicity of administration, it will probably continue to be used worldwide.

# CHAPTER 7

---

## The MACI:
### Personality Patterns, Expressed Concerns, and Clinical Syndromes

---

The Millon Adolescent Clinical Inventory (MACI)™ is a self-report inventory designed for adolescents aged 13 to 19 (Millon, 1993). As with the MCMI-III, a major advantage is that it measures personality patterns within the context of a major theory of personality and personality disorders that is consistent with the *DSM-IV* (Millon, 1996). Of particular importance to the clinician (and perhaps even more to the teenage client) is that the inventory is brief, with only 160 items. Many adolescents who cannot manage longer inventories typically complete this inventory in 20 minutes. Yet, the MACI can provide very useful hypotheses for the clinician beginning family therapy or other interventions with an adolescent.

The MACI is new, published in 1993 (Millon). The manual indicates that it is a replacement for the Million Adolescent Personality Inventory (MAPI) (1982). The MACI is designed for use with troubled adolescents. As such, the MACI norm group consists only of adolescents tested in a clinical or therapy setting. By contrast, the MAPI was developed more than a decade ago on a combined group of clinical and nonclinical adolescents. Thus, those clinicians familiar only with the MAPI need to review the MACI manual; they are also encouraged to read the "Capsule Summary of the MACI" below. Readers familiar with the MACI may wish to skip the Capsule Summary.

## CAPSULE SUMMARY OF THE MACI

The MACI consists of 160 statements about personality and behavior to which an adolescent responds "true" or "false" with reference to how the statements apply to himself or herself. A sixth-grade reading level is required. As noted, usually 20 minutes or less is needed to complete the inventory.

Many adolescents who are in crisis are not able to sustain concentration nor persevere for longer. And some of those who do persevere with longer inventories react increasingly appositionally with frustration and anger so that their cooperation with other assessment tasks is compromised.

The MACI may be administered individually, in a group, using audiotape, or the adolescent make take it directly on the computer. The last method is particularly attractive to the present generation of teens brought up on computers.

Along with mail-in and hand scoring, the most user-friendly processing option for clinicians is to utilize the computer program available from National Computer Systems (NCS) (1997). The program produces either a profile or a profile plus a several-page-long interpretive report. For the clinician using a computer-generated or hand-scored profile only, a particularly thorough knowledge of the test manual (Millon, 1993), Millon's theory (1996), and the *DSM-IV* (APA, 1994) is essential for constructing a report similar to the computer printout. Of course, anyone using the inventory should have solid knowledge of it to use it responsibly. The *Ethical Principles of Psychologists and Code of Conduct* of the American Psychological Association (1992, 2.08 (c)) states: "Psychologists retain appropriate responsibility for the appropriate application, interpretation, and use of assessment instruments, whether they score and interpret such tests themselves or use automated or other services."

Mental health professionals may use the MACI to "aid in identifying, predicting, and understanding a wide range of psychological difficulties that are characteristic of adolescents (Millon, 1993, p. 4). Millon states in the test manual: "With the exception of graduate students conducting supervised research, all individuals using the MACI should have at least a master's degree in a relevant field of mental health and should meet membership qualifications for their appropriate professional organization (American Psychological Association, American Counseling Association, American Psychiatric Association, or the National Association of Social Workers)" (p. 5). Ordering the inventory requires qualifications at the A level, defined as "Licensure to practice psychology independently, or a graduate degree in psychology in a closely related field and either a graduate-level course in Tests and Measurements or participation in an NCS-approved workshop" (NCS, 1997, p. 94).

THE MACI SCALES

Four scales are designed to modify other MACI scales to take account of response style. Twelve scales measure personality patterns based on Millon's (1996) theoretical schema. There are eight scales that focus on areas of life that reflect problems typical of troubled adolescents. Seven scales report on areas that require direct clinical intervention. Descriptions below are abridged from the MACI *Manual* (Millon, 1993).

*Modifying Indices*

These indices, in measuring response style, provide a basis on which to consider the validity of a given inventory.

> Scale X, Disclosure: The degree to which a client was open, honest, and self-revealing.
>
> Scale Y, Desirability: The degree to which the test results may have been affected by the patient's inclination to appear socially attractive, morally virtuous, and emotionally well-composed.
>
> Scale Z, Debasement: The degree to which the client was inclined to deprecate or devalue himself or herself by presenting more troublesome emotional and personal difficulties than might really be the case.
>
> Scale VV, Reliability: Based on how reasonable the response was to two highly improbable items.

*Personality Patterns*

These major adolescent personality patterns are similar to but less well-formed than the full-blown adult patterns of personality disorders that follow from Millon's (1996) theory. The adult solidified patterns are given as reference points for thoughtful dynamic consideration, but are not meant to indicate equivalency of terms or that the adolescent patterns have the same degree of crystallization as the adult personality patterns. Descriptions are of those who score high on a particular pattern.

> Scale 1, Introversive (Schizoid): Keep to themselves, indifferent to others. Appear quiet, unemotional, distant, asocial. Do not have strong, involved feelings; lack desire.
>
> Scale 2A, Inhibited (Avoidant): Appear to be distant, but actually shy, ill at ease; wanting emotional contact with others yet fearing rejection, and so keep their distance and are lonely.
>
> Scale 2B, Doleful (Depressive): Gloomy, dejected, sad, brooding, and pessimistic, perhaps since childhood. Prone to guilt and feelings of inadequacy and a sense of worthlessness.
>
> Scale 3, Submissive (Dependent): Kind, soft-hearted, and so needy in relationships that they cling and are not assertive, playing down their own positive attributes. Highly dependent-appearing.

Scale 4, Dramatizing (Histrionic): Talkative, charming, often exhibitionistic or emotionally expressive. Bored with routine, they look for excitement and relationships that are brief and intense.

Scale 5, Egotistic (Narcissistic): Confident to overconfident; self-assured, not self-doubting. Appear self-centered, often arrogant and exploitive, lacking empathy for others.

Scale 6A, Unruly (Antisocial): Act out in antisocial manner, resisting socially acceptable standards of behavior. May be pervasively rebellious leading to conflict with parents, school, and the law.

Scale 6B, Forceful (Aggressive-Sadistic): Strong-willed, tough-minded, bent on dominating others. Blunt, unkind, can abuse others, impatient with problems or weaknesses of others.

Scale 7, Conforming (Compulsive): Serious-minded, efficient, respectful, orderly, and rule-conscious. Overcontrolled in keeping emotions in check, thus tense, avoiding surprises.

Scale 8A, Oppositional (Passive-Aggressive, Negativistic): Discontented, sullen, but can alternate hostility with pleasantness. Confused and contrite about moods and lack of control over them.

Scale 8B, Self-Demeaning (Self-Defeating): Seems content to suffer; may undermine efforts of those who try to help. May deny pleasure and sabotage themselves. Their own worst enemy.

Scale 9, Borderline Tendency (Borderline): Marked emotional instability, erratic relationships, capricious, hostile, self-destructive, with fear of abandonment. Severe dysfunction.

*Expressed Concerns*

The intensity of the concern parallels an increase in scale score.

Scale A, Identity Diffusion: Not knowing who they are or where they are going. Unsure of identity, directionless, unfocused about future goals and values.

Scale B, Self-Devaluation: Sense of self, but dissatisfied. Open about feelings of low self-esteem, fearing they will fall far short of what they aspire to be.

Scale C, Body Disapproval: Discontent with perceived shortcomings of physical maturation or general physical shape. Likely to express feelings of level of attractiveness and social appeal.

Scale D, Sexual Discomfort: Sexual thoughts and feelings confusing or disagreeable. Troubled by impulses and fear sexual expression. Concerned or in conflict over roles sexuality may require.

Scale E, Peer Insecurity: Dismay and sadness over rejection by peers. Wanting approval, but may need to withdraw and become even more isolated.

Scale F, Social Insensitivity: Cool and indifferent to the welfare of others. Seek own ends by overriding others'. Lack empathy, with little interest in building warm personal ties.

Scale G, Family Discord: Families tense and full of conflict. Little emotional support, feeling of estrangement from parents. May reflect parental rejection and/or adolescent rebellion.

Scale H, Childhood Abuse: Shame and disgust about having been subjected to verbal, physical, or sexual abuse from close relations (e.g., parents, siblings, relatives, or family friends).

*Clinical Syndromes*

These typically call for direct intervention by a therapist.

Scale AA, Eating Dysfunctions: Anorexia nervosa, with an intense fear of getting fat, or bulimia nervosa, indicating uncontrolled binging followed by self-induced vomiting.

Scale BB, Substance Abuse Proneness: Alcohol or substance abuse leading to significant impairment of performance and behavior, possibly out of control, despite awareness of problems.

Scale CC, Delinquent Predisposition: Behavior leading to the rights of others being violated. Breaking rules, possibly threatening others, lying, stealing, and other antisocial behavior.

Scale DD, Impulsive Propensity: Minimal provocation leads to acting out sexual and aggressive impulses. Sudden, impetuous, and often foolhardy expression.

Scale EE, Anxious Feelings: Sense of foreboding and general apprehension about many matters. Fretful, nervous, uneasy, and disquieted, anticipating unknown torments or calamitous events.

Scale FF, Depressive Affect: Decreased level of activity, clearly distinct from the past. Decrease in effectiveness, feelings of guilt, fatigue, despair about the future, withdrawal.

Scale GG, Suicidal Tendency: Suicidal thoughts, plans, feelings of worthlessness, purposelessness. Sense that others might be better off without them, calling for professional/family alertness.

Although the scope of clinical syndromes covered is significant, McCann (1997, p. 363) has pointed out that some of the more severe forms of psychopathology are not measured, including major thought disturbances, bipolar mood disorders, and paranoid ideation. An additional limitation is the lack of a separate scale to measure posttraumatic stress disorder.

SCORE LEVELS AND PROFILE CODING

The higher the score level, the more defined is the measured descriptor. As with the MCMI-III, (1993) Millon utilized the prevalence and severity of a given disorder in the populations studied. The resulting base rates (BRs) establish anchoring points for interpretations. A BR of 60 corresponds to the median average raw score. Above 60 and below 75 suggest *features* of the dimension. A BR of 75 indicates the *presence* of the dimension, not simply a trend or feature. A BR of 85 indicates *prominence* of the dimension in the personality.

A profile is coded in the following way, as described in the MACI *Manual* (Millon, 1993, p. 51). Scores above BR 59 are placed in the MCMI code in order of their magnitude (scores below BR 59 are not included). Coding for each of the three sections, Personality Patterns, Expressed Concerns, and Clinical Syndromes, is followed by a double slash (//). Personality Pattern scores of 85 or above are placed to the left of the double asterisk notation (**). Scores at BR 75 to 84 are followed by a single asterisk (*). Scores 60 to 74 are not followed by a symbol, but simply close the set to the left of the first set of double dashes. A hyphen (-) indicates that no scale reached a BR score in that numerical range. Scores within 2 BRs from each other are underlined. This pattern is followed out through the Expressed Concerns scales placed in the second set of scores after the first slashes and before the second slashes. The Clinical Syndromes scales are listed in similar fashion after the second set of slashes and before the final slashes at the end of the code.

Coding MACI profiles provides a useful way for the researcher to categorize overall inventory results. In addition, the profiles provide the clinician with a quick way to think through levels of significance of the various bits of data and to compare with externally derived information correlated with the profile categorizations.

# Development of the MACI

The MACI was developed within Millon's (1996) theoretical structure, which provides meaningful links to broader personality aspects in the literature, rather than resting only upon empirically developed but isolated scales. Thus, the MACI can be of considerable usefulness in building rich and interweaving clinical hypotheses reflecting the complexity of personality. In developing the

MACI, Millon also ensured that the internal structure supported the conceptual framework. In addition to developing data representing empirical relationships with other inventories and special established scales, clinician judgments made without knowledge of test scores provided a beginning base of external validity data.

Although the interpretive printout developed for the MACI is based primarily on actuarial data, the report is synthesized and linkages established through utilization of Millon's (1996) systematic clinical theory. Where insufficient data existed, hypotheses deduced from the theory were developed. However, where "substantial and clear-cut data exist, the system of predictor-description relationships was determined largely by actuarial results" (Millon, 1993, p. 61).

## Why Use the MACI?

For clinicians looking for a brief inventory that can provide hypotheses on which to begin family therapy or other interventions, the MACI is an excellent choice. Its brevity is an advantage with reluctant or upset youngsters, as has been noted in the description of the inventory.

Beyond increasing the odds that adolescents will cooperate with a short inventory as compared with a longer personality inventory is the importance of its theoretical foundation. Because the MACI is based on Millon's (1996) theory of personality and personality disorder, the inventory results provide a solid basis for immediately developing hypotheses about the personality functioning of the teenager of concern. The clinician thoroughly grounded in Millonian theory can appraise the profile itself and develop logically linked ideas about the probable personality and behavioral functioning of the adolescent over time as distinct from the adolescent's immediate expressed concerns, worries, and clinical symptomatology. Thus, treatment plans can be made with the developing adolescent *person* in mind, not simply immediate problematic behavior, even though the current problems may call for immediate attention.

Without awareness of the Clinical Personality Pattern, it is all too easy to respond to, for example, substance abuse behavior accompanied by family conflict, without understanding whether their exists an Unruly (potentially antisocial) personality in the making or whether the upsetting behavior is more a function of an Oppositional (potentially passive-aggressive) pattern. One pattern, the Unruly, could call for emphasis on behavioral limit-setting and on consequences of behavior; in some circles, this might be termed "tough love." Another youngster's similar overt pattern of substance abuse, though also calling for some limit-setting, might need to be approached with psychotherapy designed to help the youngster come to grips with internal conflicts and varying moods for which he or she has not yet developed adequate self-management techniques. And, while both youngsters might be exposed to family therapy, in therapy with the Unruly adolescent, the therapist would not only concentrate on limits but would be alert to blocking those family behaviors that might reward or encourage the defiant behavior. In conducting family therapy with the Oppositional/negativistic youngster, the therapist, also concerned with limits, may be especially alert to resolving parental conflicts that have divided the family, impeding the development of the teenager who shifts sides and serves inappropriately as a mediator holding the family together (Millon, 1996, p. 567).

The MACI identifies certain frequently encountered Clinical Syndromes that are frequently found by mental health professionals. Scores in the Clinical Syndrome areas make it possible to quickly rule out the likelihood that a given adolescent is similar to other teenagers with certain clinical characteristics and rule in the possibility of being similar to others. For example, early treatment goals may be to lessen the high Depressive Affect and high Anxious Feelings in an adolescent, with less concern for exploring Eating Dysfunction and Substance Abuse Proneness if these are low or moderate level scores.

The adolescent's Expressed Concerns scores provide a way to connect to the adolescent about his or her experience. By tackling those concerns quickly, rapport can be established and the adolescent provided with appropriate respect, even though the adults around may have other concerns that appear to override the teenager's. The adolescent with high body concern and peer insecurity is likely to be responsive to any help that will begin to alleviate these worries. These may be worries that are not at the top of the parent's list of concerns.

Clinicians will find that another advantage of the MACI is that its results parallel the DSM-IV. By paralleling the DSM-IV, evolving research related to specific disorders can be correlated with the MACI findings. This provides an enriched, extended net of hypotheses for understanding and working with the troubled teenager.

## The Adolescent in the Family

The computer printout of the MACI provides hypotheses about treatment approaches, including family approaches. In addition, for thoroughly making use of the MACI results, a very useful reference for the clinician is Millon's *Disorders of Personality, DSM-IV and Beyond* (1996). In a section describing "Characteristic Experiential History," some hypotheses of possible family behavior may be found, together with suggestions for therapeutic approaches. For example, in writing about the adult negativistic personality, Millon states that the patient's family of origin dynamics might likely have been characterized by double binding, approach-avoidance conflicts. Thus, with this consideration in mind in doing family therapy with the substance abusing adolescent referred to previously, whose personality pattern is primarily Oppositional, the therapist can be alert to signs in the family sessions for contradictory hidden messages by parents, issues of loyalty in the family, and covert conflicts during which the teenager responds with negativism. These hypotheses may lead the therapist to focus on the parents in family therapy sessions and oblige the youngster to be directly assertive to make his way into the discussions, rather than be in a controlling position, be an oppositional target, or act as a go-between with his parents.

Before family therapy gained currency as a prime therapeutic medium, an oppositional youngster might have undergone individual therapy with little reference to the ongoing family process; this could have tended to maintain his negativism, and perhaps rendered therapy ineffective. With the development of family therapy, treating the substance abusing family without reference to the dynamics underlying an adolescent's overt acting-out behavior might have resulted in a misfiring of the therapeutic intervention. This misfiring would have been particularly apparent if the therapist focused only on the family setting limits for acting-out, substance abusing behavior. Instead, the therapist can now be forearmed with an etiological hypothesis suggesting the existence of a present-day family system that tends to maintain the youngster in a role that keeps the parents together focused on the teen rather than facing their marital dispute. At the same time, because the therapist assumes from the MACI results the intrapsychic Oppositional negativistic hypothesis (rather than, say, an assumption of an Unruly-antisocial teen), the odds are in favor of therapy proceeding more successfully than had therapy begun as an intrapsychically-oriented task *or* as a family reorganizational task. The MACI results and the Millon theory have provided the bridge of linking hypotheses into an action plan for a specific youngster.

## Using the MACI Interpretive Printout

Because most clinicians are likely to use the computerized interpretive printout, either in lieu of or in conjunction with their individually constructed interpretation, some assets and some limitations of the interpretive printout need to be addressed. Because of its broad, statistically developed base, generalized statements (in effect, probability statements) provide some objectivity so that the clinician can consider a wide range of hypotheses that may apply to a given case. This broad net means less likelihood of overlooking important possibilities in understanding the teenager. At the same time, the wide scope and impersonal nature of the printout means that the hypotheses presented need to be individualized for the particular teenager. The clinician does this individualizing with reference to all the information available. To the extent that the clinician has developed this skill, or art, the interpretation will have ultimate usefulness.

Although the computer printout focuses on the negative because the MACI is designed to ferret out problems, it is also important that the clinician consider the strengths of the adolescent. Inferences about strengths need to be drawn from sources of information other than the MACI, yet the MACI does provide some indicators of strengths. For example, it is this author's observation that some persons with moderate scores indicating features or even presence on Dramatizing and Conforming scales may appear clinically to have controlled expressions of affect and are able to adhere to rules and follow through with tasks to completion. Millon (1993, p. 52) also points out that distinctly low BR scores (35 and below) on Expressed Concerns may be seen as strengths, as noted above. For example, very low scores on Identity Diffusion and Self-Devaluation suggest the development of a healthy sense of self.

## Interpreting the MACI Profile

The MACI profile consists of four sections calling for a step-by-step approach to interpretation. Following a review of the purpose of the evaluation and noting patient background information, clinical observations, and other test results, a first step is to affirm that the MACI profile is valid by referring to Scale VV (Reliability). If the score reaches 2, then the MACI profile is deemed not valid and the profile should not be interpreted. On the Clinical Interpretive Report printout, the profile page will indicate whether or not the profile may be validly interpreted. In addition, even if the score reaches 1, there is very strong reason to question if not reject the profile. Research by Bagby, Gillis, and Rogers (1991) on these two items, which are also used on the MCMI, indicates that when a cutoff of one item is utilized, 95% of random responders will be identified.

The other modifying indices, though accommodated to some extent in the statistical development of the scales and their interpretation, may not be entirely compensated for. They may point to a general denial of emotional problems, excessive complaining, or an indication of degree of honesty and openness in responding to the inventory. Specifically, adolescents may tend to *deny* emotional problems, either because they don't believe that they have emotional problems or because they are putting up a good front to others (faking good); this may be reflected in a high Desirability Scale (Y). They may *complain* excessively (faking bad), seeming more upset than appears justifiable, determined by a high Debasement Scale (Z). Their Disclosure Scale (X), measuring the degree of openness, honesty, and trend toward being self-revealing, helps interpret the meaning of scales X and Z.

After assessing the meanings of the modifying indices, a next step in interpreting is to review the Personality Patterns because these reflect the foundation of the developing teenage personality. The recommended approach is to look initially at the individual scales that are elevated and then, very important, the pattern of elevated scales. A thorough understanding of Millon's (1993) description of the individual personality patterns provides the basis on which to build the clinical logic with which to propose the interweaving of the elevated scores. Emphasis is placed on the higher scores with indications of their modification by scores of lesser values. Most interpretations of Personality Patterns follow this descending/modifying logic. Occasionally, a single score may stand BR 20 points or more higher than any other personality pattern scores; in that case, reference to the cardinal type description for that score may be the main interpretive source, with very little attention paid to the significantly lower-level personality scores. Final, organized interpretation of these scores that serve as personality building blocks needs to wait until the scores on Expressed Concerns and Clinical Syndromes are evaluated.

The Expressed Concerns (A–H) of the adolescent are appraised to give insight into the conscious, phenomenological world of the teen. In this area, each of these scales, when high, reveals separate areas of the adolescent's concerns. Low scores may sometimes be seen as strengths, as noted. This is particularly likely if the BR falls below 35 (Millon, 1993, p. 52). When following testing with interviewing, a major bridge for psychologically joining with the adolescent is through discussing these acknowledged concerns and possible strengths, regardless of the primary personality pattern, without at least initial reference to Clinical Syndrome measurement outcomes.

Clinical Syndrome scales (AA–GG) need to be looked at individually first, and later considered in terms of probable covariance with the Expressed Concerns scales. The Clinical Syndrome scales provide information about the extent to which the adolescent scores similarly to the normative groups reflected in each scale, such as Eating Dysfunctions and Anxious Feelings.

In concluding the interpretive process, it is important to return to the Personality Patterns to understand how these more traitlike dimensions become modified by the Expressed Concerns and Clinical Syndromes identified. Looking at the results in this step-by-step procedure helps with the process of avoiding bias in interpretations based on prior information. The problem of bias is addressed in Chapter 12.

## What about Profiles Inconsistent with Other Data?

McCann writes, "Whenever any of the Expressed Concerns scales are expected to be elevated, but they are not, this generally reflects the adolescent's unwillingness or inability to recognize the particular area of difficulty as a concern" (in Millon, 1997b, p. 383). Some manipulation of presentation might be suggested for adolescents who score high on Submissive and Compliance scales, and yet are known to be acting out and provocative toward authorities.

Sometimes, the MACI profile seems discordant with projective test data, such as the Rorschach. If the MACI suggests little pathology and the Rorschach points to marked pathology, this type of discrepancy may indicate an ability to manage structured stimuli while becoming disorganized with unstructured stimuli. This discrepancy may thus prove useful information, even though the MACI interpreted by itself may be less helpful. This issue is taken up in Chapter 10.

It is accurate to say that no inventory/test of personality is going to cover all aspects of personality and behavior. This consideration forms part of the rationale for using a variety of tests and for the necessity of thoughtful, careful, comprehensive analysis of all data by an educated and experienced clinician. And, as with other tests, occasionally the MACI will be less useful.

Three examples of this overall interpretive process follow. They are selected to suggest general patterns of approach and to illustrate some specific procedures of interpretation.

## Case Examples

### EUGENE

Eugene is a 17-year-old high school senior. He was referred for therapy with a combination of problems. He had gotten into trouble drinking alcohol with friends in a public park and was placed on probation. His grades were barely passing even though the school psychologist reported that his verbal IQ on the Wechsler Adult Intelligence Test was higher than 95% of the general population and his SAT scores were excellent. Both the discrepancy between his grades and his ability and the drinking dismayed his parents. His father, a business executive, and his mother, a public relations expert, contrasted his performance with that of his 15-year-old sister, who, with apparently equal ability, studied consistently and made more A than B grades. Eugene's parents feared he might become alcoholic and worried that their charming and social son would never settle into study and work patterns that would spell long-range achievement. As it was, his grades would prohibit his acceptance into the universities from which his parents had obtained their degrees.

In the initial evaluative interview, the therapist had difficulty engaging Eugene into revealing his more personal thoughts and feelings, although he was superficially talkative and sociable. She reported that his affect seemed flat. Although he showed no indications of a thought disorder, the therapist did not dismiss this hypothesis. She did wonder about some depression and his apparent overt passivity as he seemed to be following her lead to see what she wanted from him in the interview. He was amenable to being administered the MACI and did not overtly object to the probability of subsequent testing, which was accomplished after the MACI results were obtained.

Eugene's MACI profile is given in Figure 7.1. It may be seen that this is a valid report. There are no test-taking attitudes that significantly distort his MACI results. Note the MACI coding: -**4-//-**-*G//-**-*FFEE//.

The Personality Patterns scale results in this instance are clear-cut. Eugene has one personality pattern that is distinctly present, although it does not reach the level of prominence that could suggest a solidifying personality disorder. This moderately high score in Dramatizing suggests that with increasing age and solidity of personality, a histrionic personality disorder could develop. With the MACI results, the data do not warrant concluding that a personality disorder is present. However, some interpreters would feel justified in referring to this pattern, because his Dramatizing score is so much higher than all other Personality Patterns scores, as at least an evolving adolescent histrionic style.

Whether his pattern is labeled dramatic or an adolescent histrionic style, certain obvious trends are suggested for follow-up observations in interviews. Following Millon's (1996, pp. 366–371) analysis of the histrionic dynamic, at a behavioral level, Eugene may be *expressively dramatic* and *interpersonally attention-seeking*. At a phenomenological level, he likely attends mightily to external events, has *cognitive flightiness*, has a *gregarious self-image*, with *poorly developed interior life* consisting, for example, of superficial memories, transient and segregated affects, and conflicts. At an intrapsychic level, one would look for *the possibility of dissociation* and a general *disjointed organization* interiorly. A generally *fickle mood*, changing and rapidly shifting, shallow emotions, might be anticipated.

As to Expressed Concerns, Eugene's MACI indicates that he is in some conflict in relation to his family. No other concerns seem present. However, it is interesting to look at the Clinical Syndromes area, which suggests features of anxious feelings and depressive affect. These scores are far higher than other scores in the Clinical Syndromes area. Comparing the findings in the Expressed Concerns area, with its somewhat elevated score in Family Discord, and the Clinical Syndromes area, with somewhat modestly elevated scores in Anxious Feelings and Depressive Affect, leads to the conclusion that whatever anxious and depressed feelings he is experiencing are likely to do with family relationships. That he may be handling these through the mechanism of dissociation is suggested by the above noted focus on an apparent dramatic/histrionic style.

A look at corollary information reveals that his life revolves around his peer group of "buddies." Drinking is done in the context of social relationships. It fits into acceptance and his dependency on this group, which is paramount in his life. He actively seeks their praise, support, and attention, finding his security in this

**MACI™**

PERSONALITY CODE:   -**4*-//-**-*G//-**-*FFEE//
VALID REPORT

| CATEGORY | | SCORE RAW | BR | PROFILE OF BR SCORES 0   60   75   85   115 | DIAGNOSTIC SCALES |
|---|---|---|---|---|---|
| MODIFYING INDICES | X | 283 | 39 | | DISCLOSURE |
| | Y | 12 | 63 | | DESIRABILITY |
| | Z | 5 | 57 | | DEBASEMENT |
| PERSONALITY PATTERNS | 1 | 11 | 27 | | INTROVERSIVE |
| | 2A | 11 | 28 | | INHIBITED |
| | 2B | 12 | 44 | | DOLEFUL |
| | 3 | 44 | 56 | | SUBMISSIVE |
| | 4 | 53 | 78 | | DRAMATIZING |
| | 5 | 42 | 55 | | EGOTISTIC |
| | 6A | 24 | 42 | | UNRULY |
| | 6B | 7 | 20 | | FORCEFUL |
| | 7 | 49 | 57 | | CONFORMING |
| | 8A | 13 | 31 | | OPPOSITIONAL |
| | 8B | 24 | 56 | | SELF-DEMEANING |
| | 9 | 11 | 38 | | BORDERLINE TENDENCY |
| EXPRESSED CONCERNS | A | 15 | 54 | | IDENTITY DIFFUSION |
| | B | 22 | 55 | | SELF-DEVALUATION |
| | C | 4 | 15 | | BODY DISAPPROVAL |
| | D | 21 | 42 | | SEXUAL DISCOMFORT |
| | E | 6 | 34 | | PEER INSECURITY |
| | F | 29 | 57 | | SOCIAL INSENSITIVITY |
| | G | 15 | 73 | | FAMILY DISCORD |
| | H | 2 | 11 | | CHILDHOOD ABUSE |
| CLINICAL SYNDROMES | AA | 7 | 18 | | EATING DYSFUNCTIONS |
| | BB | 15 | 33 | | SUBSTANCE-ABUSE PRONENESS |
| | CC | 28 | 59 | | DELINQUENT PREDISPOSITION |
| | DD | 10 | 30 | | IMPULSIVE PROPENSITY |
| | EE | 29 | 70 | | ANXIOUS FEELINGS |
| | FF | 13 | 72 | | DEPRESSIVE AFFECT |
| | GG | 5 | 21 | | SUICIDAL TENDENCY |

Figure 7.1
Millon Adolescent Clinical Inventory: Eugene
Copyright © 1994 DICANDRIEN, INC. All rights reserved.
Published and distributed exclusively by National Computer Systems, Inc.,
Minneapolis, MN 55440. Reprinted with permission by NCS.

relationship. It is a collaboratory note that he does not score high on Substance Abuse Proneness. His drinking appears not overtly based only on passive rebellion against authority but, perhaps equally likely, achieving the much-needed peer acceptance. Alcohol use or abuse does have the danger of raising his mood temporarily as it reduces his anxiety and disinhibits him so that he could behave in an impulsive way, contrary to his sober state. What parents and teachers may see as being selfish is self-centeredness focused on being accepted, rather than the manifestation of a developing sense of self. Activities that appear selfish probably reflect this marked need for acceptance by others, and, being adolescent, these others mean especially his peers.

Testing with the Rorschach (which will not be reported in detail) does indicate an extratensive problem-solving approach that is sufficiently rigid to seem pervasive. This is consistent with the dramatizing (histrionic) personality pattern on the MACI.

At this point, Eugene seems stuck with a problem-solving style oriented to a trial-and-error response to the world, with little recourse to an inner world wherein he might think things through. When he does turn inward, he tends to escape in flights of fantasies, failing to come to grips with relationships, leading to a self-imposed form of helplessness. Despite his overt style of moving into the environment interpersonally, he actually feels lonely and isolated at times. He is needy for more solid relationships.

The Rorschach findings concur in sensing a poorly developed sense of self and an inadequately developed inner life consistent with the histrionic, phenomenological suggestions on the MACI. This difficulty is complicated by his tendency to oversimplify his inputs and his cognitive processes so that he does not accurately perceive or internalize incoming information. There are indications of a thought disorder, although in reviewing his history and self-description, attention deficit disorder without hyperactivity seemed a working hypothesis. The Rorschach points to his need for excessive emotional stimulation from others. In his frustration, he is oppositional rather than directly rebellious at restrictions. His alcohol usage may have for one of its purposes the handling of anger, yet may on occasion allow for expression of anger inappropriately.

In planning treatment with this teenager with such strong traits of social dependency and need for attention and security, it is important to recognize that he is too dependent on others to be independently, narcissistically selfish. Therapy needs to be aimed at helping him become more independent, self-aware, and self-oriented in a positive way. He is not an unruly boy who acts out in an antisocial fashion. His therapist needs to be aware that the oppositional behavior needs to be turned to constructive anger. Alcohol abuse is not the primary issue, although it needs to be curbed so that he does not have this outlet for avoiding his feelings and losing the benefit of psychotherapy, delaying his personal self-development and solidifying into alcohol dependence.

Individual therapy should be client-centered or humanistic in order not to repeat an ineffective dominance-submission pattern that could reinforce his pattern to lean on others rather than encourage self-reliance in developing independence gradually over time. Along with the self-development focus in individual therapy, Eugene needs family therapy to allow him and his family to be together in laying the groundwork for furthering his steps toward independence. Family therapy must include his sister as well as his parents because of the probability of unresolved sibling rivalry issues. Psychological literature suggests that his overfocus on others may develop in the context of a family with at least one emotionally focused parent and/or in a rivalrous relationship with a sibling (Millon, 1996, p. 384). The hypothetical rivalrous relationship with his sister may have called for developing tactics that would get attention from parents. This dynamic may be repeated in relationships with other adults and also peers.

It is important for the therapist to recognize that Eugene may make initial moves toward independence to please the therapist. If he can find satisfaction from these in a personal way, he may not slide back into his more comfortable dependent role and resist genuine moves to gain independence. Therapy needs to progress slowly and cautiously, with an attempt to help him learn to pay attention to his inner processes using the humanistic or client-centered approach individually. Along with individual therapy, a more active family therapy approach would probably best be done with another therapist so as not to disturb the individual therapeutic relationship. Eugene needs his own person, the therapist, to pay attention to him, but in such a way as to foster his autonomy and independence.

The MACI serves as a focal point in discussing therapeutic goals with Eugene and helping the therapist center treatment on the long-term histrionic core issues, while ensuring that the family knot can be cut successfully. By curbing the alcohol usage, Eugene may find his way out of his troubles. Referral for possible medication to facilitate abstinence, or at least minimize abuse, may need to be considered.

## LINDA

Linda, just turned 13 and somewhat pudgy, is in the seventh grade and having difficulty adjusting to middle school. She had been in fairly protected relationships with her elementary school teachers. With the middle school shift to a number of teachers, combined with her increasing need for peer acceptance, she is having difficulty at this early adolescent level. Complicating her stance further are two facts: An older brother seems to be sailing through school easier than she, and her fairly traditional parents are manifesting more marital conflict as they face some difficult career-development choices. Apparently Linda's mother, because of the need to focus on career choices and some ensuing marital conflict, is not as available to Linda emotionally. In the past, she had been not only available but a constant, strong, guiding hand. The therapist suggested the MACI as a first step toward further understanding Linda, helping her understand herself, and planning for possible continued psychotherapy.

Figure 7.2 displays the MACI profile for Linda. The computer has calculated that her profile is valid. The remaining modifying indices fall within normal ranges, suggesting that there is no response pattern that would distort the findings. Note the MACI coding: 3**12A*8B2B//- **EB*AD//EE**FF*-//.

The Personality Patterns section points to behavior focused on the prominence of Submissive (Dependent) dynamics. This focus is modified by the presence of Introversive (Schizoid) and Inhibited (Avoidant) personality traits. Following (in part) Millon's (1996, p. 332) description of the domains for this area, behaviorally, Linda is *interpersonally submissive*. She seeks excessive advice and anticipates a mature guiding voice more than even others her age. She behaves in a withdrawn, passive way, avoiding self-expression, even though needy for relationships.

Phenomenologically, she is *cognitively naïve*, rarely disagreeing with others, is easily influenced, and tries to smooth over interpersonal difficulties. Seeing herself as weak, fragile, and inadequate, she seems more childlike than others her age. At the intrapsychic level, she is devoted to the belief that she is tightly bonded to others who are key in her life. She trusts those others to fulfill her needs. There is little internal nurturing for a sense of independent self. At a biophysical level, she is warm and noncompetitive. She seeks to avoid social tension. In summarizing the MACI, Linda's personality pattern combines passive submissive withdrawal, naïvely expecting nurturing from others without much activity on her part. Her self-depreciatory attitude seems to be blocking the development of a beginning adolescent sense of self.

At the level of Expressed Concerns, Linda clearly indicates that insecurity with peers is a problem. Her feelings of rejection are reinforcing a negative sense of self. Not shown are key items indicating emotional isolation; for example, she responds "true" to the statement "Most other teenagers don't seem to like me." Isolation within her family is suggested by her marking "true" to "There are times when nobody at home seems to care about me." So, although there is no overt family conflict expressed by her, by evaluating her response to key individual items (given in the Noteworthy Responses section of the MACI), the hypothesis is strengthened that she is missing some care within her family, in addition to suffering with isolation from peers.

All this is causing her great anxiety and depression. She is a fearful, sad teenager whose development seems blocked by the present dynamics.

Rorschach results (to be reported only briefly here) suggest an evolving major affective disorder disrupting her patterns of thinking. This disruption is of such magnitude that her thinking processes resemble those of persons suffering

MACI™

PERSONALITY CODE:   3**12A*8B2B//-**EB*AD//EE**FF*-//
VALID REPORT

| CATEGORY | | SCORE | | PROFILE OF BR SCORES | | | | | DIAGNOSTIC SCALES |
|---|---|---|---|---|---|---|---|---|---|
| | | RAW | BR | 0 | 60 | 75 | 85 | 115 | |
| MODIFYING INDICES | X | 355 | 58 | | | | | | DISCLOSURE |
| | Y | 8 | 41 | | | | | | DESIRABILITY |
| | Z | 7 | 55 | | | | | | DEBASEMENT |
| PERSONALITY PATTERNS | 1 | 41 | 78 | | | | | | INTROVERSIVE |
| | 2A | 44 | 76 | | | | | | INHIBITED |
| | 2B | 24 | 65 | | | | | | DOLEFUL |
| | 3 | 72 | 92 | | | | | | SUBMISSIVE |
| | 4 | 19 | 31 | | | | | | DRAMATIZING |
| | 5 | 11 | 19 | | | | | | EGOTISTIC |
| | 6A | 6 | 13 | | | | | | UNRULY |
| | 6B | 2 | 4 | | | | | | FORCEFUL |
| | 7 | 53 | 59 | | | | | | CONFORMING |
| | 8A | 19 | 53 | | | | | | OPPOSITIONAL |
| | 8B | 37 | 68 | | | | | | SELF-DEMEANING |
| | 9 | 23 | 57 | | | | | | BORDERLINE TENDENCY |
| EXPRESSED CONCERNS | A | 24 | 68 | | | | | | IDENTITY DIFFUSION |
| | B | 44 | 76 | | | | | | SELF-DEVALUATION |
| | C | 13 | 36 | | | | | | BODY DISAPPROVAL |
| | D | 41 | 66 | | | | | | SEXUAL DISCOMFORT |
| | E | 26 | 82 | | | | | | PEER INSECURITY |
| | F | 9 | 20 | | | | | | SOCIAL INSENSITIVITY |
| | G | 8 | 35 | | | | | | FAMILY DISCORD |
| | H | 10 | 35 | | | | | | CHILDHOOD ABUSE |
| CLINICAL SYNDROMES | AA | 12 | 27 | | | | | | EATING DYSFUNCTIONS |
| | BB | 5 | 11 | | | | | | SUBSTANCE-ABUSE PRONENESS |
| | CC | 10 | 24 | | | | | | DELINQUENT PREDISPOSITION |
| | DD | 6 | 19 | | | | | | IMPULSIVE PROPENSITY |
| | EE | 47 | 92 | | | | | | ANXIOUS FEELINGS |
| | FF | 27 | 83 | | | | | | DEPRESSIVE AFFECT |
| | GG | 8 | 26 | | | | | | SUICIDAL TENDENCY |

Figure 7.2
Millon Adolescent Clinical Inventory: Linda
Copyright © 1994 DICANDRIEN, INC. All rights reserved.
Published and distributed exclusively by National Computer Systems, Inc.,
Minneapolis, MN 55440. Reprinted with permission by NCS.

from schizophrenia. Thus, one question is whether this is an evolving schizophrenic disorder. A second hypothesis is that she has been traumatized in some way not yet known to the assessor (Briere, 1997a, pp. 120–126; Olafson, this volume).

A major underlying affect is that of oppositional anger. Her passivity and flight into fantasy are reflected in the Rorschach, and probably serve to protect her and others from her strong anger. Of course, this defense of withdrawal into fantasy buffers her from much-needed input about her behavior from others. Her self-esteem is, understandably, very poor.

Given her high level of anxiety, psychotherapy and possible psychopharmacologic intervention needs to focus on lowering her anxiety. A question may be raised as to the need for medication to help with her thought processes more directly. Once this is answered, a combination of individual and family therapy needs to begin, together with group therapy later when she is more stable and is more able to venture toward others. The therapist should not be fooled by the fact that Linda's style is to say what she thinks the therapist would like to hear. She may be suffering much more than she can say.

A female therapist for individual work might help strengthen Linda's identity and provide her with her own person apart from the family. The therapist needs to reinforce the strengths and abilities she possesses, while seeking to avoid rewarding her dependency. She may be helped to come to grips with her anger and to understand that she does not always have to appear as an incompetent or "good girl." The individual therapist must take care not to duplicate the dominance-submission pattern likely forming Linda's background. While helping her identify and change negative beliefs about herself, a general client-centered or humanistic orientation is most likely to further this young woman's development of self and general psychological maturation. As trust develops, Linda may be able to communicate about any possible traumatic experience. EMDR could facilitate desensitizing her to any trauma she might have suffered (Shapiro, 1995).

A family therapist could help with her family relationships, being alert to modifying any family rules against expression of anger. In particular, the family therapist should be especially alert not to further dominance-submission patterns in family interaction. Also, the family therapist may perceive that a major attachment figure, Linda's mother, is now not as available, and a major aspect of Linda's anxiety may be a separation anxiety. Has her mother changed from an overly coddling and overprotective relationship with Linda to, from Linda's standpoint, a rejecting one as mother pursues her own newly evolved career goals? If so, family therapy is ideal for working this out. Family sessions may also involve planning for active environmental manipulation to improve Linda's chances at success with acceptance by specialized groups of adolescents. For example, Linda's artistic capabilities can be nurtured in classes and club activities with peers with similar interests and abilities.

As Linda gains psychological strength, group therapy will be an ideal medium to spur rapid health development. Once she is less anxiously tied to her mother, has improved self-esteem, and has some beginning personal achievements, she may be more willing to risk sharing personally with peers, at least in the somewhat controlled environment of group therapy.

Thus, for Linda, the MACI, identifying the core submissive, withdrawn pattern, helps in the immediate planning for therapy and assists in anticipating evolving problems in therapy, as well as identifying her high level of anxiety. The MACI results can be said to provide the framing of the structure of the therapeutic buildings through which Linda may travel.

## DEBBIE

Debbie, 13, is an overtly highly socially successful youngster, in contrast with Linda. Debbie was administered the MACI as part of a family evaluation initiated only because Debbie's older brother, labeled a troubled delinquent by the family, continued to have problems with authorities. Family therapy was recommended and stipulated to include everyone in the family. Her brother was subtly viewed as the "bad" child in the family, she as the "good" child. Debbie was presumed not to have any problems. Originally, there had been resistance on the part of her parents to have Debbie take the MACI; they could see no point in it as the older brother was "the problem." But the parents relented, reinforced by their positive response to the MCMI-III.

In an evaluative interview with the therapist, Debbie was articulate, although hesitant and seemingly deferential in responding to the therapist as an authority. The therapist did not see this as particularly unusual for an early teenager. Debbie brightened up as she described her involvement with her friends. Much of her energy seemed devoted to working out relationships among her friends. This theme of Debbie in the role of harmonizer seemed apparent in her family relationships as well. She appeared to gloss over possible problems. She divulged no personal problems to the experienced female family therapist. Debbie was quite willing to take any actions the therapist suggested, including taking the MACI.

Figure 7.3 provides the MACI profile for Debbie. As indicated, this is a valid profile. Her disclosure level is low (Scale X). She avoids presenting any troublesome emotions and personal difficulties (Scale Z), essentially indicating that she has no problems. At the same time, there is no indication of exaggeration of need to appear socially attractive, morally virtuous, and emotionally well-composed (Scale Y). Note her code: -**-*437//-**EE*-//.

As to personality patterns, there are no indications of serious distinct characterological difficulties. Her highest scores, suggesting personality features,

MACI™

PERSONALITY CODE:   -**-*437//-**-*DGC//-**EE*-//
VALID REPORT

| CATEGORY | | RAW | BR | PROFILE OF BR SCORES 0 / 60 / 75 / 85 / 115 | DIAGNOSTIC SCALES |
|---|---|---|---|---|---|
| MODIFYING INDICES | X | 274 | 37 | | DISCLOSURE |
| | Y | 11 | 60 | | DESIRABILITY |
| | Z | 1 | 15 | | DEBASEMENT |
| PERSONALITY PATTERNS | 1 | 18 | 44 | | INTROVERSIVE |
| | 2A | 24 | 59 | | INHIBITED |
| | 2B | 7 | 21 | | DOLEFUL |
| | 3 | 51 | 64 | | SUBMISSIVE |
| | 4 | 33 | 67 | | DRAMATIZING |
| | 5 | 33 | 47 | | EGOTISTIC |
| | 6A | 15 | 31 | | UNRULY |
| | 6B | 6 | 17 | | FORCEFUL |
| | 7 | 55 | 83 | | CONFORMING |
| | 8A | 14 | 31 | | OPPOSITIONAL |
| | 8B | 20 | 46 | | SELF-DEMEANING |
| | 9 | 4 | 12 | | BORDERLINE TENDENCY |
| EXPRESSED CONCERNS | A | 7 | 29 | | IDENTITY DIFFUSION |
| | B | 19 | 44 | | SELF-DEVALUATION |
| | C | 23 | 71 | | BODY DISAPPROVAL |
| | D | 42 | 74 | | SEXUAL DISCOMFORT |
| | E | 10 | 56 | | PEER INSECURITY |
| | F | 19 | 49 | | SOCIAL INSENSITIVITY |
| | G | 14 | 72 | | FAMILY DISCORD |
| | H | 0 | 9 | | CHILDHOOD ABUSE |
| CLINICAL SYNDROMES | AA | 23 | 58 | | EATING DYSFUNCTIONS |
| | BB | 5 | 11 | | SUBSTANCE-ABUSE PRONENESS |
| | CC | 14 | 34 | | DELINQUENT PREDISPOSITION |
| | DD | 16 | 50 | | IMPULSIVE PROPENSITY |
| | EE | 36 | 84 | | ANXIOUS FEELINGS |
| | FF | 13 | 56 | | DEPRESSIVE AFFECT |
| | GG | 3 | 19 | | SUICIDAL TENDENCY |

Figure 7.3
Millon Adolescent Clinical Inventory: Debbie

Copyright © 1994 DICANDRIEN, INC. All rights reserved.
Published and distributed exclusively by National Computer Systems, Inc.,
Minneapolis, MN 55440. Reprinted with permission by NCS.

are Dramatizing, Submissive, and Conforming. These are probably subtle aspects of her personality. Thus, at a behavioral level, the observer might sense some moderately strong affect focused on engaging others, with some need for reciprocal exchange. Phenomenologically, she attends strongly to external events, and a certain internal lack of development of sense of self might be sensed; but then, she is only 13. Age could also account for some fickleness of moods as well. She would appear to be not unlike many teenagers. She does appear to be the "good" child, perhaps overly interested in others and overly conforming. Her results here are consistent with being a harmonizer in the family, as she is seen by her parents. One of the pioneer family therapists, Virginia Satir (1967, pp. 63–65), pointedly described harmonizers as "placators." Satir indicates that their private sense of self-esteem is very low: Only others really have worth.

Given the Personality Patterns results, it is interesting to consider the Expressed Concerns section. Several areas suggest some mild to moderate difficulties are being expressed: Sexual Discomfort, Body Disapproval, and Family Discord. So, some concern around her physical self is present.

To further clarify this negative note in a thus far positive picture, turning to the Noteworthy Items section of the MACI printout can sometimes be helpful. In this case, the following responses are enlightening. Debbie answered "true" to the following: "Although people tell me I'm thin, I still feel overweight"; "I'm supposed to be thin, but I feel my thighs and backside are much too big"; "I'm afraid that no matter how thin I get, I will start to gain weight if I eat"; "I'm willing to starve myself to be even thinner than I am." All these suggest anorexic tendencies. A bulimic tendency is noted in her "true" response to this item: "Although I go on eating binges, I hate the weight I gain." A hypothesis may then be developed that an evolving eating disorder may be present.

A question may be raised as to why the family and the family therapist interview were not aware of her thoughts about eating and her behavior relative to eating. The reasonable answer is that her personality style as the "good girl" without problems and the harmonizer or placator would tend to preclude this issue being raised or acknowledged interpersonally. Additionally, many times, adolescents, particularly early adolescents, are able to communicate on paper problems that are just too difficult to discuss in person.

Debbie also answers "true" to the statements "It is not unusual to feel lonely and unwanted" and "Others my age never seem to call me to get together." So, despite her seeming success, a hint of a problem is present here.

In a final Noteworthy Response, Debbie responds "true" to "Lately, I feel jumpy and nervous all the time." This suggests some generalized anxiety. In the Clinical Syndromes section, it may be seen that her score on Anxious Feelings is significantly high. Thus, despite her general appearance and her need to appear trouble-free, good, and focused on others, Debbie is having difficulty around her physical sense of self, her sexuality, and her body, as well as her family and even possibly her peers.

In following up with interpreting the inventory findings to Debbie in a one-to-one session, the family therapist can begin her comments by talking about the Expressed Concerns and asking her if she can discuss, at least somewhat, her responses to the Noteworthy Items. The therapist has an opportunity to move, on the adolescent's terms, into sex, body, and family issues that are potentially loaded. For further elaboration with these, Debbie may need some individual therapy. As to her general placating, harmonizing stance in the family, the family therapist may be able to help her define a goal in the forthcoming family therapy to get herself out of that role, at least as performed in a noninsightful, repetitive fashion. Establishing that goal for her would allow her to focus on herself in the family therapy, which would represent a significant shift right from the start of family therapy.

This example of Debbie is one in which a relatively normal MACI can provide a basis for quickly ruling out more serious evolving personality patterns, and also supplying an objective basis for understanding an adolescent's style of coping with his or her world. The specifics of her item responses and her possible problem areas when coupled with identification of her anxious feelings first help the family therapist understand where this youngster stands psychologically. Second, the therapist can plan treatment for her within and outside of the context of family therapy, even though she does not come to the therapist as the identified patient. Third, the MACI structure allows for a naturally developing structure around item and area responses that can allow for this teen to involve herself in a therapeutic process.

## Summary

This chapter has proposed that the MACI be heavily relied on for its measurements of personality patterns of troubled adolescents. Identification of personality patterns provides the overall framework for planning interventions beyond immediate alleviation of symptoms. Because this section is tied to Millon's (1996) theoretical approach, his and related literature provide a rich source of hypotheses to consider in undertaking and conducting therapy with adolescents and their family. In addition, the MACI supplies information regarding specific symptom complexes, such as anxiety and depression. The link to the teenager is that teenager's response to the Expressed Concerns area of the test. Using what the youngster says in this section helps the therapist join with the adolescent and increases the odds that the teen will see what the therapist says as credible.

# CHAPTER 8

# The PCRI, the BASC, and the STAXI:
## Assessing Special Aspects of
## Family Relationships

A number of inventories covering specialized areas of family functioning can be of assistance in understanding families and family relationships. This chapter covers three specific inventories and discusses their usefulness for augmenting the results obtained on standard clinical assessment tools: the Parent-Child Relationship Inventory (PCRI; Gerard, 1994), the Behavior Assessment System for Children (BASC; Reynolds & Kamphaus, 1992), and the State-Trait Anger Expression Inventory (STAXI; Spielberger, 1991). Although many additional inventories and scales have been developed that have been catalogued and summarized elsewhere (Corcoran & Fischer, 1987; Fredman & Sherman, 1987), the three presented in this chapter have been developed through particularly careful psychometric approaches and have clinical utility for augmenting the usefulness of the more widely known standard clinical assessment tools.

As with the tests previously discussed, the reader may wish to skip the descriptions of any of the three tests with which he or she is already familiar.

## CAPSULE SUMMARY OF THE PCRI

The PCRI was authored by Anthony P. Gerard (1994) and published by Western Psychological Services. This relatively new inventory is designed "to assess parent's attitudes toward parenting and toward their children" (p. 1). The PCRI is designed specifically to complement other assessment procedures used in evaluating children and their parents. It does not replace qualitative evaluation, but rather is designed to add quantification to the assessment of the parent-child relationship.

The PCRI is a 78-item self-report inventory that requires only a fourth-grade reading level. To each item the parent answers "strongly agree," "agree," "disagree," or "strongly agree." The marked answers are then compared through the use of scales based on an analysis of responses given by more than 1,100 parents across the United States from whom PCRI data have been collected. Items are appropriate for both mothers and fathers of children from 3 to 15. Separate norms are provided for mothers and fathers. It takes a parent about 15 minutes to fill out the answer sheet.

Several methods of scoring and reporting are available. The PCRI may be hand-scored; a mail-in service is available from its publisher (Western Psychological Services Catalogue, 1998, p. 89); and the publisher also offers a fax service at reasonable cost and a microcomputer disk service.

VALIDITY INDICATORS

If the inventory contains eight or more unmarked or double-marked items, it cannot be validly scored. Providing it can be validly scored, there are two validity indicators, Social Desirability and Inconsistency.

The Social Desirability Scale (SOC) consists of five items that are infrequently endorsed positively. A low score, 9 or less, indicates an intention to portray the parent-child relationship in an overly positive light. The Inconsistency Indicator (INC) comprises 10 pairs of highly correlated items. Each pair is scored when there is at least a two-point difference between the scores. A score of 2 or higher reflects that the client has responded inconsistently, not paid attention, or responded randomly.

PCRI CONTENT SCALES

The PCRI is normed separately for mothers and fathers. Raw scores are converted to normalized standard scores with a mean of 50 and a standard deviation of 10. Thus, about two-thirds of the comparative sample's scores fall between *T* 40 and *T* 60. A score below 40 suggests problems in the given area, with scores below 30 pointing to particularly serious problems. Percentile ranks are also provided. In the sections below, percentile ranks (PR) are given in parentheses following the *T* score reference.

*Parental Support*

This scale measures the degree to which the parent experiences "practical help and emotional support" (Gerard, 1994, p. 9). Low scores indicate the parent is under a burden with little relief. Very low scores suggest serious problems, probably feeling alone, overly burdened, or deprived.

*Satisfaction with Parenting*

This scale "reflects the enjoyment a client receives from being a parent" (Gerard, 1994, p. 10). Scoring low on this scale suggests that a parent is not finding being a parent as satisfying as anticipated. Very low scores indicate actively disliking aspects of parenting, questioning having become a parent, and having considerable discomfort in this area of life.

*Involvement*

This scale points to a parent's tendency "to seek out his or her children and manifest an interest in their activities" (Gerard, 1994, p. 10). A low score reflects less than average interest in a child's activities and not a lot of interest in spending time with a child. With a very low score, the parent may be actively avoiding contact with the child, with possible accompanying guilt and conflict.

*Communication*

This scale represents parents' "awareness of how well they communicate with their children over a variety of situations, including simple conversation" (Gerard, 1994, p. 10). The scale has a relationship with a parent's empathy for children. Low scores reflect difficulty in communication, and very low scores "indicate a serious rupture in the channels of communication. The parent may feel helpless in his or her attempts to converse with the child and to discover the child's needs and expectations" (Gerard, 1994, p. 10).

*Limit Setting*

This scale measures "the effectiveness and character of the parent's discipline techniques" (Gerard, 1994, p. 10). With a low score, a parent may not feel firmly in control and may be concerned about not always setting good limits. A sense of actually being out of control is likely the case with very low scores.

*Autonomy*

This scale reflects "the willingness of the client to promote a child's independence" (Gerard, 1994, p. 10). A low-scoring parent has difficulty accepting signs of independence that are age-appropriate. Serious problems in control of the child and identification with the child are associated with a parent scoring low on this scale; the parent likely has great difficulty with the thought of the child's growing up.

*Role Orientation*

This scale differs from all other scales in that there are no positive or negative poles. Instead, high and low scores represent different approaches to parenting.

At the high end, a parent tends toward more sharing of parental responsibilities and avoidance of behavior based on gender only. By contrast, a low-scoring parent assumes that there are markedly different roles for females and males, generally referring housekeeping tasks and child rearing to females and financial support for the family to males.

## Why Use the PCRI?

The PCRI fits a particular niche for the clinician, that of obtaining an approximate quantification of various aspects of parenting. As noted, the PCRI is not designed to supplant other assessment approaches but, instead, is designed to augment them. Specifically, by providing a normative anchor in the parenting responses of over 1,100 other parents, it provides an objective base on which to ground the qualitative impressions of parenting obtained in interviewing parents and observing parents with their children in consulting room and home settings. This grounded feature makes it particularly useful in evaluating "parent skills and attitudes, child custody arrangements, family interaction, and physical or sexual abuse of children" (Western Psychological Services, 1998, p. 89).

Because the PCRI is a recently developed inventory, it appears to reflect the changing work-family responsibilities of fathers and mothers. The parents in the normative sample showed a generally moderate, positive preference for the egalitarian model of parental responsibility (Gerard, 1994, p. 11). This result fits with the finding that only 7% of families in the United States fit the model of father-provider and stay-at-home mother–child rearer and housekeeper for two children (Philpot, Brooks, Lusterman, & Nutt, 1997, p. 42).

### THE PCRI FOR JULES AND JUDY

A case may help demonstrate the usefulness of the PCRI. Jules, 42, and Judy, 34, differing on their parenting of their daughter, Jenny, age 8, came for help. In an effort to swiftly obtain an understanding of their family situation, several psychological tests were administered, including the PCRI. The scores on that inventory presented an interesting contrast between the parents. *T*-scores and PRs are given in Tables 8.1 and 8.2.

Jules's strengths are his positive satisfaction with parenting and his adequate support with his parenting, coupled with his sufficient involvement and adequate limit-setting. It would appear, however, that he has problems with communication; this is a self-acknowledged area calling for improvement. It would seem also that he has some discomfort about allowing his daughter autonomy

Table 8.1
*Jules's PCRI*

|  | T-Score | Percentile Rank (PR) |
|---|---|---|
| Parental Support | 50 | 50 |
| Satisfaction with Parenting | 59 | 80 |
| Involvement | 50 | 50 |
| Communication | 40 | 20 |
| Limit Setting | 56 | 75 |
| Autonomy | 40 | 22 |
| Role Orientation | 53 | 60 |

appropriate to her age, suggesting that this feature may tend to impede his daughter's development. The area of communication might be helped by providing him some specific teaching in how to communicate with his child. Also, he might be influenced by education about child development and parenting approaches around the issue of independence for his child.

Judy's scores are quite high. She seems to be making a statement. Definite emphasis on discipline and limit-setting appear to be major characteristics. Her score is so high in this area that a hypothesis seems reasonable that she may be overemphasizing discipline and limit-setting. She feels quite emotionally supported in her parenting. She is satisfied with parenting. She is involved more than average, and she portrays herself as communicating adequately. She pushes her child toward autonomous actions that are appropriate for her daughter's age. Judy's role orientation falls halfway between egalitarian and traditional. Based on these inventory results, a further look at Judy's actual limit-setting behavior seems reasonable. A question raised is whether the limit-setting and discipline shades into a punishment-oriented attitude with possible underlying concern for control of the child.

Table 8.2
*Judy's PCRI*

|  | T-Score | Percentile Rank (PR) |
|---|---|---|
| Parental Support | 65 | 94 |
| Satisfaction with Parenting | 66 | 96 |
| Involvement | 57 | 75 |
| Communications | 56 | 74 |
| Limit Setting | 80 | 99+ |
| Autonomy | 59 | 77 |
| Role Orientation | 48 | 40 |

COMPARING JULES'S AND JUDY'S PROFILES

There appears to be a compatibility or role orientation in Jules's and Judy's scores, with both falling in the middle ranges between egalitarian and traditional, suggesting no conflict on this score. An area that does indicate conflict is that of autonomy for their daughter. She pushes and he holds back. As judged by their presentations, she is more communicative with their daughter, and he less. Although Jules appears firm in his discipline, Judy seems extreme, suggesting an area of conflict to be investigated and discussed.

THE PCRI RESULTS COMPARED WITH OTHER CLINICAL FINDINGS

Other tests were consistent for Jules with the hypothesis of continued difficulty in thinking (Rorschach) stemming from an accident involving head injuries a few years prior to the present testing. Indications of depression and dependency were present as well (Rorschach and MCMI-III), not surprising in the face of decreased cognitive efficiency and realistic needs to depend on others. Based on these findings, a careful, structured program was developed so that Jules could learn to parent in a way more compatible with his daughter's needs to make more age-appropriate decisions and actions. By this step and understanding these results, Judy was able to be reassured that her present situational overwhelm (Rorschach) could be lessened, and she did not have to either overprotect her daughter as much or repress her own feelings as much. Thus, although the PCRI consumed only 15 minutes of each parent's time, and minimal scoring time, plus interpreting time for the parents, it fit an important niche in one practical aspect of the task of considering the entirety of the family relationships.

# CAPSULE SUMMARY OF THE BASC

The BASC is a "multidimensional approach to evaluating the behavior and self-perceptions of children aged 4 to 18 years" (Reynolds & Kamphaus, 1992, p. 1). It has its use in a broad clinical battery focused on the personality and behavior of a child or an adolescent in a family and community system. The child 8 or older fills out a self-rating scale. The child's or adolescent's teacher responds to a scale that reflects classroom behavior. Each parent fills out a scale describing his or her offspring. In addition, one parent (sometimes both) responds to a structured developmental history. An additional form is available for recording and classifying directly observed classroom behavior, although this form is not regularly used by the present author.

The results of the BASC reflect a variety of emotional and behavioral disorders that may demonstrate themselves in the classroom setting and/or in the home. The BASC also includes scales that measure adaptive strengths. Its psychometric base is solid. Norms are based on large, representative samples, segmented by age, gender, and clinical status of the child. Reference to a complete and detailed manual facilitates appropriate, knowledgeable use of the BASC.

An outstanding feature is that scales are consistent in purpose and construct whether filled out by the teacher or the parents. Another asset is that the scales include measurement of both psychopathology and strengths. For parents and teachers, there are three sets of scales, one each to cover the preschool age, school-age, and adolescence. The self-report form consists of two levels: child (8–11) and adolescent (12–18).

The teacher form and the parent form each takes 10 to 20 minutes to fill out. The self-report form takes about 30 minutes. An audio version is available. The scales may be scored by hand, but the computer scoring and interpreting printout is strongly recommended; not only does this increase accuracy and save the clinician time, it also calculates a number of useful comparative statistics.

## THE BASC SCALES FOR VALIDITY AND RESPONSE SET

The scales include three indices of validity and response set. The F index measures the extent to which the respondent is excessively negative about the child's behaviors or self-perceptions and emotions. The L index, applicable to the adolescent level, measures a teenager's tendency to present in an overly positive light. The V index is made up of five or six nonsensical or highly implausible statements. With two or more items marked, the form may be invalid.

## THE BASC CONTENT SCALES

The scales and composite indices maintain their construct meanings and scale names across parent and teacher forms. The items and wording for parents and teachers are changed to correspond with a given age grouping for children, either preschool (4–5), school-age (6–11), or adolescent (12–18). The child and adolescent forms maintain the consistency of some construct meanings, but add others.

TEACHER SCALES AND COMPOSITES FOR
THE CHILD (6–11)

> Externalizing Problems (Composite): Aggression, *Hyperactivity*, Conduct
> Problem Scales.
>
> Internalizing Problems (Composite): Anxiety, *Depression*, Somatization
> Scales.
>
> School Problems (Composite): *Attention Problems*, Learning Problems
> Scales.
>
> Other Problems (Composite): *Atypicality*, Withdrawal Scales.
>
> Adaptive Skills (Composite): Adaptability, Leadership, Social Skills,
> Study Skills Scales.
>
> Behavior Symptoms Index (Composite of scales italicized).

TEACHER SCALES AND COMPOSITES FOR THE
PRESCHOOL CHILD (4–5)

These consist of all teacher-rated scales and composites listed for the child 6
to 11, except Conduct Problems, School Problems, Learning Problems, Leadership, and Study Skills.

TEACHER SCALES AND COMPOSITES FOR THE
ADOLESCENT (12–18)

These consist of all scales and composites listed for the teacher-rated child 6
to 11, except Adaptability.

PARENT SCALES AND COMPOSITES FOR THE CHILD (6–11)

These consist of all teacher-rated scales and composites listed for the child 6
to 11, except School Problems and Study Problems.

PARENT SCALES AND COMPOSITES FOR
THE PRESCHOOLER (4–5)

These consist of all teacher-rated scales and composites listed for the preschool child (4–5), except Leadership.

PARENT SCALES AND COMPOSITES FOR THE
ADOLESCENT (12–18)

These consist of all teacher-rated scales and composites listed for the adolescent (12–18), except School Problems and Learning Problems.

SELF-RATING SCALES AND COMPOSITES FOR THE
ADOLESCENT (12–18)

These consist of the composite Clinical Maladjustment, made up of *Anxiety,* *Atypicality,* Locus of Control, *Social Stress,* and Somatization. Also included are the composite of School Maladjustment, comprising Attitude to School, Attitude to Teachers, and Sensation Seeking. In addition, the composite Other Problems is included, consisting of *Depression* and *Sense of Inadequacy.* Finally, these include the composite Personal Adjustment, comprising Relations with Parents, *Interpersonal Relations, Self-Esteem,* and Self-Reliance. Scales in italic make up the Emotional Symptom Index.

## Why Use the BASC?

The BASC provides, in effect, various windows into the personality and behavior of a particular child or adolescent, including the child's self-perception. These consciously derived views have a degree of built-in similarity that permits comparisons among child, parents, and teacher. The BASC covers a broad range of distinctive dimensions appropriately normed against a cross-section of the population. Along with these advantages, the forms are user-friendly in that they require little time. A number of clues may be unearthed that point the way toward broader assessment techniques, or the results may stand alone, serving as an initial screening.

## BASC Case Example

Following her parents divorce, Amy, 10 and a half, was caught between her mother (and stepfather) and her biological father, who had visitation on alternate weekends and a midweek dinner on the nonvisitation weekend. Her mother felt that Amy had marked problems; her father did not. Having joint legal custody, he was able to resist the mother's wish to refer Amy for therapy. He was able to go along with an evaluation, however, out of which could come recommendations for Amy. One of the psychological assessment tools used was the BASC.

Her mother's rating of Amy produced numerous significant scores. By PR on the BASC Clinical Scales, the scores fell as follows: Withdrawal, PR 99; Anxiety, PR 98; Depression, PR 97; Somatization, PR 97; Hyperactivity, PR 95; Aggression, PR 95. Atypicality, at PR 76, was not quite significant. On the Adaptive Scales, the Leadership PR reached 92, but the Adaptability PR was 14. Significant Composite Indices were Internalizing Problems, PR 99; Behavioral Symptom Index, 96; and Externalizing Problems, 94 PR.

The mother indicated several critical items, marking "sometimes" on "(Amy) threatens to hurt others; says 'I want to kill myself'"; "has eye problems"; "says, 'I want to die' or 'I wish I were dead'"; "sleeps with parents." These items are obviously important to follow up in interview with the mother and suggest areas to explore with Amy.

From the mother's scores, a conclusion is that this girl is very upset. The focus may be on general withdrawal characterized by depression, anxiety, and somatization, indicating an internalization of problems. However, it is also evident from the mother's standpoint that externalization is present. Not surprisingly, given these scores, as viewed by the mother at least, Amy has a hard time adapting to circumstances. That the Atypicality score is up at all raises a question of possible psychotic process. Clearly, her mother views Amy as burdened with serious psychological problems, despite having some definite strengths. Talking to her about any treatment proposals would emphasize alleviating her daughter's suffering.

Amy's father, by contrast, has few significant scores in rating Amy. His significant Clinical Scale scores for Amy fall as follows: Withdrawal, PR 85; Attention Problems, 84. As to the Adaptive Scales, he sees her as significantly poor: Adaptability, PR 9; Social Skills, PR 3, and Leadership, PR 5.

On the Composite Indices, the father's score of Externalizing Problems at PR 80 is significant. Adaptive Skills overall rate a PR of 4. Thus, it appears that her father does not see Amy as someone with major overt psychological symptomatology, but as someone who does lack general adaptive, psychologically healthy aspects. In considering any treatment proposals, talking to the father might well emphasize the need for Amy to develop positive social and other skills needed for adaptation.

Critical items on the father's form are sometimes "has toileting accidents"; "sleeps with parents." These may be followed up with father to further understand these responses.

Amy's teacher responds with major concerns on the Clinical Scales of Withdawal, PR 91; Depression, PR 89; and Anxiety, PR 88. She also rates Amy as low in the Adaptive Scales area: Adaptability, PR 14; Social Skills, PR 24; and Leadership, PR 30.

Amy rates herself as relatively average overall in the Clinical Scales area. She does, however, acknowledge some elevated level of Anxiety, but in the average range, PR 78. Some scales are quite low, suggesting no indication of problems.

In the Adaptive Scales area, Amy does indicate that her Self-Esteem is distinctly low, PR 17.

High and low scores by Amy's stepfather fall similarly with Amy's mother. He does, however, view Amy as having fewer Social Skills (PR 20) than does her mother, more in line with the biological father's score.

Although some people might raise the question of whose view is correct, the answer is everyone *and* no one. The assumption is that each person's view of Amy is reflective of their relationship, which is influenced by both parties to the dyad. Amy's teacher may have the most objective view, being least personally connected. Yet even her view does not reflect how Amy is with the other adults in her life or how Amy views herself.

Certain observations can be made that guide the clinical assessment enterprise. Except for her father, everybody, including Amy, sees her as somewhat to highly anxious. Some see her as withdrawn and depressed, and everyone questions some aspect of Amy's adaptive skills. Amy's response indicates low self-esteem; who better than the child to comment on her own self-esteem? Thus, there are a number of hypotheses that can be drawn from BASC results for comparison with other assessment information.

## THE BASC RESULTS COMPARED TO OTHER CLINICAL FINDINGS

Interviews and Rorschach findings identified that Amy has a far less favorable estimate of her own self-value than others her age. The Rorschach pointed to some level of thinking disorder, with unnecessary narrowing of her cognitive focus, distortion of reality perceptions, and distortions during her thinking-through process. Yet, there seemed to be overreliance on thinking things through not in keeping with her young age. Inner resources were fewer than expected, leading to the possibility of being overwhelmed. She appeared to push away feelings and avoided emotional involvement with others. Interviews and Rorschach supported the issue of her rigidity. Thus, the BASC was used as a screening instrument to guide further assessment that proved fruitful. In turn, the discussion of assessment findings was facilitated by returning to the different views of Amy.

## CAPSULE SUMMARY OF THE STAXI

The STAXI (Spielberger, 1991) has a useful and unique place in addressing family situations where anger between the parents is an important feature. It provides an initial assessment of key features of the direction of anger, useful when there are concerns for normal and abnormal expressions of anger as well as the potential contribution of anger to health conditions, including hypertension, coronary heart disease, and cancer.

The STAXI was developed by Charles D. Spielberger (1991), a psychologist expert in this area of test development (and respected by his colleagues, as reflected in his election as president of the American Psychological Association). This inventory fills a particular niche, that of measuring the experience and expression of anger, which has been found to relate directly to health. Measurement of anger is also important in the many situations addressed by clinicians when negative feelings are strong between parents. The obvious situation is that of separation and divorce. There also is a place for use of this inventory when couples are trying to work out their relationship in a positive way for themselves and their children. In addition, the STAXI has been used in studies on the effect of anger on health.

Spielberger (1991) writes:

> State anger is defined as an emotional state marked by subjective feelings that vary in intensity from mild annoyance or irritation to intense fury and rage . . . the intensity of state anger varies as a function of perceived injustice, attack or unfair treatment by others, and frustration resulting from barriers to goal-directed behavior. Trait anger is defined as the disposition to perceive a wide range of situations as annoying or frustrating, and the tendency to respond to such situations with more frequent elevations in state anger. (p. 1)

Spielberger (1991, p. 1) considers anger in terms of three major components. The first component is outward expression of anger toward people or objects (Anger-out). Holding or suppression of anger is the second component (Anger-in). A third component consists of individual differences in the extent to which an individual attempts to control anger expression (Anger Control). Thus, based on this conceptualization, he has developed the following scales:

State Anger (S-Anger): A 10-item scale which measures the intensity of angry feelings at a particular time.

Trait Anger (T-Anger): A 10-item scale which measures individual differences in the disposition to experience anger. The T-Anger scale has two subscales:

Angry Temperament (T-Anger/T): A 4-item T-Anger subscale which measures a general propensity to experience and express anger without a specific provocation.

Angry Reaction (T-Anger/R): A 4-item T-Anger subscale which measures individual differences in the disposition to express anger when criticized or treated unfairly by other individuals.

Anger-in (AX/In): An 8-item anger expression scale which measures the frequency with which angry feelings are held in or suppressed.

Anger-out (AX/Out): An 8-item scale which measures the frequency with which an individual attempts to control the expression of anger.

Anger Control (AX/Con): An 8-item anger expression scale which measures the frequency with which an individual attempts to control the expression of anger.

Anger Expression (AX/EX): A research scale based on the responses to the 24 items of the AX/In, AX/Out, and AX/Con scales which provides a general index of the frequency that anger is expressed, regardless of the direction of expression. (Spielberger, 1991, p. 1).

The STAXI may be administered to those 13 and older with at least a fifth-grade reading level. Clients complete the STAXI in 10 to 15 minutes. Hand-scored and machine-scored test forms are available. With training following instructions in the manual, clerical personnel may administer this inventory. A professional with adequate psychometric knowledge and understanding of the concepts of anger is needed to interpret this test. Results are interpreted by gender. Norms are given for a general adult population, a college population, and an adolescent population. They are also provided for special interest groups, including medical and surgical patients, prison inmates, and military recruits.

As abstracted from the manual, these are the interpretation of high scores (Spielberger, 1991, p. 5):

S-Anger: Relatively intense angry feelings that are likely to be situationally determined.

T-Anger: Angry feelings associated with, ordinarily, feeling that one is treated unfairly.

T-Anger/T: Quick temper and ready expression of angry feelings with minimal provocation.

T-Anger/R: Anger experienced because of high sensitivity to criticism and affronts.

AX/In: Anger frequently experienced, but with a tendency to suppress anger.

AX/Out: Anger frequently experienced that is expressed aggressively.

AX/Con: Anger monitored and overcontrolled, possibly resulting in passivity and depression.

AX/EX: Anger experienced intensely, then suppressed or expressed aggressively, or both.

## Why Use the STAXI?

The STAXI is ordinarily included with other instruments in a battery. Because it usually takes less than 15 minutes, it doesn't add appreciably to the client's test-taking time. By being specifically about anger as a dimension, the results provide a basis for discussion about the role of anger and anger expression in a couple relationship. This is especially useful because a couple coming to therapy to improve their marriage likely has some anger generated within their relationship. If they are being evaluated in connection with a divorce, it is important for the clinician to know how their anger may be handled to work on coparenting effectively.

## STAXI Case Example

Ann, 30, and Dick, 34, a divorced couple, were administered the STAXI in connection with a child custody evaluation. Their two children, a boy 11 and a girl 9, were at issue. They had shared coparenting satisfactorily for two years, with Dick having primary physical custody. Ann had liberal visitation, almost half time. Dick had an offer of a job in a city 500 miles away that he couldn't refuse for the sake of his career and increased income to support the children. He planned to take the children to live with him and fly them regularly to visit Ann. Ann objected. The child custody evaluation ensued. Both parents are living with new partners.

Dick, a mild-mannered, technically oriented man, had STAXI scores within the 40th to 60th percentile range except for T-Anger at PR 70, T-Anger/R at PR 27, and AX/In at PR 34. None of the scores are extreme. The modestly elevated T-Anger suggests some angry feelings; believing that he is being treated unfairly, he appears to process anger in such a way as to not turn it clearly outward or inward. The low scores suggest that he is not sensitive to criticism (T-Anger/R), and he does not frequently experience angry feelings that must be suppressed.

By contrast, Ann has one very high score, AX/OUT, a PR of 98. This indicates that she frequently experiences anger and expresses this anger in aggressive behavior. It turns out that she has a "temper" and is prone to throwing things, as well as having a sharp tongue. These behaviors had contributed significantly to the original breakup of Ann and Dick. Dick had some concern that this behavior may be repeated with the children. Ann had only one other score of even modest importance, T-Ang/R at 70 PR. This suggests some tendency for her to be overly sensitive to criticism and to respond with intense feelings.

Interestingly, Dick's MMPI-2 included a highly significant Overcontrolled Hostility score along with a compulsive style suggested on the MCMI-III. Compulsive personalities often work to contain inner anger from breaking through, and his MCMI-III suggested occasional surges of resentment that break through. Apparently, for the most part, Dick contains his anger and is able to manage it. His Rorschach does not indicate anger as a major element in his personality.

Ann did not score high on the Overcontrolled Hostility score on the MMPI-2. She doesn't restrain her anger. Her MCMI-III results suggest a histrionic style, if not disorder, wherein she may have struggled, not always successfully, at controlling her anger. The Rorschach reflects her laxity at controlling her emotions, and she has a significant level of chronic oppositional hostility (4S).

In interpreting the findings to these former partners, their consciously expressed thoughts about anger as reflected in the STAXI provided an avenue for discussion. The evaluator's broader understanding of the dynamics was held privately as a way to understand the more complex dynamics underlying the responses to the STAXI.

## Summary

This chapter considered three inventories that are ordinarily best used in a battery of tests. The PCRI provides insight into major dimensions of parenting, at least as viewed consciously by the parent. The BASC is an excellent screening tool that covers problem personality dimensions and adaptability as viewed through the eyes of each parent, teacher, and child (8 and older). The STAXI provides a look at one major dimension important in problematic couple relationships—that of anger. All three inventories have an excellent psychometric base, and because of their brevity are cost-effective.

## PART II

# INTEGRATED TEST USAGE
# WITH COUPLES AND FAMILIES

# CHAPTER 9

## Using Inventories with Couples: Selection, Strategic Use, and Feedback

Chapters 2, 3, and 4 provided a basic understanding of the MMPI-2, the MCMI-III, and the 16PF as used with couples. This chapter first briefly compares the usefulness of the inventories in screening for serious psychopathology, an important responsibility of any clinician. Attention is then focused on how to choose which inventory to use with a given couple, and whether to use more than one inventory. The concluding sections address the challenge of feeding back inventory findings to enhance the effectiveness of couple therapy as well as the process of blending the testing results into couple therapy.

## Screening for Individual Psychopathology

One responsibility of the clinician is to be alert to more extreme symptomatology, mood state problems, or marked, serious personality disorders. Identification of more extreme problems may require intrapersonally oriented intervention instead of, or in addition to, couple or family work. Referral for medication evaluation may be needed. In a rare situation, hospitalization may need to be considered.

All three inventories provide some basis for screening individuals for psychopathological indications. With the MMPI-2, clinical scale $T$-scores above 65, especially those 75 and above, point to symptomatic or mood state problems of various sorts, such as depression, paranoia, or manic activity. In addition, many two-point codes above $T$ 65 provide descriptions of problem traits and behaviors because of the identified correlates of many high two-point codes.

The MCMI-III provides screening for symptomatology and problematic mood states similar to the MMPI-2, although with less empirically based breadth than the MMPI-2. However, the MCMI-III includes specific scales parallel with Axis I of the *DSM-IV* (APA, 1994). High scores on Axis I–related Severe Syndromes (Thought Disorder, Major Depression, and Delusional Disorder) are particularly likely to call for individual intervention. When scores are high on

175

Severe Personality Pathology scores (Schizotypal, Borderline, and Paranoid), which parallel Axis II of *DSM-IV*, further individual screening may also be called for. In general, very high scores on any personality disorder, Clinical Personality Patterns, raise a question of possible individual intervention.

Although the 16PF provides measurement primarily of normal personality dimensions, problems in emotional stability are to some extent subject to screening through one scale; also, high anxiety is measured. So, even the 16PF can screen for more extreme individual psychopathology.

## How to Decide Which Inventory to Use with a Couple

Although clinicians may reasonably decide to use a given inventory based on their general understanding of and experience with a specific inventory, making explicit the advantages and disadvantages of the MMPI-2, the MCMI-III, and the 16PF can provide a more reasoned basis for choosing which inventory to use with a particular couple.

The MMPI-2 is a broad-scale measure of psychopathology. Because of the breadth and depth of its database, which references an enormous body of literature, the MMPI-2 is particularly useful as a screening measure for a very wide range of psychological problems. Thus, if clients are drawn from a large, heterogeneous population, a broad socioeconomic range, or a population believed to include in its numbers significantly emotionally disturbed people, the MMPI-2 would be particularly appropriate. One application of this guideline suggesting the MMPI-2 is providing service to patients in a large community mental health center that draws from an impoverished area where people who have difficulty coping on a daily basis and/or people with serious mental illness might be overrepresented. On the negative side is that the MMPI-2 takes typically an hour and a half to complete; patients in crisis may not have the wherewithal to complete an inventory requiring this length of time. And, for marital partners who function quite well in general, the MMPI-2 may not provide much significant information when clinical scores fall in the normal ranges. Additionally, the pathologically oriented language may put off these less symptomatic, "normal" couples.

The 16PF may be the instrument of choice when referrals come from a more highly functioning population within which overt, classical psychopathological patterns are not as frequently found. People functioning at high levels at work and socially are more likely to have their couple interactional problems identified by this instrument. Private counseling centers, for example, in more privileged neighborhoods, are likely to find the 16PF to their liking. Taking slightly less time to complete than the MMPI-2 and having normalized items make the 16PF less off-putting to this population of couples. The availability of a computer program designed specifically for marital couples enhances the usability of this test for the clinician, as well as broadening the interactional hypotheses to be considered as results are discussed with a couple (Institute for Personality and Ability Testing, 1998, p. 17).

The MCMI-III for use with a couple may be the choice for the clinician who wants some screening for serious symptom and mood state problems and at the same time is committed to intervention approaches taking account of personality style or disorder. A clinician/researcher quite helpful in this situation is Retzlaff, who presents his strategic approach using the MCMI-III in his *Tactical Psychotherapy of the Personality Disorders* (1995).

Based on the personality style or disorder of individuals as reflected in the MCMI-III, an interaction picture of styles or disorders in couple relationships can be constructed by the experienced clinician, as was done in Chapter 3. An assumption may be made that a style or disorder manifests itself in particular ways of interaction between the marital partners. With that interaction may come individual symptoms of some sort, such as depression. Sometimes, however, the dysfunctional marital interaction (such as fighting and blaming) staves off the development of symptoms or problem mood states, or at least conscious awareness of individual psychopathology, such as depression. Identification of the interlocking styles or disorders provides a focus for intervening with the marital partners' interactions. Though strong on identifying problem personality styles and/or disorders, the MCMI-III has less applicability to individually well-functioning marital partners, as well as having less applicability to very disturbed individuals.

## Using Two Inventories with a Couple

Inventory results with couples may be thought of as snapshots that catch an aspect of the personality functioning of each partner in a couple relationship. Thus, although, as noted, there are overlaps among the three inventories, each has some unique contributions to make. So, under some circumstances, there is real value in administering more than one inventory. Systematic research exists only on relationships between the MMPI and the MCMI.

MMPI/MMPI-2 PATTERNS CLARIFIED BY MCMI PATTERNS

Research with the MMPI reveals that addition of the MCMI-III to the MMPI-2 helps sort out the meaning of some ambiguous MMPI/ MMPI-2 patterns. Antoni

(1997, pp. 106–123) studied some original MMPI high-point patterns that had internally inconsistent descriptions. High-point patterns on the original MMPI were sorted out by analysis with reference to findings on the original version of the MCMI. Out of a sample of over 3,000 cases, MCMI patterns were reported that clarified the meaning of several frequently found MMPI high-point patterns: 28/82, 24/42, 89/98, and 78/87. Although the research was carried out on earlier versions of these inventories, because of a reasonable degree of consistency between earlier to later versions of the inventories, there are implications for interpreting the MMPI-2 and the MCMI-III.

Patients with the MMPI pattern 2/8, 8/2 (Depression/Schizophrenia) all had an avoidant high-point pattern on the MCMI. However, three different subgroups were identified. One group, in addition to the avoidant high point, had a schizoid high point. This group was described as an *interpersonally acting-in group*. The second avoidant group had a negativistic (passive-aggressive) high point along with the avoidant high point, and was labeled the *emotionally acting-out group*. A third group, avoidant plus dependent, was described as the *emotionally acting-in group*.

A second MMPI pattern, 2/4, 4/2, was studied. Recall that MMPI 2 is Depression and 4 is Psychopathic Deviate. This combination clustered into three subtypes, with one of these having two variants. An *interpersonally acting-out group* was identified, which consisted of an MMPI 24/42 high point characterized by MCMI antisocial spike, antisocial coupled with narcissism, or compulsive narcissistic. These MCMI findings indicate overall that for these 24/42 MMPI people, the core is Scale 4, with Scale 2 up because they have been unable to acquire the psychological reinforcements they need. However, Antoni (1997) indicates that these 2/4, 4/2 MMPI people react to stress with impulsive and outwardly directed actions. Within this group, the MCMI high points in addition to the antisocial peak further individualize the three subgroups.

The second major MMPI 2/4, 4/2 subtype is labeled the *interpersonally acting-in group*. People in this group are usually high in schizoid, dependent, and negativistic MCMI scores. They put themselves down, are withdrawn, and appear overall intrapunative. They are likely to be indifferent to social standards and possess low self-esteem.

Still another MMPI 2/4, 4/2 group has dependent/histrionic or high negativism with either dependent or histrionic scales up. This group is tabbed the *emotionally acting-out group*. They tend to display poorly modulated affect and lability of affect and draw attention to themselves by their emotional acting-out. They may be seen as seeking to regain some lost sense of support.

Each of these groups is defined more elaborately by Antoni (1997). However, even the abbreviated descriptions presented here may make it clear that those classified by the MMPI as 4/2, 2/4 high-point people can be differentiated usefully by using the MCMI.

Individuals with the 8/9, 9/8 high-point profile on the MMPI appear to be a more heterogeneous group than the 2/4, 4/2s when considered from the vantage point of the MCMI. Specifically, three subtypes were developed by Antoni (1997, pp. 117–118): the *interpersonally acting-out group*, the *interpersonally grandiose group*, and the *emotionally acting-out group*.

The interpersonally acting-out group is primarily characterized by elevations on the MCMI antisocial scale. Some in this group also have elevations on narcissism and also sometimes schizoid and compulsive. Generally, the entire group responds to stress by impulsive, outwardly directed, and projected responses. They can be explosive, driven by fear and mistrust, with a need to vindicate past injustices.

The interpersonally grandiose group has primary elevations on narcissism on the MCMI. They are arrogant, disregard social convention, may be charming, but easily act out under stress.

Another group of the 8/9, 9/8 MMPI categorization primarily scores high on the MCMI scales of negativism (passive-aggressive) and dependent. They are labile in emotionality, unpredictable, and intense in expression. This is the emotionally acting-out group.

The last group identified by Antoni (1997) is an MMPI categorization of the 7/8, 8/7 code type. This group consists of diverse groups as identified on the MCMI: the *interpersonally acting-in*, the *emotionally acting-out*, and the *emotionally acting-in group*.

The MCMIs of the interpersonally acting-in group elevate on schizoid and avoidant scales. Thus, they tend to react with indecision, anxiety, and general withdrawal. Many are likely to reach a level of obsessive-compulsive disorder.

Another subgroup of 7/8, 8/7 code type people are more outwardly expressive. These constitute the emotionally acting-out group. They are labile and may alternate between angry defiance and sullen moodiness, according to Antoni (1997, p. 120).

The final subgroup of 7/8, 8/7 people consists of individuals with avoidant and dependent MCMI high points. Antoni (1997) calls these the emotionally acting-in group. They suffer through feelings of loneliness, anxiety, anger, guilt, sadness, and considerable internalized conflict.

Given the relationships found between the MMPI and the MCMI, it is reasonable to assume that similar findings might be uncovered were the MMPI-2 and the MCMI-III researched together. Results of these early studies suggest that when any one of these four MMPI-2 codes (2/8, 8/2; 2/4, 4/2; 8/9, 9/8; 7/8, 8/7) appears, administration of the MCMI-III may well clarify some of the ambiguities and help anticipate problems with the therapeutic process. For example, providing clues pointing to a propensity to act out interpersonally could be helpful for the couple therapist in anticipating one partner's response to stress before therapy adds to an already stressed marriage relationship.

These findings also suggest that the routine use of the MCMI-III with the MMPI-2 when time is available could result in clarifying hypotheses about the couple's functioning, regardless of whether either partner has one of the four identified MMPI-2 high-point codes. The use of these two inventories together with a couple would be feasible if, of course, the clinician has a thorough understanding of each instrument.

Although this discussion, because of the research at hand, has treated the MMPI as the primary inventory indexed by the MCMI, it is not intended that either the MMPI or the MMPI-2 be considered the primary inventory. In fact, a strong theoretical case can be made for the MCMI-III to be primary. The MCMI-III, by virtue of its measurement of personality traits and disorders, provides a more fundamental starting point because these ongoing styles or disorders interacting with the environment of the family (and elsewhere) may breed a dysfunctional couple and family interactional pattern. This pattern may result in problem symptoms or mood states or, on the other hand, may help contain the development of symptoms because of the power of the family system.

Combining the MCMI-III with the 16PF could prove to be an interesting mix. The MCMI-III provides information about personality style or disorder to target in planning intervention strategies and to anticipate what sort of psychological symptoms might develop under increased stress. The MCMI-III could also help screen for immediate symptoms or problem mood states, including screening for such prevalent problems as addictive potential and posttraumatic stress disorder. Results from the 16PF could then be the primary findings on which to base feedback to the couple. No research on this combination of inventories has come to this writer's attention, however.

## Normalizing Test Inferences Preparatory to Feedback

A major recommendation is to *consider normalizing the feedback language to avoid technical psychopathological terms and jargon because these are likely to be misunderstood by the couple.* Because couples frequently are functioning reasonably in life, except in their close relationship, providing them with information in more normal terms will usually encourage their acceptance of test results. In relation to this guideline, the 16PF already has an advantage over the other inventories in that its measurements focus on normal dimensions of personality, and so the language describing the scales sounds more ordinary and "normal." The MMPI-2 and the MCMI-III, on the other hand, are usually interpreted in psychopathological terms because the inventories measure psychopathology. It is possible, however, to reframe MMPI-2 and MCMI-III findings in language that remains accurate but at the same time does not increase the resistance of the couple to the meaning of the inventory results.

NORMALIZING THE MMPI-2

Rodgers (personal communication, 1998) has some suggestions for reframing the MMPI/MMPI-2. He sees MMPI/MMPI-2 clinical scores as reflecting a person's means of coping under stress. High scores may represent desperate attempts at personal management, rather than indications of psychiatric pathology analogous to medical diseases. If Rodgers's reasoning is accepted, a much more charitable attitude toward the meanings of significant MMPI/MMPI-2 scores follows. For example, consider L, called the Lie score.

The name Lie scale sets a negative tone suggesting deceitfulness. Butcher (1990), first author of the MMPI-2, writes:

> Individuals who score high on L appear to be naive and low in psychological mindedness; they tend to be defensive and are characterized by denial and "hysteroid" thinking. They are often rigid in their thinking and adjustment and have a strong need to "put up a good front." (p. 28)

Particularly by using the words "denial," "hysteroid," "rigid," and "put up a good front," this description is suggestive of pathology, unlike Rodgers's (1998) approach, which emphasizes coping effectiveness and ineffectiveness under life stresses. The former language may be interpreted by a client as saying that he or she is somehow bad or sick, as compared with Rodgers's view that the client is coping the best he or she can, although that coping response may present some problems.

As an example of MMPI-2 normalizing, Rodgers (1998) proposes defining L as follows: " L - Lie. An indication that the person does not trust open communication of negative behavior or negative feelings, is doubtful that others would be accepting of behavior that is less than completely rectitudinous and virtuous" (p. 5). Discussing the possible meanings of the L score from the standpoint of coping strategies holds the potential for a therapeutic discussion. The negative connotation of high L, as in the quote from Butcher (1990), is more likely to lead to defensiveness as the client may more easily feel accused.

Although Butcher (1990) pathologies in describing scores such as the L score, he does recognize that an elevated L score may also reflect an individual's coping with a particular circumstance, such as the purpose for which the test is administered. For example, he indicates that people seeking to create a favorable impression, such as in a personnel selection situation or child custody evaluation, are expected to have elevated L scores, as do ministers from certain denominational backgrounds and people from certain subcultural groups (p. 28). Greene (1991, p. 109), who has written a seminal text on the MMPI/MMPI-2, has made similar comments. Thus, among widely accepted experts, there is a useful mix of meanings of MMPI/MMPI-2 clinical scores between those stressing traditional psychopathology connotations and those suggesting coping responses focused on human effectiveness. For the therapist interpreting couple MMPI-2s, Rodgers's (1998) approach, which is focused unambiguously on effectiveness of coping skills, offers a better platform for couple therapy that itself aims at improving the effectiveness of the couple's interaction in the face of life's stresses.

Taking Rodgers's (1998) coping strategy approach and truncating his descriptions, while referring also to Greene (1991) as well as considering the thinking of Kunce and Anderson (1976) and Duckworth and Anderson (1986), listed below are some suggestions for interpreting the MMPI-2 in terms of positive therapeutic issues for the couple. Definitions refer to elevated scores.

L: A need to be self-controlled, presenting consistently in terms of favorable impression, perhaps being overly cautious, even fearful, of admitting or presenting negative behavior or feelings;

F: Needing to stress the severity of distress, which may accurately reflect feelings or a need to overemphasize distress so that others will pay attention;

K: A self-protective approach, presenting a fairly sophisticated, positive picture of oneself;

HS: Somatic preoccupation, possible fears of deficient physiologic integrity, such as with older people, and could result from actual physical illness; valuing maintaining a state of physical well-being more than coping through an intellectual understanding or emotional comfort; a careful attitude;

D: A sad mood, unhappiness with the world, self, or life as one would want it, quite possibly relating to the reason for seeking help; perhaps a self-protective retreat from the world; may be seen as a realistic response to situations;

HY: An overall naïve yet sensitive optimism; at moderately high levels, looking on the bright side of life, coping by looking for more simplistic solutions to problems; under stress, a sick role develops seeking caring, yet still denying psychological problems;

PD: An assertive and social expectation that problems reside with others, and so a fighting stance, often against authority; at moderate levels, fights against perceived worldly injustice; at higher levels, general anger and fighting; under crisis, especially marital, the score may rise;

MF: For males, more culturally, intellectually, esthetically oriented; for females, avoidance of the traditional female role;

PA: Interpersonally sensitive, but with increased elevation may become hypersensitive and hostilely personalize others' actions; helps maintain a naïve belief of the world as a caring place while trying to explain a personal lack of ability to benefit from a positive world, which breeds an inquiring, questioning attitude;

PT: Anxiety of a chronic nature; as a coping strategy, focuses on the future to avoid difficulties; in a way, results from anticipating that the world will be like one's expectations rather than adapting one's expectations to be like the world; anxiety can set in motion organized, thorough responses if not so high that it is disorganizing;

SC: At moderate levels, can be a divergent, imaginative thinker, but can lead at higher levels to isolation, remoteness, and alienation, difficulties in logic and concentration, with a sense of lack of control in a chaotic world such that seeking help is a reflection of motivation to find a way through a very confusing time;

MA: Hyperactive, enthusiastic zest for life, energetic to overactive, coping with a high level of force; when controlled and harnessed, can result in significant productivity; a need to watch that things do not get out of hand;

SI: A withdrawal that may come as a coping strategy maintaining autonomy in the face of interpersonal challenges; if comfortable for a person, this strategy may be okay; otherwise, this shy, introverted style, rather than reflecting independence and self-reliance, may need modification to obtain some positive interpersonal interaction.

## NORMALIZING THE MCMI-III

Theodore Millon (1994a) has developed scale cutoffs and profile interpretations to fit the majority of patients. He writes that the MCMI-III is applicable to those displaying disturbances in the midrange, not for those with marked, manifest, clinical disturbances, for whom this book is not intended (p. 7). He also states that the MCMI-III is not designed for those whose difficulties are essentially normal (p. 7). As was evident in Chapter 3 in this book, the MCMI-III in couple and family work appears to have value not only as a screening tool, but also in providing clues with people who appear to be functioning more normally, but who have interlocking patterns reflective of their personality styles or disorders as measured on the MCMI-III. For this group, it is useful to maintain in a faithful way Millon's descriptions of scale-reflected psychopathology, and also to seek more user-friendly words for interpretation to clients (without denying the pathology). More acceptance and less defensiveness encourage a client or client couple to be more open to working on "problems."

Usually, a couple consists of two adults in a marriage or other close relationship. Sometimes in the course of family work, it is necessary to work with a parent-adolescent dyad, such as mother-daughter or father-son. The language of the personality pattern scales of the MACI (Millon, 1993) provides a basis for developing more normal trait language with which to communicate in these relationships. Adapting some of this language for use with the adult couple can also prove helpful in communicating in a less pejorative way. Below are some suggestions applicable to both adult couples and adult-adolescent dyads for scale descriptors drawn from the *Manual* for the MACI (Millon, 1993) with reference to the *Manual* for the MCMI-III (Millon, 1994a):

Scale 1, Schizoid. Introversive: Distant, quiet, uninvolved, not socially interested, neither appearing to need nor gain much pleasure or pain from relationships with others; should pain arise, coping by separation from others.

Scale 2A, Avoidant. Inhibited: Often socially distant, reflecting a coping strategy to avoid pain in relationships, always being on guard; wanting relationships, unlike the Schizoid; a careful, step-by-step therapeutic approach might help the inhibited out of his or her shell.

Scale 2B, Depressive. Doleful: Sad, unhappy, a long-standing pattern of which the client is somewhat aware; a sense of a generally pessimistic outlook, often from early losses breeding a sense of loss of hope; perhaps understanding this stance and modifying it in therapy can help the couple relationship, if only by the acceptance of both partners that stance is perhaps a given for the depressive, then to move ahead to some satisfactions so that joy can be retrieved to some extent.

Scale 3, Dependent. Submissive: Cooperative persons who form strong attachments, but then let others make decisions for them; positive relationships become exceedingly important.

Scale 4, Histrionic. Dramatic: Colorful, charming, seek stimulation; others are exceedingly important; tending to be demanding and controlling in keeping a relationship.

Scale 5, Narcissistic. Egotistic: Confident and independent-minded; feel sure of superiority in some ways, and often may work hard to demonstrate that they are superior; when things are going well, can often be psychologically together, even with some flexibility; often feel special; tend to expect a spouse to orient life around them.

Scale 6A, Antisocial. Unruly: Independent of social standards; unruly; an "every man for himself" (or "woman for herself") attitude; apt to believe themselves no more exploitive than others, but will readily take advantage of a situation.

Scale 6B, Sadistic. Aggressive: Forceful, tough, fearless competitor; tend to be hard and cold, disdaining any sign of weakness; at higher levels, tend to exploit and dominate others who seem weaker; need for power a major feature.

Scale 7, Compulsive. Conforming: Respectful, prudent, controlled, and perfectionistic; concerned about being law-abiding; at higher levels, organized, controlled cover papers over considerable resentment, even marked anger.

Scale 8A, Passive-Aggressive. Oppositional: Struggle between working for own rewards and the rewards of others; sometimes deferent, sometimes defiant/negativistic; moods change quickly, and anger tends to be expressed indirectly.

Scale 8B, Self-Defeating. Self-demeaning. Sensitive: Obsequious and self-sacrificing; tend to be exploited by others; put themselves down unnecessarily; "shoot themselves in the foot"; own worst enemies.

Interpretation of these 11 basic patterns may be further elaborated by reference to Millon's (1996) recent book and the computer-interpretive printout developed by Millon and colleagues (1994a) covered in Chapter 3.

## Feedback and Discussion of Inventory Results

Following an initial couple session, presenting and discussing the results of psychological testing with each marital partner separately has several important purposes. First, when results are discussed between the clinician and one marital partner in a separate session, presentation of overall test or inventory findings can serve to mirror and consensually validate the individual's sense of self. This engenders a beginning sense of confidence in the results, which forms a basis for subsequently introducing aspects of personality that may run counter to the individual's self-picture. For the individual who experiences losing himself or herself in a relationship, this discussion helps restore personal boundaries and redefine a sense of self. For the person who has a generally shaky, insecure sense of self, this mirroring helps solidify a psychological sense of self, the "who I am" sense.

A second purpose of discussing inventory results is to expand the individual's sense of self beyond easily accepted conceptions, even to those that run contrary to the person's self-picture. Third, looking at the results individually with the clinician and without the presence of the partner provides an environment more open to exploratory discussion, including considering the implications for this particular personality in a relationship. Thus, the entire individual process, when done in a collaborative way with the client, is intended to turn the client's energies in a constructive way on himself or herself.

The intent is to carry this openness and self-questioning into the subsequent couples session.

It is important to understand that the process of feedback includes discussing not only the positive but also the negative features of a personality. Finn and Tonsager (1992), who have demonstrated the effectiveness of feedback of MMPI-2 findings in a controlled study with college students, discuss why people in their study felt better even when negative things about them were brought to light, such as depression, impulsive style, and self-centeredness. They cite as a possible explanation Swann's (1983) self-verification theory. This theory posits that "individuals seek feedback from others that fits their own conceptions of themselves, even if such feedback is negative" (Finn & Tonsager, 1992, p. 284). Although people desire praise, it may be more important that others see them as they see themselves. Finn and Tonsager do not speculate why this is so; it may be that a sense of being known as one knows oneself counters a sense of alienation, being misunderstood and misread by others, and lessens a feeling of isolation. With couples in therapy, whose relationship is disrupted in some fashion by virtue of their presenting for couples therapy, it seems particularly important that the therapist convey, empathetically and supportively but objectively, an understanding of each spouse separately. Test-based feedback provides this opportunity. It provides a basis for connection between the couple therapist and each spouse separately and serves as a basis for the couple sessions to follow. The therapist may subsequently be seen to temporarily enter the couple system, taking charge to make it a triangular system for therapeutic purposes.

In the individual feedback session, the clinician not only uses normative language, as discussed earlier, but also a conscious approach that takes into account the client's personality style (or disorder). For example, in working with a narcissistic style or disorder underlining the attributes and realistic accomplishments (and sidestepping for the moment an overly inflated self-picture) will make it much easier to discuss where some "moderate shifting of behavior" (perhaps major shifting) might serve the client more effectively. The aim here is to build toward a cooperative relationship, not get into a competitive contest, while recognizing the hypersensitivity to any judgments. Supportively catching the self-defeating person in self-depreciatory statements will help achieve some consensual verification of personality style. With the depressive personality, awareness that the client is likely to interpret all comments negatively will alert the clinician to block those automatic expressions by reinforcing reality, which, even in the worst of situations, is unlikely to be all bleak. Knowing the histrionic personality will have little experience with or inclination toward introspection can further the clinician's patience in gently returning regularly to helping the client consider his or her internal processing somewhat, even though feeling compelled to focus on behavior oriented toward others. With the dependent personality's ready acceptance of interpretations by the clinician, the clinician can avoid being seduced into thinking that ideas are being absorbed as well as they might seem to be.

When beginning the feedback session, the recommendation is to restate the purpose of the session within the context of couples therapy. Specifically, it is useful to remind clients of the issues already identified in the intake session, their questions regarding the marital relationship, the dissatisfactions, and so on. It furthers session development to indicate that toward the end of the hour to hour and a half time limit, these issues will be revisited and discussed in light of the consideration of test findings. Making this statement enables the clinician to make the therapeutically important choice of when to begin to actively link the individual test results with the identified issues. Clients are reminded that the first part of the feedback session is to focus on the inventory findings as pertaining to them as individuals. Then, it is useful to talk about inventory and test results never being 100% accurate, and, furthermore, that words the test interpreter uses will at times have a different meaning for the client. It is necessary therefore for the feedback session to be a collaborative one, in which the interpreter will be raising ideas for a mutual discussion to see how the findings fit the client as a specific, unique person, living in a particular relationship with a particular partner. In fact, from now on in the session, the therapist will not be thinking in terms of feedback, but instead will be focusing on presenting ideas for mutual discussion. Feedback suggests that an active professional dispenses information to a passive client; the session must become a mutual exploration to be helpful. This concept is conveyed directly to the client.

In the session, the recommended approach is to identify those symptom and mood state elements with which the client is likely to agree. It may also be possible to identify something of the ongoing personality pattern: personality features, traits, or style (which may or may not reach the level of disorder). In starting with data on which agreement is anticipated, this stage is similar to Finn's (1993) Category I Findings presentation, "which verify clients' usual ways of thinking about themselves and which will be accepted easily in the feedback session" (p. 4). An apparent difference with Finn's Category I is that, as noted above, data indicating conscious experience, such as discouragement and anxiety, are discussed along with the client's usual way of thinking and behaving.

The second level of discussion in the session, Finn's (1993) Category II, attends to elements that describe the usual ways with which the client copes in the world, and then modifies or amplifies them, in Finn's terms. Caution is necessary, however, to avoid attacking or threatening core elements of the personality or self-esteem of the client. The emphasis is on pushing the envelope. It is possible at this stage, when the modification or amplification is accepted, to speculate on what way this expanded self-knowledge might apply to the couple relationship. When looking at the application, it is important to consider both positive and negative implications for the couple relationship. For example, the compulsive person who is careful, thoughtful, and methodical may realize that the original attraction for a vivacious, optimistic (histrionic) partner makes sense, in that the emotional stirring makes the compulsive feel more alive. At the same time, the process of living together on a day-to-day basis means that the perfectionistic, compulsive partner may have great impatience with the scattered, flighty ways of the colorful, social (histrionic) partner in that partner's handling of household finances and organization.

Following Finn's (1993) lead, the third step is to present those findings that are so novel in relation to or so discrepant from the client's self-perception that they are liable to raise opposition, anxiety, and rejection. Many people whose personality styles do not reach the level of personality disorder may be able to discuss, accept, and think through the new ideas and creatively consider how these aspects of personality might be affecting the couple relationship. Those with personality disorders, however, may take in little that is new, or if they appear to, such as with the dependent personality disorder, the taking in is "skin deep," done in service of seeking immediate approval. It may be possible in some cases to present findings that are seemingly strange to the client by introducing them as follows: "This may sound crazy to you, but in all fairness, I need to present to you all the findings. Maybe we can figure out together why the inventory might have come out this way."

The fourth step in inventory interpretation occurs within the couple session that follows the individual test feedback session. The purpose of this session is to use the results in such a way that they further discussion between the partners, encouraging them to look in broader ways at themselves and each other, as well as find confirmation for longer-standing perceptions of their partner. A way to do this is to suggest to the clients, "Please share with each other the most important outcomes from your individual feedback session that you are willing to share with your partner. I will help clarify and further a constructive discussion about what you present, and add to what you say if it seems useful." Asking for any additional remembrances from the feedback sessions can encourage hesitant partners. Clinicians may also state, "If there is anything that I see as really important that either of you have omitted, I will make suggestions to see if you are willing to discuss the omitted information or topic." It may be helpful to encourage each partner to acknowledge what the other says, even if he or she doesn't agree. This tends to ensure that partners have heard accurately what has been said. Then, each partner should respond to the other with his or her reaction to what has been said. The clinician should do considerable summarizing toward the end of this session because new insights easily recede out of consciousness in the face of overwhelming old, destructive behavior patterns. In subsequent sessions, the clinician can refer back to the self-perceptions raised in this first postfeedback session.

## A Strategic Framework for Feedback: Case Example

This section demonstrates a strategic framework for approaching feedback with a couple. The process described here can be used as a model for interpreting any personality inventory administered to a couple, although in this instance, the MCMI-III was chosen. The MCMI-III profiles for Ann and Ron are provided in Figures 9.1 and 9.2.

Ann and Ron, both 42, were highly achieving people who jointly ran their own financially successful personal services business. They came in to discuss problems with their teenage daughter, Shirley. Shirley was 18, had done well in an academically demanding high school, but was now floundering in her first year in community college. The parents observed that Shirley didn't seem to follow through on assignments and appeared to them to have gone on too many trips out of town with friends; this "irresponsibility" cut into her class time, they argued, and lowered her grades. Yet, Shirley hoped to graduate from community college and transfer to a nearby major state university. Shirley kept telling her parents not to worry, she would pull her grades up, but she continued to party. The parents observed to the therapist in the initial interview that they understood they did not have the control over Shirley they had when she was younger, and they knew that they had to trust her. Ron tended to blame Ann (very subtly) for her leniency with Shirley, and Ann blamed Ron (very directly) for his leniency with Shirley. Overall, Ron looked up to Ann, but Ann seemed truly ambivalent in her attitude toward him. They presented themselves as "stuck," even though they had undergone many sessions of couple therapy two years previously with another therapist and despite their availing themselves of many self-help resources throughout their marriage in their quest to better themselves and their relationship. They felt dismayed as their daughter's behavior damaged her chances at college success and, it turned out, tarnished their image as good, effective, and loving parents. Following a breakup with a boyfriend, Shirley had been in therapy for a number of months at the time Ron and Ann came to the present therapist. After the first conjoint interview with the therapist, the parents took the MCMI-III and subsequently met individually with the therapist before having their second conjoint couple session.

Strategically, the therapist had positioned himself as their consultant (Nurse, 1996) when he heard clearly (especially from Ann) that they had come in for help with their parenting. Even discussing the parents' differences did not change her position, which seemed rooted in her personality. She appeared to be somewhat reluctant to look at herself psychologically or at their marriage.

Ron seemed rather global, warm, and willing to go along with Ann's statements about what they needed, expressing that he held Ann in great esteem. He did acknowledge that he slipped into brief angry outbursts at her on rare occasions.

MCMI-III™

MILLON CLINICAL MULTIAXIAL INVENTORY - III
CONFIDENTIAL INFORMATION FOR PROFESSIONAL USE ONLY

Valid Profile

PERSONALITY CODE:   5 4 ** - * 7 + 6A " 1 6B 3 2B 8A 2A 8B ' ' // - ** - * //
SYNDROME CODE:   - ** - * // - ** - * //

| CATEGORY | | SCORE | | PROFILE OF BR SCORES | | | | | DIAGNOSTIC SCALES |
|---|---|---|---|---|---|---|---|---|---|
| | | RAW | BR | 0 | 60 | 75 | 85 | 115 | |
| MODIFYING INDICES | X | 71 | 45 | | | | | | DISCLOSURE |
| | Y | 19 | 89 | | | | | | DESIRABILITY |
| | Z | 2 | 38 | | | | | | DEBASEMENT |
| CLINICAL PERSONALITY PATTERNS | 1 | 3 | 30 | | | | | | SCHIZOID |
| | 2A | 0 | 0 | | | | | | AVOIDANT |
| | 2B | 1 | 7 | | | | | | DEPRESSIVE |
| | 3 | 2 | 13 | | | | | | DEPENDENT |
| | 4 | 23 | 90 | | | | | | HISTRIONIC |
| | 5 | 24 | 115 | | | | | | NARCISSISTIC |
| | 6A | 3 | 36 | | | | | | ANTISOCIAL |
| | 6B | 2 | 24 | | | | | | AGGRESSIVE (SADISTIC) |
| | 7 | 20 | 74 | | | | | | COMPULSIVE |
| | 8A | 1 | 7 | | | | | | PASSIVE-AGGRESSIVE |
| | 8B | 0 | 0 | | | | | | SELF-DEFEATING |
| SEVERE PERSONALITY PATHOLOGY | S | 5 | 61 | | | | | | SCHIZOTYPAL |
| | C | 5 | 38 | | | | | | BORDERLINE |
| | P | 0 | 0 | | | | | | PARANOID |
| CLINICAL SYNDROMES | A | 1 | 12 | | | | | | ANXIETY DISORDER |
| | H | 0 | 0 | | | | | | SOMATOFORM DISORDER |
| | N | 8 | 66 | | | | | | BIPOLAR: MANIC DISORDER |
| | D | 1 | 7 | | | | | | DYSTHYMIC DISORDER |
| | B | 1 | 25 | | | | | | ALCOHOL DEPENDENCE |
| | T | 1 | 25 | | | | | | DRUG DEPENDENCE |
| | R | 3 | 30 | | | | | | POST-TRAUMATIC STRESS |
| SEVERE SYNDROMES | SS | 5 | 43 | | | | | | THOUGHT DISORDER |
| | CC | 1 | 8 | | | | | | MAJOR DEPRESSION |
| | PP | 2 | 60 | | | | | | DELUSIONAL DISORDER |

Figure 9.1
MCMI-III: Ann

Copyright © 1994 DICANDRIEN, INC. All rights reserved.
Published and distributed exclusively by National Computer Systems, Inc.,
Minneapolis, MN 55440. Reprinted with permission by NCS.

**MCMI-III™**

## MILLON CLINICAL MULTIAXIAL INVENTORY - III
### CONFIDENTIAL INFORMATION FOR PROFESSIONAL USE ONLY

Valid Profile

PERSONALITY CODE:   4 ** - * 5 6A 6B + 7 " 3 8A 2B 1 2A 8B ' ' // - ** - * //
SYNDROME CODE:   - ** - * // - ** - * //

| CATEGORY | | SCORE | | PROFILE OF BR SCORES | | | | | DIAGNOSTIC SCALES |
|---|---|---|---|---|---|---|---|---|---|
| | | RAW | BR | 0 | 60 | 75 | 85 | 115 | |
| MODIFYING INDICES | X | 69 | 43 | | | | | | DISCLOSURE |
| | Y | 16 | 74 | | | | | | DESIRABILITY |
| | Z | 1 | 34 | | | | | | DEBASEMENT |
| CLINICAL PERSONALITY PATTERNS | 1 | 0 | 0 | | | | | | SCHIZOID |
| | 2A | 0 | 0 | | | | | | AVOIDANT |
| | 2B | 1 | 20 | | | | | | DEPRESSIVE |
| | 3 | 3 | 30 | | | | | | DEPENDENT |
| | 4 | 24 | 92 | | | | | | HISTRIONIC |
| | 5 | 18 | 73 | | | | | | NARCISSISTIC |
| | 6A | 9 | 67 | | | | | | ANTISOCIAL |
| | 6B | 8 | 61 | | | | | | AGGRESSIVE (SADISTIC) |
| | 7 | 9 | 36 | | | | | | COMPULSIVE |
| | 8A | 3 | 22 | | | | | | PASSIVE-AGGRESSIVE |
| | 8B | 0 | 0 | | | | | | SELF-DEFEATING |
| SEVERE PERSONALITY PATHOLOGY | S | 0 | 0 | | | | | | SCHIZOTYPAL |
| | C | 6 | 60 | | | | | | BORDERLINE |
| | P | 2 | 24 | | | | | | PARANOID |
| CLINICAL SYNDROMES | A | 1 | 20 | | | | | | ANXIETY DISORDER |
| | H | 0 | 0 | | | | | | SOMATOFORM DISORDER |
| | N | 7 | 64 | | | | | | BIPOLAR: MANIC DISORDER |
| | D | 1 | 20 | | | | | | DYSTHYMIC DISORDER |
| | B | 6 | 70 | | | | | | ALCOHOL DEPENDENCE |
| | T | 12 | 73 | | | | | | DRUG DEPENDENCE |
| | R | 1 | 15 | | | | | | POST-TRAUMATIC STRESS |
| SEVERE SYNDROMES | SS | 1 | 15 | | | | | | THOUGHT DISORDER |
| | CC | 0 | 0 | | | | | | MAJOR DEPRESSION |
| | PP | 1 | 25 | | | | | | DELUSIONAL DISORDER |

Figure 9.2
MCMI-III: Ron

Copyright © 1994 DICANDRIEN, INC. All rights reserved.
Published and distributed exclusively by National Computer Systems, Inc.,
Minneapolis, MN 55440. Reprinted with permission by NCS.

In looking at Ann's MCMI-III profile (Figure 9.1), the therapist considered a narcissistic-histrionic personality disorder. But how could a personality disordered person be so successful? In the particular personal services business engaged in by the couple, qualities of self-care and self-focus, coupled with an entrepreneurial spirit to further the business and the interpersonal seduction of repetitive sales seemed to be very consistent with a narcissistic-histrionic disorder. Her disorder or pronounced style involved a superior attitude toward others, not allowing easily for a patient role. This attitude was compatible with the therapist's assumption of consultant role; she could tolerate a consultant or coach to assist her in correcting her temporarily blemished parent image. The therapist would have to be careful not to fall into becoming a satellite to Ann, as her husband appeared to be.

There were no clear symptoms in Ann's profile, although a cyclothymic mood might be a possibility. Thus, unlike some clients, there was no overt anxiety or depression indicated to serve as a lever in sessions. The marked indications of narcissism in the face of apparently fallible parenting was to be a lever in the couple sessions.

In the individual feedback session with Ann, the therapist had an uneasy sense that he was being looked down upon, which was probably true. Having anticipated this possibility, it was easier for him to ignore this attitude, and so he maintained a positive attitude toward her, discussing her success in planning and working in the business and how, when earlier problems had arisen, she had gotten herself and her family into productive therapy. He suggested to her that perhaps she could use some of that same attitude and energy now in solving her family's present problems, and congratulated her on coming for consultation with her husband. He then focused on how much she had needed to pay attention to her self-development. In furthering the business, at times she might not have had the patience to develop the needed empathy for her daughter, Shirley. The therapist also made the suggestion that, having succeeded in so many ways, Ann could perhaps turn her good personal skills on her family in a different way, one that would take into account her daughter's growing individuation. Ann, now, for her own growth, needed to stretch herself so that she would be more aware of what Shirley needed, not simply what Ann thought her daughter needed. It was stressed that both parents needed to do this, so part of Ann's task was to improve working as a parenting team with her husband, while both of them needed to work to understand their daughter's psychological needs. Thus, with the self-other polarity in mind, this self-focused person was encouraged to work toward considering the "other" end of the polarity in a more active fashion with her daughter and her husband. The therapist's having initially laid the groundwork by reviewing her accomplishments made it easier for Ann to consider the therapist's mildly challenging statements that followed.

As shown in Figure 9.2, the therapist was faced with the good possibility that Ron also fit the category of personality disorder. However, in his case, the emphasis was on the histrionic aspects, with the narcissistic features as secondary. The question was raised again: How could a person with a personality disorder be this successful? Ron's role in the personal services business required that he be personable, charming, immediately cheerful, and focused in order to influence and persuade (manipulate) people. In the individual session, this was discussed with Ron. Then the question was raised about what he needed as an individual. Because he spent his days focused on clients and his off hours focused on Ann and his daughter, where was he in the picture? What sort of consideration might he give himself in his own development? Though he might focus some time on his daughter, the therapist suggested that by paying more attention to himself and less to responding as others wanted, he might in the long run give more to his daughter and his wife personally. Even though Ann sometimes liked him orbiting around her, it might be that both of them were becoming a bit tired of the distancing and lack of fulfillment in their relationship. Perhaps he could explore this with her in therapy. Though his affirmative answer reflected in part his need to please the therapist, it set the stage for a therapeutic conflict between pleasing the therapist and pleasing the spouse in the ensuing couple sessions.

The therapist observed that the MCMI-III profile suggested possible drug and/or alcohol dependence. Ron responded that he had been dependent on pain killers for a time after an operation and that he was fearful of the side of him that could become addicted. He indicated that at one point in his life, he had been overly dependent on alcohol but now seldom drank.

In the couple's next session, they were asked to share with each other their main reactions stemming from their individual sessions. Ron told Ann that he wanted to talk with her about some ideas he had about parenting that fit his own need for being a more effective parent. Ann indicated to him that she needed to be more open to others' ideas, including his. She also planned to take a trip with her daughter. Perhaps she might be able to engage her more, not simply push her own conceptions of what might be good for her daughter. They made a contract to work with each other with those goals in mind. It became obvious, too, that a family session with Shirley was needed to let their daughter discuss her own ideas with them. A family consultation session was proposed.

As Ann and Ron began to discuss their planet-satellite/wife-husband relationship, modifying that became a goal in couple sessions with their therapist. They were provided reading material describing a more egalitarian marital relationship, which furthered this discussion.

During the entire process, the personality styles/disorders were not attacked directly, which would have been to no avail, particularly in brief therapy.

Instead these were reinforced as having positive effects. Then it became possible to let the partners relax, consider the negative sides of the styles, and propose other slightly different ways of relating while still feeling positive about how their approaches led to professional/business success. The immediate administration of the MCMI-III led to more quickly focusing on what needed changing minimally for the couple to have a chance at getting what they came for in terms of their family members' development.

## Summary

This chapter presented some of the strengths and weaknesses of the principal inventories—the MMPI-2, the MCMI-III, and the 16PF—for providing screening for serious psychopathology. In addition to this screening function, the chapter discussed choosing which inventory to use to augment the effectiveness of couples therapy and how that choice is based particularly on the nature of the general population served by the couples therapist. Attention was paid to the process of providing both partners with their own inventory results and suggesting ways that these results might be blended into the beginning couple therapeutic process. The chapter concluded with an example of a couple whose personality disorders were reinforced in their business life, thus discouraging the need to modify their personality styles (disorders); yet, the couple decided, through therapy, to work toward modifying their styles (disorders) sufficiently to improve their family relationships.

# CHAPTER 10

## Using Test Batteries with Families: Integration, Strategy, and Interpretation

This chapter presents an approach to the special situation in which a psychological assessment requires administering to each member of a family a full battery of psychological tests. Administering a battery of tests to each family member is appropriate and may be extremely helpful when major family problems are at issue. These instances include, for example, when allegations of child maltreatment or abuse could require potentially drastic child protection actions, or when child custody decisions are in the offing that could affect the lives of all family members and their relationships for years to come. Similarly, when parents are divorcing, even when they are reasonably considerate of each other out of concern for their children, the application of a full battery to all family members can be useful in facilitating effective coparenting that is mindful of the needs of the children.

In working with a large amount of test information about each family member, it is necessary to address some of the crucial influences that may bias the assessment process, including test interpretation. Because certain sources of bias are so important to keep in mind in considering family test information, this chapter begins by examining the problem of assessor bias. An approach toward integrating test data is subsequently presented, followed by a consideration of ways to systematically interrelate data from various family members.

## The Bias Base in Family Assessment

The clinician evaluating a family in depth finds himself or herself subject to a number of influences beyond the task of objectively, carefully generalizing and synthesizing from psychometric and other information. In fact, the idea of being able to always assume an objective or impartial stance in evaluating families is unrealistic, as R. Saunders, Gindes, Bray, Shellenberger, and Nurse (1996, p. 33) have pointed out. More appropriate is a goal of being as thorough as possible while conducting the assessment process with as much awareness as possible of biasing influences. These forces are particularly strong when parents are in conflict. In this instance, the assessing clinician is pulled emotionally first one way and then another by powerful family forces. Getting to know each family member through the individual assessment process places the evaluating clinician in a position to be drawn toward an alliance with each family member as that member is assessed, despite their conflicting views of the family situation. The unwary clinician occasionally can be repulsed by a given family member, but more often is easily swayed by a member into (even unwittingly) viewing the family primarily through the eyes of that one person. This dynamic is similar to the experience of an individual family member's therapist. It is a difficult task to simultaneously empathize sufficiently with a given person's family position in order to understand that position, yet maintain a broader view of the family as a whole. However, the ability to extricate oneself after being momentarily caught in the family maelstrom may provide the assessing clinician an important perspective for comprehending the family system, just as it does for the family therapist who, by being trapped briefly in the family system, thereby learns about it.

In addition to the impact of the family forces on the evaluator during the assessment, several specific forms of bias are considered below: gender bias, the need to rescue, the availability heuristic, and confirmatory bias. By understanding these, a balance may more easily be maintained or regained as the assessor proceeds through the evaluation process. Specific recommendations are presented for minimizing bias during the assessment process.

GENDER BIAS

A core of societal relational changes in the last half of this century accompanied the changing roles of men and women. This occurred as women experienced more choices in how they lead their lives. As a member of the culture, the assessing clinician is likely to have developed significant awareness of his or her assumptions about overt male and female family roles and also, hopefully, to have developed a sense of possible subtler influences, including those seemingly inherent in simply being male or female. Research studies in this area, however, suggest that the assessing clinician may not be as unbiased as he or she might think.

One would expect that having professional experience should further being able to make nonbiased judgments about a family. It probably can sometimes. However, a study reported in the *Journal of Family Psychology* resulted in disconcerting findings (Ivey & Conoley, 1994). A comparison of ratings by 70 naïve observers and 70 experienced family therapists viewing videotapes of actors performing a mother-led and a father-led family interaction indicated that experienced clinicians may be no less vulnerable to gender bias than inexperienced raters: Sex-role stereotypes appeared to influence the ratings in that the male-led family was rated more positively than the female-led family. It is note-worthy that almost two-thirds of the naïve and experienced observers were women. Gender bias appears to be a complicated and subtle issue.

In another study, this one of experienced professionals doing child custody evaluations, male and female evaluators significantly favored their own gender and were highly critical of the opposite gender in rather specific ways (Bradshaw & Hinds, 1997). Both groups tended to view the opposite-gender parent as "weak," and recorded many more negative statements about that parent than they did about the same-gender parent. Female evaluators were especially harsh when they saw fathers as immature, reflected in their seeming isolation, apparent indif-ference, and fears of vulnerability. Male evaluators were particularly critical when they saw mothers as passive, unable to cope with adult life, and easily disorga-nized by stress. The nature of the evaluators' bias is of interest: As a group, eval-uators were most critical of the downside of the cultural values imposed on the opposite gender. In other words, then criticized the downside of the traditional male values of independence and invincibility—isolation, apparent indifference, and fear of vulnerability—and the downside of the traditional female values of cooperation, sinking help through relationships and emphasis on feelings—pas-sivity, inability to cope, and disorganization under emotional stress. These and other findings in this study that suggest general same-gender support lead to questioning whether an evaluator can be significantly free from gender bias, the first bias of concern in this analysis.

How can gender bias be counterbalanced? Issues of potential gender bias by the assessing clinician can sometimes be neutralized by using a consultant of the opposite gender with whom to discuss the experiences of the males and females in the family being assessed. Preferably, the evaluation itself can be conducted by a male-female team. If the latter is the case, it is suggested that the initial inter-view with each parent be done by the same-gender coevaluator. Toward the end of the process, when considerable information has been assembled, each evalua-tor, cautioned by the availability of test information at hand, should interview the opposite-gender parent. This is particularly useful when the issues are about custody and the parents are in significant conflict, viewing their changing fam-ily situation quite differently.

THE NEED TO RESCUE

When an assessing clinician sees parents who are so caught up in their battle that their child is overlooked and/or caught in the fight, that clinician under-standably may be angry at both parents and feel protective toward the child. Should the clinician have any unresolved fantasies about rescuing a child from wicked parents and being a superior parent himself or herself, these fantasies may interfere with a balanced look at the family. Obviously this need to rescue

can present a problem. The clinician should be aware of psychological boundaries in this situation and yet be able to empathize to understand in what way
the child is being hurt in the family conflict. Hopefully, the assessing clinician
will have significant self-understanding, probably promoted by his or her own
psychotherapeutic experiences as well as checked through case conferences with
colleagues.

## THE AVAILABILITY HEURISTIC

Another very important source of bias is labeled the availability heuristic
(Ganellen, 1996, pp. 64–65). With the availability heuristic, clinicians'

> choice among several, equally plausible alternative explanations for a particular
> situation can be influenced by how familiar they are with and how recently they
> have been exposed to the different explanations: the explanation the individual
> has been exposed to most recently is the one most likely to be chosen, presumably
> because it is cognitively more accessible than other, competing explanations.
> (Ganellen, 1996, p. 64, citing Hogarth, 1987)

For example, a clinician who has recently attended a workshop on intergenerational transfer of symptomatology will have that theoretical framework in mind
more readily than other frameworks when he or she next assesses a family.
Awareness of the phenomenon of the availability heuristic will help compensate
for this bias. In addition, an important safeguard is for the assessing clinician to
let some time pass (usually weeks) after exposure to a new framework. This allows for the analysis of data and report writing to be revisited after the glow from
the exciting stimulus of a workshop or training process has worn off and the new
knowledge has settled into the context of the clinician's overall approach. In
these days of increasing mandatory continuing education requirements for reli-
censure, watching for this bias takes on even more importance.

## CONFIRMATORY BIAS

In psychological assessment, a particularly insidious and damaging form of bias
is labeled confirmatory bias (Ganellen, 1996, pp. 60–62). The best and most experienced assessment clinicians can inadvertently have otherwise logical trails of
thinking consistently slanted by confirmatory bias. Confirmatory bias occurs
when an assessor (or other clinician) makes an initial judgment prematurely and
this initial judgment influences the acceptance or rejection (or minimizing) of
data during the information gathering process. This bias can lead to dismissing
out of hand evidence that would contradict the initial judgment. For instance,

having early reached a decision that child sexual abuse is likely to have occurred could sensitize the clinician to those pieces of information consistent with this hypothesis, encouraging the belief that they confirm the hypothesis, and may incline the clinician to make light of or ignore information inconsistent with the hypothesis of child abuse.

A methodology of data collection that keeps open various hypotheses and their related lines of thinking can help to avoid the problems inherent in confirmatory bias. One such methodology will be discussed subsequently in this chapter.

## Integrating a Family Member's Test Results

Before contrasting and comparing family members' test findings, it is necessary to look at each family member's test results by themselves. One useful way to begin the intertest analysis for an individual is adopted from an approach by Finn (1996), who has developed a methodology for feeding back to clients their results on the MMPI/MMPI-2 and the Rorschach.

### COMPARING THE MMPI/MMPI-2 AND THE RORSCHACH

The MMPI/MMPI-2 consists of cognitive, digital, structured tasks drawing specifically on conscious awareness, as described in Chapter 2. This inventory is interpersonally impartial in that the stimulus material is the written (or taped) word. It lends itself to a self-presentation inclined toward either a positive, negative, or more neutral, objective appearance. The pilot who wants to return to flying after treatment for alcoholism (Butcher, Morfitt, & Rouse, 1997) or the parent seeking child custody in a divorce (Bathurst, Gottfried, & Gottfried, 1997) are both inclined to underreport psychological symptoms while putting their best foot forward. By contrast, the person seeking help for personal problems may color his or her responses negatively, perhaps overreporting in hopes that this approach may elicit the needed help (Greene, 1991, p. 116).

By contrast, the Rorschach presents stimuli in an interpersonal context; stimuli may be unstructured or semistructured. Some people are made anxious by the need to respond to the ambiguity of the inkblots, and there is a tendency to respond affectively, particularly to shadings and colors.

Thus, the possibility exists, so Finn (1996) suggests, to initially divide the overall test results by whether or not they present a high degree of psychological disturbance as revealed on the MMPI/MMPI-2 profile and on the structural summary of the Rorschach. This results in four possibilities: high disturbance on the MMPI/MMPI-2 and Rorschach; low disturbance on the MMPI/MMPI-2 and high disturbance on Rorschach; high disturbance on the MMPI/MMPI-2 and low disturbance on the Rorschach; and low disturbance on both the MMPI/MMPI-2 and the Rorschach.

Finn (1996) proposes different interpretations of the four categories, which are expanded here. These are subsequently modified by analysis of the MCMI-III by the present author, as described below. As to the first category, when disturbance is present on both the MMPI/MMPI-2 and the Rorschach, most probably the client is aware of difficulties in coping on a day-to-day basis and ordinarily has a history confirming that difficulty.

A more complex situation exists when the MMPI/MMPI-2 clinical scales fall within the normal ranges while the Rorschach shows significant disturbance. Normal MMPI/MMPI-2 findings suggest a conscious lack of awareness of underlying difficulties. Or, if the client has something to gain by appearing "normal," these scores may simply mean underreporting. An awareness of the possible uses of the tests as viewed by the client should indicate which of the two possibilities are more likely. If there appears to be no gain for underreporting the results, it is likely that psychological disturbance appears under stressful, emotionally arousing, interpersonal situations provoking a momentary regression, despite ordinarily maintaining an adequate adjustment in familiar surroundings that can be handled by intellectualization.

When the disturbance is high on the MMPI/MMPI-2 and low on the Rorschach, Finn (1996) offers two possible interpretations: The client may be overreporting on the MMPI/MMPI-2, which reflects malingering or, alternatively, a "cry for help." This assumes an adequate Rorschach has been obtained. On the other hand, if the Rorschach is defensive, constricted, and generally shut down, it may be the client can respond accurately on the impersonal inventory while needing to be protective in the interpersonal, emotionally arousing context of the Rorschach; thus, MMPI/MMPI-2 high scores may not represent overreporting, particularly if the situation involves no anticipated gain for expressing psychopathology.

The final category, low disturbance on both the MMPI/MMPI-2 and the Rorschach, is not usually found clinically, except occasionally in marital and family evaluations, but may be seen in research or employment screening. Both partners may have little in the way of psychological disturbance, yet they may need to enhance their relationship. Or they may be so ill-matched, perhaps even through positive development on both their parts, that they need to find a successful way to relate, coexist, or divorce. Sometimes, their couple pathology is such that they are trapped in unsatisfying roles, but their problematic interaction inhibits the development of psychopathology on one or both partners' parts. Interlocking personality styles or even disorders may be more evident on the MCMI-III, to be discussed below, which hold them "neurotically together," but the marked styles or even disorder may not be reflected in psychological disturbance on the MMPI/MMPI-2 or Rorschach. And, of course, one partner may show low disturbance on the MMPI-2 coupled with low disturbance on the Rorschach that may reflect a well-functioning person. However, if the Rorschach indicates low disturbance but features a relatively low (but not invalidly low) number of responses, high L, and low EA, this may reflect either a protective pattern specific to the testing situation itself or it may indicate a general constricted, shut down pattern in life. Interview information, history, and feedback from collateral sources of information may be helpful in sorting this out.

## THE MCMI-III AND THE MMPI/MMPI-2 AND RORSCHACH FOUR CATEGORIES

The MCMI-III shares characteristics of the MMPI/MMPI-2 in that it is digital, draws on conscious awareness, and is impersonal in administration. The MCMI-III is different in that it is designed to maximize its concordance with both its base in personality theory and the official diagnostic schema, the *DSM-IV* (Millon, 1994a). As noted in Chapter 3 of this book, both its measurement of specific clinical syndromes and personality patterns closely parallel Axis I and Axis II, respectively, of the *DSM-IV*. In the first overall look at disturbance as revealed on the MMPI/MMPI-2, it may be useful to factor in reasoning based on the MCMI-III personality pattern results.

Personality pattern score elevation can provide a guide to the overall feature, trait, style, or disorder of a given client to be considered in relation to which of the four MMPI/MMPI-2 categories best fit a client. Of particular importance is that, when the data of the MMPI/MMPI-2 and Rorschach diverge, a cursory consideration of the MCMI-III may help further clarify the seeming divergence. The narcissistic personality disorder and the dependent personality pattern scales are examples of clarification. The narcissistic person may have great difficulty describing himself or herself in other than self-aggrandizing terms consciously on the MMPI/MMPI-2, while minimizing awareness of psychological problems. In contrast to the underreporting on this inventory, the Rorschach may pick up considerable psychological disturbance. The identification of a dependent personality disorder may indicate a propensity to overreport symptoms on the MMPI/MMPI-2 to establish a relationship. The anticipation of the dependent personality may be that appearing needy is necessary to be cared for and therefore loved. Yet, the Rorschach may indicate relatively little disturbance.

## DETAILED ANALYSES AND CATEGORIZATION OF TEST RESULTS

Having considered the individual client's overall pattern of response to the MMPI/MMPI-2, Rorschach, and the MCMI-III, the thoroughness that continues to be needed throughout the test interpretive process may be furthered by a careful, methodical approach aimed at producing a balanced, detailed analysis. A critical feature for ensuring a methodical, thorough approach is for *the detailed results of each test or inventory to first be interpreted separately* without regard for any other information. These pieces of information can be organized according to a common set of categories, which pushes the clinician/assessor to create a process that structures salient and relevant data. This tends to work against bias and against overlooking or downplaying important information whose significance may not be readily apparent.

One set of categories is that proposed by Beutler and Berren (1995, Chapter 2) in their volume *Integrative Assessment of Adult Personality*. They propose the following categories: approach and validity/reliability, cognitive functioning and ideation, affect/mood/emotional control, conflict areas, intra- and interpersonal cuing strategies, diagnostic impression, and treatment recommendations. Another author, Ganellen (1996b), indicating a slightly different set of categories, states that psychological evaluations ordinarily include "an assessment of profile validity, current symptomatology, interpersonal relationships, self-concept, defenses and dynamics" (p. 45).

A set of categories that draws partially on the recommendations of Beutler and Berren (1995), Ganellen (1996b), and Finn (1996) is proposed: approach and validity/reliability, disturbance overall, situationally related psychological symptoms and mood state problems, ongoing personality feature/trait/style/disorder, self-concept, defenses, interpersonal relationships, and special features. Special features include anger and its control, parenting characteristics, and beliefs about one's own children.

When this approach is followed, the assessor/clinician's search is for solid information with each procedure for each category, as opposed to a potentially bias-inducing process of leading from hypotheses to the data. Only when all categories for all procedures have been summarized should careful and complete cross-checks be undertaken. Then, when hypotheses begin to be shaped, they will benefit from the data-informed, rigorous process described here, and be less susceptible to overinfluence from theory and the sorts of bias described above. When the test reports are prepared for comparison and theorizing about family relationships, the ultimate result will be more grounded and less likely to be biased overall.

## Integrating Results from the Rorschach with the Inventories

Because some relationships between the MMPI and the MCMI were already covered in the previous chapter, only relationships between the Rorschach and the MMPI-2 and the Rorschach and MCMI-III will be approached here. Remarkably, only a small number of studies have formally studied the ways the MMPI/MMPI-2 and the Rorschach interact, despite the huge number of separate publications on these two tests. Because the MCMI-III has only been developed over the last 25 years, it is not surprising that few studies have investigated its relationship with the Rorschach.

Systematic integration of the MMPI/MMPI-2 with the Rorschach was addressed in a series of articles in the *Journal of Personality Assessment* in 1996. In a major volume, Ganellen (1996b) explored issues of integrating the MMPI/MMPI-2 with the Rorschach, in which Ganellen provided several useful summaries of test interrelationships (pp. 48–53). The tables cover mood states, psychotic and paranoid disorders, self-evaluations, coping and defense mechanisms, plus, particularly important for the scope of this book, interpersonal functioning. Interpersonal functioning as measured by each test is broken down into four areas: rebelliousness/conflict with authority, social discomfort/avoidance, dependence/passivity, and interpersonal manipulation/exploitation. Scales and indices related to the four areas are presented below:

*Rebelliousness/Conflict with Authority.* See MMPI-2 Scale 4; 4/9, 9/4; ASP (Antisocial Personality); Pd2 (Authority Conflict); Ma1 (Amorality); MAC-R; and CYN (Cynicism). For the Rorschach, see S > 2; Fr + rF > 0; a:p > 2:1; Egocentricity ratio > .45; and PER.2.

*Social Discomfort/Avoidance.* See MMPI-2 Scale 0; Scale 7; SOD (Social Discomfort); LSE (Low Self-Esteem); Hy1 (Denial of Social Anxiety)-low; Pd3 (Social Imperturbability)-low; Si1 (Shyness/Self-Consciousness); Si1 (Social Avoidance); and Ma3 (Imperturbability)-low. For the Rorschach, see FT + TF + T = 0; COP = < 1; Isolate cluster > .25; HVI positive; CDI = > 4; H < (H) + Hd + (Hd).

*Dependence/Passivity.* See the MMPI-2 Scale 3; Scale 4-low; Scale 5 (males high, females low); Hy2 (Need for Affection); Ma4 (Ego Inflation)-low; S/3 (Self/Other Alienation); LSE (Low Self Esteem); Do (Dominance)-low. For the Rorschach, see p > a + 1; Mp > Ma; Food > 0; FT + TF + T > 1; Populars > 8.

*Interpersonal Manipulation/Exploitation.* See MMPI-2 Scale 4, Scale 9; ASP (Antisocial Practices); Pa3 (Naivete)-low, Ma1 (amorality); Ma4 (Ego Inflation). For the Rorschach, Fr + rF > 0; Egocentricity index > .45; AG = > 2 *and* COP = < 1; H < (H) + Hd + (Hd).

Listings in the four areas can serve as checkpoints to avoid overlooking any major variables that might pertain to a particular broad psychological descriptive category. The reader is cautioned that, although scales on these tests and the MCMI-III may carry similar labels, scales may measure different aspects of an overall concept. The concept of depression is one example. Despite their overlap, the following depression scales all have slightly to distinctively different meanings: MCMI-III of Major Depression, Depressive Personality Pattern, and Dysthymia, plus on the MMPI-2 Scale 2, Depression, four of the Harris-Lingoe Depression subscales and the DEP (Depression), and, finally the Rorschach's DEPI (Depression) index.

A fair generalization, following the observations in the above paragraph, is that *scales carrying the same name more likely than not represent somewhat different aspects of a complex, dynamic concept.* This statement emphasizes that to have accurate understanding of test results, which is required for studying their interrelationships, *the clinician/assessor must have solid knowledge of the actual descriptions of the scales and their scientific basis.* It should not be surprising that people will score variably on scales that carry the same name, and that this thorough understanding of the basis of the scales will provide the basis for understanding the seeming discrepancy among the scales and will result in writeups that are more precise in their descriptions of individuals.

To illustrate some of the principles, recommendations, and suggestions presented, the case of one difficult family is presented.

## Case Example

Jack, 31, having earned an Associate of Arts degree, works in a subengineering, technical position. His wife, Jill, age 30, has one year of college and works in a clerical managing position. They have a daughter, age 9, named Mary. The couple initiated a divorce, after arguing regularly for several years. Unfortunately, Mary is sometimes a witness to the arguments. Her teacher reports that she is not working up to her intellectual potential and does not relate well to her classmates. As the divorce has dragged on, each partner has begun a new live-in relationship.

Each family member took a full battery of tests as part of a child custody evaluation. Information was gathered from a number of sources, including their new partners, interviews, home visits, discussions with collaterals, letters, legal documents, and data from other sources; the case as presented here will focus on the test results of mother, father, and daughter and their probable interrelationships and usage. The intent is to show a pattern of how the test results may be processed and utilized. After surveying the MMPI-2 profile and the Rorschach structural summary to discern a pattern of degree of overall disturbance, then surveying the MCMI-III, each person's battery results are assembled first by categories of information for each test. Then, each category is summarized separately, and a brief summary report is presented. After the reports are presented, probable family interaction patterns are discussed (see the chapters covering specific tests for references used in checking the inferences below). The category approach is adapted primarily from *Integrative Assessment of Adult Personality* (Beutler & Berren, 1995), with reference to Ganellen (1996b) and Finn (1996).


JACK

Following Finn (1996), the MMPI-2 and the Rorschach results for Jack suggest that his is a test pattern of low disturbance level on the MMPI-2 and the Rorschach. The Rorschach's high L, low EA, and relatively low R suggests a constricted, shut-down person, either in life in general or specifically in responding to the testing situation. His MCMI-III profile indicates little if any disturbance and is consistent with an overall controlled, organized, possibly constricted person.

*Jack's MMPI-2 (Figures 10.1 and 10.2)*

Approach (validity/reliability): He responded with considerable defensiveness. He is attempting to present himself very favorably. He is likely to view the world in extremes. Issues are right and wrong, good and bad, with little or no gray in between. With his denying and avoiding unacceptable feelings, he probably has restricted insight into his own motivations.

Disturbance level: On this test, the overall indication in one of nondisturbance, as noted above. Given that he is in the middle of a divorce, this is an unusual finding.

Situational reactions (psychological symptoms and mood state problems): He may be holding back his anger, however, only to express it periodically, but rarely, when the stress becomes too great.

Personality feature/trait/style/disorder: He is probably mildly histrionic at a level of personality feature, but not to a level of trait or disorder.

Self concept: There are no indications of faulty self-concept.

Defenses: These probably include some mild focus on denial, suppression, and repression.

Interpersonal relationships: He is neither socially isolated nor withdrawn. He probably meets well and talks well with other people. He is relatively at ease and not overly anxious.

*Jack's MCMI-III (Figure 10.3)*

Approach (validity/reliability): On this inventory, he carefully avoids much self-disclosure. He may be naturally protective in this evaluative situation; on the other hand, he may lack psychological-mindedness.

Disturbance level: Overall, as noted above, this is a nondistressed psychological picture, which is unusual, given that this is a divorce situation.

Situational reactions (psychological symptoms and mood state problems): Jack admits to being only mildly stressed at the present time.

**MMPI-2**

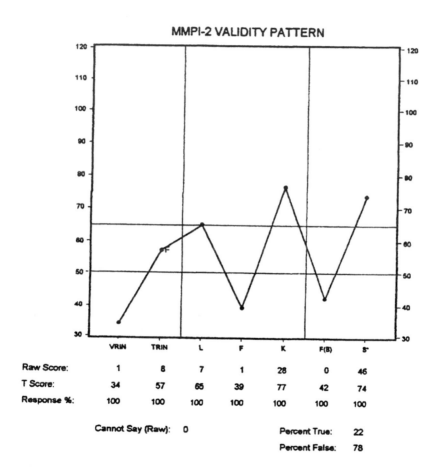

**MMPI-2 VALIDITY PATTERN**

| | VRIN | TRIN | L | F | K | F(B) | S* |
|---|---|---|---|---|---|---|---|
| Raw Score: | 1 | 8 | 7 | 1 | 28 | 0 | 46 |
| T Score: | 34 | 57 | 65 | 39 | 77 | 42 | 74 |
| Response %: | 100 | 100 | 100 | 100 | 100 | 100 | 100 |

Cannot Say (Raw):  0          Percent True:   22

Percent False:  78

*Experimental

Figure 10.1
MMPI-2 Validity Pattern: Jack

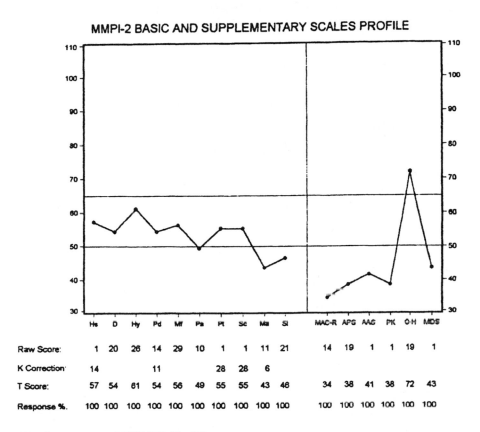

Figure 10.2
MMPI-2 Profile: Jack

Personality features/traits/style/disorder: Results suggest a well-functioning individual with no major personality disturbances. It is likely important to him that he appear composed, virtuous, and conventional in behavior. He tends toward easy conformity and suitability and downplays emotional problems, tending to avoid, deny, or suppress feelings. There may be some times when he experiences oppositional feelings to others and perhaps a cynical attitude. He fears that if he were to express some feelings he might lose his emotional control. Moderate surges of resentment may at times break through his

MCMI-III™

---

## MILLON CLINICAL MULTIAXIAL INVENTORY - III
### CONFIDENTIAL INFORMATION FOR PROFESSIONAL USE ONLY

Valid Profile

PERSONALITY CODE:   - ** - * 7 4 5 + 2A " 1 6A 2B 3 6B 8A 8B ' ' // - ** - * //
SYNDROME CODE:   - ** - * // - ** - * //

| CATEGORY | | SCORE | | PROFILE OF BR SCORES | | | | | DIAGNOSTIC SCALES |
|---|---|---|---|---|---|---|---|---|---|
| | | RAW | BR | 0 | 60 | 75 | 85 | 115 | |
| MODIFYING INDICES | X | 38 | 0 | | | | | | DISCLOSURE |
| | Y | 14 | 65 | | | | | | DESIRABILITY |
| | Z | 0 | 0 | | | | | | DEBASEMENT |
| CLINICAL PERSONALITY PATTERNS | 1 | 1 | 30 | | | | | | SCHIZOID |
| | 2A | 2 | 42 | | | | | | AVOIDANT |
| | 2B | 0 | 18 | | | | | | DEPRESSIVE |
| | 3 | 0 | 18 | | | | | | DEPENDENT |
| | 4 | 14 | 64 | | | | | | HISTRIONIC |
| | 5 | 10 | 64 | | | | | | NARCISSISTIC |
| | 6A | 1 | 26 | | | | | | ANTISOCIAL |
| | 6B | 0 | 18 | | | | | | AGGRESSIVE (SADISTIC) |
| | 7 | 13 | 72 | | | | | | COMPULSIVE |
| | 8A | 0 | 18 | | | | | | PASSIVE-AGGRESSIVE |
| | 8B | 0 | 18 | | | | | | SELF-DEFEATING |
| SEVERE PERSONALITY PATHOLOGY | S | 0 | 10 | | | | | | SCHIZOTYPAL |
| | C | 0 | 10 | | | | | | BORDERLINE |
| | P | 0 | 10 | | | | | | PARANOID |
| CLINICAL SYNDROMES | A | 0 | 10 | | | | | | ANXIETY DISORDER |
| | H | 0 | 10 | | | | | | SOMATOFORM DISORDER |
| | N | 0 | 10 | | | | | | BIPOLAR: MANIC DISORDER |
| | D | 0 | 10 | | | | | | DYSTHYMIC DISORDER |
| | B | 0 | 10 | | | | | | ALCOHOL DEPENDENCE |
| | T | 0 | 10 | | | | | | DRUG DEPENDENCE |
| | R | 0 | 10 | | | | | | POST-TRAUMATIC STRESS |
| SEVERE SYNDROMES | SS | 0 | 10 | | | | | | THOUGHT DISORDER |
| | CC | 0 | 10 | | | | | | MAJOR DEPRESSION |
| | PP | 0 | 10 | | | | | | DELUSIONAL DISORDER |

Figure 10.3
MCMI-III: Jack

Copyright © 1994 DICANDRIEN, INC. All rights reserved.
Published and distributed exclusively by National Computer Systems, Inc.,
Minneapolis, MN 55440. Reprinted with permission by NCS.

surface composure. It seems that conformity and adherence to the rules and values in life are important to him.

Self concept: There are no suggestions of a negative self-concept.

Defenses: These appear to be focused on pushing feelings away and doing what he considers to be the right behavior in situations. Defenses fall within normal ranges.

Interpersonal relationships: He likely relates to others in an easy way but still retains restraint on expression of his own feelings.

*Rorschach (Figure 10.4)*

Approach (validity/reliability): There is an adequate, although small number of responses, so the Rorschach is deemed valid. At the same time, there is a restriction of focus and a lack of availability of affect, suggesting some deficiency of depth and lack of richness in his Rorschach record.

Disturbance overall: This record is not overtly markedly disturbed in the sense of subjective distress, nor are there indications of depression, discouragement, or stress.

Situational reaction: He has a general tendency to narrow and simplify stimulus experiences. Thus, he does not react much to ideational stimuli. When he reacts, he may push feelings away even before they come into consciousness. He does not have more than the average amount of anger or hostility.

Personality features/traits/styles/disorder: He seems to be investing a great deal of personal resource reservoir to significantly contain emotions. There are indications that he is somewhat vulnerable to being overwhelmed by his feelings. At those times, he may not be very stringent about modulation of his emotional discharges. Some of his feelings just now are intensely negative, probably very painful emotions. These may spill over, being feelings that can disrupt his emotional functioning at present. This process suggests possible histrionic features, alternately placing a cap on his feelings, then periodically but infrequently expressing them forcefully.

Self-concept: He apparently has a reasonable balance between focus on himself and concern for others. He appears to be neither more nor less concerned with himself than most other people. There are, however, indications that his mental process includes some rumination about personality features that he perceives to be undesirable. This sort of thinking often leads to a sense of dissatisfaction with the self and promotes depression. Some of this rumination may relate to feelings of guilt, shame, or remorse.

======================= STRUCTURAL SUMMARY =======================

| LOCATION FEATURES | DETERMINANTS | | CONTENTS | S-CONSTELLATION |
|---|---|---|---|---|

LOCATION FEATURES · DETERMINANTS (BLENDS / SINGLE) · CONTENTS · S-CONSTELLATION

```
LOCATION              DETERMINANTS            CONTENTS        S-CONSTELLATION
FEATURES        BLENDS          SINGLE                        NO..FV+VF+V+FD>2
                                          H   = 4, 0          NO..Col-Shd Bl>0
Zf    = 10      FC'.FV        M   = 3     (H) = 0, 0          NO..Ego<.31,>.44
ZSum  = 30.0    M.FD          FM  = 2     Hd  = 0, 0          NO..MOR > 3
ZEst  = 31.0                  m   = 0     (Hd)= 0, 0          NO..Zd > +- 3.5
                              FC  = 0     Hx  = 0, 0          YES..es > EA
W  =  9                       CF  = 0     A   = 6, 0          NO..CF+C > FC
 (Wv = 0)                     C   = 0     (A) = 0, 0          YES..X+% < .70
D  =  7                       Cn  = 0     Ad  = 2, 0          NO..S > 3
Dd =  1                       FC'= 0      (Ad)= 0, 0          NO..P < 3 or > 8
S  =  1                       C'F= 0      An  = 0, 1          NO..Pure H < 2
                              C'  = 0     Art = 0, 0          NO..R < 17
   DQ                         FT  = 0     Ay  = 0, 0           2.....TOTAL
.........(FQ-)                TF  = 0     Bl  = 0, 0
 +  =  3   ( 0)               T   = 0     Bt  = 1, 0         SPECIAL SCORINGS
 o  = 14   ( 2)               FV  = 0     Cg  = 1, 0                  Lv1    Lv2
 v/+ = 0   ( 0)               VF  = 0     Cl  = 0, 0        DV   =   0x1    0x2
 v  =  0   ( 0)               V   = 0     Ex  = 0, 0        INC  =   0x2    0x4
                              FY  = 0     Fd  = 0, 0        DR   =   0x3    0x6
                              YF  = 1     Fi  = 0, 0        FAB  =   0x4    0x7
                              Y   = 0     Ge  = 0, 0        ALOG =   1x5
   FORM QUALITY               Fr  = 0     Hh  = 0, 0        CON  =   0x7
                              rF  = 0     Ls  = 0, 0        Raw Sum6  =    1
      FQx  FQf  MQual  SQx    FD  = 0     Na  = 0, 0        Wgtd Sum6 =    5
 +  =  0    0     0     0     F   = 9     Sc  = 0, 0
 o  = 11    6     3     1                 Sx  = 0, 0        AB  = 0     CP  = 0
 u  =  4    1     1     0                 Xy  = 1, 0        AG  = 0     MOR = 0
 -  =  2    2     0     0                 Id  = 2, 2        CFB = 0     PER = 0
none=  0    --    0     0      (2) =  6                     COP = 0     PSV = 0
```

=============== RATIOS, PERCENTAGES, AND DERIVATIONS ===============

```
R = 17           L =  1.13          FC:CF+C = 0: 0      COP = 0      AG = 0
                                    Pure C  =    0      Food         = 0
EB = 4: 0.0   EA =   4.0   EBPer= 4.0   SumC':WSumC= 1:0.0   Isolate/R  =0.06
eb = 2: 3     es =   5     D =   0       Afr      =0.70       H:(H)Hd(Hd)= 4: 0
              Adj es = 5   Adj D =  0    S        = 1         (HHd):(AAd)= 0: 0
                                        Blends:R= 2:17       H+A:Hd+Ad  =10: 2
FM = 2  :  C'= 1   T = 0                 CP       = 0
m  = 0  :  V = 1   Y = 1
                          P    = 4      Zf  =10          3r+(2)/R=0.35
a:p    =  5: 1   Sum6  = 1   X+% =0.65      Zd   = -1.0         Fr+rF   = 0
Ma:Mp  =  3: 1   Lv2   = 0   F+% =0.67      W:D:Dd = 9: 7: 1    FD      = 1
2AB+Art+Ay= 0    WSum6 = 5   X-% =0.12      W:M  = 9: 4         An+Xy   = 2
M-     =  0      Mnone = 0   S-% =0.00      DQ+  = 3            MOR     = 0
                            Xu% =0.24      DQv  = 0
```

```
SCZI = 0     DEPI = 4     CDI = 3     S-CON = 2     HVI = No     OBS = No
```

Figure 10.4
Rorschach: Jack. Reproduced with permission.

Defenses: As implied above, defenses are more constrictive and orderly as well as repressive and oppressive in character, suggesting mild compulsive and histrionic personality features.

Interpersonal relationships: He needs to maintain his distance from other people as a way to cope with them because he easily sees them as potentially threatening, demanding, and nongiving. His psychological distance and delays while thinking things through in problem solving are such that he tends to make individualistic translations even in those situations in which socially expected translations are obvious.

Others may therefore likely regard him at times as eccentric or deviant. He may compound this impression by his occasional bad judgment, hastened by his struggles in dealing with his feelings.

*Additional Inventory-Derived Information*

On the PCRI, there are indications of significant involvement with his child. From his standpoint, communications are adequate with the child. He gains significant satisfaction from parenting and has adequate emotional support with his parenting. He limit-sets well, at least by this measure. When compared with other parents, he neither pushes his child extremely toward autonomy nor holds her back. In terms of his general father role, he is at neither extreme of being markedly androgenous nor markedly chauvinistic. On the STAXI, all scales fall within the broad normal ranges, so no conscious awareness of anger as a problem area is indicated.

*Categorical Summary for Jack*

Approach: All tests are valid. As many do when evaluated, he carefully presented himself in a good light. Results do suggest that he may not be psychologically sophisticated and that he tends to see the world in terms of black and white, good and bad.

Disturbance level: He seems not consciously aware of disturbance, nor is he markedly distressed. This is unusual in an evaluative situation. He seems to be expressing himself very cautiously. Perhaps he has processed the divorce process well.

Situational reactions: Jack does not present with psychological symptoms or mood state problems. He may be mildly stressed. Although he may react rapidly, his defenses swing in to prevent, deflect, or push away feelings, but within relatively normal bounds.

Personality features/traits/style/disorder: His style is to expend considerable energy repressing feelings and reactions that do not fit with his sense of himself. Thus, he is able to appear composed, virtuous, and conventional in behavior. The emotional cost to him is significant in that his feelings are not readily available to him. His underlying resentment, pushed out of the way for long, can break through, spill over, but with the pressure released, he can reconstitute his repressive and constrictive pressure to enable him to maintain a seemingly calm, orderly presence. He also keeps himself under control by perceiving the world narrowly and overly simplistically, but misses some important input by this narrowing of his perceptual processes.

Self-concept: He has a good balance between paying attention to himself and to others. However, he is now ruminating about negative features of himself, which probably include infrequent outbursts, the intensity of which probably bothers him. This thinking may promote some depression along with a general sense of dissatisfaction, plus related feelings of guilt, shame, or remorse. But no indication of marked clinical depression appears in the testing.

Defenses: Moderate constriction of affect and mild repression and suppression appear to be his major defenses.

Interpersonal relationships: He likely meets and talks well with others on a superficial or businesslike level. However, it is clear that he keeps his emotional distance from others, even as he keeps a distance from his own feelings. He is an individualist and does not want to be overly stimulated by others who might stir up his angry side. In his isolation, he may make bad decisions and act inappropriately and out of character as he struggles to maintain himself as a good person with few negative aspects (of some of which he is now becoming aware).

Additional information: He responds as an involved, effective parent who probably has the ability to set limits productively.

*Summary Testing Report for Jack*

Jack is a 31-year-old technician who is requesting primary custody of his child, Mary, age 9. He is open to liberal visitation by the child's mother. Although no psychological tests were invalidated, Jack worked carefully to present himself in a strongly positive way, as would ordinarily be expected in a child custody evaluation. His guardedness does mean that some possible psychological symptoms may not have come to the attention of the assessing psychologist.

Jack's overall psychological disturbance and present distress is minimal. In fact, considering what he has at stake, the minimal indications of consciously expressed distress are surprising. He does not report psychological symptoms nor mood state problems and appears to be only mildly stressed.

His apparent minimal reactivity in this situation is probably typical for him when he faces difficult, important situations. His style is to sidestep dealing with his feelings by pushing them away or avoiding awareness of them at all. Complementing this generally repressive style is a perceptual processing style in which he narrows and simplifies information as it comes to him. He is able to maintain an appearance and substance of composure, virtue, work efficiency, and conventionality in his behavior.

This combination of dampening or pushing down his feelings with his avoidance of looking at the bigger picture has its downside. It overly restricts his spontaneous expression of feelings that could be important in his parenting with his daughter (and relating to his new partner). Moreover, this constricting, repressive/suppressive defensive process feeds underlying resentment, which periodically can break through. Once expressed, his internal pressure lessens, and he can reconstitute his internal balance, yet he may not have dealt with the issues stimulating the buildup of resentment nor the process of dampening his feelings.

There is some indication in the test findings that he is ruminating about some self-perceived negative features in his personality and behavior. This may be promoting some depression and related feelings of guilt, shame, or remorse. Thus, he may be open to some modification of his general style by carefully planned, cognitively structured individual therapy. As with many men, the cognitive approach would be less threatening yet provide a route to help him eventually deal with his feelings more comfortably.

The lever for him to make any modifications may be in stressing his relationships with his daughter and his new partner. If they are to be a family unit, whether or not he obtains primary custody, the interpersonal stimulation of short-term, interactionally oriented family therapy with father, daughter, and father's new partner would hold considerable promise for his developing a freer, more expressive emotional relationship with his daughter. The testing does suggest that he already has some positive parenting skills and attitudes. To consider this possibility of family therapy requires considering his daughter's psychological state and assessing the new partner's openness and willingness to consider this intervention.

## JILL

Jill's MMPI-2 profile (Figures 10.5 and 10.6) indicates low disturbance. (By contrast, the Rorschach points to a significant level of disturbance.) Thus, although psychologically disturbed, she either presents herself positively, as do typical persons in custody disputes, and is consciously aware of psychological difficulties, or it may be that in general she is denying her psychological disturbance. The MCMI-III (Figure 10.7) indicates psychological disturbance, scoring as do people with anxiety disorders. The anxiety symptomatology appears in the context of a histrionic personality disorder, also an indication of disturbance.

*Jill's MMPI-2 (Figures 10.5 and 10.6)*

Approach: Though the results are valid, she approached the test in a defensive and very cautious manner. She was evasive and unwilling to admit many personal faults. Responding this way is not unusual in an evaluative situation.

Disturbance level: There is little or no apparent conscious awareness of disturbance. Given that she is in the middle of a divorce, this is an unusual finding.

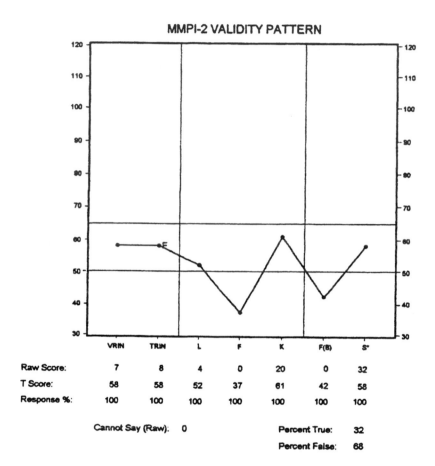

Figure 10.5
MMPI-2 Validity Pattern: Jill

Situational reactions (psychological symptoms and mood state problems): Although a few items suggested some somatic problems, her scores do not suggest problematic situational reactions.

Personality features/trait/style/disorder: She is an outgoing, extroverted person. She is sociable and needs to be around others. Her extroversion

**MMPI-2**

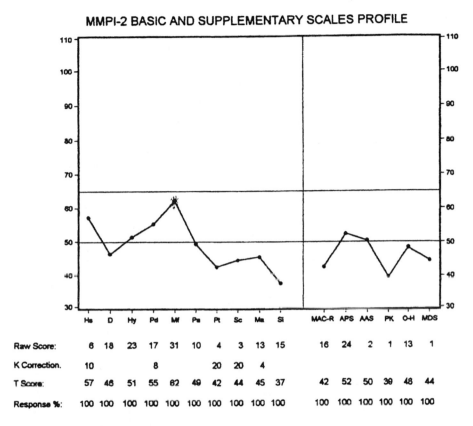

MMPI-2 BASIC AND SUPPLEMENTARY SCALES PROFILE

|  | Hs | D | Hy | Pd | Mf | Pa | Pt | Sc | Ma | Si | | MAC-R | APS | AAS | PK | O-H | MDS |
|---|---|---|---|---|---|---|---|---|---|---|---|---|---|---|---|---|---|
| Raw Score: | 6 | 18 | 23 | 17 | 31 | 10 | 4 | 3 | 13 | 15 | | 16 | 24 | 2 | 1 | 13 | 1 |
| K Correction. | 10 | | 8 | | | | 20 | 20 | 4 | | | | | | | | |
| T Score: | 57 | 46 | 51 | 55 | 62 | 49 | 42 | 44 | 45 | 37 | | 42 | 52 | 50 | 39 | 48 | 44 |
| Response %: | 100 | 100 | 100 | 100 | 100 | 100 | 100 | 100 | 100 | 100 | | 100 | 100 | 100 | 100 | 100 | 100 |

Welsh Code (new):   5-143/62987:0# K-U:F#
Welsh Code (old):   4-3516 89/270: K-U/F?:
Profile Elevation:   48.60

Figure 10.6
MMPI-2 Profile: Jill

appears to be a traitlike characteristic. She has a significant degree of assertiveness.

Self-concept: There are no negative indications.

Defenses: No clear defensive pattern is indicated.

Interpersonal relationships: As noted above, she appears typically outgoing and sociable. She has a strong need to be in relationships with others. It is possible that she may take a significant part of her personal definition from her relationships with others, more than others do.

MCMI-III™

## MILLON CLINICAL MULTIAXIAL INVENTORY - III
### CONFIDENTIAL INFORMATION FOR PROFESSIONAL USE ONLY

Valid Profile

PERSONALITY CODE:   4 ** - * 7 5 6B + 3 2B 6A " 8A 1 8B 2A ' ' // - ** - * //
SYNDROME CODE:   - ** A * // - ** - * //

| CATEGORY | | SCORE | | PROFILE OF BR SCORES | | | | | DIAGNOSTIC SCALES |
|---|---|---|---|---|---|---|---|---|---|
| | | RAW | BR | 0 | 60 | 75 | 85 | 115 | |
| MODIFYING INDICES | X | 85 | 54 | | | | | | DISCLOSURE |
| | Y | 18 | 84 | | | | | | DESIRABILITY |
| | Z | 11 | 64 | | | | | | DEBASEMENT |
| CLINICAL PERSONALITY PATTERNS | 1 | 3 | 30 | | | | | | SCHIZOID |
| | 2A | 1 | 8 | | | | | | AVOIDANT |
| | 2B | 7 | 46 | | | | | | DEPRESSIVE |
| | 3 | 8 | 53 | | | | | | DEPENDENT |
| | 4 | 20 | 89 | | | | | | HISTRIONIC |
| | 5 | 15 | 68 | | | | | | NARCISSISTIC |
| | 6A | 3 | 36 | | | | | | ANTISOCIAL |
| | 6B | 7 | 63 | | | | | | AGGRESSIVE (SADISTIC) |
| | 7 | 19 | 72 | | | | | | COMPULSIVE |
| | 8A | 5 | 33 | | | | | | PASSIVE-AGGRESSIVE |
| | 8B | 2 | 23 | | | | | | SELF-DEFEATING |
| SEVERE PERSONALITY PATHOLOGY | S | 1 | 14 | | | | | | SCHIZOTYPAL |
| | C | 7 | 51 | | | | | | BORDERLINE |
| | P | 3 | 45 | | | | | | PARANOID |
| CLINICAL SYNDROMES | A | 10 | 82 | | | | | | ANXIETY DISORDER |
| | H | 9 | 66 | | | | | | SOMATOFORM DISORDER |
| | N | 8 | 66 | | | | | | BIPOLAR: MANIC DISORDER |
| | D | 5 | 33 | | | | | | DYSTHYMIC DISORDER |
| | B | 2 | 60 | | | | | | ALCOHOL DEPENDENCE |
| | T | 1 | 25 | | | | | | DRUG DEPENDENCE |
| | R | 6 | 60 | | | | | | POST-TRAUMATIC STRESS |
| SEVERE SYNDROMES | SS | 9 | 63 | | | | | | THOUGHT DISORDER |
| | CC | 7 | 52 | | | | | | MAJOR DEPRESSION |
| | PP | 0 | 0 | | | | | | DELUSIONAL DISORDER |

Figure 10.7
MCMI-III: Jill

Copyright © 1994 DICANDRIEN, INC. All rights reserved.
Published and distributed exclusively by National Computer Systems, Inc.,
Minneapolis, MN 55440. Reprinted with permission by NCS.

*MCMI-III (Figure 10.7)*

Approach (validity/reliability): She has a need to present herself in a strong, positive light, not unusual in an evaluation. She appears to be naïve about psychological matters and may have a possible deficit in general self-knowledge.

> Disturbance level: Indications of disturbance are present. Symptomatically, she is extremely anxious. Her clinical personality pattern points to the prominence of a histrionic disorder.

> Situational reactions (psychological symptoms and mood state problems): Her anxiety is such that she reaches a level of disorder. She is sensitive to criticism and public censure. Apparently, her normally controlled emotions are exposed, and as a consequence, she is experiencing considerable discomfort. Despite a conscientious attitude toward work, she seems to be having considerable self-doubt. Symptoms present indicate that she may have insomnia and abdominal pain. She is apprehensive about being open to public exposure.

> Personality features/traits/style/disorder: Results suggest a histrionic personality disorder. She is very concerned about the approval of others. She is hyperalert to the desires of others and that enables her to anticipate their needs and avoid their ire. She is concerned about the approval of those with status and those in authority. She can entertain people with her sociability and her charming and controlled façade. Underneath this charm, there are negative emotions. She fears losing control of these negative emotions. Usually, her style hides her repressed resentment. Surges of resentment periodically break through her surface attractiveness and restraint. With her strong control, she tends to develop somatic disorders.

> Self-concept: Her exterior orientation toward people hides the fact that underneath that exterior she sometimes feels bad about herself. She is actually insecure and fearful that her anger can burst through and be destructive to her relationships with others.

> Defenses: She tends to repress, suppress, and deny as a way of handling and resolving conflicts. She is also subject to developing somatic symptoms as an unconscious way to handle her conflicts.

> Interpersonal relationships: She is charming and sociable, as noted above, and very much oriented to entertaining and meeting the needs of other people. An aspect of this is that she seeks publicly attractive partners or institutional affiliations; these give her a sense of status, she believes. She works hard in her relationships because she fears rejection. She also has some awareness that when her surges of

resentment burst forth, others back away. Her interest in them is often their use to her more than the intrinsic satisfaction of the relationship.

*Rorschach (Figure 10.8)*

Approach (validity/reliability): A sufficient number of responses were given. She has a basic response style in which she oversimplifies incoming information, thus easily neglecting some important bits of information. Thus, at times, she may not appropriately meet some social demands or expectations.

================================ STRUCTURAL SUMMARY ================================

| LOCATION FEATURES | DETERMINANTS BLENDS | SINGLE | CONTENTS | S-CONSTELLATION |
|---|---|---|---|---|
| | | | H = 3, 0 | NO..FV+VF+V+FD>2 |
| | | | (H) = 1, 0 | NO..Col-Shd Bl>0 |
| Zf = 19 | FT.Fr | M = 3 | Hd = 2, 1 | YES..Ego<.31,>.44 |
| ZSum = 61.5 | FM.Fr | FM = 1 | (Hd)= 1, 0 | NO..MOR > 3 |
| ZEst = 63.0 | Fr.CF | m = 0 | Hx = 0, 0 | NO..Zd > +- 3.5 |
| | F.C | FC = 0 | A =10, 0 | NO..es > EA |
| W = 16 | | CF = 0 | (A) = 2, 0 | YES..CF+C > FC |
| (Wv = 1) | | C = 1 | Ad = 2, 0 | YES..X+% < .70 |
| D = 8 | | Cn = 0 | (Ad)= 0, 0 | YES..S > 3 |
| Dd = 3 | | FC'= 0 | An = 0, 1 | YES..P < 3 or > 8 |
| S = 4 | | C'F= 0 | Art = 1, 0 | NO..Pure H < 2 |
| | | C' = 0 | Ay = 0, 0 | NO..R < 17 |
| DQ | | FT = 1 | Bl = 0, 0 | 5.....TOTAL |
| ........(FQ-) | | TF = 0 | Bt = 0, 1 | |
| + = 7 ( 2) | | T = 0 | Cg = 0, 0 | SPECIAL SCORINGS |
| o = 19 ( 3) | | FV = 2 | Cl = 0, 0 | Lv1  Lv2 |
| v/+ = 0 ( 0) | | VF = 0 | Ex = 0, 0 | DV = 1x1  0x2 |
| v = 1 ( 0) | | V = 0 | Fd = 0, 0 | INC = 2x2  0x4 |
| | | FY = 0 | Fi = 1, 0 | DR = 0x3  0x6 |
| | | YF = 0 | Ge = 0, 0 | FAB = 0x4  0x7 |
| | | Y = 0 | Hh = 0, 1 | ALOG = 0x5 |
| FORM QUALITY | | Fr = 1 | Ls = 2, 1 | CON = 0x7 |
| | | rF = 0 | Na = 0, 0 | Raw Sum6 = 3 |
| | | FD = 0 | Sc = 0, 0 | Wgtd Sum6 = 5 |
| FQx FQf MQual SQx | | F =14 | Sx = 2, 0 | |
| + = 1  0  0  0 | | | Xy = 2, 0 | AB = 0  CP = 0 |
| o = 15  9  2  2 | | | Id = 0, 1 | AG = 0  MOR = 1 |
| u = 5  3  1  1 | | | | CFB = 0  PER = 0 |
| - = 5  2  0  1 | | (2) = 4 | | COP = 0  PSV = 0 |
| none= 1  --  0  0 | | | | |

========================= RATIOS, PERCENTAGES, AND DERIVATIONS =========================

R = 27          L = 1.08

| | | | FC:CF+C = 0: 3 | COP = 0    AG = 0 |
|---|---|---|---|---|
| | | | Pure C = 2 | Food = 0 |
| EB = 3: 4.0 | EA = 7.0 | EBPer= N/A | SumC':WSumC= 0:4.0 | Isolate/R =0.15 |
| eb = 2: 4 | es = 6 | D = 0 | Afr =0.50 | H:(H)Hd(Hd)= 3: 5 |
| | Adj es = 6 | Adj D = 0 | S = 4 | (HHd):(AAd)= 2: 2 |
| | | | Blends:R= 4:27 | H+A:Hd+Ad =16: 6 |
| FM = 2 : C'= 0 | T = 2 | | CP = 0 | |
| m = 0 : V = 2 | Y = 0 | | | |
| | | P = 9 | Zf =19 | 3r+(2)/R=0.59 |
| a:p = 3: 2 | Sum6 = 3 | X+% =0.59 | Zd = -1.5 | Fr+rF = 4 |
| Ma:Mp = 2: 1 | Lv2 = 0 | F+% =0.60 | W:D:Dd =16: 8: 3 | FD = 0 |
| 2AB+Art+Ay= 1 | WSum6 = 5 | X-% =0.19 | W:M =16: 3 | An+Xy = 3 |
| M- = 0 | Mnone = 0 | S-% =0.20 | DQ+ = 7 | MOR = 1 |
| | | Xu% =0.19 | DQv = 1 | |

| SCZI = 2 | DEPI = 4 | CDI = 2 | S-CON = 5 | HVI = No | OBS = No |
|---|---|---|---|---|---|

Figure 10.8
Rorschach: Jill. Reproduced with permission.

Disturbance level: Psychological pain, neediness, and major indications of opposition and hostility point to inner disturbance.

Situational reactions (psychological symptoms and mood state problems): She is experiencing considerable distress. She feels lonely and grief-stricken about a significant emotional loss. Some of her discomfort appears to stem from her tendency to ruminate about personal characteristics that she sees as negative. Guilt, shame, or remorse appear to be provoking her rumination. A major reaction is that of anger. She is very lax about controlling her emotions. Probably when she does not control herself adequately, her responses are inappropriate and are not helpful to her adaptation.

Personality features/traits/styles/disorder: A core part of her self-image is a narcissistic feature, if not a trait. She overvalues her personal worth, and this inflated sense of herself influences all her perceptions of the world. She has a great need for affirmation of herself and probably works hard to earn this. When the praise for her performance and herself is not forthcoming, she can be devastated. The shadow of her narcissism can interfere with her ability to actively empathize with others even though she has the capacity to empathize. Another aspect of her personality (noted in the approach section) is her tendency to narrow her perceptions so that she overlooks some important pieces of information; this narrowing helps her momentarily cope more effectively because of the simplicity of her view.

Self-concept: She focuses strongly on the external world to see what the world can do for her. She is very needy. Thus, her apparent interest in others reflects back on her as a reference point. She is more involved with herself in that sense than are other people typically. With her narcissism, she tends to overvalue her personal worth. She has an inflated sense of herself. However, at this time, she seems aware of aspects of herself that she sees as undesirable, and in response is having some tendencies toward ruminations that may relate to guilt, shame, and remorse as well as depression.

Defenses: When she fails, she indulges in rationalization, denial, and externalization as ways to defend herself against looking at those negative aspects of her image. Repression and suppression are used by her as well. It is possible that she uses her core of anger not only to express her irritation, but also as a way to cope with and demand from others.

Interpersonal relationships: Because of her involvement with herself and her inflated sense of herself, she has difficulty making and maintaining deep relationships. Her opposition and her general hostility also interfere with her generally overtly positive attitude toward people. Her strong individualistic orientation tends to keep her psychologically distant from other people. She appears to project off her own hostility, and therefore often perceives the environment as threatening, demanding, and ungiving. Thus, despite her overt interest in people, she does not expect positive interactions with people routinely.

## Unique Information

She does not have a major style for solving problems. She neither focuses primarily on thinking things through nor does she involve herself interpersonally in consistently working things out through interaction with other people. She lacks consistency. This makes her more likely to make errors in judgment as well as more likely to reverse earlier decisions.

## Additional Inventory-Derived Information

As indicated in the PCRI, although she feels an average amount of support and satisfaction in parenting, she is not as involved as the average parent. She is particularly adamant about limit-setting. Her communication skills are similar to others. She neither pushes autonomous action by her child, nor does she hold onto her too much. She would not be characterized as falling at an extreme of either a traditional or nontraditional mother.

She frequently experiences anger, which she is prone to express as hostile, aggressive behavior, as reflected in her responses to the STAXI. Her anger is likely to be directed toward other persons or objects rather than being self-directed. It is possible that it may be expressed in physical ways, such as in assaulting other persons or slamming doors. More likely, it will be expressed verbally in the form of criticism, sarcasm, insults, threats, and the extreme use of profanity.

## Categorical Summary for Jill

Approach: As is expected in a typical evaluation, she works to present herself in a strong, positive manner. She is careful and cautious in her approach. She may be naïve about psychological matters.

Disturbance level: Results are mixed. The MMPI-2 results do not suggest disturbance. However, the MCMI-III profile points to an anxiety disorder, which would indicate subjective distress. Perhaps the combination of a need to present well in an evaluation and a histrionic disorder with its denial and repression indicated on the MCMI-III are sufficient to account for the mixture of findings.

Situational reactions: Despite some denial and her presentation of a good front, she is likely suffering from a marked anxiety disorder (as indicated above). Her conscious anxiety may stem from many sources, including the fact that she is being evaluated. More important, her distress is probably linked to deeper problems. She is grief-stricken about a significant emotional loss. This may be a stimulus for her ruminations and doubts about negative parts of herself that are at great variance from her inflated, more externalized view of herself. Guilt, shame, or remorse may be provoking her as well. Somehow, this mix arouses her anger, which she expresses freely with little control. When she does control herself, she is susceptible to somatic symptoms.

Personality features/traits/styles/disorder: She is an outgoing, extroverted person who has great need to be around others. Although she has the capability for empathizing, she is interested in people not so much for themselves as for what they can do for her in reflecting and helping her sustain her inflated sense of herself. This narcissistic core is central, coloring all her views of the world. She can be so angry and raging that this characteristic must be considered a major trait, not simply a reaction to not getting what she needs in the world. Affecting the efficiency with which she manages her world is her cognitive style, which restricts and narrows incoming information so that she oversimplifies situations and is susceptible to misjudging them.

Self-concept: Her insecurity and fear coupled with her need to reinforce her inflated self-image combine to push her to see what the world can do for her rather than what she can do for the world. Her sense of self is not solid. Her self-image is in part tarnished and she has some awareness of depressiveness, coupled with guilt, shame, and remorse. But her narcissism remains central in considering her self-concept.

Defenses: She uses repression and suppression, along with rationalization, denial, and externalization. Even her anger may be used as a way to cope with and demand from others, even though it is an expression in itself of her distress and frustration midwifed by her problems of self-regulation.

Interpersonal relationships: Jill is oriented toward others. She has the charm and social skills to make headway toward getting what she wants. Because of her manipulative approach and because her hostility is just below the surface, when her anger does not show openly, her relationships tend to be superficial and/or nonlasting.

## Unique Information

She does not have a predominant style for solving problems. She neither prefers to think things through nor does she involve herself interpersonally as a chosen principal style. She vacillates, changes her mind, and exhibits an unsureness. Errors in judgment follow.

### Additional Comments

On the anger inventory, it is clear that she is very aware that she regularly experiences anger that is turned outward. She has the potential for assaultive behavior, either with things or people. She is verbally expressive in the form of criticism, sarcasm, insults, threats, and the extreme use of profanity.

### Summary Testing Report on Jill

Jill is 30 years old, works in a clerical managing position, and is requesting primary custody of her daughter, Mary, age 9. She is open to liberal visitation with Mary by the father, Jack. Jill approached the testing process carefully and cautiously, working to present herself in a strong, positive manner. She evidences some naïveté about psychological matters. To be protective and careful in an important evaluative situation is expected and reflects to some extent good social reality testing, or at least social sensitivity, on her part.

Despite the appearance of putting up a good front and revealing disturbance on one test, results of the other measures do reveal some distress. Of course, this is not surprising given the conflict over primary custody of her daughter. The nature of the distress identified is that of a high anxiety level, reaching the level for classification as an anxiety disorder. At a dynamic level, she is grief-stricken about a significant emotional loss. From the testing, it is not possible to tell if this condition comes about in response to the present reduced time with her daughter, or whether it is anticipatory grief stemming from fears of losing her daughter to her former husband, or whether something else is going on about which we have not been told. In going over the test results with her, this issue will be a major one about which to tactfully but comprehensively inquire.

Jill's testing reveals a personality style or disorder that has important implications for her parenting. She behaves socially in an often charming and effective way, reflecting at least a histrionic style if not disorder. Unfortunately, this seeming attention toward other people appears motivated less by her interest in them for themselves than by what they can do for her. She is fearful of rejection and, in particular, needs constant reassurance that in various ways she is the superior, effective person she strives to be. The supposition is that she believes she must be this superior person to be accepted and loved. But, regardless of what the origins may be of this mental process, the unfortunate part of the narcissistic core is that the self-focus may be so strong that it can interfere with her ability to extend herself toward her daughter as her daughter evolves into an increasingly independent person. It is important to understand that she does have some capability for empathizing, however.

Major features of her personality about which to be concerned are her temper, her rage reactions, and her lax emotional controls over expressing this anger as well as other feelings. Her readiness for underlying hostility to break through and the actual breakthrough is expected to upset other household members. The potential violence of her verbal and, sometimes, physical outbursts are at a level to be potentially damaging for a child. The ubiquitousness of her underlying hostility means that her relationships, with adults and children, are likely to be more superficial. She will put people off. And apparently even her defenses of repression and suppression are not sufficient to push down her hostile feelings, given their strength and her inadequate or lax controls.

Although maintaining an inflated sense of herself, there are indications that she could see negative sides of herself. She has some awareness of depressiveness coupled to guilt, shame, and remorse, pointing to a mildly tarnished self-image. This would be a topic for inquiry when test results are discussed.

Jill has not developed a workable problem-solving style. Some people predominantly think things through, then reach a decision; others, more typically, actively extend themselves in their relations with others to work things out in the interaction. She vacillates, goes back and forth, unsure about which way is better for her. She reverses decisions, thus having a hard time depending on herself. (In effective individual therapy, this style could be modified and solidified to be more predominantly extroversive or introversive.)

## MARY

Mary's Rorschach suggests high disturbance. Conflicting results on the BASC (not shown) indicate high disturbance as viewed by mother and low disturbance as seen by father.

*Rorschach (Figure 10.9)*

> Approach (validity/reliability): There are a sufficient number of responses for the Rorschach to be usable.

> Disturbance level: Considerable disturbance is indicated by an unusually high level of anger, lax controls, thinking problems, and low self-esteem.

> Situational reactions (psychological symptoms and mood state problems): Anger is the major mood state problem. It interferes significantly with her cognitive processing. Limited concentration and interruptions in the flow of deliberate thinking are likely. Her thinking is seriously disturbed. Disorganization and inconsistent decision-making patterns are both to be expected. Perceptual inaccuracy and impairment in reality

```
============================= STRUCTURAL SUMMARY =============================

LOCATION          DETERMINANTS              CONTENTS       S-CONSTELLATION
FEATURES          BLENDS        SINGLE                     ..FV+VF+V+FD>2
                                        H    = 3, 0        ..Col-Shd Bl>0
Zf   = 25        M.FC'         M   = 3   (H)  = 1, 0        ..Ego<.31,>.44
ZSum = 80.5      M.C          FM   = 9   Hd   = 0, 1        ..MOR > 3
ZEst = 84.5      FM.M          m   = 0   (Hd) = 2, 0        ..Zd > +- 3.5
                              FC   = 0   Hx   = 0, 0        ..es > EA
W   = 23                      CF   = 0   A    =17, 0        ..CF+C > FC
 (Wv = 2)                     C    = 2   (A)  = 3, 0        ..X+% < .70
D  =  5                       Cn   = 0   Ad   = 1, 0        ..S > 3
Dd =  2                       FC'  = 0   (Ad) = 0, 0        ..P < 3 or > 8
S  =  7                       C'F  = 0   An   = 0, 0        ..Pure H < 2
                              C'   = 0   Art  = 0, 0        ..R < 17
   DQ                         FT   = 0   Ay   = 0, 0       x.....TOTAL
.........(FQ-)                TF   = 0   Bl   = 0, 0
 +  =  7  ( 3)                T    = 0   Bt   = 0, 0       SPECIAL SCORINGS
 o  = 21  (12)                FV   = 0   Cg   = 0, 3             Lv1      Lv2
v/+ =  0  ( 0)                VF   = 0   Cl   = 0, 1       DV   = 0x1     1x2
 v  =  2  ( 0)                V    = 0   Ex   = 1, 0       INC  = 1x2     0x4
                              FY   = 0   Fd   = 1, 0       DR   = 0x3     0x6
                              YF   = 0   Fi   = 0, 0       FAB  = 2x4     0x7
                              Y    = 0   Ge   = 0, 0       ALOG = 2x5
   FORM QUALITY               Fr   = 0   Hh   = 0, 0       CON  = 1x7
                              rF   = 0   Ls   = 0, 0       Raw Sum6 =   7
      FQx FQf MQual SQx       FD   = 0   Na   = 0, 0       Wgtd Sum6 =  29
 +  =  0   0    0    0        F    =13   Sc   = 0, 0
 o  =  3   2    0    0                   Sx   = 0, 0       AB  = 0    CP  = 0
 u  = 10   5    3    1                   Xy   = 0, 0       AG  = 0    MOR = 2
 -  = 15   6    3    6                   Id   = 1, 2       CFB = 0    PER = 0
none=  2  --    0    0        (2) =  4                     COP = 0    PSV = 0

=================== RATIOS, PERCENTAGES, AND DERIVATIONS ===================

R = 30        L =  0.76        FC:CF+C = 0: 3    COP = 0      AG = 0
-----------------------------  Pure C  =    3    Food       = 1
EB = 6: 4.5  EA = 10.5  EBPer= N/A  SumC':WSumC= 1:4.5  Isolate/R =0.07
eb =10: 1    es = 11    D =    0    Afr    =0.43   H:(H)Hd(Hd)= 3: 4
           Adj es = 11  Adj D =  0  S      = 7     (HHd):(AAd)= 3: 3
-----------------------------  Blends:R= 3:30    H+A:Hd+Ad =24: 4
FM =10  :  C'= 1    T = 0        CP     = 0
m  = 0  :  V = 0    Y = 0
                              P   = 4       Zf  =25        3r+(2)/R=0.13
a:p   = 13: 3   Sum6  = 7    X+% =0.10      Zd  = -4.0     Fr+rF  = 0
Ma:Mp =  4: 2   Lv2   = 1    F+% =0.15   W:D:Dd =23: 5: 2  FD     = 0
2AB+Art+Ay= 0   WSum6 = 29   X-% =0.50      W:M =23: 6     An+Xy  = 0
M-    =  3      Mnone = 0    S-% =0.40      DQ+ = 7        MOR    = 2
                             XuX =0.33      DQv = 2

=============================================================================
 SCZI = 5*   DEPI = 4   CDI = 3   S-CON =N/A   HVI =YES   OBS = No
=============================================================================
```

Figure 10.9

Rorschach: Mary. Reproduced with permission.

testing is present. This thinking disorder, though it appears to be a situational reaction, may subsequently turn out to be a more stable characteristic. Her emotions are not consistent, and she can be overcome by emotions when they become intense, more so than other children her age.

Personality features/trait/style/disorder: She is a hypervigilant child. She has considerable energy and maintains a state of hyperalertness and general guardedness. Because of the above noted thinking disorder, it is of concern that she may develop paranoidlike characteristics as an exacerbation of her hypervigilant state.

Self-concept: Her sense of her personal worth is very poor. She judges herself far less favorably in comparison to others. This self-judgment may likely give rise to feelings of futility and may also call forth episodes of depression.

Defenses: She avoids emotional stimuli. This is probably because reacting to emotions might be expected to stir up her anger and depression, which might be acted out in her environment.

Interpersonal relationships: Her hyperalertness has its origins in a mistrusting attitude toward the environment. She feels quite vulnerable, and as a consequence, is cautious in her behavior. She is concerned about her own personal space. She does not anticipate positive interaction among people; therefore, she stays on the periphery during group interactions. This reactive behavior very importantly cuts out the learning that she could have by being in more constant interaction with others. Without the opportunity to learn through feedback from peers, she stands to increasingly fall behind in acquiring age-appropriate behaviors.

*Additional Inventory-Derived Information*

On the parent form of the BASC, Mary's father responded validly. His answers suggest that she has no problem areas that he sees. As he marks her, her social skills are very high and her general adaptability is excellent.

By contrast, her mother, also with a valid inventory, marks Mary so that Mary reaches the 95th percentile on a scale designed to measure externalizing, or acting-out of inner tensions. Her mother sees her as hyperactive and at risk for aggressive behavior, although she does not score as a conduct disorder. Her mother also sees her as a child who internalizes problems, the 94th percentile, in contrast with her father who, as noted above, views her as symptomless. With her mother's view of her as an internalizer, Mary scores as having a significant level of depression and is at risk for debilitating anxiety. On individually significant items, her mother marked that Mary almost always "argues with parents," "is critical of others," and "complains about rules."

*Kinetic Family Drawing*

Mary identifies her family as her father, stepmother (father's new partner), and her aunt and uncle (who are temporarily staying with her father) and their son. Strikingly, Mary does not include her mother in her picture.

*Summary Test Report on Mary*

Mary's testing was sufficiently valid to allow for interpretation. Mary is a very angry girl. Her distress as reflected by her anger is marked. Its power and ubiquitous character is such that it appears to interfere with Mary's ability to think things through without internal disruptions. She is disorganized under her present stress. Her inconsistent decision-making patterns create an unsettled state, and she suffers from poor reality testing accompanied by distortions in her ways of thinking about the world. Perhaps it is this internal disorganization that makes her feel so vulnerable, which results in a hypervigilant stance in the world.

A linking hypothesis is that she may have suffered sufficient trauma that she must be constantly hyperalert, lest (unconsciously) that trauma descend on her again. It may be that her past exposure to her mother and father fighting has traumatized her. Or it may be that mother's volatile anger and lax control has been especially damaging to Mary. She has reason to be angry simply because her parents separated. Whatever the causes, Mary clearly needs help in dealing with her anger. She also needs help to alleviate her negative feelings about herself. The testing reveals that her sense of personal worth is very poor and her need for safety is significant. She is overly concerned about personal space and is likely to remain on the periphery of group interaction, which can restrict her ability to learn from other children.

These test scores that suggest the probability of strained interpersonal relationships, an instability of reaction including inconsistent control over expression of feelings, being overwhelmed with the intensity of her anger, her poor sense of self-worth, and her cognitive difficulties do point to a flawed developmental process.

A puzzle that will need to be addressed is that her mother views her as very disturbed, seeing Mary as acting-out and acting-in, with depression and probable high anxiety. This relationship between mother and daughter is reinforced by the fact that Mary does not include her mother in her family drawing. Her father does not see disturbance. Possibly both are correct. Their different views of Mary may reflect their different relationships with her. That is, the mother-daughter relationship may reflect conflict and difficulty, whereas the relationship with her father may be relatively free of problems.

## THE FINAL STEPS IN DEVELOPING THE PSYCHOLOGICAL
## TEST REPORT

In this stage of developing a final test report summary of this father, mother, and daughter, the summary test reports on each person are reviewed. The summary categories, the individual test categories, and the test data summaries are also reviewed, together with referring to original test interpretation printouts and standard references, such as those noted in the test chapters in this book. By this time, considerable information has been collected through individual interviews, mother-daughter and father-daughter observations, and other sources of data. This information is factored in through the category system described here for the test data. So, the final report has been prepared with this broader synthesis of information. However, because the focus here is on integration of test results, the extensive, extratest information will not be addressed other than incidentally.

## RELATIONSHIP OF JACK, JILL, AND MARY AS INFERRED
## FROM TEST RESULTS

A cardinal overt problem in this father/mother/daughter grouping is that of angry expression. Mother, Jill, has not only a temper, but a ubiquitous angry quality underlying her relationships, despite an overt orientation to charm others. This readiness for hostility to break through her social, other-oriented exterior is made worse by her inadequate controls over expression of feelings, including anger. Her anger appears matched by her daughter Mary's marked hostility, also untempered by lack of adequate controls, even in comparison with other 9-year-olds. History (not included in this chapter) indeed confirms a long history of flare-ups between mother and daughter that have become more prevalent since the parental breakup. It is likely that stoking this fire is the daughter's feeling of abandonment when mother left, leaving her to her father, although mother returned to visit regularly. And, despite mother's action in leaving the family home, mother's sense of loss and accompanying loneliness is likely significantly related to her frayed connection with her daughter. She can acknowledge her unhappiness at not having more contact with her daughter and, hence, fighting in a custody "battle" for her, precipitating this evaluation. Were she not to fight so strongly she would need to confront and deal with the guilt for, in many ways, rejecting her daughter.

Father, Jack, does not have the same problem of overt ubiquitous anger that his wife displays. He holds in all feelings, including anger, until, rarely, the provocation is strong enough; then he can explode. The mix of anger between them created a cyclical fight dynamic.

Mary was traumatized and responded with her fearfulness by identifying with her aggressive mother even while being very angry with her. Mary's anger overwhelms her, disrupting her thinking process, particularly when confronted with her mother's anger or in the wake of it. Mary's reaction generalizes to others. She is hyperalert, wary, and mistrustful, and does not easily mix with other children. This standoffish attitude means that she cannot benefit from the day-to-day feedback from peers so necessary for adequate development. Her personality development is faltering at present.

TREATMENT AND CUSTODY RECOMMENDATIONS

Based on these findings, Mary needs some individual play therapy, and perhaps EMDR (Shapiro, 1995), to handle her builtup trauma. Her mother, Jill, likewise needs individual therapy, and possibly EMDR, to learn to manage her anger and find more constructive ways to respond under pressure. Then the two of them need sessions with a family therapist to work on their relationship. A final healing process is for mother, daughter, and father to meet with the family therapist to rework the child's trauma with them and establish a working coparenting relationship. In the meantime, with father continuing to have primary physical custody and the parents having joint legal custody, relatively short, two- to four-hour mother-daughter visits would occur frequently (perhaps three times per week). Mother can utilize ongoing long-term therapy to help her modify her histrionic style and her narcissistic traits.

FEEDBACK OF RESULTS TO JACK AND JILL

The clinician/assessor met with each adult separately to review their individual test results. Most people are very interested in knowing about their own test results, and under the ethics code of the American Psychological Association (1992), the psychologist has an obligation to discuss these findings with clients. Each parent was presented with the findings on his or her own tests. Results from one parent were not discussed with the other. In a joint session with the evaluator, each parent was encouraged to share as much as he or she was willing with the other parent. With the parents together, the circular problem of the anger dynamic with the three of them and the mother-daughter conflict was discussed, and feedback to the parents about Mary's testing was provided. Mary's results were not discussed with Mary because of her age. (Had she been a teenager, however, her results would have been discussed first with her privately, and then she would have been helped to tell her parents in a joint session with the therapist what she considered most important about her test results. The therapist would have supported her and filled important gaps in feedback for the parents.)

*A Further Note about Feedback of Test Results*

When the findings are presented to each individual parent about himself or herself, the first feedback information, following Finn (1996, pp. 548–550), has to do with their approach to the testing and the degree of disturbance, including whether or not disturbance appeared on the structured inventories and/or on the more ambiguous Rorschach. Presenting information tentatively can help further the cooperative attitude required to make personal meaning out of the results. Using information positively is very important.

## Summary

This chapter addressed the special situation wherein testing is conducted with an entire family, such as with a family in the transition of divorcing, changing from a nuclear to a binuclear form. Various forms of bias were discussed: gender bias, the need to rescue, the availability heuristic, and confirmatory bias. A process was proposed for integrating the test results of an individual, then suggesting ways for relating the test information from each family member. Finally, a case example was presented.

# CHAPTER 11

## Using Testing When Family Violence and Child Abuse Are Issues

ERNA OLAFSON, Ph.D., Psy.D.

> What if the instruments of the social scientists have been calibrated to filter out the insistent static of posttraumatic pain that is central to the origins of violence and emotional disturbance?
>
> —Roland Summit (1988, p. 51)

The first thing the examiner needs to keep in mind when embarking on these challenging cases is that even if asked to evaluate violent or sexually assaultive families for treatment purposes only, the examiner may well end up in court, with all case records subpoenaed. Although criminal prosecutions in cases of family violence tend to be relatively uncommon, sexual abuse, rape, and physical assault within the family are criminal acts, and cases may go to criminal or juvenile courts (Salter, 1995). In addition, parents in families where there has been battering or incest may separate or divorce, and contentious custody or visitation disputes often follow.

## The Complexities of Assessing Family Violence

For these reasons, it is absolutely essential to define in writing the purposes, boundaries, and confidentiality limits of a psychological assessment to family members at the outset of the very first contact with the family, so that treatment and forensic tasks remain distinct and goals defined. Many psychologists charge higher fees for forensic assessments than they do for treatment, and some lawyers may try to cut costs by coaxing a forensic expert opinion out of an examiner who has done a psychological assessment for treatment purposes alone. Familiarity with state laws and ethical codes about the differences between fact witnesses and expert witnesses, about the handling of raw psychological data, and about privilege and confidentiality are especially important when evaluating family members whose troubles include violence or sexual assault. It goes without saying that records in such cases should be meticulously maintained and all contacts with family members, including a fully informed and signed consent to treatment, should be carefully documented. Any contacts with lawyers should also be documented, and the examiner should bear in mind that even the client's lawyer is outside of the circle of confidentiality unless the client has signed a release.

Second, a wide variety of behaviors are gathered under the rubrics of sexual abuse and family violence, and their consequences vary. As Finkelhor and Berliner (1995) remind us, sexual abuse is an experience, not a disorder or a syndrome, and it seems to be associated with a very wide range of symptom patterns in its victims. Sexually abusive behaviors to children are diverse; they can range from a single act of fondling to repeated, violent rape. The contexts, meanings, durations, and emotional contents of child sexual abuse also vary. In addition, a one-time psychological assessment will provide only a limited and potentially misleading snapshot of abuse effects; Putnam and Trickett (1997; Putnam, 1997b), in their longitudinal comparative study of sexually abused girls, have demonstrated that symptom patterns change over time as these girls develop and mature. The same applies to battering, which is an experience, not a disorder or syndrome. Battering victims and witnesses may suffer from a variety of psychological symptoms or apparently none at all at the time of an assessment.

The psychological picture for family perpetrators of sexual and emotional violence is equally complex. There is no single pedophile profile, just as there is no single batterer profile, and the absence of psychological symptoms does not constitute evidence that a person has *not* perpetrated violence or sexual assault upon family members. Such a null finding is without probative value; it is evidence of nothing at all. Indeed, many—perhaps a majority—of perpetrators appear to be psychologically normal upon standard clinical and psychological assessment. As Salter (1995) writes, "Frequently, there is simply nothing wrong with sex offenders other than aberrant sexuality, which offenders usually deny" (p. 34). About battering, Pagelow (1992; see also Hamberger, 1993) writes that "the stereotypes of mental disturbance do not apply to the vast majority of abusers and victims" (p. 108). Straus and Gelles (1990) have developed a sociological rather than psychological model to explain woman-battering. Feminist theoreticians have expanded the depathologizing of perpetrators into a social-political model of gendered violence within patriarchy (Yllö & Bograd, 1988).

To add to the complexities in these cases, standard psychological batteries are insufficient (and in some cases misleading) when the effects of interpersonal violence on victims are being assessed. The standard tests and diagnostic categories were not originally designed to measure the effects of trauma and interpersonal victimization, although trauma subscales have been incorporated into some recent revisions. The standard instruments can miss some trauma effects and distort others, for example, by identifying dissociative symptoms as schizophrenia or posttraumatic hypervigilance as paranoia (Briere, 1997a). Fortunately, a number of excellent trauma-specific instruments for children and adults have been developed and normed within recent years. Most are commercially available and summarized in comprehensive recent manuals and books (Briere, 1995, 1996, 1997a; Carlson, 1997; Friedrich, 1997; Putnam, 1997a; Wilson & Keane, 1997).

As an additional caveat, the psychologist should be warned that shoehorning the complex consequences of interpersonal family violence into the categories of the American Psychiatric Association's *Diagnostic and Statistical Manual of Mental Disorders* (*DSM-IV*, 1994) is often impossible, no matter what test has been applied. Herman (1992) writes, "In general, the diagnostic categories of the existing psychiatric canon are simply not designed for survivors of extreme situations and do not fit them well" (p. 118). A competent assessment will cover the full range of specificity and complexity each case presents.

Finally, because most diagnostic interviews and psychological instruments depend upon client self-disclosure of symptoms, individual and cultural reporting styles affect client responses. Traumatized individuals often employ avoidance strategies such as minimization, denial and dissociation to manage their pain. Indeed, where abuse and violence are chronic in families, denial and numbing can become predominant family coping styles. Norms for emotional expressiveness vary greatly by culture, so that a restricted range of affect may have different meanings depending on whether a client is from the dominant American culture or is, for example, Native American or from a first-generation Chinese or Japanese American family. Researchers have found that traumatized Southeast Asian refugees more readily admit to somatic symptoms than to psychological ones (Lee & Lu, 1989). As Carlson (1997) writes, "There is also cultural variation in willingness to report psychological symptoms. In fact, mainstream U.S. culture probably has fewer prohibitions against such reports than almost any other culture or any American subculture" (p. 175).

Stress responses themselves appear to be culture-bound. For example, dissociative and somatic symptoms appear to be more common stress responses in some cultures than among the mainstream North Americans in whom the posttraumatic stress disorder diagnosis was first identified in the years after the Vietnam war ended (Marsella, Friedman, & Spain, 1996). Marsella and colleagues have published an edited volume about cultural considerations in assessing posttraumatic stress disorder; other resources about cultural factors in trauma assessment are listed in Briere (1997a, pp. 47–49) and Carlson (1997, p. 175).

## Symptoms

For adults, interpersonal victimization correlates with a wide range of symptom patterns, depending on its nature and duration, prior stressors and traumas, and individual and cultural characteristics. For children, medical researchers are finding that the developmental age at which stress or trauma occurs is psychobiologically crucial and that children may be more susceptible to stressful experiences at biologically critical periods (Cicchetti & Toth, 1998; Perry, Pollard, Blakely, Baker, & Vigilante, 1996; Putnam, 1997a; Trickett & Putnam, 1993). Herman (1992) states it succinctly: "Repeated trauma in adult life erodes the structure of the personality already formed, but repeated trauma in childhood forms and deforms the personality" (p. 96). A number of research studies have shown that prior exposure to traumatic events may sensitize individuals to subsequent ones, making them more vulnerable to posttraumatic stress disorder (PTSD) (Bremner, Southwick, Johnson, Yehuda, & Charney, 1993; Wilson & Keane, 1997). It has also been found that adult women with childhood physical and sexual abuse histories appear to dissociate more following assaults than do victims without child abuse histories, and a tendency to dissociate appears to make victims more vulnerable to the development of PTSD if they are traumatized again (Dancu, Riggs, Hearst-Ikeda, Shoyer, & Foa, 1996).

Except in rare instances, the *DSM-IV* does not give etiologies for mental disorders, but it does make exposure to an extreme traumatic stressor essential to the diagnosis of posttraumatic stress disorder, acute stress disorder, and brief psychotic disorder with marked stressor. It also mentions that physical and sexual abuse, neglect, hostile conflict, and early parental loss or separation are "more common" in the childhood histories of those with borderline personality disorder (APA, 1994, p. 652). The *DSM-IV* links the dissociative disorders with histories of trauma, although in most cases not exclusively (Briere, 1997a).

For both adults and children, then, the trauma-linked disorders include posttraumatic stress disorder, acute stress disorder, and psychotic disorder with marked stressor. The adjustment disorders also identify the presence of a stressor, albeit not an extreme traumatic one. Dissociative amnesia, dissociative fugue, dissociative identity disorder (the *DSM-IV* term for multiple personality disorder), and depersonalization disorder can all be correlated with an experience of extreme trauma. Other possibly trauma-related diagnoses include conversion disorder, somatization disorder, and some personality disorders (borderline, avoidant).

Not all interpersonal victimization produces posttraumatic symptoms. Anxiety and mood disorders, physical health problems, self-esteem deficits, passivity, substance-related disorders, and sleep disorders can all be triggered or exacerbated by the experience of domestic violence or sexual assault, but these are not trauma-specific disorders and all have other possible etiologies.

A diagnosis to account for the complex and enduring sequelae of prolonged, repeated interpersonal violence and trauma, described by Herman (1992) as complex posttraumatic stress disorder and intended to remedy the lack of a comprehensive and accurate diagnosis for such victims, was proposed, field-tested, and ultimately rejected by the committees that put together the DSM-IV. Unlike the International Classification of Diseases, 10th edition (ICD-10), the DSM-IV does not include complex PTSD, although its omission from DSM-IV nomenclature was controversial (Roth, Newman, Pelcovitz, van der Kolk, & Mandel, 1997). This proposed and rejected diagnosis, also known as "disorders of extreme stress not otherwise specified," or DESNOS, has been given a DSM-IV paragraph that describes "an associated constellation of symptoms" of posttraumatic stress disorder that is more common with an interpersonal stressor such as childhood sexual or physical abuse or domestic battering, torture, and so forth than with naturally occurring catastrophes such as floods or fires (APA, 1994, p. 425). Briere (1997a) points out that complex PTSD is significant in incorporating symptoms often associated with Axis II personality disorders such as borderline personality disorder. It includes enduring symptom patterns having to do with affect regulation, identity disturbances, self-destructive behaviors, and interpersonal difficulties, a constellation of symptoms associated with exposure to severe and prolonged interpersonal trauma.

Research on DESNOS indicates that sexual abuse histories increase the risk for adults to have complex PTSD. The DSM-IV field trial for PTSD found that women sexually and physically abused in childhood were at greatest risk for developing complex PTSD (DESNOS), followed by women with child sexual abuse alone, and then by women with child physical abuse alone (Roth et al., 1997). Another study showed increased DESNOS symptoms of somatization, dissociation, hostility, anxiety, alexithymia, social dysfunction, maladaptive cognitive schemas, self-destructive behaviors, and adult revictimization among 74 adult female survivors of child sexual abuse when compared with 34 nonabused women. The DESNOS symptoms were found to be significantly related to the sexual abuse histories, but this finding was confounded by the fact that many of the sexually abused women had also experienced childhood physical abuse (Zlotnick et al., 1996).

In children, child sexual abuse is often correlated with disturbances in sexual functioning, as well as with a range of other mental disorders (Kendall-Tackett, Williams, & Finkelhor, 1993). Traumatic sexualization of a child can unfold developmentally into a variety of sexual dysfunctions. Sexually abused children may engage in age-inappropriate sexualized behaviors, may be vulnerable to revictimization, may become sexually promiscuous or dysfunctionally avoidant of sex as they mature, and may victimize others (Finkelhor & Browne, 1985; Olafson & Boat, in press). Recently normed instruments designed to assess these sexual disorders include Briere's Trauma Symptom Inventory for

Children (1996), Briere's Trauma Symptom Inventory (1995), and Friedrich's Child Sexual Behavior Inventory (1997), all described in detail below. A history of being raped during childhood has been found more likely to predict PTSD among adult women when it was accompanied by life threat and/or physical injury, when there was anal or oral rape or a higher number of types of rape, and/or when the child victim was forced to testify in court (Epstein, Saunders, & Kilpatrick, 1997).

For children who have been beaten or have witnessed their mothers being beaten, symptoms cover the range of psychiatric disorders, from anxiety and depression through the trauma-specific disorders, including complex PTSD (Kolbo, Blakely, & Engleman, 1996). Carmen, Rieker, and Mills (1984) have suggested that physical abuse by a parent may have the effect of exaggerating sex-role characteristics in children as they mature, with girls becoming more passive and boys more aggressive. Physically abused boys are statistically more likely to become hyperaggressive, abusive adolescents and adult men than are non-abused boys (Jenkins & Bell, 1994; Malamuth, Sockloskie, Koss, & Tanaka, 1991). There is a growing literature on the psychological impact on children who witness violence; a child need not be assaulted to be traumatized (Wolak & Finkelhor, 1998).

Geffner (1998) reminds us to screen for neuropsychological damage when testing both batterers and their victims. He states that the presence of central nervous system damage in such families may often be missed. Children born to women who have been beaten in the abdomen during pregnancy (a tragically common scenario) may suffer central nervous system damage while in utero. Both frontal lobe and temporal lobe damage are known to affect impulse control and judgment. It seems possible that the impulsive rages of some batterers and the apparently flawed judgment of some battered women have neurological components, but this issue needs further research. It is recommended that a referral be made for a complete neuropsychological evaluation when battering has included assault to the abdomen of a pregnant woman or has included violent shaking or head trauma to a child or adult.

Perry (1994) points out that victimized children do not receive the diagnosis of posttraumatic stress disorder as often as they should and are often misdiagnosed with behavior disorders or attention deficit hyperactivity disorder (ADHD). He argues that many of these children are hypervigilant rather than inattentive and may be experiencing physiological hyperarousal, hyper-reactivity, sleep disturbances, hypertension, increased heart rate, startle reactions, and muscle tension. Putnam and Trickett have found that over 30% of the sexually abused girls in their longitudinal study are identified in their schools as having attention deficit hyperactivity disorder, in contrast to a rate below 10% for the matched comparison group in their study (Putnam, 1997b). A victimized child who cannot sit still may be suffering from the effects of severe trauma. If misdiagnosed as hyperactive and prescribed Ritalin rather than trauma-specific treatment and medication, the child's chances of recovery are likely to be greatly impeded.

There also appear to be gender differences in children's responses to interpersonal trauma and victimization. Research shows that more abused and traumatized boys display externalizing disorders such as ADHD, behavior disorders, and delinquency, and more girls than boys appear to display internalizing symptoms such as dissociation or depression (Chandy, Blum, & Resnick, 1996; Perry et al., 1996).

## Ascertaining Victimization and Trauma History

Trauma cannot be effectively treated until it is stopped. Ongoing family victimization will often continue until outside intervention puts a stop to it. A number of studies have shown that victims of ongoing interpersonal violence do not generally disclose their experiences unless asked directly about them (Briere, 1997a; Herman, 1992; Salter, 1995). It is therefore imperative to ask. Abuse histories should be a routine part of medical and mental health intakes, whether by a family physician, a divorce counselor, or a psychologist embarking on a standard psychological assessment (Olafson & Boat, in press). For obvious reasons, family members must be separated for such questioning, because victims do not generally report ongoing abuse in the presence of perpetrators or even when nonabusive parents are present. Questions should be clear and focused without being leading. Victimized subjects who respond in the negative to general questions about physical abuse or sexual abuse may recall and describe such experiences only when asked more specific questions about being hit, touched, or penetrated against their will. In similar fashion, many battered women reframe their victimization as fighting or wrestling because they have learned to avoidantly minimize or have internalized the batterer's distortions, so that specific questions may be called for here as well (Briere, 1997a; Salter, 1995). Studies show that sexually abused children in independently confirmed cases characteristically minimize or deny the sexual abuse when first questioned, and many subsequently retract after disclosure (Lawson & Chaffin, 1992; Sorenson & Snow, 1991).

Briere (1997a) lists a number of structured interview protocols for interviews with adults and offers a "customized" traumatic events interview (pp. 89–91). Carlson (1997) summarizes interview protocols and measures of traumatic experiences for children and adults (pp. 203–214). Boat (1995) reminds us of the very high co-morbidity between wife-battering, child sexual and physical abuse, and animal abuse and has developed a questionnaire for children that assesses their animal-related experiences. The overlap between adult domestic violence and child maltreatment is found in 30% to 60% of the families studied, so that assessments of battered women should include inquiries about the safety of children in the home, as well as inquiries about dependent adults and the frail elderly (American Psychological Association Presidential Task Force on Violence and the Family, 1996; Edleson, 1998, in press).

## Using Standard Test Batteries to Assess Family Victimization in Adults

The WAIS-III, MMPI-2, MCMI-III, and Rorschach constitute one standard battery generally administered, often supplemented by drawings. Although these instruments were not originally designed to assess the effects of trauma and victimization, they do offer information about general symptom patterns, personality, responding style, and perceptual accuracy. When trauma and victimization are at issue, the standard battery must be supplemented by trauma-specific measures, for, as Carlson (1997) writes, "results from a standard psychological test battery are unlikely to yield the information you need for a systematic assessment of trauma responses" (p. 8).

### THE WECHSLER ADULT INTELLIGENCE SCALE-III (WAIS-III)

The WAIS-III can be administered in whole or part. The Vocabulary and Block Design subtests screen for general verbal and visual-spatial abilities and give the examiner necessary information about reading level. Because self-report measures such as the MMPI-2 require an eighth-grade reading level, it is necessary to ascertain reading ability at the outset of testing. Administration of the entire WAIS-III can screen for neurological deficits that would require further evaluation, and it might also indicate the presence of anxiety and depression that subjects may minimize in the self-report personality measures. The Picture Arrangement and Comprehension subtests can reveal information about social judgment, which is often relevant in the assessment of both victims and perpetrators. However, administration of the entire WAIS-III is time-consuming and expensive, and decisions about its complete administration will be on a case-by-case basis.

### MINNESOTA MULTIPHASIC PERSONALITY INVENTORY-2 (MMPI-2)

The MMPI-2 can pose problems for some victims. Individuals who are very distressed, deeply depressed, or in a state of dissociative fragmentation may find answering the 567 questions of the MMPI-2 a formidable task. Empathizing with

client complaints and providing a quiet and reassuring atmosphere for administration is often enough to encourage such clients to complete the test. However,
as with all cases, but especially here, it is essential to check for excessive omis-
sions or random response patterns.

Interpreting validity scales for traumatized patients presents special difficulties. Although the F scale (atypical responding) can elevate when a client over-
reports or exaggerates symptoms, studies of Vietnam veterans and child abuse
survivors who have posttraumatic stress disorder and/or affective dysregulation
also show elevations in this scale (Briere, 1997a; Carlson, 1997). Some studies
have shown, however, that although the F scores of traumatized individuals average close to three standard deviations above the mean, the average scores of those
who are "faking bad" are generally even higher. In addition, the raw F-K index appears to discriminate between the two groups (Briere, 1997a). Examiners are cautioned not to automatically assume overreporting when individuals with known
trauma and victimization histories have high F scores. Carlson and Armstrong
(1994) warn that the F scale is often elevated in subjects not only with PTSD but
also with dissociative disorders. Briere (1997b) writes,

> It is likely that, for some abused individuals, elevated F scores reflect the ten-
> dency for trauma-related dissociative and intrusive symptomology to produce
> unusual experiences and chaotic, disorganized internal states. Under such con-
> ditions, an elevated F scale may not suggest a 'fake bad' response or invalid
> protocol as much as an accurate portrayal of extreme stress or internal disorga-
> nization (p. 51).

Underreporting in any individual case is also difficult to detect, although
validity indicators may point in this direction. As with overreporting, the examiner can consider information from the range of tests including the projective
measures, the clinical interview, and the client's history and culture. Because
many individuals cope with severe trauma through avoidant minimization,
bravado, and the numbing of feeling, the examiner should be alert to possible
underreporting of symptoms (Briere, 1997b). Clients may also present psychological symptoms as somatic complaints, a coping pattern that might show clinical elevations only in scores 1 and 3 on the MMPI-2, with a possible additional
elevation on Overcontrolled Hostility.

As for the standard clinical scales, a number of them can be elevated in
traumatized adults, commonly an F-8-2 profile, indicating affective disturbances,
intrusive and dissociative symptoms, and severe levels of distress and fragmentation (Briere, 1997a; Munley, Bains, Bloem, & Busby, 1995). Rage, suspiciousness,
worry, distrust, and anxiety can elevate scales 4, 6, and 7 as well. One study finds
that battered women show F-4-6-8 MMPI-2 profiles, with additional elevations on
the new PTSD measures, PS and PK (Khan, Welch, & Zillmer, 1993). Indeed, a

variety of elevated profiles are possible when PTSD, depression, and dissociation are present, so that the MMPI-2 profiles of traumatized adults often have a Himalayan appearance (Munley et al., 1995). Computerized clinical reports may misdiagnose these traumatized patients as psychotic, paranoid schizophrenic, or bipolar, so that clinicians should carefully examine the subscales and especially the critical items in each elevated scale. The elevated profiles of trauma can also resemble the 2-4-6-8 "floating" profile associated in clinical lore with borderline personality disorder. It is to be hoped that before long, the diagnosis of complex PTSD will replace the borderline diagnosis as a more accurate and less derogatory diagnostic label for these patients.

The new PTSD scales developed for the MMPI are the PS scale (Schlenger et al., 1989) and the more commonly used PK scale, developed by Keane and others in 1984 and revised for the MMPI-2 (Briere, 1997a). Because the 46 items in Keane's PK scale had to be drawn from existing MMPI-2 questions, they do not cover the full range of posttraumatic symptoms, such as intrusive experiences (flashbacks) or emotional numbing (Carlson, 1997). The scale has also been criticized because it was developed and validated primarily on Vietnam veteran samples and appears to have somewhat less validity for civilian PTSD (Briere, 1997a; Gaston, Brunet, Koszycki, & Bradwejn, 1996). Carlson (1997) writes, "The PK subscale may be useful if you have access to MMPI results and no other options for measuring PTSD, but it is not optimal for that purpose" (p. 7). Norris and Riad (1997) agree that use of the PK Scale may make the most sense in settings where the MMPI-2 is administered routinely.

Adult survivors of child sexual abuse can also show MMPI-2 elevations on scales F, 4, and 8 that can lead to suspicions of symptom overreporting as well as misdiagnoses. Other scores that may elevate for adult survivors include 2, 6, and 7. Chronic health problems often seen in sexual abuse survivors may elevate scales 1 and possibly 3. Substance abuse, which is statistically more common among adult survivors, can elevate the MacAndrew-R Scale (Briere, 1997b; Cole & Putnam, 1992). Standard interpretations of these elevations for abuse survivors (as in computerized printouts) must be viewed with caution, and careful examination of subscales and critical items is likely to give a more accurate picture (Briere, 1997a; Carlin & Ward, 1992). Briere (1997b) writes that because the effects of chronic child maltreatment can be pervasive and can generalize and elaborate over time, these effects are difficult to assess adequately with any one instrument, and multiple measures are necessary to evaluate them.

The MMPI and MMPI-2 do not contain sufficient items to measure the dissociation construct, although dissociative patients may show elevations on Scale 8 (the schizophrenia scale) and may therefore be mislabeled as psychotic. Recent dissociation-specific instruments with good reliability and validity are now available and are described below.

Finally, average MMPI scores vary to some extent according to subculture, socioeconomic status, and religious belief. As is standard for all evaluations, the examiner should interpret profiles while taking into account information about client circumstances and culture. Elevations on scales that contain unusual responses may reflect religious belief systems rather than thought disorders, and paranoid elevations may reflect victimization by racism or homophobia, to name just two possible examples.

## MILLON CLINICAL MULTIAXIAL INVENTORY-III (MCMI-III)

Although the Millon scales are increasingly widely used, the MCMI-III is relatively recent (Millon, 1994a) and is a substantial revision of the MCMI-II, with 95 new items out of a total of 175. There are still many more external criterion validity and factor-analytic studies on the MCMI-II (McCann & Dyer, 1996). In addition, the MCMI-III's cross-validation sample ($N = 398$) contained very few African Americans, Asians, or Hispanics, so that results should be applied with special caution to clients from those groups (Millon, 1994a). McCann and Dyer suggest that until further research on the MCMI-III has been completed, forensic evaluators should continue to use the earlier version.

Nevertheless, for the assessment of trauma survivors the MCMI-III has advantages over the MCMI-II. It contains a new scale to assess PTSD, the R Scale. Briere (1997a) notes that only 6 of this scale's 16 items tap *DSM-IV* diagnostic criteria for PTSD, and these focus more on intrusive experiences than on avoidance or hyperarousal. Data are not yet available on this new scale's discriminant validity. The MCMI-III has also added questions about child abuse experiences.

Studies using earlier versions of the MCMI have focused primarily on Vietnam veterans and adult survivors of child maltreatment. Veterans with PTSD have shown various combinations of avoidant, schizoid, and/or borderline personality patterns, as well as Axis I elevations for anxiety and depression (Briere, 1997a). Child abuse survivors have shown a wider variety of disorders than veterans, testing with dependent personality disorder in addition to the avoidant, schizoid, and borderline patterns (Briere, 1997a). On Axis II, child abuse survivors show anxiety and more severe depressive symptoms than do veterans. Briere writes that elevations on MCMI scales for delusional disorder or thought disorder among adult survivors may reflect, not psychosis, but rather posttraumatic symptoms and/or chaotic internal states, especially if subjects have elevated PTSD scores.

In spite of the MCMI's shortcomings, Briere (1997a; Herman, 1992) recommends that it is useful to administer where posttraumatic symptoms may coexist with personality disorders or where complex PTSD, the enduring characteristics of which resemble personality disorders, is an issue.

RORSCHACH (EXNER SYSTEM)

For trauma survivors, the Rorschach can be especially useful, because as a projective measure, it avoids client overreporting or underreporting of symptoms. However, because the Exner diagnostic classification system has accounted insufficiently for the sequelae of victimization and trauma such as PTSD and dissociation, Rorschach results have misdiagnosed traumatized Vietnam veterans and child sexual abuse survivors as psychotic (Saunders, 1991; van der Kolk & Ducey, 1989). The computer printout for the Exner System states that patients who meet full criteria on the Schizophrenia Index are very unlikely not to have this diagnosis. However, clinical experiences with traumatized but nonpsychotic child sexual abuse victims and their parents show many false positives on the Schizophrenia Index for both children and adults. Therefore, as with the MCMI and the MMPI, examiners should exercise caution in interpreting Rorschach results that indicate psychosis if patients have trauma histories or are parents of children severely traumatized outside of the home.

Studies are appearing that identify posttraumatic indicators on the Rorschach (Levin & Reis, 1997). Posttraumatic hypervigilance can elevate the Hypervigilance Index (Levin & Reis, 1997); posttraumatic numbing and avoidance can show up as very high Lambdas and low Affective Ratios (Afr) as clients avoid responses to emotional stimuli such as color (Briere, 1997a). Posttraumatic intrusions such as flashbacks can show up in the color band ratio, with unstructured color responses outnumbering the structured ones, in a manner reminiscent of children's relatively unmodulated Rorschach responses (Briere, 1997a). The defensive coping strategies of many trauma victims may reveal themselves in a record that is devoid of movement and color, has a very high Lambda and a low Affective Ratio, but has one or two unstructured color responses. This profile suggests a strategy of avoiding stimuli that trigger emotional responses, because emotions are typically experienced as raw, inchoate, and overwhelming when they do break through. Scores that correlate with situational stress, such as Inanimate Movement responses (m) and Diffuse Shading responses (Y), are often elevated and suggest feelings of powerlessness, helplessness, and anxiety. Already in 1966, Schachtel had described the inanimate movement response as the "attitude of the impotent spectator" (cited in Levin & Reis, 1997, p. 538).

Survivors of chronic trauma, such as long-standing child abuse and adult revictimization (a common clinical presentation), may produce Rorschach protocols that reflect personality disorders, or to be more accurate, may reflect personality styles formed and deformed to adapt to chronic trauma. One such pattern is a numb, avoidant, constricted record with brief responses, a very high Lambda, a low Affective Ratio, no Texture responses, and indications of stress or depression in Achromatic Color (C'), Vista (V), Inanimate Movement (m), Diffuse Shading (Y) and/or Morbid responses (Levin & Reis, 1997). Together these patterns suggest a long-term avoidant adjustment with constricted affect, painful introspection, enduring depressive symptoms, and overwhelming helplessness. Wounded, stoical, distrustful, and isolated, these clients deny even normal desires for closeness, so that their bleak, colorless, static, scanty responses contain no Texture responses. Often, their initial records are too brief to score and must be readministered.

The examiner may also find that another Rorschach pattern for the complex PTSD of chronic trauma resembles the characteristic Rorschach protocols for patients with borderline personality disorder. These clients may appear to have impaired reality testing, thought disorders or cognitive slippage, poor form quality responses, and special scores such as Fabulized combinations and Confabulations. Intrusive re-experiencing of symptoms may show themselves in extensive unstructured color responses and frequent Blood, Morbid, Sexual, Aggressive, and Anatomy responses.

A promising Rorschach trauma content scale has been developed by Armstrong and Loewenstein (1990). Armstrong initially tested this *Trauma Content Index* (TC/R) on 14 dissociative patients with known trauma histories and is continuing to study it with a larger sample (Briere, 1997a). This index adds the Sex, Blood and Anatomy content scores to the Morbid and Aggressive special scores and divides their sum by the total number of responses. It has shown good preliminary results.

One study of female psychiatric inpatients with and without child sexual abuse histories correctly classified over 90% of them when indicators on a new *Sexual Abuse Index* were applied. This index, devised by Leavitt and Labott (1996), is made up of eight content indicators: sexual activity, sexual anxiety, sexual violence, damage to the body, imagery of adults as victims, imagery of children as victims, imagery of fearful adults, and imagery of fearful children. Elevated scores on the Armstrong content index and the Leavitt and Labott sexual abuse index may reflect fixated traumatic material that emerges when triggered by the stimulus of the Rorschach cards, rather than psychologically primitive, regressive, primary-process materials (Briere, 1997a; Carlson & Armstrong, 1994; Levin & Reis, 1997).

The results of Kaser-Boyd's (1993) Rorschach study of 28 battered women who had killed their battering spouses showed similarities to veterans with post-traumatic stress disorder. Cognitively and emotionally constricted, these women experienced those emotions they did have as intense and unmodulated. Their reality testing was distorted. Unlike thought disordered patients, but like traumatized veterans, they had no parallel increase in special scores. They appeared to have no consistent decision-making style and to have limited internal resources to cope with stress.

Levin and Reis (1997) summarize Rorschach results across numerous studies on a variety of trauma victims (including war veterans) and offer a useful table of *DSM-IV* trauma categories correlated with possible Rorschach variables

(p. 540). They point out that Rorschach research on traumatized populations is relatively recent, and that both larger sample sizes and correlations with trauma-specific measures such as the Dissociative Experiences Scale would be useful in future studies. Their summary shows that the single most consistent finding across Rorschach studies of traumatized populations is the presence of elevated inanimate movement (m) scores, a finding that may relate to situational stress, helplessness, and/or the presence of dissociation (p. 538). A related elevation across subject groups is diffuse shading (Y), related both to feelings of helplessness and anxiety. Unstructured color responses, which appear to measure the presence of raw and unmodulated affect, are often elevated, although numbly avoidant subjects may have no color responses at all.

PERSONALITY ASSESSMENT INVENTORY (PAI)

There is now a relatively new self-report measure, the Personality Assessment Inventory (PAI), that covers both Axis I and II disorders, is psychometrically sound, and at 344 items is far briefer for clients to fill out than the 742 questions of the combined MMPI-2 and MCMI-III (Morey, 1991). The PAI provides the same range of diagnoses as the MMPI-2 and the MCMI-III (Morey, 1991). It also contains a PTSD scale. However, because this instrument is quite recent, there is not yet sufficient research to assess its sensitivity and specificity for trauma and abuse victims. Examiners should look for studies on the PAI, and if it fulfills its early promise, consider using it in future assessments.

# Specific Trauma and Victimization
# Measures for Adults

In recent years, a number of self-report measures have been developed to assess trauma effects; books by Briere (1997a), Carlson (1997), and Wilson and Keane (1997) describe them in detail. To assess violence and trauma in families, most of these new measures are not applicable. Many were developed for and normed on combat veteran populations, and many are designed as research measures only. Briere has a good critical summary of their strengths and weaknesses.

However, two new measures, Briere's (1995) Trauma Symptom Inventory and Carlson and Putnam's (1993) Dissociative Experiences Scale, should be included in batteries of adults where family trauma and violence are at issue. They are targeted to assess the sequelae of victimization and trauma in themselves, and they also can assist in interpreting otherwise puzzling elevations on the more standard older instruments such as the MMPI-2.

TRAUMA SYMPTOM INVENTORY (TSI)

Briere's (1995) Trauma Symptom Inventory is a 100-item, self-report test designed to measure both acute and chronic posttraumatic stress in adults aged 18 and over. The test has 3 validity scales and 10 clinical scales, which yield T-scores. The validity scales are Response Level, which measures underendorsement of items or the attempt to appear symptom-free; Atypical Response, which measures extreme distress or the attempt to appear dysfunctional/disturbed; and Inconsistent Response. The 10 clinical scales are Anxious Arousal, Depression, Anger/Irritability, Intrusive Experiences, Defensive Avoidance, Dissociation, Sexual Concerns, Dysfunctional Sexual Behavior, Impaired Self-Reference, and Tension Reduction Behavior. The instrument was standardized on a general population sample and on military personnel. Norms are available for four groups: men and women aged 18–54; and men and women age 55 and above. TSI scores vary by about 2% to 3% as a function of race.

The advantages of using the TSI are several. The three components of PTSD are broken out into the separate scales of Anxious Arousal, Intrusive Experiences, and Defensive Avoidance, a clear advantage over other instruments, which generally have a single PTSD scale and often skimp on one component or another. Trauma-linked sexual dysfunctions are assessed in separate scales that measure both concerns and behaviors. Other components of complex posttraumatic symptomology, such as dissociation and chronic anger or irritability, have their own scales. There is a scale for the pervasive impairments in self-reference and identity that are often found in patients with child abuse and neglect histories. On standard instruments, impaired self-reference is likely to receive a personality disorder diagnosis. Finally, there is a scale to measure the tension reduction behaviors, such as self-mutilation or aggressive acts, by which many victimized and traumatized patients attempt to externalize their distress.

Research by Briere and colleagues (Briere, Elliott, Harris, & Cotman, 1995) with the Trauma Symptom Inventory supports the clinical impression that sexual traumas for both children and adult predict symptoms across the clinical range and "are especially and uniquely injurious," when compared with other forms of interpersonal victimization.

A general population study using the TSI and other measures found that among those subjects who reported child abuse histories, those who had recently recalled child sexual abuse after a period of amnesia had higher levels of symptomology on all ten TSI scales than did three other groups: nonabused subjects, abused subjects without amnesia, and abused subjects whose recall after amnesia had not been recent (Briere, Elliott, Harris, & Cotman, 1995). The highest levels of distress for the recent recall group were in posttraumatic intrusion and avoidance, dissociation, and impaired self functioning. Treatment status did not predict recall status, nor did race, socioeconomic status, or gender.

Because this instrument is very new, validity has been established only by correlation with other measures. In the next few years, we should be seeing publication of studies of this scale's predictive validity, that is, its sensitivity and specificity, for stress and trauma disorders.

DISSOCIATIVE EXPERIENCES SCALE (DES)

The Dissociative Experiences Scale (DES) is a 28-item self-report measure for adults aged 18 and over of the frequency of dissociative experiences in daily experience. It is not commercially sold but is freely available. It is printed as Appendix One in Putnam's (1997a) *Dissociation in Children and Adolescents.* Carlson and Putnam (1993), who authored the scale, write that the measure was designed to quantify dissociative experiences, to assist in determining the degree of dissociation in various psychiatric disorders, and to screen for dissociative disorders. The DES was not intended as a diagnostic instrument; the authors recommend a structured interview for diagnosis. Various studies have shown that populations diagnosed with PTSD, multiple personality disorder, and dissociative disorder NOS have DES scores of 30 or higher. General population studies have shown median scores of 3.7 to 7.8 on the DES (Carlson & Putnam, 1993). Individuals with diagnoses such as schizophrenia or anxiety average scores in the midrange between population norms and posttraumatic stress disordered or dissociative subjects. A multicenter ($N = 883$) discriminant analysis of the DES as an instrument to screen for multiple personality disorder showed that it performed quite well in terms of sensitivity and specificity (Carlson et al., 1993).

# Adult Perpetrators of Sexual and Physical Abuse

The thorough evaluation of perpetrators of physical and sexual abuse crosses into forensic and criminological specialties beyond the scope of a chapter on family assessment. There will, however, be instances when examiners are asked to evaluate treatment potential for family offenders. There have to date been fewer systematic studies of perpetrators of violence than of their victims, but this is a rapidly developing area of inquiry.

As has long been known, the examiner cannot take most of these individuals at their word when they describe the extent and nature of their violence to others (Jacobson & Gottman, 1998; Salter, 1995). Offender minimizing, denying and outright lying are common in these cases. Psychology has as yet no practical science to discriminate liars from truth-tellers, and intuition and experience fare no better. Ekman has shown that even experienced judges, magistrates, police officers, and psychologists who are convinced that they can discern truth-tellers from liars score no better than chance in laboratory studies (Ekman & O'Sullivan, 1991). Although polygraphs have ardent defenders, their science is uncertain at best (Cross & Saxe, 1992). In our current state of knowledge, if a well-dressed, personable, respectable man assures the examiner with convincing sincerity that he is puzzled and hurt by the accusations and certainly did nothing at all like what his vindictive, unstable wife and brainwashed children are saying he did, psychology offers no practical science to tell us whom to believe.

The sexual abuse of children is a crime, although perhaps fewer than 5% of child molesters are caught. Criminal convictions and imprisonment are estimated to occur in fewer than 1% of cases (Salter, 1995). Because the assessment and treatment of sexual offenders is highly specialized and contains a large literature replete with controversy, the subject will be covered only briefly here. The examiner should be aware, however, that sexual offending is generally a compulsive, repetitive, and intransigent behavior, that sexual offenders are skilled at lying, manipulating, and denying, and that the protection of a child from a potential molester should be paramount in a family intervention where child sexual abuse is at issue (Salter, 1995).

Child sexual abusers are heterogeneous and can vary from psychologically normal to pathologically disturbed. Herman (1990) writes, "The most striking characteristic of sex offenders, from a diagnostic standpoint, is their apparent normality" (p. 180). Myers and his colleagues (1989) state, "Sex offenders are a heterogeneous group with few shared characteristics apart from a predilection for deviant sexual behavior. Furthermore, there is no psychological test or device that reliably detects persons who have or will sexually abuse children" (p. 142). Abel, Mittelman and Becker (1985) find that 60% in their sample of over 200 outpatient child molesters have no psychopathology other than sexual deviancy. Becker and Quinsey (1993) argue that because the question of whether or not a person has committed a sexual offense is not one that clinical assessment can address, the matter is best left to detectives and the courts (p. 169).

We do know, however, that most, but not all, sexual offenders are male (Kaufman, Wallace, Johnson, & Reeder, 1995). Child sexual abuse is less clearly correlated with the stresses of lower socioeconomic status than are physical abuse or neglect (Salter, 1995). The French physician Claude Bernard made the discovery in the late 19th century, and it has been confirmed by late 20th-century research, that men who appear to be well-educated, prosperous, respectable, and otherwise law-abiding, can be child molesters (Masson, 1984; Salter, 1995). If men who are doing this choose to deny it in clinical interview, as most do, psychologists have no special skills to ascertain that they are lying. In clinical interview and psychological testing they can appear to be normal.

Most child sexual abusers do not meet *DSM-IV* criteria for pedophilia, and there is no pedophile profile that can diagnose them. Many child molesters have multiple paraphilias (Salter, 1995). Much of what we thought we knew in the 1970s about child molesters has been challenged by recent research. In contrast to the beliefs of Giaretto (1982) and other early child sexual abuse experts that "a failing marriage is, invariably, one of the precursors to incest" (p. 54), or that mothers promote incest "by abandoning and frustrating their husbands sexually" (Sarles, 1975, quoted in Salter, 1988, p. 36), we now know that child molesters can be outwardly normal, heterosexually active married men (Salter, 1995). Groth's (1978) regressed-fixated offender distinction has also been challenged by subsequent research, which has revealed that a great many incest offenders have extrafamilial histories of sexual assault, child molesting, and rape (Abel, Becker, Mittelman, Cunningham-Rathner, Rouleau, & Murphy, 1987). One subgroup of child molesters and incest offenders also engage in a variety of other antisocial acts, from armed robbery to white collar crimes such as tax fraud (Salter, 1995).

The examiner may find that deficiencies in empathy characterize many child molesters. These deficiencies may be evident in antisocial or narcissistic personality disorders on the MCMI and the absence of human movement and human contents on the Rorschach. Impulse control problems may also be evident, with elevations on MMPI scales 4 and 9 and unstructured color responses on the Rorschach. Deviant thinking patterns may be evident on the WAIS-III Comprehension or Vocabulary subtests or may show up on MMPI critical items or Rorschach responses. But although test results such as these may offer the examiner hints that all is not well, the great majority of narcissistic men who have impulse control problems are not child sexual abusers.

Batterers are heterogeneous as well. The male batterer may beat his wife or girlfriend for reasons that have little to do with psychopathology. Perhaps the majority of men who are violent at home have no mental disorders measurable by current tests (Pagelow, 1992, 1993; Straus & Gelles, 1990; Tolman & Bennett, 1990). These men may, for example, belong to subcultures where wife battering is accepted, as it was in much of the Western world until the recent past (Gordon, 1988; Gelles & Loseke, 1993). Pagelow (1992) writes that there are no psychological characteristics that predispose women to choose battering partners, although when women emerge from violent relationships, they may show posttraumatic symptoms, anxiety, depression, and other signs of distress (Herman, 1992). Only recently has attention been directed to battering within gay or lesbian relationships, and it is believed that its incidence has been greatly underestimated. Treatment programs for both victims and perpetrators in homosexual relationships are scarce.

Gondolf (1997) writes that one promising direction to assess dangerousness as well as treatment potential lies in research on batterer typology. In addition to the "normal" batterer, Gondolf suggests that there appear to be at least two categories of batterer: psychopathic/antisocial and impulsive/manipulative.

Psychopathic/antisocial batterers are not confined to the criminal classes; these often charming men may be successful entrepreneurs, contractors, or investors. Psychopathic/antisocial batterers are characterized by deficits in empathy and remorse, a pattern of especially severe and pervasive violence, and negative treatment indicators (Gondolf, 1997). A recent study suggests that their partners are less likely to get free of them than are the partners of other violent men (Gottman et al., 1995, cited in Gondolf, 1997). The antisocial tendencies and distorted thinking of these men may or may not show up on standard measures. They may display elevations on Scales 4 and 6 of the MMPI-2 and the Antisocial or Sadistic scales on the MCMI-III. Their Rorschachs may contain very few human movement responses, a high number of Aggressives, and no Cooperatives.

Jacobson and Gottman (1998) have divided batterers into two groups, which they label "pit bulls" and "cobras." They find significant physiological differences between them. During polygraphed laboratory arguments with their wives, pit bulls show physiological arousal, whereas cobras calm down internally during arguments. In their sample of 63 battering relationships, Jacobson and Gottman found that at the two-year follow-up, 38% of the wives had escaped the battering relationship, but none of the women who left were the wives of cobras, most likely because cobra wives were more frightened. Cobras are more dangerously violent, more willing to use lethal weapons, and more likely to engage in antisocial behaviors outside of marriage.

Many batterers have prior childhood or combat trauma histories (Jacobson & Gottman, 1998; Tolman & Bennett, 1990). They may test with patterns similar to borderline personality disorder, PTSD, or complex PTSD (Dutton, 1994, 1995; Tolman & Bennett, 1990). Many of these men also abuse alcohol (Tolman & Bennett, 1990). One subtype may show a dependent personality disorder on the MCMI-III and a high number of Texture responses on the Rorschach, whereas another may disguise dependency needs in a manipulative histrionic/somatizing pattern with corresponding scale elevations. Impulsivity may show up in elevated 4 and 9 scales and possibly Over-controlled Hostility (OH) on the MMPI-2. On the Rorschach, unstructured color responses often outnumber structured ones. Some batterers have a paranoid edge that may be revealed in the MMPI-2 or the MCMI-III.

Hamberger and Hastings (1991) have used the MCMI to measure personality correlates of men who batter. They compared convicted batterers in treatment with two groups of men in the community: batterers in the community never convicted or treated, and nonviolent men. The treatment group contained no men convicted of felony-level domestic assaults, so that it was not representative of all batterers Results showed a personality-disordered pattern for the batterers in treatment who were also alcohol abusers, but only moderate elevations in avoidant, negativistic, and borderline characteristics for the non-alcoholic identified batterers. MCMI scores for alcoholic batterers differed significantly from those of nonviolent men for aggression, hypomania, and psychotic thinking. Alcoholic batterers also reported the highest levels of disruption (victimization, witnessing abuse, divorce, parental addictions) in their families of origin. There were no differences between the community-batterer group and the nonviolent group.

Men who batter their wives are significantly more likely to sexually or physically abuse their children than are nonbatterers (American Psychological Association Task Force, 1996; Edleson, in press; Wilson, 1998). Battered women are also more likely to neglect or abuse their children than are nonbattered women (Crimmins, Langley, Brownstein, & Spunt, 1997). Exposing children to adult violence in the home is in itself psychological maltreatment (American Psychological Association Presidential Task Force on Violence and the Family, 1996). Child witnesses, even when not hit or injured themselves, are emotionally and behaviorally disordered when they have to live with chronic violence (Graham-Bermann & Levendosky, 1998; Kolbo, Blakeley, & Engleman, 1996; Wolak & Finkelhor, 1998). Obviously, then, any assessment of adults in violent homes should include child interviews. The children must be seen alone and out of the presence of either parent.

## Psychological Assessment of Victimized Children

Children from violent families are often subjected to more than one form of child maltreatment: physical abuse, sexual abuse, neglect, psychological maltreatment, and the witnessing of violence against their parents. When it is not the family itself who seeks help, it is generally reports to social services by those outside the family, such as neighbors or teachers, that bring abusive families to the attention of the authorities and eventually to the psychologist's office for assessment. School referrals of traumatized children to assess for attention deficit hyperactivity disorder constitute a second common referral path by which abused children may come for psychological assessment. ADHD is too often misdiagnosed and erroneously medicated in traumatized children who are distracted or unable to sit still because they have posttraumatic or dissociative symptoms, acute anxiety, or agitated depression. A thorough history that includes questions about victimization, abuse, and violence should be part of every ADHD testing protocol. It is now well-established that children do not as a rule volunteer information about ongoing family victimization to outsiders. It will not help agitated, traumatized children to give them Ritalin and send them home for more abuse.

The standard batteries for children vary by age but include child and youth self-report measures, parent- and teacher-report measures, and ability and projective tests with the child. For children believed to have been victimized, a number of trauma-specific measures have recently been developed and validated. Although parents are generally seen as the single most reliable source of information about children (Achenbach, 1991a), this is not always the case. As part of the abusive dynamics of violent families, parents may minimize or deny their children's symptoms. On the other hand, if the context is forensic (e.g., lawsuits, child custody), parents may consciously or unconsciously exaggerate their children's symptoms. Achenbach (1991a; Achenbach, McConaughy & Howell, 1987) has reported that mothers are generally more valid reporters than fathers of children's behavior problems, although maternal and paternal reports tend to be significantly correlated. Foster mother and natural mother reports also correlate; Friedrich (1997) found no significant difference on total raw scores for his Child Sexual Behavior Inventory between foster mothers and natural mothers.

## WECHSLER INTELLIGENCE SCALE FOR CHILDREN-III (WISC-III)

The WISC-III should be administered if competent, recent ability testing is not available from school or other records. The WISC-III offers information not only about ability level but also about possible psychological symptoms. Performance scores that are significantly lower than verbal scores may signal the psychomotor retardation symptomatic of depression. This discrepancy may also alert the examiner to possible brain damage in children whose interpersonal victimization included severe shakings or blows to the head or brain injury before birth from battering to the mother's abdomen. Depressed Third Factor scores that signal distractibility can correlate with posttraumatic or anxiety symptoms. A significant pattern of intra- or intertest scatter can correlate with dissociative symptoms or the intrusive experiences of PTSD. Examiners should be aware that the anxiety, depression, and posttraumatic symptoms from which many victimized children suffer can depress full-scale intelligence scores, so that test results on these children may not reflect their true abilities.

## THE ACHENBACH CHECKLISTS: CHILD BEHAVIOR CHECKLIST (CBCL), TEACHER REPORT FORM (TRF), AND YOUTH SELF-REPORT (YSR)

The Child Behavior Checklist (Achenbach, 1991a) has two versions, one for children aged 4–18 and one for children aged 2–3. It consists of 112 items about a child's behavior for which the parent responds Not True, Somewhat or Sometimes True, and Very True or Often True. There are also a number of general questions about the child's activities, chores, friends, siblings, academic performance, illnesses or handicaps, parental concerns about the child, and the best things about the child. Fathers and mothers with reading skills at the fifth-grade level can fill out the form, which is then scored by hand or computer to generate a profile. It is possible to calculate correlations among parent, youth, and teacher forms on a single child to look for similarities and differences across multiple informants.

The three CBCL Competence Scales are Activities, Social, and School. The eight CBCL syndromes are: Withdrawn, Somatic Complaints, Anxious/Depressed, Social Problems, Thought Problems, Attention Problems, Delinquent Behavior, and Aggressive Behavior. For the CBCL but not the YSR or TRF, a syndrome for Sex Problems can also be generated. (If sexual problems are of clinical concern, additional measures such as the Trauma Symptom Checklist for Children and the Child Sexual Behavior Inventory should also be administered.) T-scores of between 67 and 70 are in the borderline clinical range, and T-scores above 70 are more clearly in the clinical range. Clinical scales can also be grouped into two categories: the Internalizing group is made up of Withdrawn, Somatic Complaints, and Anxious/Depressed; and the Externalizing group is made up of Delinquent Behavior and Aggressive Behavior. Achenbach (1991a) writes, "These groupings of syndromes reflect a distinction that has been detected in numerous multivariate analyses of children's behavioral/emotional problems" (p. 60).

The Youth Self-Report Form (Achenbach, 1991c) is intended for children aged 11–18, and it is very similar to the parent-report measure in structure and scoring. Profiles of syndromes and syndrome groupings are identical to those generated by the parent form. Like the CBCL, the YSR requires that the subject have a fifth-grade reading level.

The Teacher's Report Form (Achenbach, 1991b) resembles the parent and youth forms in that it consists of 112 questions and generates a similar clinical profile and syndrome groupings. The TRF also contains additional items about the child's level of performance in academic subjects, as well as achievement and aptitude test scores.

The Achenbach instruments are well-established and have good reliability and validity. Because they can be computer-correlated across informants, they are especially useful. Although the Achenbach instruments are not abuse- or trauma-focused, they should be an essential part of any battery to assess a child believed to have been victimized by abuse or violence, as well as to assess children who are themselves abusive or violent.

## THE MILLON ADOLESCENT CLINICAL INVENTORY (MACI)

The adolescent version of the Millon measures, the MACI, which can be administered to adolescents aged 13–18, is recommended as part of the battery for adolescent victims and adolescent offenders (Millon, 1993). In addition to the scales for personality patterns and clinical syndromes, the MACI is especially useful when assessing victims because of the 8-scale section on Expressed Concerns. This section includes scales labeled Identity Diffusion, Self-Devaluation,

Sexual Discomfort, and Body Disapproval, concerns that can reflect normal adolescent preoccupations but that can become more marked when there has been abuse. There is a scale for childhood abuse. As part of the evaluation of adolescents who may be themselves violent or abusive, the MACI has scales for anti-social tendencies, Social Insensitivity, Substance-Abuse Proneness, Delinquent Predisposition, Impulsive Propensity, and Borderline Tendency.

## THE RORSCHACH

The Rorschach has many potential advantages for use with traumatized children. It can be administered to youngsters as young as five. It will often reveal the presence of distress that a child may deny on self-report measures. Carlson (1997) writes that until the Armstrong and Lowenstein (1990) Trauma Content Index becomes a part of the standard Rorschach scoring system, the Rorschach may be of limited usefulness in the psychometric assessment of children's trauma responses but can generate clinical hypotheses. Both the Trauma Content Index (Armstrong & Loewenstein, 1990) and the Leavitt and Labott (1996) Sexual Abuse Index can be applied to abused children.

Leifer, Shapiro, Martone, and Kassem (1991) find that Rorschach results with sexually abused African American girls show more disturbed thinking, significantly more preoccupation with sexuality, and lower adaptive coping resources than the control group Rorschachs results show. Friedrich and his colleagues (Friedrich, Jaworski, Huxsahl, & Bengston, 1997) find that sexually abused children in psychiatric populations are significantly likelier to provide sexual content in their Rorschach responses than are a nonpsychiatric clinical sample and a psychiatric sample with no known sexual abuse histories.

The administration of the Rorschach as part of a more complete battery is recommended as long as its trauma assessment limitations and the potential for misinterpretation are clearly understood. Readers are referred to the section in this chapter on the uses of the Rorschach with victimized adults for additional commentary and references. It is expected that further research will appear in the next few years as publications in this area proliferate.

## THE TRAUMA SYMPTOM CHECKLIST FOR CHILDREN (TSCC)

The Trauma Symptom Checklist for Children (TSCC) is the child version of the Trauma Symptom Inventory (Briere, 1996). A 54-item self-report measure, it is intended for children aged 8–16, although it can be administered to children one year older or one year younger (Briere, 1996). The measure can be hand- or computer-scored and yields profiles for males and females aged 8–12 and 13–16. To address the concerns of some parents or caretakers in cases where child sexual abuse is not suspected, a 44-item version of the TSCC, the TSCC-A, which contains no reference to sexual issues, is also available. Briere (1996) writes, "In the interests of a more complete evaluation, however, and because some children may have experienced sexual traumas and symptoms that have not been disclosed, the full TSCC is recommended over the TSCC-A when there are no factors to preclude its use" (p. 3).

The TSCC has two validity scales and six clinical scales. Validity Scales measure under-responding and hyperresponding, and clinical scales measure anxiety, depression, anger, posttraumatic stress, dissociation, and sexual concerns. The profile form shows one score for dissociation and two dissociation subscales: Overt Dissociation (DIS-O) and Fantasy (DIS-F). The Sexual Concerns Scale also contain two factors: Sexual Preoccupation (SC-P) and Sexual Distress (SC-D). Sexual preoccupation varies by age, so that a raw score that is atypical for an 8-year-old boy will be within normal limits for one who is 16 (Briere, 1996). The Sexual Preoccupation scale is also sensitive to cultural differences. High scores on Sexual Distress reflect sexual fears and conflicts or sexual thoughts and behaviors that are ego-dystonic to the child. The SC-D is generally the most elevated of all TSCC scales and subscales in samples of sexually abused children (Briere, 1996). The TSCC and TSCC-A also contain critical items that may need immediate attention by the examiner, such as suicidal ideation or the fear of being killed. The TSCC can be administered at intervals to assess treatment progress. It is an indispensable instrument for children and adolescents with trauma and victimization histories.

Lanktree and Briere (1995) administered the TSCC every three months to 105 male and female child sexual abuse victims aged 8–15 who were in an outpatient, abuse-focused treatment program. They found that all symptom scales except Sexual Concerns declined somewhat after three months of therapy. Sexual Concerns first showed a decline at six months but increased again at nine months. Dissociative symptoms showed no further decline after the initial reduction at six months, and Anger did not change after initial drops at three and six months. At one year into treatment, those still in treatment showed continued decrements in Anxiety, Depression and Posttraumatic Stress, but not in Anger and Dissociation.

Because many adolescents with aggressive or abusive behavior problems have child abuse histories, the TSCC should be a standard part of their psychological evaluations as well.

## CHILD DISSOCIATIVE CHECKLIST (CDC)

The Child Dissociative Checklist is a 20-item, observer-report, screening measure for dissociation (Putnam, Helmers, & Trickett, 1993; Putnam & Peterson, 1994). It can be filled out by parents, teachers, or other observers. The CDC is available without cost as an appendix to Putnam, 1997a. The targeted age group is 5–14, but the instrument can also be administered for older or younger children. The instructions ask informants to respond about the present and the prior 12 months, but Putnam (1997a) writes that clinicians are free to specify another time frame when, for example, the instrument is administered periodically to measure treatment progress. Observers respond to 20 questions according to a 3-point scale (not true, somewhat or sometimes true, very true), and total scores can range from 0 to 40. Although younger children score slightly higher than older ones, children who do not have maltreatment histories generally have very low CDC scores. In general, scores of 12 or above indicate the possibility of pathological dissociation warranting further evaluation. Putnam (1997a) warns that a high score does not prove the presence of a dissociative disorder, because individual children's behaviors and observer's reports can vary greatly. Although further studies are needed to assess the influence of gender, class, and culture on scores, the instrument has shown good reliability and the general ability to discriminate children who have pathological dissociation from those who do not. The authors emphasize that the CDC is a screening measure rather than a diagnostic one.

### THE ADOLESCENT DISSOCIATIVE EXPERIENCES SCALE (A-DES)

Armstrong, Putnam, and Carlson (1997a) have recently developed a 30-item self-report Adolescent Dissociative Experiences Scale that is now undergoing validation. Preliminary results suggest that A-DES scores of 4.0 or higher may indicate pathological dissociation. However, the mean for older adolescents who have psychotic disorders approaches the 4.0 cutoff. The score for normal adolescents averages 2.4 (p. 254).

### CHILD SEXUAL BEHAVIOR INVENTORY (CSBI)

Friedrich's (1997) Child Sexual Behavior Inventory (CSBI) is a 38-item measure that uses maternal or primary female caretaker report of sexual behavior in children aged 2–12. It is commercially available from Psychological Assessment Resources. Although the content of several scale items was derived from items in Achenbach's CBCL, the CSBI contains more items that pertain to sexual behaviors than the Achenbach measures do. Discriminant analyses have shown that the CSBI outperforms the CBCL on sensitivity and specificity for all age and gender groups. If sexual abuse is suspected or known to have occurred, the Child Sexual Behavior Inventory should always be part of a child's battery of psychological tests.

The CSBI covers children's sexual behaviors in nine domains: boundary problems, exhibitionism, gender role behavior, self-stimulation, sexual anxiety, sexual interest, sexual intrusiveness, sexual knowledge, and voyeuristic behavior. Results are tabulated into three clinical scales: CSBI Total, Developmentally Related Sexual Behavior (DRSB), and Sexual Abuse Specific Items (SASI). DRSB score for nonabused children correlates with age, family nudity and sexuality, and other behavior problems, and it may also correlate with a general pattern of externalizing behavior on the part of a child (Friedrich, 1997). It also elevates when a child has been sexually abused. High Sexual Abuse Specific (SASI) scores are likely to be related to sexual abuse, and coexisting physical abuse and inconsistent parenting may further elevate these scores.

Validity studies have shown consistent differences in total CSBI raw scores between sexually abused and non-abused children at different ages (Friedrich, 1997). However, many children in the nonabused normative samples were reported to engage in some sexual behaviors such as touching their sex parts at home or trying to look at other people when they were nude. By contrast, among boys and girls in the nonabused normative groups aged 6 and above, there were certain CSBI items (all SASI) in which no single nonabused child was reported to have engaged; these included trying to put items into their vaginas or rectums, putting mouths on the sex parts of others, and trying to have intercourse. That is, although there are certain sexual behaviors in which many nonabused children engage, there are other sexual behaviors that are extremely rare or that seem to occur not at all among nonsexually abused children.

The CSBI can be administered periodically to children in therapy to monitor treatment progress or as part of a complete assessment in forensic contexts. However, in the CSBI manual Friedrich (1997) states that although the CSBI provides useful information, "sexual behavior alone is not proof of sexual abuse" (p. 17). False positives and false negatives are possible. Friedrich also warns that CSBI data should not be used to question the validity of a child's statements when CSBI scores are not elevated. For example, in the validity studies for this measure, one in four sexually abused girls aged 10–12 did not receive CSBI scores that would classify them in the abused group. Many sexually abused children do not display sexualized behaviors, and not all sexually inappropriate behavior by children, especially sexually coercive behaviors, correlate with sexual abuse histories.

## Summary

In the conclusion of his 1997 book about the psychological assessment of posttraumatic states, Briere (1997a) writes, "Traditional psychological instruments have tended to misinterpret what are now understood to be posttraumatic states, generally repackaging them as psychosis, personality disorder, and other less relevant psychological conditions" (p. 164). Nevertheless, Briere recommends that the standard instruments be used as part of batteries for assessing traumatized individuals to evaluate for non trauma-specific psychological symptoms and disorders. These should be supplemented by diagnostic interviews and by the newly developed trauma-specific instruments.

Because the assessment of the psychological correlates of family violence is a relatively recent and developing area of inquiry, it is expected that much new information will emerge in the next few years. For the examiner to keep current with this research, it is recommended not only that the standard psychological journals be routinely scanned but also that specialized trauma- and abuse-focused publications such as *Child Abuse and Neglect*, *Child Maltreatment*, *The Journal of Interpersonal Violence*, and *The Journal of Traumatic Stress* be regularly reviewed.

# CHAPTER 12

## Using Testing in the Context of Divorce

Psychological testing results can play an important and sometimes vital role in a clinician's understanding of parents and children going through a divorce. Tests may be used in differing contexts, ranging from hotly contested, high-conflict divorces involving child custody issues to more ordinary but painful negotiated divorces, to mediation for issues around marital dissolution, to the cooperative process in the newly developing Collaborative Divorce[sm] (Nurse & Thompson, 1997).

This chapter begins by addressing the salience of psychological testing in child custody evaluations designed to lead to settlement. The critical application of tests in the Collaborative Divorce process is then evaluated. A discussion of principal considerations in the general use of tests in divorce is followed by focusing on the attributes of specific tests as applied to divorce, making up the majority of this chapter.

## The Salience of Testing in Child Custody Evaluations

Tests are routinely used by psychologist evaluators, ordinarily court-appointed as independent experts, to provide opinions to the court about child custody issues (Ackerman, 1995, pp. 100–118). Typically, a psychologist evaluator both interviews and tests the parents and the children. The systemically oriented evaluator may be expected to interview and test other parent-figures in the family system, such as new live-in relationships. Testing and interviewing findings are used in the context of information gathered from teachers, therapists, and others familiar with the case. Available documents, past assessments, and many other sources of information are sought as the evaluator places the testing in the context of data reflecting the overall life of the family as viewed from many nontest resources. The evaluating psychologist is then prepared to report in writing and verbally to inform the court in making its decision. Results usually are reviewed by the attorney for each parent and the parties themselves. Many times, the logic of the report and the information presented is such that the parents and their attorneys are able to reach a settlement without having to argue the case in court in front of a judge. In some instances, however, the case goes to court, where the evaluator's report, recommendations, and expert testimony are ordinarily given significant weight in the ultimate decision made by the court. The psychological testing results lie at the heart of the assessment report and must have been done in a highly professional, knowledgeable, and effective way. Inappropriate and unskilled use of testing may bias the psychologist's report, rendering the report not simply useless, but, in fact, misleading and, therefore, potentially harmful to family members.

## Testing Results as Guideposts in Collaborative Divorce

Collaborative Divorce is a new, nonadversarial, interdisciplinary approach that places a premium on facilitating personal and family transitions, but also attends fairly to the financial and legal aspects of divorce (Fagerstrom et al., 1997; Nurse & Thompson, 1997; Nurse, Thompson, Wolfrum, & Wilde, 1998). Collaborative Divorce services are provided through an interdisciplinary team (including the attorneys) that signs an agreement *not* to go to court. The adults and children undergo some psychological testing as in a child custody evaluation, although the amount of testing will vary depending on the clinician's judgment of the case (Nurse & Thompson, 1997). Each parent has a same-gender mental health professional (usually a psychologist) to meet with individually. Guided by inventory result-generated hypotheses, the mental health professionals work to improve the parents' management of emotions and teach new communication skills. Based on this therapeutically oriented but problem-focused experience, the parents then work with the mental health professionals in a four-way meeting designed to improve their ability to coparent and aimed at developing specific coparenting plans. The children are assessed separately, and the child psychologist providing this service meets with the parents and the divorce counselors (psychologists) to provide feedback on the children; this feedback is designed to inform the coparenting planning discussions and decision making. Tests are administered to both parents and children as a part of assessment, but, as noted, the amount and type of testing may be modified with reference to the needs of the children and their parents. In the Collaborative Divorce process, each parent has his or her own collaborative law attorney who works cooperatively with the other attorney. The parents frequently have one joint finance person who helps with organizing financial information and advising (sometimes teaching) the couple about practical budgeting matters. Among the assessment findings shared with the attorneys and the financial person is information about the interpersonal style (possibly disorder) manifested by the parents. When these other professionals gain knowledge of the interpersonal style or disorder early in the collaborative process, they are better able, with the help of psychologists, to develop a successful strategy for productively working as a team with the parents.

## Principal Considerations in Using
## Tests in Divorce

The context in which tests, especially inventories, are used influences how people respond in taking the tests. The assessor must consider test-taking attitudes in interpreting the test results. Professional literature is only recently beginning to evolve that the clinician may review in interpreting test findings in a child custody evaluation. In this situation, parents are expected to put their best foot forward. They are highly motivated to appear as good parents and to deny, or at least soft-pedal, their problem areas. The clinician assessor must take this motivation into account; indeed, when it seems not to be operating in the data and the parent is very candid, as if asking for help, this calls for explanation. By contrast with the child custody evaluation, in the Collaborative Divorce process the test-taking attitudes may soften. Although some clients may remain wary and intend to put their best foot forward while minimizing problems, many will appropriately view Collaborative Divorce as a problem-solving situation in which they work collaboratively with a team of professionals, and so take tests as they would in other help-seeking contexts. The clinician must make the judgment call on how much weight to put on various sets of normative data in the analysis of the clients' scores.

It is also important for the clinician assessor to consider whether a test finding of apparent psychopathology is more likely to come about from situational pressures or is a long-standing feature, trait, style, or disorder. For example, the state of being upset, anxious, and depressed in a divorcing situation may well be situational, as well as being a typical response to divorce. This finding can reflect the psychology of someone who, for most of her or his life, did not manifest these symptoms. Or it may be an aggravated finding for someone with a long-standing dysthymia and anxiety disorder.

The next section of this chapter considers each test or inventory as used in the context of marital dissolution, whether specifically a child custody evaluation or a variant of the Collaborative Divorce process. The assessing clinician needs to analyze the data in both contexts with reference to usual normative test standards and whatever divorce-specific norms are available. As Stricker and Trierweiler (1995) have written, taking account of local settings and particular persons along with considering broader norms helps bridge the gap between the empirical science base in psychology and the practice of psychology. The relative interpretive emphasis of general as compared with specific population norms is a matter of the clinician's sophisticated judgment of the individual case.

# Major Tests

## MMPI/MMPI-2

Given the expectation that parents undergoing evaluation for the court in child custody matters want to appear in a favorable light and with minimal or no psychological problems, it is not surprising when their validity pattern on the MMPI-2 shows a defensive pattern. James Butcher (1990, p. 33), lead developer of the MMPI-2, reports a typical pattern of high L ($T$ 66), high K ($T$ 70), and low F ($T$ 44) common for a parent in a child custody evaluation. This pattern of exaggerated positive mental health, outstanding virtue, and low self-disclosure on the validity scales is accompanied by moderate to low clinical scales.

Batthurst, Gottfried, and Gottfried (1997) report normative MMPI-2 data on 508 litigants in child custody cases, thus providing for the first time reasonable norms derived within the context of disputed issues in divorce, with its accompanying strife. Mean MMPI-2 $T$ scores are L 56, F 45, K 59, HS 48, D 47, HY 52, PD 51, MF 51, PA 52, PT 47, SC 47, MA 48, SI 43, and OH 60. Thus, overall mean average clinical scores fall within the normal ranges. Consistent with Butcher (1990) as noted above, these scores reflect a defensive pattern of presenting oneself in a positive light, denying or minimizing psychological problems. It is barely conceivable that on average, no or few psychological problems are present, despite the situational stress of divorce.

In looking at the validity score data in their sample of 508 people, Batthhurst et al. (1997, p. 208) were unable to determine whether their high L, low F, and high K pattern might be interpreted as an overestimate of mental health in a psychologically healthy population or as an attempt by psychologically disturbed individuals to conceal symptomatology. A reasonable conclusion is that there are problems of underidentification (false negatives) if the MMPI-2 is used as a screen for psychopathology in the divorcing context. The use of additional tests and other sources of information beyond the MMPI-2 is required to more fully screen for psychopathology.

*Frequent High-Point Code Types*

The data in the Batthurst et al. (1997, p. 207) study do provide some hypotheses about the within-normal types of high-point codes to anticipate in the divorcing population. Three codes are most typical: 34/43, 36/63, and 46/64. In terms of the percentages of the normative population, the code groupings represent (rounded) for 34/43, 12%; for 36/63, 19%; and for 46/64, 12%. The authors state that "Although these mean average 2-point code types do not meet the general rule of well-defined code-types (Graham, 1993), there is clinical support for their credibility" (p. 207).

Experts characterize the 34/43 code type as having problems interpersonally around chronic anger that may be expressed explosively, sometimes alternating with a more contained appearance (see Butcher, 1990; Caldwell, 1997a; Graham, 1990; Greene, 1991). More aggressive behavior may be expected when Scale 4 is higher. Impulsive, stormy, and difficult interpersonal relationships are anticipated, with a readiness to blame others. High 4 persons may have had flawed relationships with their own parents and perhaps as a result have shallow peer relationships. Caldwell (pp. 69–70) indicates that there may be a kind of upwardly mobile role playing that appears phony, and they may initially idealize a partner, only to become disillusioned and resentful subsequently.

The 36/63 pattern points to a denial of personal problems, similar to the 34/43. Considerable hostility may surface indirectly with blame being projected on others, particularly those in their family. People with the 36/63 pattern tend to divide others into two groups: those who are on their side and those who are against them. Overall, they appear uncooperative and self-focused.

The third pattern, 46/64, also is characterized by considerable anger and blaming of others. A history of social maladjustment is likely (Greene, 1991, p. 275). They may be "immature, narcissistic, and self-indulgent" (Graham, 1990, p. 98). And, as noted above, the higher Scale 4 points to more interpersonal disruption and aggressiveness.

*Parenting*

Alex Caldwell (1997a, pp. 66–75) summarizes what literature there is on parenting. Reports from child guidance clinics and related facilities indicate that "profiles of parents in such settings are *on the average* (1) more disturbed than the profiles of 'normal' or 'control' samples . . . , but they are (2) less disturbed than the profiles of adult patients seeking individual psychotherapy" (p. 66).

Consistent with Batthurst et al. (1997), Caldwell (1997, p. 69) states that the 34/43, 36/63, and 46/64 high-point codes are the three most common in custody conflict situations. Caldwell writes that "none are good patterns for parenting (particularly with increasing elevations on scale 4-Pd in the 34/43 and 46/64 codes)" (p. 71). Greene (1991, p. 155) notes that a higher Scale 4 along with a

good social façade coupled with underlying rebelliousness and hostility anticipates unreliability, egocentricity, and irresponsibility. As Caldwell (1997a, p. 71)
states, "attention to the child or children is typically uneven and undependable
over time. It is apt to vary from dramatic showings of attention and favor to moments of coldness to the child's wants or even to occasions of failure to respond
to the child's urgent distress." Caldwell goes on to elaborate that the problem of
an elevated scale 4-Pd is that of deficient bonding. He believes that the parent
scoring with this elevation was likely not lovingly and warmly bonded to his or
her own parents, and this limitation or shallowness of emotional attachment is
apt to be recapitulated with that individual's children (p. 72).

There are problems with the parenting when adults have the 36/63 code. A
rigidity may be expected that may entail "both over-identifying alliances with
the child and severity when the child fails to comply with high parental standards and expectations" (Caldwell, 1997a, p. 71). This pattern may be associated with alienation of a child from the other parent as, particularly, the
school-age child has strong emotional pressure from the 36/63 parent to take
sides.

With the 43/34 profile, the parent may appear to make all the right moves
as a parent in order to obtain help, yet be lacking in the spontaneous warmth
needed to nourish the child (Caldwell, 1997a, p. 71). Explosive, inconsistent,
superficial parenting might be anticipated.

### Some Additional Observations on MMPI/MMPI-2 Profiles

Marc Ackerman (1995, pp. 110–113) in the *Clinician's Guide to Child Custody
Evaluations* agrees with Caldwell in opinions cited on the 34/43, 36/63, and
46/64 profiles. With the 46/64 profile, Ackerman also notes that with the addition of a third high score—Scale 8 Schizophrenia, Scale 9 Mania, or both 8 and
9 together—a parent may present a danger to the child. The reason is that elevation on Scale 8 points to confusion in thinking that may interfere with a parent's
ability to organize and structure his or her own life and the child's; an elevation
on Scale 9 indicates impulsivity and excitement that may preclude a parent from
placing the child's needs first (Ackerman, 1995, p. 111). Ackerman also points
out that a high 49/94 profile predicts lack of responsibility and putting blame on
others, particularly when anxiety scores are not high (p. 111). However, regardless of the profile high points, when anxiety scores are high, the anxiety may be
so debilitating as to interfere with parenting (p. 112). A high 2 Depression also
may signal such distress that a parent has difficulty functioning as a parent
(p. 110). Because therapy is often recommended for parents, consideration of
TRT (Negative Treatment Indicators scale) is warranted. A high score reflects
the parent's belief that no one can be of help and that there is no need to
change anything in his or her life anyway (p. 113). Use of this scale underlines
the necessity for scoring all major scales and identifying critical items, rather

than calculating only the basic validity and clinical scales. To do only the latter, indicates Ackerman (p. 114), raises ethical issues associated with not using the entire MMPI/MMPI-2.

*Cautions in Applying High-Point Codes*

In applying these descriptions of the 34/43, 36/63, and 46/64 profiles, the reader is reminded that these pattern descriptions were developed with the MMPI; because little research is yet available on the MMPI-2 codes, the recommendation is to use both MMPI and MMPI-2 patterns. Note also that these are more marked descriptions of clinically significant pictures, so that with profiles less than $T$ 70 on the MMPI and $T$ 65 on the MMPI-2, the patterns may be of only moderate intensity. Furthermore, in the crisis of divorce, people are likely to respond with more symptoms and temporary rigidity than is normal to their general characterologic structure. In particular, whereas the mild 46/64 pattern may reflect the moment, it may not appear on retaking the MMPI/MMPI-2 sometime after the divorce. With a change from active family discord to a new positive family association, Scale 4 may be lowered. In the old relationship, the former spouse may really have been out to get the person and persecute him or her. About half the items on Scale 6 are persecutory ones, so that scale 6-Pa would go down when the client is in a new, positive, cooperative, and helpful relationship. Of some help is the NCS printout, which can provide an indication of definition of the profile, which has implications of its stability over time. Despite these limitations, the MMPI/MMPI-2 profiles may provide a significant source of data for reasoning about the family, particularly in the context of other assessment information.

MCMI-III

There has been a question about the use of the iterations of the MCMI with custody evaluations. Ackerman (1995, p. 115), for example, states that the MCMI-II "is a test that is designed to be used only in clinical settings, not in custody disputes or other circumstances where the individuals are not seeking psychological treatment." More recently, however, Dyer (1997, p. 134) pointed out that "since 1993 Millon trainers have been stating in workshops that the test author explicitly permits use of the (Millon) Inventories" in child custody evaluations. Dyer's rationale is that if the litigation reaches the point where a child custody evaluation is ordered, this reflects that the interpersonal relationships in the family are sufficiently disturbed to "label the evaluation as a clinical case" (p. 134). In the *MCMI-III Manual*, Millon (1994a, p. 5) clarifies that while the MCMI-III "is not a general personality instrument to be used for normal populations . . . assessments for forensic purposes—such as child custody . . . —are appropriate, owning to the presence of many such cases in the MCMI-III normative sample."

Clinicians now have normative data available on child custody evaluations with the MMPI/MMPI-2, but norms specific only to the divorce context are not yet available for the MCMI-III. However, because its development was in part based on divorcing parents, the MCMI-III has applicability to the divorcing population.

As discussed in Chapter 2 of this volume, a unique feature of the MCMI-III is its measurement of personality features, traits, styles, and disorders. In addition, the MCMI-III measures a number of clinical syndromes. The MCMI-III provides hypotheses that can clue the clinician into the personal qualities, strengths, and weaknesses of the divorcing parents. Of particular importance is that with approximately 20 minutes of the client's time and an approximate $11 investment in NCS profile scoring, a clinician can, early on, develop a theoretical platform upon which to structure thinking against other assessment data. The "early on" aspect is particularly important for the divorcing couple because a couple often separates in the context of a crisis. Quick identification of both problem symptoms and mood states together with personality styles or disorders can provide guidance for the clinician's intervention process.

*Selected Clinical Syndromes, Divorce Implications*

It is important to emphasize that a *DSM-IV* diagnostic label per se does not automatically discredit a parent. However, because the MCMI-III is designed in parallel with the *DSM-IV*, these diagnostic categories are referenced. MCMI-III results help identify targets for modifying interventions that aim at improving parenting. For example, in the area of clinical syndromes, the identification of an anxiety disorder and/or a dysthymic disorder may call for medication evaluation and a recommendation for cognitive therapy. A significant score on Alcohol Dependence or Drug Dependence may call for specific interventions and safeguards about substance use and potential abuse. A high score on major depression would alert to appraisal of not only symptoms of depression, but possible inability to function adequately as a parent. This might call for various interventions, including medication evaluation, concern for suicide potential and possible hospitalization, along with temporarily relieving the adult of independent parenting responsibilities.

*The MCMI-III and Clinical Personality Patterns*

As with couples who are not divorcing, the MCMI-III provides unique assistance to the divorcing couple in that it supplies hypotheses for the clinician regarding the ongoing features, traits, styles, or disorders of the spouses. These hypotheses can be given in-depth and enriched meaning by reference to Millon's (1996) descriptions in *Disorders of Personality, DSM-IV and Beyond*. With these in mind, reference to the couple literature, including reference to *The Disordered Couple* (Carlson & Sperry, 1998), may prove of assistance in teasing out the possible spousal dynamics.

For example, Table 12.1 displays a schema for considering the relationship system in a dependent/narcissistic couple (Nurse, 1998, p. 323). The MCMI-III results suggest the hypothesis that this couple is caught in a dependent/narcissistic bind. In the divorcing situation, one of the partners, often the dependent one, often the female, is maturing and no longer wants a relationship of this type wherein she has increasing resentment against what feels like an oppressive partner. The narcissistic person feels betrayed that homage is no longer given to his superior status and is consequently increasingly resentful. Although overtly, all the clinician may see is the overload of anger of both spouses over a range of petty instances, developing a grasp on the actual interlocking of personality styles (or disorders) and the consequent relationship can let the clinician see to the more covert and important issue of the threat of increasing independence on the part of the dependent personality. Knowing the underlying personality structure means that both the divorce counselor/therapist/psychologist and the attorney for the dependent woman can encourage independence with support but, very importantly, not fall into the trap of becoming the client's new person on whom to depend. As for handling the narcissistic male, his divorce counselor/therapist and his attorney can provide support for his positive qualities, not undermine him, yet carefully

Table 12.1
*Relationship System of the Dependent/Narcissistic Couple*

| Level | Dependent Spouse | Narcissistic Spouse |
|---|---|---|
| **Behavioral** | | |
| Expressive | Incompetent, helpless | Haughty, extracompetent |
| Interpersonal | Submissive, needs strong other | Exploitive, entitled, unempathetic |
| **Phenomenological** | | |
| Cognitive | Naïve, overagreeable thoughts | Expansive, self-glorifying thoughts |
| Self-Image | Inept, inadequate | Admirable, special |
| Internalizations | Immature images, easily overwhelmed | Contrived, readily refashioned |
| **Intrapsychic** | | |
| Mechanism | Inseparable bond with other | Rationalizations, self-focused |
| Organization | Inchoate, underdeveloped | Spurious, solid look yet actually flimsy |
| **Biophysical** | | |
| Mood | Pacific, warm, noncompetitive | Insouciant, feigned tranquillity |

*Note:* Adapted from *Disorders of Personality: DSM-IV and Beyond*, Chapters 9 and 11 (Millon, 1996).

help him become more empathetic with his divorcing spouse and particularly his children, at the same time not furthering his egocentric, self-focused behavior.


## RORSCHACH INKBLOT TEST

As discussed in Chapter 5, during the past 30 years, a scoring and interpreting system was developed by John Exner and associates (1991, 1993). Exner's Comprehensive System provides a sturdy base for using the Rorschach in child custody disputes. It is strongly recommended that the Rorschach be administered, scored, and interpreted following the approach by Exner and associates because of the excellent research base underpinning this system. For divorce disputes involving custody evaluations, the reader is referred specifically to Exner and Weiner's (1995) *The Rorschach: A Comprehensive System, Volume 3: Assessment of Children and Adolescents*, second edition. This book includes a chapter titled "Custody Issues," which is discussed below.

Unfortunately, two recent guidebooks for psychologists conducting custody evaluations underplay the usefulness of the Rorschach with divorcing families. Ackerman (1995, p. 116), although endorsing the Exner scoring system, believes that the Rorschach may also be administered without inquiry and scoring, and the resulting responses may be interpreted intuitively by the examiner. Ackerman provides no specific tactics for using the Rorschach in child custody evaluations.

In the other recent guidebook in this area, *Conducting Child Custody Evaluations*, Stahl (1994, p. 55) states: "The Rorschach can provide a good understanding of the adult's affect, organization skills, and reality testing, but, except for the most dysfunctional parent, it will not do much to answer questions about day-to-day parenting." Though there is some literal truth to Stahl's statement about day-to-day parenting, Exner's Comprehensive System provides well-established indices designed to identify serious psychological problems, a significant responsibility for the assessing psychologist. The Rorschach findings are very helpful in identifying various characteristics potentially interfering with adequate parenting, such as an extreme self-focus and deficiencies in ability to empathize, problems of control, and difficulties in the areas of anger and aggression. As with Ackerman, Stahl presents no examples of the Rorschach's usefulness in child custody evaluations.

### The Rorschach as Applied to Parenting Appraisal in Child Custody Evaluations

Exner and Weiner (1995, pp. 381–416) address issues about the Rorschachs of parents in a chapter titled "Custody Issues" in their recent book on children and adolescents. The Rorschach has value, as noted, in identifying extreme psychopathological conditions that are likely to interfere with effective parenting.

The parent with a high SCZI will ordinarily be found to have a problem in thinking that can result in poor judgment in making decisions about a youngster, even if not found by other criteria to reach the threshold suggesting a diagnosis of schizophrenia. A positive HVI points to a parent who invests considerable energy in being constantly prepared for hostile attacks or even gestures of closeness from others; at an extreme, this very suspicious attitude reaches paranoidlike levels. This positive HVI is likely to foster a fearful, distancing attitude on the part of a child. The parent who is so depressed as to reach a DEPI greater than 5 is functioning questionably, having problems in both cognitive and affective realms, or emphasizing one more than another. Depression, whether the focus of the psychopathology or an accompaniment of other psychological problems, means that a parent has difficulty managing and extending himself or herself in a warm, feeling way toward a child.

Exner and Weiner (1995) point out:

> once marked pathology is ruled out, however, there is no personality description that always and automatically determines a judge's decision in a case of contested custody, and there is no personality pattern that has been found to preclude a parent's being granted custody or to prevent him or her from functioning effectively in the parental role. (p. 386)

Although there is no profile to define the good parent or the bad parent, Rorschach findings can provide some important clues that need to be factored into all of the information regarding a parent.

Exner and Weiner (1995, p. 386) state that "the person with zero T, at least one reflection, and a high Egocentricity Ratio is probably less parentally oriented than a person whose record is free from these deviations from normative expectation." This is the person who is likely to be self-centered and selfish, deficient in ability to form attachments, and not likely to be realistically self-sacrificing in parenting behavior.

Additionally, parents who fail to modulate their emotional expressions (higher right than left side of the FC:CF + C ratio) and have a large number of S responses may be found to have moments of out-of-control anger reactions toward their children, in contrast to parents who simply experience annoyance and express themselves in more controlled ways. The former parents are likely to instill fear and an accompanying hypervigilant reaction on the part of their children.

The assessor should pay attention to parents who have few human contents and few pure H responses. These parents, especially when demonstrating no COP scores, are likely to be deficient in interest and emotional empathy with their children.

The Rorschachs of some parents experiencing the chaos that can occur during the divorce crisis may produce *little m* responses, suggesting a sense of being

out of control. Still other parents, separated, lonely, and feeling isolated, may produce a higher number of T responses. In research conducted in the early 1970s to
assist in the development of the Comprehensive System, Exner and Bryant (Exner,
1993, pp. 384–385) found an average of four T responses in 30 recently separated
nonpatient adults. Retested 10 months later, about two-thirds of these people were
in new or reconstructed relationships and gave significantly fewer responses. The
remaining one-third all produced three or more T responses. Thus, the Rorschach
can provide information suggestive of both traitlike and state-specific qualities
useful in understanding parenting behavior.

Various other features of the Rorschach may provide clues about problems
in parenting. The uncertain style of the ambient, in contrast with the introversive or extroversive styles, suggests the potential for exhibiting a lack of structure
in parenting. A passive style may present some problems in being sufficiently
assertive with children, including setting realistic boundaries. The difficulty in
coping predicted by a significant CDI points to problems in management on a
day-to-day basis that would affect parenting behavior negatively.

Rorschach scores such as these point to potential problems in personality
dynamics that negatively affect parenting. One practical problem in using this information in a custody case is that frequently, the separating parents function at
a problematic developmental level, manifesting similar or interlocking personality
problems. This can be very discouraging to the evaluator who may seem to have
no good recommendations for the court because both parents appear to have significant problems. However, the positive aspect of negative findings is that these
results can help identify specific targets for modification through therapy and
other interventions. Uncovering these problems enables the evaluator not simply
to recommend therapy in a general sense, but instead to be very specific about
what needs to be changed through therapy and, quite often, therefore, what kind
of therapy might prove most effective.

### The Rorschach as Applied to Children in Child Custody Evaluations

The major reference in considering children's Rorschachs is the volume mentioned above by Exner and Weiner (1995). Summarizing its useful data is beyond the purposes of the present writing. However, several features of their work
are particularly salient for child custody evaluations. First, Exner and Weiner
supply normative data year by year, beginning at year 5 and extending through
16. This provides guideposts for the normal development of youngsters against
which to consider the meaning of scores that are divergent in a particular child's
results. Second, because the constructs mean the same regardless of age, there is
a consistent, anchoring conceptual framework within which to think through
the ideographic meaning of the individual Rorschach. Finally, Exner and Weiner
provide ways of thinking about children's problems, including the faltering personality development, that may be of particular concern in appraising the child

of divorce. One reason that the faltering personality pattern is of particular importance is because recent research on children of high-conflict divorcing couples shows that these children appear to manifest some of these characteristics (Johnston & Roseby, 1997, pp. 151–154). These patterns are believed to frequently serve as precursors to developing personality disorders, particularly borderline personality disorders.

Exner and Weiner (1995) describe the core problems of flawed or faltering personalities as (a) overly intense emotions, (b) poor self-control, (c) illusory social adaptation, (d) strained interpersonal relationships, and (e) persistence of problems. The conditions begin early in life, gradually become identifiable during the developmental years, and are egosyntonic.

Problems in coping styles and stress tolerance are discussed by Exner and Weiner (1995, p. 237). There are several indicators of which to be especially aware. When a high Lambda style continues steadily into adolescence, it may signal some avoidance of complexity that can limit growth experiences. An ambient state continuing into adolescence indicates the lack of development of either the more stable introversive or extroversive style. The ambient style is of particular concern if there is an EA of less than 7 in a youngster 10 or older. In this case, that child is vulnerable to emotional overload, which can provoke impulsive and unpredictable behavior. A lag in personal development may be indicated by an Adjusted D of −2 or lower.

Cognitive difficulties are signaled by significant scores on those measurements suggesting elements of disordered thinking that, in extreme cases, may lead to a significant SCZI. An introversive style prior to age 13 is suspect, and such a style under the age of 9 or 10 points to a problem. Children at these younger ages are not sufficiently neurophysiologically developed to be able to think through and weigh issues as can adult introversives; instead, their thinking is concrete and often peculiar (Exner & Weiner, 1995, p. 238). The introversive style is particularly a problem if they tend to escape into fantasy, as suggested by a considerably higher ratio of passive to active Human Movement.

A major area of concern is that of affective difficulties. Affective problems may show in various ways, according to Exner and Weiner (1995, pp. 238–240). More than four space responses indicates traitlike major hostility and negativism, probably a reflection of experiencing being particularly put upon by the intrusions and manipulations of others on the one hand, or feeling abandoned by those around them on the other hand. Another indication of affective problems could be more than two pure C responses in someone older than 8. Sometimes, the presence of many more CF + C responses than FC responses points to affective difficulties in someone 14 or older. Another reaction to potential emotional disturbance is avoidance. When an Afr is below .40, this may be the situation. Combined with WsumC low and a number of C' answers, a cutoff from an interchange of feelings with others, an obvious growth inhibitor, may be suggested.

Problems in self-concept are to be considered. A low Egocentricity index may be encountered coupled with some negative ruminations about the self, "indicated by the presence of Vista answers, and the presence of more than one Color-Shading blend, indicating a marked confusion about feelings" (Exner & Weiner, 1995, p. 240). Analysis of the pure H content may provide clues about the quality of human identification. Being ambivalent about the self may manifest in pairs of figures that are perceived in different ways. By adolescence, most Reflection responses should be gone; if they remain, an evolving narcissistic personality disorder may be suspect.

Another clue to the character of interpersonal problems is the texture score. No T at all is likely with socially and emotionally isolated children; they have limited ability to be close to others. At age 10 or above, a T-less record is cause for concern. Some clinicians refer to this picture as the "burnt child syndrome." Having been hurt in past close relationships, they tend to avoid developing present close ones.

Multiple Ts also pose a problem. They may reflect a recent situation of loss. If not, they may represent unmet needs for closeness and "a propensity for clinging, dependent, and demanding relationships with others" (Exner & Weiner, 1995, p. 243). There may be themes of loneliness or abandonment. Therefore, when parents are divorcing and the child has little contact with one of them, taking note of T in the Rorschach record is very useful. As with adults, an inflated T count may reflect an immediate situation. If a recent loss is not identified, the ongoing emotional loss and hunger for relationships may be a long-standing, traitlike characteristic of the child.

Rorschach findings can suggest problems in interpersonal relationships. One key index is CDI. Shy, withdrawn, and avoidant youngsters may have poor social skills, and this may be indicated by a significant CDI of 5 or more. It is important to target the deficit in social skills rather than assume that the unhappiness and lack of satisfaction is depression that must be treated with psychotherapy. An elevated DEPI is likely to reflect the more depressive condition. Thus, these Rorschach scores help define treatment objectives and differential intervention approaches to apply when aiming to head off development of an entrenched, disordered pattern.

It is particularly important to note that the high CDI may appear with youngsters who seem to be developing normally. "Typically, they are bright, talented, and/or attractive to adults. They may do well in the classroom, be admired for their appearance, or earn praise for their artistic or academic prowess, but they are suffering from an arrest in social development and are unlikely to be enjoying rewarding peer relationships or to be feeling good about themselves" (Exner & Weiner, 1995, p. 242). These children seem to be similar to children caught in high-conflict divorces who have been studied and treated at the Center for Families in Transition in Corte Madera, California (Johnston & Roseby, 1997).

*Rorschachs of Children Caught in High-Conflict Divorces*

When the conflict between parents is intense and chronic, children experience a lack of support, often feeling alienated from one (or both) parents, and a self-protective, distrusting, distancing pattern often emerges, according to Johnston and Roseby (1997) with the Center for Families in Transition. This pattern is not always detectable. These children "tend to excel at picking up cues about what is expected of them and can mask their own vulnerabilities as a matter of survival" (Johnston & Roseby, 1997, pp. 151–152). These writers go on to say: "Not surprisingly, observational checklists and cursory interviews often indicate they are performing adequately in the classroom, in sports, or other areas of performance but fail to capture the fragile and layered quality of their competence" (p. 152). These are children who may be described as "cardboard kids," seemingly managing outwardly but inwardly impoverished, with a damaged sense of self, and lacking actual relationships in depth (Nurse, 1996). Johnston and Roseby use the same expression: "There is an almost cardboard quality to the performances of pseudo competent children" (p. 150).

The damaged developmental core may be identified on the Rorschach by considering $T$, the Egocentricity Ratio, and $S$, according to results of a study by Roseby, Erdberg, Bardenstein, and Johnston (1995). In studying a school-age sample, they discovered that 90% of their sample of children in high-conflict divorces had no $T$ responses in their Rorschachs, as contrasted with 12% of nonpatient 10-year-olds. This finding suggests deficits in basic attachment for the clinical group. The reader may wish to review the Rorschach structural summary presented in Figure 10.9, for Mary, age 9, suggesting a damaged developmental core.

Over half the children of high-conflict divorces in the Roseby et al. (1995) study were characterized by low Egocentricity scores, in contrast to only 3% of the nonpatient comparison group. During the school- or latency-age period, it is expected that the focus of children will be more on themselves than on others. Children from divorced families apparently orient themselves to others, particularly parents, as a function of the need to survive. Energy is expended on reflecting and responding to the external world, and centrally to a fragile parent(s). This is energy that in normal development would be expended toward the developing self; thus, the developing self suffers. Some of these children appear to be achieving sufficient energy and focus, meeting society's expectations, but in actuality they are the "cardboard kids" (Nurse, 1996) mentioned earlier, having little inner substance despite a patina of outward success.

It is perhaps not unexpected that children in this divorcing family context harbor significant anger. Sixty percent of the Roseby et al. (1995, p. 8) study children had high levels of space responses. This contrasts with 12% of the non-patient group. A number of responses to white space on the Rorschach reflects an oppositional, alienated stance for the clinical group children. The researchers suggest that this finding of underlying anger "likely captures the rage which is evoked by relationships" (p. 8).

These three characteristic markers on the Rorschach reflect personality features that, though instigated in service of survival in the family crisis, because of their intrinsic characteristics tend to solidify the developing personality, including the sense of self, so that the child is isolated from usual interactive corrective and developmentally positive experiences.

This problem of self-development is further aggravated by problems in processing affective and interpersonal information. Rather than processing affective information, these children of high-conflict divorce maintained distance from their feelings, shutting the feelings down, as reflected in a low affective ratio (Roseby et al., 1995, p. 9). Fifty percent of the high-conflict group as compared to 13% of the nonpatient group scored in this way.

Nearly two-thirds of the high-conflict sample fell in the high Lambda category, as contrasted with 11% of the nonpatient group (Roseby et al., 1995, p. 9). High Lambda suggests internal processing designed to restrict and oversimplify the range of experiences, either internal or external in origin. Thus, this process serves to narrow the experiential world into one of "predictable and controllable sameness," according to the researchers (p. 9).

Expectations about relationships indicate problems in the high-conflict sample. These expectations are reflected in a significant Hypervigilance index, super-introversion, and compromised reality testing. Roseby et al. (1995, pp. 9–10) report that 40% of their sample were positive on the Hypervigilance index as compared with no children in the nonpatient sample. This would indicate an anxious scanning of the interpersonal world that is anticipated as potentially hostile and dangerous. Given the affective shutdown so characteristic of this group, it is not surprising that 40% of the study group was superintroversive (p. 10). That is, they relied too heavily on just their ideational activity for working out problems. Thus, they were not sufficiently open to input from others or their own affect, restricting experiences that would further a modifying and developing process centered on steady self-development.

One hundred percent of the children of high-conflict divorce demonstrated a clinically significant level of unusual or markedly distorted percepts, as contrasted with only 10% of the nonpatient 10-year-old comparison group (Roseby et al., 1995, p. 11). This finding may not be so surprising given the problems of these children's psychological functioning, wherein the damaged developmental core, the restriction in affective interpersonal information, and the narrowed experiences of relationships were significant. Given these processes, the children did not, seemingly could not, engage themselves in experiences that would have impacted their internally generated view of the world, resulting in uncorrected distortions. The researchers describe that these children tended by this process to solidify their view of the world as a dangerous place. Their own distorted processes, however, served to protect them against the dangers, even though the researchers could observe that the distorted processes inhibited the development of a healthy sense of self and relationships. The clinicians state that it was very difficult to get the children to give up their model of the world and their relation to it (p. 12).

*When to Use the Rorschach with Children in Divorcing Families*

Parents and attorneys are sometimes resistant to this use of the Rorschach with children who appear to have no observable problems, fearing the situation of the Rorschach testing will put a child under unnecessary stress. In these cases, it is necessary to point out that children sometimes spend all their energy to meet adult standards of success while failing to develop an adequate sense of self, leading to an emptiness and continued restriction or blocking of personal development. Particularly if a child is highly intelligent, the child may appear to be meeting external standards very effectively, but his or her internal development is so diminished that future problems of a serious nature are to be anticipated. Thus, it is recommended that in any child evaluation in the context of divorce, especially of the high-conflict sort, the Rorschach be administered not simply to the identified problem child, but also to the child who appears to have no problems.

# Case Example

Amy, 10, has been at the center of a controversy between her parents for several years. Even though legally divorced, her parents have solidified their angry relationship through a series of accusations and counteraccusations that center on describing the other parent as being bad for Amy. The father, Roger, blames the mother, Celia, for "alienating" Amy from him. Celia blames Roger for negligent, abusive, parenting when Amy had unsupervised visits with him. Mutual restraining orders keep the parents separate from each other. Amy now reluctantly goes to professionally supervised visits with her father a few hours once a week. Psychological testing is administered to the child and parents in the context of a court-ordered reevaluation by an independent psychologist who is charged with making custody recommendations to the court.

Though no single family case can illustrate all psychological testing results, the findings do provide a considerable number of examples found with high-conflict families.

CELIA

Celia, 38, is employed in a technical management capacity in a quasi-public agency. Her general ability tests in the average ranges on the WAIS-R. She has a belief that her ex-husband should not be allowed alone with "her" daughter because of his instability and her fear that when angry he will get out of control. Celia is fearful also that his anger will result in physical violence toward her. She argues that his documented verbal abuse of her will lead to the next step of physical violence, although there is some dispute as to whether he has actually been physically violent toward Celia.

## MMPI/MMPI-2

Celia's MMPI-2 profile is presented in Figure 12.1, and her derivative MMPI profile is given in Figure 12.2. Unlike the typical defensive pattern, this validity pattern is unusually open, candid, and fairly well-balanced. The tendency toward self-disclosure and perhaps acknowledgment of present distress raises a question as to whether this woman has adequate defenses. As the typical custody evaluation parent, her clinical scales fall within the normal ranges. Her moderate elevation on scale 10 Si suggests someone who often prefers to be alone or with only close associates, not needing to interact much with others. Her 16/61 profile within the normal range suggests that she may tend to be mildly hostile and to somatize. That she may express some hostility directly is suggested by the somewhat low K and OH (not shown), which in falling at the normative average level, is low for a person undergoing child custody evaluation. Given her very low Scale 4 Pd, she is likely to appear as a conforming and submissive person. Her conventional, concrete view of life is borne out by her low Scale 8 Schizophrenia.

## MCMI-III

Figure 12.3 presents Celia's MCMI-III profile. It is a valid profile. As anticipated with child custody evaluations, she attempts to show herself in a positive light (high Desirability score and high Compulsive score). Her high Compulsive score may be inflated by her need to put her best foot forward, but a score that high indicates the prominence of compulsive dynamics. She may be somewhat psychologically naïve. Behaviorally, she is likely disciplined and highly structured with a well-organized approach to life, although perfectionism may interfere with her decision-making capabilities. She will appear respectful, formal, and correct, playing by the rules in a very conscientious way. Fearful of error, cognitively constricted, in her inner world she presses to keep unwanted feelings out of awareness. Intrapsychically, she defends through reaction formation and compartmentalization. She is solemn and hardworking, even grim. Her compulsive style or disorder is accompanied by some affect as suggested by the Histrionic and Narcissistic features in the profile. Of some concern are her paranoid, suspicious personality features,

MMPI-2™

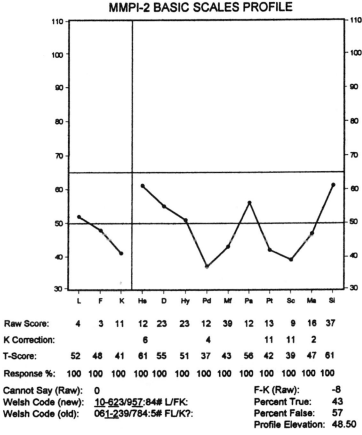

## MMPI-2 BASIC SCALES PROFILE

| | L | F | K | Hs | D | Hy | Pd | Mf | Pa | Pt | Sc | Ma | Si |
|---|---|---|---|---|---|---|---|---|---|---|---|---|---|
| Raw Score: | 4 | 3 | 11 | 12 | 23 | 23 | 12 | 39 | 12 | 13 | 9 | 16 | 37 |
| K Correction: | | | | 6 | | | 4 | | | 11 | 11 | 2 | |
| T-Score: | 52 | 48 | 41 | 61 | 55 | 51 | 37 | 43 | 56 | 42 | 39 | 47 | 61 |
| Response %: | 100 | 100 | 100 | 100 | 100 | 100 | 100 | 100 | 100 | 100 | 100 | 100 | 100 |

Cannot Say (Raw):　0
Welsh Code (new):　10-623/957:84# L/FK:
Welsh Code (old):　061-239/784:5# FL/K?:

F-K (Raw):　　　　-8
Percent True:　　43
Percent False:　　57
Profile Elevation:　48.50

Figure 12.1
MMPI-2 Profile: Celia

as reflected in her Paranoid score. Symptomatically, a question is raised by the slightly elevated scores on Delusional Disorder and Bipolar Manic Disorder. These scores suggest the hypothesis that a compulsive personality disorder might be protecting against a potentially psychotic state.

### Rorschach

Although a thorough use of the Rorschach findings would include a consideration of the sequence of scores, the content of the responses, and the narrative printout

**MMPI-2™**

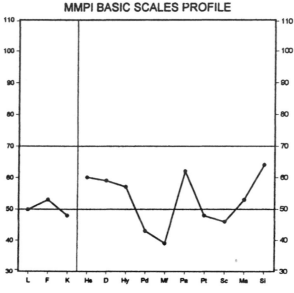

Figure 12.2
MMPI Profile: Celia

of numerous hypotheses following Exner's (1991) strategies of interpretation, this analysis will focus only on major implications of the Structural Summary, Ratios, Percentages, and Derivations, the data are presented in Figure 12.4. Major Rorschach variables are listed in parentheses.

In her overall response style, she evidences a marked tendency to look at the world in an oversimplified, narrow fashion (high L). This style promotes overlooking significant inputs from her environment, although it can serve to help her avoid an affect that might prove unpleasant. Furthermore, she has a hasty scanning process that inclines her toward overlooking significant pieces of information (Zd). Her approach to problem solving is inconsistent and irregular; she neither regularly settles back to think things through nor does she interact

MCMI-III™

## MILLON CLINICAL MULTIAXIAL INVENTORY - III
### CONFIDENTIAL INFORMATION FOR PROFESSIONAL USE ONLY

Valid Profile

PERSONALITY CODE:   7 ** - * 4 5 6B 3 + 2A 8B " 2B 1 8A 6A ' ' // - ** - * //
SYNDROME CODE:   - ** - * // - ** - * //

| CATEGORY | | SCORE RAW | SCORE BR | 0 | 60 | 75 | 85 | 115 | DIAGNOSTIC SCALES |
|---|---|---|---|---|---|---|---|---|---|
| MODIFYING INDICES | X | 87 | 55 | | | | | | DISCLOSURE |
| | Y | 19 | 89 | | | | | | DESIRABILITY |
| | Z | 4 | 45 | | | | | | DEBASEMENT |
| CLINICAL PERSONALITY PATTERNS | 1 | 3 | 30 | | | | | | SCHIZOID |
| | 2A | 5 | 43 | | | | | | AVOIDANT |
| | 2B | 5 | 33 | | | | | | DEPRESSIVE |
| | 3 | 9 | 60 | | | | | | DEPENDENT |
| | 4 | 15 | 68 | | | | | | HISTRIONIC |
| | 5 | 15 | 68 | | | | | | NARCISSISTIC |
| | 6A | 0 | 0 | | | | | | ANTISOCIAL |
| | 6B | 9 | 65 | | | | | | AGGRESSIVE (SADISTIC) |
| | 7 | 25 | 99 | | | | | | COMPULSIVE |
| | 8A | 3 | 20 | | | | | | PASSIVE-AGGRESSIVE |
| | 8B | 3 | 36 | | | | | | SELF-DEFEATING |
| SEVERE PERSONALITY PATHOLOGY | S | 1 | 15 | | | | | | SCHIZOTYPAL |
| | C | 1 | 8 | | | | | | BORDERLINE |
| | P | 10 | 70 | | | | | | PARANOID |
| CLINICAL SYNDROMES | A | 2 | 24 | | | | | | ANXIETY DISORDER |
| | H | 2 | 17 | | | | | | SOMATOFORM DISORDER |
| | N | 8 | 66 | | | | | | BIPOLAR: MANIC DISORDER |
| | D | 0 | 0 | | | | | | DYSTHYMIC DISORDER |
| | B | 3 | 61 | | | | | | ALCOHOL DEPENDENCE |
| | T | 0 | 0 | | | | | | DRUG DEPENDENCE |
| | R | 2 | 20 | | | | | | POST-TRAUMATIC STRESS |
| SEVERE SYNDROMES | SS | 0 | 0 | | | | | | THOUGHT DISORDER |
| | CC | 2 | 15 | | | | | | MAJOR DEPRESSION |
| | PP | 3 | 65 | | | | | | DELUSIONAL DISORDER |

Figure 12.3
MCMI-III: Celia

Copyright © 1994 DICADRIEN, INC., All rights reserved.
Published and distributed exclusively by National Computer Systems, Inc.,
Minneapolis, MN 55440. Reprinted with permission by NCS.

================== STRUCTURAL SUMMARY ==================

| LOCATION FEATURES | DETERMINANTS BLENDS | SINGLE | CONTENTS | S-CONSTELLATION |
|---|---|---|---|---|
| | | | H   = 3, 0 | NO..FV+VF+V+FD>2 |
| Zf   = 18 | | M   = 3 | (H) = 0, 0 | NO..Col-Shd Bl>0 |
| ZSum = 56.0 | | FM  = 3 | Hd  = 2, 0 | NO..Ego<.31,>.44 |
| ZEst = 59.5 | | m   = 0 | (Hd)= 1, 0 | NO..MOR > 3 |
| | | FC  = 2 | Hx  = 0, 0 | NO..Zd > +- 3.5 |
| W   = 11 | | CF  = 2 | A   =21, 1 | NO..es > EA |
| (Wv = 0) | | C   = 0 | (A) = 0, 0 | NO..CF+C > FC |
| D   = 18 | | Cn  = 0 | Ad  = 3, 1 | YES..X+% < .70 |
| Dd  = 6 | | FC'= 0 | (Ad)= 0, 0 | YES..S > 3 |
| S   = 4 | | C'F= 0 | An  = 4, 0 | NO..P < 3 or > 8 |
| | | C'  = 0 | Art = 0, 0 | NO..Pure H < 2 |
| DQ | | FT  = 1 | Ay  = 0, 0 | NO..R < 17 |
| .........(FQ-) | | TF  = 0 | Bl  = 0, 0 | 2.....TOTAL |
| +   =  7  ( 0) | | T   = 0 | Bt  = 0, 1 | |
| o   = 28  ( 8) | | FV  = 0 | Cg  = 0, 0 | SPECIAL SCORINGS |
| v/+ =  0  ( 0) | | VF  = 0 | Cl  = 0, 0 |           Lv1   Lv2 |
| v   =  0  ( 0) | | V   = 0 | Ex  = 0, 0 | DV  =  0x1   0x2 |
| | | FY  = 1 | Fd  = 0, 0 | INC =  0x2   1x4 |
| | | YF  = 0 | Fi  = 0, 0 | DR  =  0x3   0x6 |
| | | Y   = 0 | Ge  = 0, 0 | FAB =  0x4   1x7 |
| FORM QUALITY | | Fr  = 0 | Hh  = 0, 0 | ALOG = 0x5 |
| | | rF  = 0 | Ls  = 0, 0 | CON =  0x7 |
| FQx FQf MQual SQx | | FD  = 1 | Na  = 0, 0 | Raw Sum6 =    2 |
| +  =  0    0    0    0 | | F  =22 | Sc  = 0, 0 | Wgtd Sum6 =   11 |
| o  = 19   12    2    1 | | | Sx  = 0, 0 | |
| u  =  8    5    1    1 | | | Xy  = 0, 0 | AB  = 0    CP  = 0 |
| -  =  8    5    0    2 | | | Id  = 1, 0 | AG  = 0    MOR = 0 |
| none=  0   --    0    0 | | (2) = 14 | | CFB = 0    PER = 0 |
| | | | | COP = 0    PSV = 0 |

================ RATIOS, PERCENTAGES, AND DERIVATIONS ================

| | | | | | | |
|---|---|---|---|---|---|---|
| R = 35 | | L = 1.69 | | FC:CF+C = 2: 2 | COP = 0 | AG = 0 |
| | | | | Pure C  =   0 | Food    = 0 | |
| EB = 3: 3.0 | EA = 6.0 | EBPer= N/A | | SumC':WSumC= 0:3.0 | Isolate/R =0.03 | |
| eb = 3: 2 | es  = 5 | D = 0 | | Afr    =0.46 | H:(H)Hd(Hd)= 3: 3 | |
| | Adj es = 5 | Adj D = 0 | | S      =  4 | (HHd):(AAd)= 1: 0 | |
| | | | | Blends:R= 0:35 | H+A:Hd+Ad =25: 7 | |
| FM = 3 : C'= 0 | T = 1 | | | CP     =  0 | | |
| m  = 0 : V = 0 | Y = 1 | | | | | |
| | | | P   = 4 | Zf  =18 | 3r+(2)/R=0.40 | |
| a:p  = 3: 3 | Sum6 = 2 | X+% =0.54 | Zd  = -3.5 | Fr+rF  = 0 | |
| Ma:Mp = 2: 1 | Lv2  = 2 | F+% =0.55 | W:D:Dd =11:18: 6 | FD      = 1 | |
| 2AB+Art+Ay= 0 | WSum6 = 11 | X-% =0.23 | W:M =11: 3 | An+Xy   = 4 | |
| M-    = 0 | Mnone = 0 | S-% =0.25 | DQ+ = 7 | MOR     = 0 | |
| | | Xu% =0.23 | DQv = 0 | | |

| SCZI = 3 | DEPI = 3 | CDI = 1 | S-CON = 2 | HVI = No | OBS = No |
|---|---|---|---|---|---|

Figure 12.4
Rorschach: Celia. Reproduced with permission.

immediately with others in problem-solving efforts (EB ambient). She probably finds making firm decisions difficult. Not surprisingly, she views the world consistently with a significant degree of inaccuracy (low X + %). Her thinking appears seriously disturbed, although she does not score as do those likely to be diagnosed as schizophrenic. Flawed judgment and problems in conceptualization are likely present. With fewer inner resources available than would be anticipated (low EA), she is vulnerable to being overwhelmed by usual, everyday stresses. Thus, when faced with complexity, she may behave in a disorganized fashion, lacking control, and possibly quite inappropriately.

More intense emotions may overwhelm her (EB ambient), and she does not work to control expressions of her feelings as much as might be expected (FC:CF + C). Of great importance is the role of anger in her makeup (S): It appears to be fundamental to her attitude toward others. She may be quick to respond negatively in situations that others might find only mildly annoying. Therefore, consistent interpersonal difficulties with those close to her might be anticipated. She herself does not anticipate positive relationships with others (COP, AG).

Though she appears to have a reasonable balance between self and others (3r[2]/R), she seems to have an overconcern with her bodily processes (An + Xy). But her sense of self is likely to be based more on imagination (Hd: [H] + Hd + [Hd]).

### Additional Test Results: PCRI and STAXI

PCRI findings (not given) suggest that she perceives her parenting behavior as falling much like average parents' in the normative comparison group. She does tend to perceive herself as somewhat more lenient in limit-setting, and perhaps her personal satisfaction with parenting is not up to the level of the typical parent. The STAXI results suggest typical anger expression scores, that is, in the moderate ranges.

## ROGER

Roger, 44, has been steadily employed in a routine job with a public agency. His verbal abilities fall in the average ranges, but his performance abilities exhibit some marked deficits. He comes across as generally angry. When the subject of Celia arises, his face flushes and he is likely to commence a tirade centered on how despicable she is in her alienating his daughter from him and engaging in various legal "shenanigans" aimed at him. He seems to be having an adult version of a temper tantrum. The professional supervisor reports that during visits with his daughter he appears awkward in her presence and either backs off or dictates to her what activities they are to do during the visitation. The supervisor reports that he can become easily frustrated and momentarily angry with his daughter.

### MMPI/MMPI-2

Roger's MMPI-2 profile is given in Figure 12.5 and his MMPI profile in Figure 12.6. The basic validity scores, L-F-K, form a defensive pattern typical of child custody evaluation cases. Except for the slightly higher scale 3 Hy, clinical scales fall at or below normative mean averages for custody evaluation parents. The slightly elevated Hy scale does suggest extroversion, some naïveté, lack of insight, and a tendency to deny unwanted feelings. That Hy is the peak score is

MMPI-2™

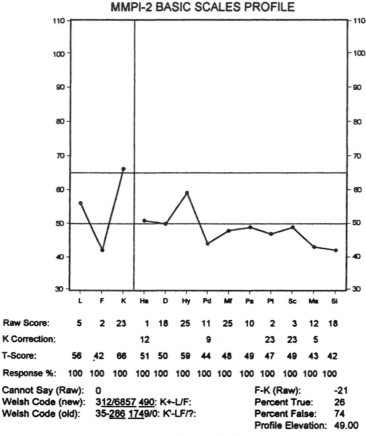

**MMPI-2 BASIC SCALES PROFILE**

| | L | F | K | Hs | D | Hy | Pd | Mf | Pa | Pt | Sc | Ma | Si |
|---|---|---|---|---|---|---|---|---|---|---|---|---|---|
| Raw Score: | 5 | 2 | 23 | 1 | 18 | 25 | 11 | 25 | 10 | 2 | 3 | 12 | 18 |
| K Correction: | | | | 12 | | | 9 | | | 23 | 23 | 5 | |
| T-Score: | 56 | 42 | 66 | 51 | 50 | 59 | 44 | 48 | 49 | 47 | 49 | 43 | 42 |
| Response %: | 100 | 100 | 100 | 100 | 100 | 100 | 100 | 100 | 100 | 100 | 100 | 100 | 100 |

Cannot Say (Raw): 0
Welsh Code (new): 312/6857 490: K+-L/F:
Welsh Code (old): 35-286 1749/0: K'-LF/?:

F-K (Raw): -21
Percent True: 26
Percent False: 74
Profile Elevation: 49.00

Figure 12.5
MMPI-2 Profile: Roger

consistent with the custody normative data, however. OH (not shown) at a T of 65 is above the child custody sample elevated score of T 60. This score implies that even more than the typical child custody evaluee, he is holding back his hostility and may feel socially alienated.

*MCMI-III*

As may be seen in Figure 12.7, Roger's overall pattern is very defined. Although the pattern is valid, he clearly is presenting himself in a markedly favorable light,

**MMPI-2™**

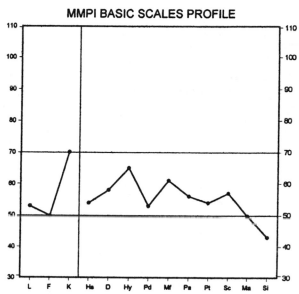

MMPI BASIC SCALES PROFILE

Original
MMPI T-Score * :     53   50   70   54   58   65   53   61   56   54   57   50   43

Welsh Code:   35-286 1749/0: K'-LF/?:

* The T scores include K-scale corrections for scales Hs, Pd, Pt, Sc, and Ma.
They are derived from Appendix K of the MMPI-2 Manual for Administration and Scoring.

Figure 12.6
MMPI Profile: Roger

implying composure, high virtue, and positive appearance. With his histrionic score so high that it predicts a personality disorder, behaviorally, he is expressively dramatic, impulsive, emotional, and volatile, demanding of attention. Phenomenologically, he is cognitively flighty, avoiding introspective thinking. He may be superficially social, but lacks deeper relationships. Intrapsychically, he may dissociate, avoiding reflecting on unwanted thoughts. His personality organization is disjointed and not well-integrated. There are no indications of any psychological symptoms, as would usually be the case with a man in a custody battle.

**MCMI-III™**

---

## MILLON CLINICAL MULTIAXIAL INVENTORY - III
### CONFIDENTIAL INFORMATION FOR PROFESSIONAL USE ONLY

Valid Profile

PERSONALITY CODE:   4 ** - * 7 5 + 3 " 6A 1 2A 2B 6B 8A 8B ' ' // - ** - * //
SYNDROME CODE:   - ** - * // - ** - * //

| CATEGORY | | RAW | BR | PROFILE OF BR SCORES | DIAGNOSTIC SCALES |
|---|---|---|---|---|---|
| MODIFYING INDICES | X | 63 | 37 | | DISCLOSURE |
| | Y | 20 | 94 | | DESIRABILITY |
| | Z | 0 | 0 | | DEBASEMENT |
| CLINICAL PERSONALITY PATTERNS | 1 | 0 | 0 | | SCHIZOID |
| | 2A | 0 | 0 | | AVOIDANT |
| | 2B | 0 | 0 | | DEPRESSIVE |
| | 3 | 4 | 40 | | DEPENDENT |
| | 4 | 24 | 92 | | HISTRIONIC |
| | 5 | 16 | 61 | | NARCISSISTIC |
| | 6A | 1 | 8 | | ANTISOCIAL |
| | 6B | 0 | 0 | | AGGRESSIVE (SADISTIC) |
| | 7 | 23 | 67 | | COMPULSIVE |
| | 8A | 0 | 0 | | PASSIVE-AGGRESSIVE |
| | 8B | 0 | 0 | | SELF-DEFEATING |
| SEVERE PERSONALITY PATHOLOGY | S | 0 | 0 | | SCHIZOTYPAL |
| | C | 0 | 0 | | BORDERLINE |
| | P | 0 | 0 | | PARANOID |
| CLINICAL SYNDROMES | A | 0 | 0 | | ANXIETY DISORDER |
| | H | 0 | 0 | | SOMATOFORM DISORDER |
| | N | 3 | 36 | | BIPOLAR: MANIC DISORDER |
| | D | 0 | 0 | | DYSTHYMIC DISORDER |
| | B | 0 | 0 | | ALCOHOL DEPENDENCE |
| | T | 1 | 15 | | DRUG DEPENDENCE |
| | R | 0 | 0 | | POST-TRAUMATIC STRESS |
| SEVERE SYNDROMES | SS | 0 | 0 | | THOUGHT DISORDER |
| | CC | 0 | 0 | | MAJOR DEPRESSION |
| | PP | 0 | 0 | | DELUSIONAL DISORDER |

Figure 12.7
MCMI-III: Roger
Copyright © 1994 DICADRIEN, INC. All rights reserved.
Published and distributed exclusively by National Computer Systems, Inc.,
Minneapolis, MN 55440. Reprinted with permission by NCS.

*Rorschach*

The basic Rorschach data is given in Figure 12.8. Roger has fewer personal resources with which to respond as compared to others (EA). Given this deficiency in control, more typical of younger persons, and the indications that he
is under significant situational stress and distress (Y), this markedly extratensive person (EB) is easily overwhelmed by his affect (FC:CF + C). His behavior
may be quite inappropriate, especially given his social ineptness, which renders
day-to-day coping problematical (CDI). Emotions are overly intense when released (C). Apparently having some awareness of this problem, he tries to avoid

================= STRUCTURAL SUMMARY =================

| LOCATION FEATURES | | DETERMINANTS BLENDS | SINGLE | | CONTENTS | | S-CONSTELLATION |
|---|---|---|---|---|---|---|---|
| | | | | | | | NO..FV+VF+V+FD>2 |
| | | | | | H = 1, 0 | | YES..Col-Shd Bl>0 |
| Zf = 5 | | C.Y | M = 1 | | (H) = 0, 0 | | NO...Ego<.31,>.44 |
| ZSum = 10.0 | | | FM = 0 | | Hd = 1, 0 | | NO..MOR > 3 |
| ZEst = 13.5 | | | m = 0 | | (Hd)= 0, 0 | | NO..Zd > +- 3.5 |
| | | | FC = 1 | | Hx = 0, 0 | | NO..es > EA |
| W = 5 | | | CP = 0 | | A = 5, 0 | | YES..CF+C > FC |
| (Wv = 2) | | | C = 1 | | (A) = 0, 0 | | YES..X+% < .70 |
| D = 8 | | | Cn = 0 | | Ad = 2, 0 | | NO..S > 3 |
| Dd = 2 | | | FC'= 0 | | (Ad)= 0, 0 | | NO..P < 3 or > 8 |
| S = 0 | | | C'F= 0 | | An = 0, 0 | | YES..Pure H < 2 |
| | | | C' = 0 | | Art = 1, 0 | | YES..R < 17 |
| DQ | | | FT = 0 | | Ay = 0, 0 | | 5.....TOTAL |
| ........(FQ-) | | | TF = 0 | | Bl = 0, 0 | | |
| + = 3 ( 0) | | | T = 0 | | Bt = 0, 0 | | SPECIAL SCORINGS |
| o = 9 ( 0) | | | FV = 0 | | Cg = 0, 1 | | Lv1 Lv2 |
| v/+ = 0 ( 0) | | | VF = 0 | | Cl = 0, 0 | | DV = 0x1 0x2 |
| v = 3 ( 0) | | | V = 0 | | Ex = 0, 0 | | INC = 0x2 0x4 |
| | | | FY = 1 | | Fd = 0, 0 | | DR = 0x3 0x6 |
| | | | YF = 0 | | Fi = 0, 0 | | FAB = 0x4 0x7 |
| | | | Y = 1 | | Ge = 0, 0 | | ALOG = 0x5 |
| FORM QUALITY | | | Fr = 0 | | Hh = 0, 0 | | CON = 0x7 |
| | | | rF = 1 | | Ls = 0, 0 | | Raw Sum6 = 0 |
| FQx FQf MQual SQx | | | FD = 0 | | Na = 2, 0 | | Wgtd Sum6 = 0 |
| + = 0 0 0 0 | | | F = 8 | | Sc = 0, 0 | | |
| o = 6 4 1 0 | | | | | Sx = 0, 0 | | AB = 0 CP = 0 |
| u = 6 4 0 0 | | | | | Xy = 0, 0 | | AG = 0 MOR = 0 |
| - = 0 0 0 0 | | | | | Id = 3, 0 | | CFB = 0 PER = 1 |
| none= 3 -- 0 0 | | | (2) = 3 | | | | COP = 0 PSV = 0 |

================= RATIOS, PERCENTAGES, AND DERIVATIONS =================

| | | | | | | |
|---|---|---|---|---|---|---|
| R = 15 | L = 1.14 | | | FC:CF+C = 1: 2 | COP = 0 | AG = 0 |
| | | | | Pure C = 2 | Food = 0 | |
| EB = 1: 3.5 | EA = 4.5 | EBPer= 3.5 | | SumC':WSumC= 0:3.5 | Isolate/R =0.27 | |
| eb = 0: 3 | es = 3 | D = 0 | | Afr =0.36 | H:(H)Hd(Hd)= 1: 1 | |
| | Adj es = 1 | Adj D = +1 | | S = 0 | (HHd):(AAd)= 0: 0 | |
| FM = 0 : C'= 0 | T = 0 | | | Blends:R= 1:15 | H+A:Hd+Ad = 6: 3 | |
| m = 0 : V = 0 | Y = 3 | | | CP = 0 | | |
| | | P = 3 | | Zf = 5 | 3r+(2)/R=0.40 | |
| a:p = 0: 1 | Sum6 = 0 | X+% =0.40 | | Zd = -3.5 | Fr+rF = 1 | |
| Ma:Mp = 0: 1 | Lv2 = 0 | F+% =0.50 | | W:D:Dd = 5: 8: 2 | FD = 0 | |
| 2AB+Art+Ay= 1 | WSum6 = 0 | X-% =0.00 | | W:M = 5: 1 | An+Xy = 0 | |
| M- = 0 | Mnone = 0 | S-% =0.00 | | DQ+ = 3 | MOR = 0 | |
| | | Xu% =0.40 | | DQv = 3 | | |

| SCZI = 1 | DEPI = 4 | CDI = 5* | S-CON = 5 | HVI = No | OBS = No |
|---|---|---|---|---|---|

Figure 12.8
Rorschach: Roger. Reproduced with permission.

emotional stimuli when possible, leading to social constraint and isolation (Isolate/R). His orientation is very self-focused, narcissisticlike, and leads him to overvalue his personal worth (Fr). He is naïve in his conception of self and others. As a result of these various conditions, his relationships are shallow, reinforced by his need to keep his distance from others (T). He does not anticipate that contact with others will be positive. He tends to view the world in an oversimplified way (L), further aggravated by his hasty and inconsistent scanning of the world, by which he neglects critical pieces of information (Zd). His interpretations of what he sees are likely to be unconventional (P). Being out of step with the world in his perception process—influenced by an emotional overload—he has confrontations with authorities and perceives the environment as threatening, demanding, and ungiving.

## Additional Test Results: PCRI and STAXI

On the PCRI (not shown), he scores as do those who feel a lack of support for their parenting efforts. His efforts do bring him satisfaction, though. His level of involvement, ability to communicate, ability to limit-set, and the degree to which he pushes his daughter to age-appropriate autonomy are very close to the inventory normative average. He does hold a more traditional view of the roles of males and females. On the STAXI, Roger acknowledges experiencing relatively intense angry feelings that are situationally determined. There are indications that he works harder than average to monitor and exert control over his anger.

## AMY

Amy, 10, evidences a general ability level higher than her parents. On the WISC-R, she scored in the superior range verbally, and significantly lower (although in the average range) on performance tasks. Reports indicate that Amy is doing well enough at school, although a rather withdrawn and isolated child. Her mother has had primary custody since a divorce when Amy was 4 or 5. She initially had regular visitation with her father. A series of conflicts between the parents has been accompanied by accusations from the mother of neglect by the father and accusations by the father that the mother systematically works to poison Amy's mind about him. For some months, Amy has balked at visiting her father, except recently under court order of professional supervision.

## Rorschach

Figure 12.9 presents the Structural Summary, Ratios, Percentages, and Derivations for Amy. In many ways Amy resembles the children caught in high-conflict divorces, as described by Roseby et al. (1995), and children with faltering

=========================== STRUCTURAL SUMMARY ===========================

| LOCATION FEATURES | DETERMINANTS BLENDS | SINGLE | CONTENTS | S-CONSTELLATION |
|---|---|---|---|---|
| | | | H = 3, 0 | ..FV+VF+V+FD>2 |
| Zf = 13 | M.CF | M = 3 | (H) = 1, 0 | ..Col-Shd Bl>0 |
| ZSum = 38.5 | | FM = 1 | Hd = 0, 1 | ..Ego<.31,>.44 |
| ZEst = 41.5 | | m = 0 | (Hd)= 0, 0 | ..MOR > 3 |
| | | FC = 0 | Hx = 0, 0 | ..Zd > +- 3.5 |
| W = 11 | | CF = 0 | A =10, 1 | ..es > EA |
| (Wv = 0) | | C = 0 | (A) = 0, 0 | ..CF+C > FC |
| D = 6 | | Cn = 0 | Ad = 1, 0 | ..X+% < .70 |
| Dd = 1 | | FC'= 0 | (Ad)= 0, 0 | ..S > 3 |
| S = 2 | | C'F= 0 | An = 1, 1 | ..P < 3 or > 8 |
| | | C' = 0 | Art = 0, 0 | ..Pure H < 2 |
| DQ | | FT = 0 | Ay = 0, 1 | ..R < 17 |
| .........(FQ-) | | TF = 0 | Bl = 0, 1 | x.....TOTAL |
| + = 5 ( 2) | | T = 0 | Bt = 0, 0 | |
| o = 13 ( 5) | | FV = 0 | Cg = 0, 1 | SPECIAL SCORINGS |
| v/+ = 0 ( 0) | | VF = 0 | Cl = 0, 0 | Lv1    Lv2 |
| v = 0 ( 0) | | V = 0 | Ex = 0, 0 | DV = 0x1    0x2 |
| | | FY = 0 | Fd = 0, 0 | INC = 1x2    0x4 |
| | | YF = 0 | Fi = 0, 0 | DR = 0x3    0x6 |
| | | Y = 0 | Ge = 0, 0 | FAB = 1x4    0x7 |
| FORM QUALITY | | Fr = 0 | Hh = 0, 0 | ALOG = 1x5 |
| | | rF = 0 | Ls = 1, 0 | CON = 0x7 |

| | FQx | FQf | MQual | SQx | FD = 0 | Na = 0, 0 | Raw Sum6 =    3 |
|---|---|---|---|---|---|---|---|
| + = | 0 | 0 | 0 | 0 | F =13 | Sc = 0, 0 | Wgtd Sum6 =   11 |
| o = | 8 | 6 | 2 | 0 | | Sx = 0, 0 | AB = 0    CP = 0 |
| u = | 3 | 3 | 0 | 1 | | Xy = 0, 0 | AG = 0    MOR = 2 |
| - = | 7 | 4 | 2 | 1 | | Id = 1, 0 | CFB = 0    PER = 0 |
| none= | 0 | -- | 0 | 0 | (2) = 4 | | COP = 0    PSV = 0 |

This record has rejections and may not be interpretively valid.

=============== RATIOS, PERCENTAGES, AND DERIVATIONS ===============

| R = 18 | L = 2.60 | | FC:CF+C = 0: 1 | COP = 0    AG = 0 |
|---|---|---|---|---|
| | | | Pure C = 0 | Food = 0 |
| EB = 4: 1.0 | EA = 5.0 | EBPer= 4.0 | SumC':WSumC= 0:1.0 | Isolate/R =0.06 |
| eb = 1: 0 | es = 1 | D = +1 | Afr =0.50 | H:(H)Hd(Hd)= 3: 2 |
| | Adj es = 1 | Adj D = +1 | S = 2 | (HHd):(AAd)= 1: 0 |
| | | | Blends:R= 1:18 | H+A:Hd+Ad =15: 2 |
| FM = 1 : C'= 0 | T = 0 | | CP = 0 | |
| m = 0 : V = 0 | Y = 0 | | | |
| | | P = 6 | Zf =13 | 3r+(2)/R=0.22 |
| a:p = 4: 1 | Sum6 = 3 | X+% =0.44 | Zd = -3.0 | Fr+rF = 0 |
| Ma:Mp = 3: 1 | Lv2 = 0 | F+% =0.46 | W:D:Dd =11: 6: 1 | FD = 0 |
| 2AB+Art+Ay= 1 | WSum6 = 11 | X-% =0.39 | W:M =11: 4 | An+Xy = 2 |
| M- = 2 | Mnone = 0 | S-% =0.14 | DQ+ = 5 | MOR = 2 |
| | | Xu% =0.17 | DQv = 0 | |

| SCZI = 4* | DEPI = 3 | CDI = 3 | S-CON =N/A | HVI = No | OBS = No |
|---|---|---|---|---|---|

Figure 12.9
Rorschach: Amy. Reproduced with permission.

personality development whose picture is sketched out by Exner and Weiner (1995). Amy restricts and narrows her range of experiences so as to make her world more manageable (Lambda). In service of this restriction, she relies too heavily on ideational activity for working through problems with little affective input (EB superintroversive, only one color response). These styles interfere with her ability to make use of both inner affective clues and external input that would help her develop and modify her thinking. Her thinking, therefore, demonstrates serious problems (significant SCZI). Her ideas are fragmented and conceptualization is faulty, leading to poor judgment, flawed logic, and errors in decision making. Distortion of reality is considerable (low X + %). Her internal resources are poor (low EA). It would be expected that some of her behaviors would be inadequate to meet situations over time and she would easily become overwhelmed.

Similar to 90% of children in a study by Roseby et al. (1995), she fails to produce any texture responses ($T$ 0). She likely is socially and emotionally isolated. This way of being in the world may help her maintain her present restricted, superintroversive way of problem solving, but, as noted, without input from others she does not have the interpersonal resources to develop her sense of self and mastery. She tends to keep her distance from others.

Not surprisingly, Amy's sense of self is suffering (egocentricity ratio lower than any child in the normative sample for 10-year-olds). Her estimate of self-worth is much more negative than it should be. It may be that she pays more attention to others than to herself, despite keeping her own space in relationships.

## Additional Test Results: BASC

Appropriate forms of the BASC (not shown) were completed by Amy, her teacher, and her parents. (See Chapter 8 for a discussion of this instrument.) On this screening inventory, Amy sees herself as somewhat anxious, in the upper ranges of the average in the normative group: the 78th percentile. Her self-esteem seems at risk; she scores at the 17th percentile.

Her mother views her as having serious difficulties. On her mother's rating, Amy internalizes (99th percentile) and externalizes (94th percentile). Anxiety, depression, somatization, aggression, hyperactivity, and general behavioral symptoms fall at better than the 95th percentile by her mother's description. By contrast, her father rates Amy as overall in the average ranges, but at risk for withdrawal, attention problems, adaptability, social skills, and leadership. Amy's teacher, while providing rating within the average ranges, marks the inventory so that Amy appears at risk for problems of anxiety, depression, withdrawal, and adaptability. One explanation for these various views of Amy is because the three respondents experience her in very divergent relationships.

In summary, Amy experiences some anxiety and does not feel very good about herself. Amy's teacher sees Amy in the structured classroom situation and sees only moderate potential problems; by the Rorschach, Amy does better in structured environments. Roger's experience of Amy now is very limited and highly structured; we also know that he tends to deny and may not see problems. Celia, on the other hand, not only does not deny but also is very angry, upset, and rigid while having contact with Amy of the most unstructured, day-to-day, problem-solving sort. So each person's view may have some truth to it.

SOME CUSTODY IMPLICATIONS OF TEST FINDINGS ON
MOTHER, FATHER, AND DAUGHTER

*The Parents*

This is the sort of case where, for the parents, if only the MMPI/MMPI-2 were to be used for screening, individually demonstrated severe psychopathology would not be predicted. The MCMI-III highlights a probable personality disorder for both parents, compulsive (with paranoid trends) for the mother, histrionic (with compulsive trends) for the father. The Rorschach results further clarify some ways that these parents experience their world, together with marked distortions, projection, and a perpetual anger dynamic at work. Thus, the Rorschach provides the key to the assessor's responsibility to evaluate for the existence and type of individual psychopathology that might interfere with effective parenting. In this case, both parents have marked psychopathology as individuals, in addition to the destructive pathological relationship in which they are enmeshed.

Both parents fit the category described by Finn (1996) as low disturbance on the MMPI-2, high disturbance on the Rorschach. Following Finn, these clients may function adequately in "familiar, structured situations when they can use intellectual resources to deal with anxiety" (p. 546). Recall that both ex-spouses do have average verbal intellectual abilities. So, in the case of Roger at least, his MMPI/MMPI-2 normal clinical profile may be a function of not only defensiveness, but his ability to function adequately when bolstered by a regular structure in which he is not interrupted by novelty. His work is fairly routinized and he is not called upon to problem-solve new situations. Given the lack of defensiveness in Celia's MMPI/MMPI-2 profile, she may not only function adequately with structure and poorly in unstructured situations, she may also have little insight into her psychological dynamics and problems. Given her paranoid trends and apparent lack of insight, Celia may be maintaining her composure by having an enemy to blame, namely Roger. Roger is uninsightful in a different way, by being naïve and inept interpersonally.

The apparent rigidity of their personality disorders would probably lead an evaluator to accept the proposition that these parents are going to parallel parent, not coparent. Thus, the more that transitions can be routinized and handled so that the parents do not face each other, the less is their daughter likely to be caught actively between them. The schedule of the child's visitation needs detailed structuring.

*The Daughter*

This little girl is in trouble. Her present psychological organization precludes much openness to either her own inner cues or to outside affective stimuli. She gets lost and confused in her own thinking processes. Thus, she may tend to reject overtures to closeness from either parent as she works to maintain her own space. She must continue to pay attention externally so that she can be safe and so that she can learn to manipulate the environment. Her self-development falters as she is caught in her process that discourages emotional interaction. She is not even aware how needy she is.

## Child Custody Recommendations

An evaluator in this situation, based on the testing, would not propose that the parents learn to coparent together. They need to improve their parallel parenting. This could be done by each person having his or her own helping therapist/coach. Father-daughter sessions would allow for direct assistance in parenting skills focusing on father learning to listen to what the child says and planning brief excursions in detail, so that father and daughter would be clear about what to expect. Mother and daughter might be seen by their therapist to help them talk and provide more direct emotional input to each other; because both may deny the need for this, they may learn more about emotional contact so as to break out of their sense of isolation. Of course, it would be of additional help if each had her own individual therapist who had regular contact conjointly with the parenting therapists/coaches. Evaluation for psychoactive medication might be broached, especially for Celia. If Roger were at all willing, a structured parenting or time-defined men's group could prove of help with his social ineptness.

An evaluator might plan in a detailed way the general activities of the child with each parent, to be followed up by the therapists/coaches. Of major importance, a commitment needs to be made by both parents to support the child in long-term individual therapy and, at an appropriate time, additional group therapy for her. Consultation with the child's teacher might help the teacher find some intellectual or other activity or skill (Amy has a verbal level surpassing 90% of children) that might result in achievements bolstering her self-esteem. Parents could be alerted about this need as well.

# Summary

This chapter pointed to the use of psychological testing in context of divorce. When momentous decisions must be made affecting all family members, it is crucial to obtain information from all reasonable sources. Thus, in collaborating divorce situations, tests can provide important input for cooperative planning. In the adversarial context, tests are routinely used by psychological evaluators to collect information from parents and children, teachers, and others. Research was reviewed on major testing instruments administered to divorcing parents and children caught in the divorce process.

# CHAPTER 13

## Family and Couple Assessment in Perspective

In this concluding chapter, following a restatement of the purpose of this book, several overall questions are addressed. The first of these is whether or not to "test." In relationship to this, the cost of testing is subsequently discussed after reviewing considerations of inventories for couples and full batteries for families. Next, some standards are explicated for the education, training, and supervision required to conduct various kinds of tests. In this chapter, the reader is reminded that this book focuses on classical standardized tests of personality; in working with couples and families, other instruments may at times be needed. Several of these new and promising personality measures are identified, with the suggestion that the clinician keep an eye on these because, as their research base grows and they gain increased general acceptance by practitioners, these measures may provide additional assistance for the clinician working with couples and families.

## Family Assessment

*Family assessment* is about applying to couple and family matters psychological (personality) tests that have been well-developed scientifically and have stood the test of time with practitioners in the field. Although the tests (and inventories, technically speaking) were developed to evaluate individuals, the major complaints of persons seeking help have continued to be about their couple and family relationships. Given the development of understanding of families and the growth of family therapy during the past quarter of a century, it seems high time to explicitly explore psychological testing within this context. This book has attempted to do that, along with providing some practical recommendations for the clinician in everyday practice.

289

## To Test or Not to Test

The observation of this author is that psychological tests and inventories are underutilized by mental health professionals who intervene to assist couples and families. Often, thinking seems to follow a dichotomous approach, framing the question as Do we test or not? This line of thinking seems to be stuck in the belief that testing means always using a battery of tests involving many professional hours and a high cost. As implied in this book, the more appropriate, realistic way of considering testing is to reflect on the case-related questions being asked and consider what the specific test results may potentially contribute to decision making and treatment planning. Then it would follow to weigh the cost of specific testing against the potential emotional and behavioral costs of errors in decision making without testing.

## Couple Relationships and Inventories

For some situations where a couple is functioning fairly well but is seeking to modify problematic interactions and improve their relationship, use of a marital report form of the 16PF may provide a sufficient basis to begin brief counseling in an expeditious manner. For another, more entrenched couple, the MCMI-III and/or the MMPI-2 may supply sufficient information for the therapist. However, a complex divorce situation involving children and apparent abuse, may call for an array of psychological tests and inventories to be administered by a psychologist skilled at a very high level with tests, understanding of families, and knowledge of features of divorce and abuse dynamics.

## Cost

In planning couple therapy, what may be overlooked is that for about a third of the cost of a single treatment hour, the clinician can obtain an interpretive printout of an inventory. And for about a third of *that* cost, a profile (without the interpretive printout) on an inventory (MMPI-2, MCMI-III) can be procured. This latter choice can be a particularly attractive option for the clinician experienced with these inventories and who has at hand pertinent references, books, and journals to facilitate a thorough personal interpretation. Thus, the use of inventories is truly cost-effective when the cost is balanced by what may be learned about a couple or family and how treatment may be improved and often shortened.

Of course, the use of a battery of tests with a family is costly because of the large number of professional hours involved. However, it is important to weigh the momentous nature of decisions to be considered with families in crisis, such as coparenting arrangements in divorce or supervised visitation in abuse situations. Any input from psychological test results that will help maximize the accuracy of interventions and avoid the emotional cost for children of a poor decision is worth the extra initial financial investment. Skimping here by not testing could be truly penny-wise and pound-foolish.

## Clinicians' Education, Training, and Supervision

This rational consideration for testing needs to be based on the potential for the contribution of testing to understanding and treating couples and families. This means that any therapist working with couples and families needs to have basic education and training in using inventories and tests. Supervision and/or consultation in the use of particular inventories is essential.

Couple and family therapists of the various mental health disciplines with education, training, and supervision along with supervision in the use of specific inventories will find the tests useful in planning treatment and as guides for conducting therapy. Couples can often make good use of skilled feedback. This background, plus professional knowledge of the specific assessment situation, such as couples communication or divorce, is a requirement for ethical practice. Of course, use of a projective measure such as the Rorschach requires much more specialized training and supervision to the extent only at present found regularly in the curriculum for the professional, doctoral-level psychologist.

## Some Limitations of This Volume and the Future of Family Assessment

With this plea for a thoughtful, considered use of traditional, time-honored psychological tests, it needs to be noted also that there are new clinical measures and normal-focus measures unexplored in this book that may expand the boundaries of testing and may address issues in new ways for testing couples and families. For example, the Personality Assessment Inventory (PAI; Morey, 1991) assesses adult psychopathology in an objective format that allows the client to rate items on a four-point scale. The NEO Personality Inventory–Revised (NEO PI-R; 1992) provides for adults measures of five normal personality domains that result from decades of personality structure research. Also aimed at the normal adult population is the Millon Index of Personality Styles (MIPS; 1994), with its basis in Theordore Millon's theoretical approach to personality. For adolescents, the MMPI-A (1992) stands out as a major tool developed in the tradition of the MMPI. Among the newer ones that may prove of considerable help in evaluating depression in children and adolescents in the family context is the Children's Depression Inventory (CDI; 1992) developed by Maria Kovacs.

There are also some relatively new scales designed to measure parent behavior and couple relationships. These include the Parent Stress Index (PSI, third edition, 1998), the Marital Satisfaction Inventory, Revised (MSI-R; 1998), the Bricklin Perceptual Scales (BPS; 1984), Perception of Relationships Test (PORT; 1989), and the Parent Awareness Skills Survey (PASS; 1990), designed for custody situations.

In addition to these new measures, there are many short scales of proven usefulness with a long history, such as the Beck Depression Inventory-II (BDI-II; 1996) and the Spielberger State-Trait Anxiety Inventory (STAI), which had an equal right to be included in this volume, had there been more space.

Utilization of cognitive measures, including intelligence tests, as applied to the family context were not within the purview of this book because it was designed to focus on traditional clinical personalty tests and inventories. However, with family assessment, the need for cognitive assessment may arise, particularly with children and adolescents. With children, adolescents, and adults who have been physically abused, concern for brain dysfunction or brain damage may call for neuropsychological testing.

The recommendation is that explorative use of these additional measures be undertaken in conjunction with the core traditional tests and inventories reviewed in this book. The extensive research and clinical knowledge accrued about these classical measures provides a solid base of information on which to build knowledge about new instruments, specific scales, and cognitive measures. Information gained on the newer scales, the cognitive tests, and the neuropsychological instruments can also enhance the usefulness of these core personality measures.

# References

Abel, G. G., Becker, J. V., Mittelman, M., Cunningham-Rathner, J., Rouleau, J. L., & Murphy, W. D. (1987). Self-reported sex crimes of nonincarcerated paraphiliacs. *Journal of Interpersonal Violence, 2,* 3–25.

Abel, G. G., Mittelman, M. S., & Becker, J. V. (1985). Sexual offenders: Results of assessment and recommendations for treatment. In M. R. Ben-Aron, S. J. Huckle, & C. D. Webster (Eds.), *Clinical criminology: The assessment and treatment of criminal behavior* (pp. 191–205). Toronto: M & M Graphic.

Abidin, R. (1998). Parenting stress index (PSI) (3rd ed.). In *Catalogue.* Odessa, FL: Psychological Assessment Resources.

Achenbach, T. M. (1991a). *Manual for the child behavior checklist: 4–18 and 1991 profile.* Burlington: University of Vermont Department of Psychiatry.

Achenbach, T. M. (1991b). *Manual for the teacher's report form and 1991 profile.* Burlington: University of Vermont Department of Psychiatry.

Achenbach, T. M. (1991c). *Manual for the youth self-report and 1991 profile.* Burlington: University of Vermont Department of Psychiatry.

Achenbach, T. M., McConaughy, S. H., & Howell, C. T. (1987). Child/adolescent behavioral and emotional problems: Implications of cross-informant correlations for situational specificity. *Psychological Bulletin, 101,* 213–232.

Ackerman, M. (1995). *Clinician's guide to child custody evaluations.* New York: Wiley.

Allport, G. (1937). *Personality: A psychological interpretation.* New York: Holt.

American Psychiatric Association. (1994). *Diagnostic and statistical manual of mental disorders* (4th ed.). Washington, DC: Author.

American Psychological Association. (1992). Ethical principles of psychologists and code of conduct. *American Psychologist, 47*(12), 1597–1611.

American Psychological Association Presidential Task Force on Violence and the Family. (1996). *Violence and the family.* Washington, DC: American Psychological Association.

Antoni, M. (1997). Integrating the MCMI and the MMPI. In T. Millon (Ed.), *The Millon instruments* (pp. 106–123). New York: Guilford Press.

Archer, R. P., Griffin, R., & Aiduk, R. (1995). MMPI-2 clinical correlates for ten common codes. *Journal of Personality Assessment, 65*(3), 491–507.

Armstrong, J. G., & Loewenstein, R. J. (1990). Characteristics of patients with multiple personality and dissociative disorders on psychological testing. *Journal of Nervous and Mental Disease, 178*, 448–454.

Bagby, R. M., Gillis, J. R., & Rogers, R. (1991). Effectiveness of the Millon Clinical Multiaxial Inventory validity index in the detection of random responding. *Psychological Assessment, 3*, 285–287.

Batthurst, K., Gottfried, A., & Gottfried, A. (1997). Normative data for the MMPI-2 in child custody litigation. *Psychological Assessment, 9*(3), 206–211.

Beck, A., Steer, R., & Brown, G. (1996). *Beck depression inventory—II*. New York: Psychological Corporation.

Becker, J. V., & Quinseg, V. L. (1993). Assessing suspected child molesters. *Child Abuse and Neglect, 17*, 169–194.

Ben-Porath, Y. S., & Tellegen, A. (1995). How not to evaluate the comparability of MMPI and MMPI-2 profile configurations. A reply to Humphrey and Dahlstrom. *Journal of Personality Assessment, 65*(1), 52–57.

Beutler, L., & Berren, M. (1995). *Integrative assessment of adult personality*. New York: Guilford Press.

Blake, S., Humphrey, L., & Feldman, L. (1994). Self-deliniation and marital interaction: The Rorschach predicts structural analysis of social behavior. *Journal of Personality Assessment, 63*(1), 148–166.

Boat, B. W. (1995). The relationship between violence to children and violence to animals: An ignored link? *Journal of Interpersonal Violence, 10*, 229–235.

Bradshaw, E., & Hinds, R. (1997). The impact of client and evaluator gender on custody evaluations. *Family and Conciliation Courts Review, 35*(3), 317–335.

Bremner, J. D., Southwick, S. M., Johnson, D. R., Yehuda, R., & Charney, D. S. (1993). Childhood physical abuse and combat related posttraumatic stress disorder in Vietnam veterans. *American Journal of Psychiatry, 150*, 235–239.

Bricklin, B. (1984). *Bricklin perceptual scales*. Doylestown, PA: Village.

Bricklin, B. (1989). *Perception-of-relationships-test*. Doylestown, PA: Village.

Bricklin, B. (1990). *Parent awareness skills survey*. Doylestown, PA: Village.

Briere, J. (1995). *TSI: Trauma symptom inventory: Professional manual*. Odessa, FL: Psychological Assessment Resources.

Briere, J. (1996). *TDCC: Trauma symptom checklist for children: Professional manual*. Odessa, FL: Psychological Assessment Resources.

Briere, J. (1997a). *Psychological assessment of adult posttraumatic states*. Washington, DC: American Psychological Association.

Briere, J. (1997b). Psychological assessment of child abuse effects in adults. In J. P. Wilson & T. M. Keane (Eds.), *Assessing psychological trauma and PTSD* (pp. 43–68). New York: Guilford Press.

Briere, J., Elliott, D. M., Harris, K., & Cotman, A. (1995). Trauma symptom inventory: Psychometrics and association with childhood and adult victimization in clinical samples. *Journal of Interpersonal Violence, 10,* 387–401.

Burns, R. (1982). *Self-growth in families: Kinetic family drawings (K-F-D) research and application.* New York: Brunner/Mazel.

Burns, R., & Kaufman, H. (1970). *Kinetic family drawings (K-F-D).* New York: Brunner/Mazel.

Burns, R., & Kaufman, H. (1972). *Actions, styles, and symbols in Kinetic family drawings (K-F-D).* New York: Brunner/Mazel.

Butcher, J. (1989). *User's guide/the Minnesota report: Adult clinical system, MMPI-2.* Minneapolis: National Computer Systems.

Butcher, J. (1990). *MMPI-2 in psychological treatment.* New York: Oxford University Press.

Butcher, J., Dahlstrom, G., Graham, J., Tellegen, A., & Kaemmer, B. (1989). *MMPI-2: Manual for administration and scoring.* Minneapolis: University of Minnesota Press.

Butcher, J., Morfitt, R., & Rouse, S. (1997). Reducing MMPI-2 defensiveness: The effect of specialized instructions on retest validity in a job applicant sample. *Journal of Personality Assessment, 68*(2), 385–401.

Butcher, J., Williams, C., Graham, J., Archer, R., Tellegen, A., Ben-Porath, Y., & Kaemmer, B. (1992). *MMPI-A: Manual for administration and scoring.* Minneapolis: University of Minnesota Press.

Caldwell, A. (1988). *MMPI supplemental scale manual.* Los Angles: Caldwell Report.

Caldwell, A. (1997a). *Forensic questions and answers on the MMPI/MMPI-2.* Los Angles: Caldwell Report.

Caldwell, A. (1997b). Whither goest our redoubtable mentor, the MMPI/MMPI-2? *Journal of Personality Assessment, 68*(1), 47–67.

Carlin, A. S., & Ward, N. G. (1992). Subtypes of psychiatric inpatient women who have been sexually abused. *Journal of Nervous and Mental Disease, 180,* 392–397.

Carlson, E. B. (1997). *Trauma assessments: A clinician's guide.* New York: Guilford Press.

Carlson, E. B., & Armstrong, J. (1994). Diagnosis and assessment of dissociative disorders. In S. J. Lynn & J. W. Rhue (Eds.), *Dissociation: Theoretical, clinical, and research perspectives* (pp. 159–174). New York: Guilford Press.

Carlson, E. B., & Putnam, F. W. (1993). An update on the Dissociative Experiences Scale. *Dissociation, 6,* 16–27.

Carlson, E. B., Putnam, F. W., Ross, C. A., Totem, M., Coons, P. M., Dill, D. L., Loewenstein, R. J., & Braun, B. G. (1993). Validity of the dissociative experiences scale in screening for multiple personality disorder: A multicenter study. *American Journal of Psychiatry, 150,* 1030–1036.

Carlson, J., & Sperry, L. (Eds.). (1998). *The disordered couple.* New York: Brunner/Mazel.

Carmen, E. H., Rieker, P. R., & Mills, T. (1984). Victims of violence and psychiatric illness. *American Journal of Psychiatry, 141,* 378–383.

Cattell, R. (1949). *Sixteen personality factor questionnaire.* Champaign, IL: Institute for Personality and Ability Testing.

Cattell, R., Cattell, A., & Cattell, H. (1993). *Sixteen personality factor questionnaire* (5th ed.). Champaign, IL: Institute for Personality and Ability Testing.

Cattell, R., Eber, H., & Tatsuoka, M. (1988). *Handbook for the sixteen personality factor questionnaire (16PF).* Champaign, IL: Institute for Personality and Ability Testing.

Cattell, R., & Nesselroade, J. (1967). Likeness and completeness theories examined by sixteen personality factor measures on stably and unstably married couples. *Journal of Personality and Social Psychology, 7*(4), 351–367.

Cattell, R., & Nesselroade, J. (1968). Note on analyzing personality relations in married couples. *Psychological Reports, 22,* 381–382.

Chandy, J. M., Blum, R. W., & Resnick, M. D. (1996). Gender-specific outcomes for sexually abused adolescents. *Child Abuse and Neglect, 20,* 1219–1231.

Choca, J., Stanley, L., & Van Denburg, E. (1992). *Interpretive guide to the Millon clinical multiaxial inventory.* Washington, DC: American Psychological Association.

Choca, J., & Van Denburg, E. (1997). *Interpretive guide to the Millon clinical multiaxial inventory* (2nd ed.). Washington, DC: American Psychological Association.

Cicchetti, D., & Toth, S. (Eds.). (1998). *The effects of trauma and the developmental process.* New York: Wiley.

Cole, P. M., & Putnam, F. W. (1992). Effect of incest on self and social functioning: A developmental psychopathology perspective. *Journal of Consulting and Clinical Psychology, 60,* 174–88.

Colligan, R. C., Osborne, D., Swenson, W. M., & Offord, K. P. (1993). *The MMPI: A contemporary normative study.* New York: Praeger.

Corcoran, K., & Fischer, J. (1987). *Measures for clinical practice.* New York: Free Press.

Costa, P., & McCrae, R. (1992). *The NEO PI-R.* Odessa, FL: Personality Assessment Resources.

Cowan, C., & Cowan, P. (1992). *When partners become parents: The big life change for couples.* New York: Basic Books.

Crimmins, S., Langley, S., Brownstein, H. H., & Spunt, B. J. (1997). Convicted women who have killed children: A self-psychology perspective. *Journal of Interpersonal Violence, 12,* 49–69.

Cross, T. P., & Saxe, L. (1992). A critique of the validity of polygraph testing in child sexual abuse cases. *Journal of Child Sexual Abuse, 14,* 19–33.

Dancu, C. V., Riggs, D. S., Hearst-Ikeda, D., Shoyer, B. G., & Foa, E. B. (1996). Dissociative experiences and posttraumatic stress disorder among female victims of criminal assault and rape. *Journal of Traumatic Stress, 9,* 253–267.

Dicks, H. (1967). *Marital tensions: Clinical studies towards a psychoanalytic theory of interaction.* London: Routledge & Kegan Paul.

Duckworth, J., & Anderson, W. (1986). *MMPI interpretation manual for counselors and clinicans.* Muncie, IN: Accelerated Development.

Dutton, D. G. (1994). Behavioral and affective correlates of borderline personality organization in wife assaulters. *International Journal of Law and Society, 17,* 265–279.

Dutton, D. G. (1995). Trauma symptoms and PTSD-like profiles in perpetrators of intimate abuse. *Journal of Traumatic Stress, 8,* 299–316.

Dyer, F. (1997). Application of the Millon inventories in forensic psychology. In T. Millon (Ed.), *The Millon inventories: Clinical and personality assessment.* New York: Guilford Press.

Edleson, J. L. (1998). Responsible mothers and invisible men: Child protection in the case of adult domestic violence. *Journal of Interpersonal Violence, 13,* 294–298.

Edleson, J. L. (in press). The overlap between child maltreatment and woman battering. *Violence Against Women.*

Ekman, P., & O'Sullivan, M. (1991). Who can catch a liar? *American Psychologist, 46,* 913–920.

Epstein, J. N., Saunders, B. E., & Kilpatrick, D. G. (1997). Predicting PTSD in women with a history of childhood rape. *Journal of Traumatic Stress, 10,* 573–588.

Exner, J. (1969). *The Rorschach systems.* New York: Grune & Stratton.

Exner, J. (1974). *The Rorschach: A comprehensive system* (Vol. 1). New York: Wiley.

Exner, J. (1991). *The Rorschach: A comprehensive system. Interpretation* (Vol. 2, 2nd ed.). New York: Wiley.

Exner, J. (1993). *The Rorschach: A comprehensive system. Basic foundations* (Vol. 1, 3rd ed.). New York: Wiley.

Exner, J., Armbruster, G., & Viglione, D. (1978). The temporal stability of some Rorschach features. *Journal of Personality Assessment, 42,* 474–482.

Exner, J., & Ona, N. (1995). *Rorschach interpretation assistance program, 3.1.* Odessa, FL: Psychological Assessment Resources.

Exner, J., & Sanglade, A. (1992). Rorschach changes following brief and short term therapy. *Journal of Personality Assessment, 59,* 59–71.

Exner, J., & Weiner, I. (1995). *The Rorschach: A comprehensive system: Assessment of children and adolescents* (Vol. 3, 2nd ed.). New York: Wiley.

Fagerstrom, K., Kalish, M., Nurse, A., Ross, N., Thompson, P., Wilde, D., & Wolfrum, T. (1997). *Divorce: A problem to be solved not a battle to be fought.* Orinda, CA: Brookwood.

Fairbairn, R. (1954). *An object relations theory of the personality.* New York: Basic Books.

Fals-Stewart, W., Birchler, G. R., Schafer, J., & Lucente, S. (1994). The personality of marital distress: An empirical typology. *Journal of Personality Assessment, 62*(2), 223–241.

Feldman, L. (1992). *Integrating individual and family therapy.* New York: Brunner/Mazel.

Finkelhor, D., & Berliner, L. (1995). Research on the treatment of sexually abused children: A review and recommendations. *Journal of the American Academy of Child and Adolescent Psychiatry, 34,* 1408–1423.

Finkelhor, D., & Browne, A. (1985). The traumatic impact of child sexual abuse: A conceptualization. *American Journal of Orthopsychiatry, 55,* 530–541.

Finn, S. (1993). *Using psychological assessment as a therapeutic intervention.* Continuing education workshop. Annual convention, Society for Personality Assessment, San Diego.

Finn, S. (1996). Assessment feedback integrating MMPI-2 and Rorschach findings. *Journal of Personality Assessment, 67*(3), 543–557.

Finn, S., & Tonsager, M. (1992). Therapeutic effects of providing MMPI-2 test feedback to college students awaiting psychotherapy. *Personality Assessment, 3,* 278–287.

Framo, J. (1982). Marriage therapy in a couples group. In J. Framo (Ed.), *Explorations in marital and family therapy* (pp. 141–151). New York: Springer.

Fredman, N., & Sherman, R. (1987). *Handbook of measurements for marriage & family therapy.* New York: Brunner/Mazel.

Friedrich, W. N. (1997). *CSBI: Child sexual behavior inventory: Professional manual.* Odessa, FL: Psychological Assessment Resources.

Friedrich, W. N., Jaworski, T. M., Huxsahl, J. E., & Bengston, B. S. (1997). Dissociative and sexual behaviors in children and adolescents with sexual abuse and psychiatric histories. *Journal of Interpersonal Violence, 12,* 155–170.

Gacomo, C., & Meloy, R. (1994). *The Rorschach assessment of aggressive and psychopathic personalities.* Hillsdale: Erlbaum.

Ganellen, R. J. (1996a). Comparing the diagnostic efficiency of the MMPI, MCMI-II, and Rorschach: A review. *Journal of Personality Assessment, 67*(2), 219–243.

Ganellen, R. J. (1996b). *Integrating the Rorschach and the MMPI-2 in personality assessment.* Mahwah, NJ: Erlbaum.

Gaston, L., Brunet, A., Koszycki, D., & Bradwejn, J. (1996). MPI profiles of acute and chronic PTSD in a civilian sample. *Journal of Traumatic Stress, 9,* 817–832.

Geffner, R. (1998, January). *Assessment of family violence and incest offenders: Forensic issues and practical techniques.* Workshop presented at the San Diego Conference on Responding to Child Maltreatment, San Diego, CA.

Gelles, R. J., & Loseke, D. R. (Eds.). (1993). *Current controversies in family violence.* Newbury Park: Sage.

Gerard, A. (1994). *Parent-child relationship inventory (PCRI).* Los Angles: Western Psychological Services.

Giaretto, H. (1982). *Integrated treatment of child sexual abuse: A treatment and training manual.* Palo Alto, CA: Science and Behavior Books.

Goldenberg, H., & Goldenberg, I. (1998). *Counseling today's families* (3rd ed.). Pacific Grove, CA: Brooks/Cole.

Gondolf, E. W. (1997). Batterer programs: What we know and need to know. *Journal of Interpersonal Violence, 12,* 83–98.

Gordon, L. (1988). *Heroes of their own lives. The politics and history of family violence.* New York: Viking Penguin.

Gottman, J. (1994). *Why marriages succeed or fail.* New York: Simon & Schuster.

Graham, J. R. (1990). *MMPI-2: Assessing personality and psychopathology.* New York: Oxford University Press.

Graham, J. R. (1993). *Assessing personality and psychopathology* (2nd ed.). New York: Oxford University Press.

Graham, J. R., Timbrook, R. E., Ben-Porath, Y. S., & Butcher, J. N. (1991). Code-type congruence between MMPI and MMPI-2: Separating fact from artifact. *Journal of Personality Assessment, 57,* 205–215.

Graham-Bermann, S. A., & Levendosky, A. A. (1998). Traumatic stress symptoms in children of battered women. *Journal of Interpersonal Violence, 13,* 111–128.

Greene, R. L. (1991). *The MMPI-2/MMPI: An interpretive manual.* Boston: Allyn & Bacon.

Groth, A. N. (1978). Pattern of sexual assault against children and adolescents. In A. W. Burgess, A. N. Groth, L. L. Holmstrom, & S. M. Sgroi (Eds.), *Sexual assault of children and adolescents* (pp. 3–24). Lexington, MA: Lexington Books.

Groth-Marnat, G. (1990). *Handbook of psychological assessment* (Rev. ed.). New York: Wiley.

Hamberger, L. K. (1993). Comments on Pagelow's myth of psychopathology in woman battering. *Journal of Interpersonal Violence, 8,* 132–136.

Hamberger, L. K., & Hastings, J. E. (1991). Personality correlates of men who batter and nonviolent men: Some continuities and discontinuities. *Journal of Interpersonal Violence, 6,* 131–148.

Handler, L., & Habenicht, D. (1994). The Kinetic family drawing technique: A review of the literature. *Journal of Personality Assessment, 63*(3), 440–464.

Harris, R. E., & Lingoes, J. C. (1955). *Subscales for the MMPI: An aid to profile interpretation.* Unpublished manuscript, University of California.

Hathaway, S. R., & McKinley, J. C. (1943). *The Minnesota multiphasic personality inventory.* Minneapolis: University of Minnesota Press.

Hedlund, J. L., & Won Cho, D. (1991). MMPI data research tape for Missouri department of mental health patients. In R. L. Greene (Ed.), *MMPI-2/MMPI: An interpretive manual.* Boston: Allyn & Bacon.

Hendrix, H. (1988). *Getting the love you want: A guide for couples.* New York: Harper-Collins.

Herman, J. L. (1990). Sex offenders: A feminist perspective. In W. L. Marshall, D. R. Laws, & H. E. Barbaree (Eds.), *Handbook of sexual assault: Issues, theories, and treatment of the offender.* New York: Plenum Press.

Herman, J. L. (1992). *Trauma and recovery.* New York: Basic Books.

Hjemboe, S. (1991). The marital distress scale (MDS). *MMPI-2 News & Profiles, 2*(1), 8–9.

Hodges, W. (1991). *Interventions for children of divorce: Custody, access, and psychotherapy.* New York: Wiley.

Holtzman, W. (1968). Holtzman inkblot technique. In A. I. Ragin (Ed.), *Projective techniques in personality assessment* (pp. 136–170). New York: Springer.

Humphrey, D. H., & Dahlstrom, W. C. (1995). The impact of changing from the MMPI to the MMPI-2 on profile configurations. *Journal of Personality Assessment, 64,* 428–439.

Institute for Personality and Ability Testing. (1998). *Catalogue.* Champaign: IPAT.

Ivey, D., & Conoley, C. (1994). Influence of gender in family evaluations: A comparison of trained and untrained observer perceptions of matriarchal and patriarchal family interviews. *Journal of Family Psychology, 8*(3), 336–346.

Jacobson, A. (1993). *A study of Kinetic family drawings of public school children, ages six through nine.* Unpublished doctoral dissertation, University of Cincinnati.

Jacobson, N. S., & Gottman, J. M. (1998). *When men batter women: New insights into ending abusive relationships.* New York: Simon & Schuster.

Jenkins, E. J., & Bell, C. C. (1994). Violence among inner city high school students and posttraumatic stress disorder. In S. Friedman (Ed.), *Anxiety disorders in African Americans.* New York: Springer.

Jensen, A. (1958). Personality. *Annual Review of Psychology, 9,* 395–422.

Johnson, S. (1987). As cited in M. Scarf, *Intimate partners: Patterns in love and marriage* (pp. 190–405). New York: Ballantine Books.

Johnston, J., & Roseby, V. (1997). *In the name of the child.* New York: Free Press.

Kaser-Boyd, N. (1993). Rorschachs of women who commit homicide. *Journal of Personality Assessment, 60,* 458–470.

Karol, D., & Russell, M. (1995). Summary of recent research: 16PF 5th edition questionnaire and relationship adjustment. In M. Russel (Ed.), *The 16PF fifth edition couple's counseling report user's guide* (pp. 23–49). Champaign, IL: Institute for Personality and Ability Testing.

Karson, S. (1985). *Interpretive hypotheses for the 16PF.* Unpublished report.

Karson, S., & O'Dell, J. (1976). *Clinical use of the 16 PF.* Champaign, IL: Institute for Personality and Ability Testing.

Kaslow, F. (1990). *Voices in family psychology* (Vol. 1). Newbury Park: Sage.

Kaufman, K. L., Wallace, A. M., Johnson, C. F., & Reeder, M. L. (1995). Comparing male and female perpetrators' modus operandi. *Journal of Interpersonal Violence, 10,* 322–333.

Kendall-Tackett, K. A., Williams, L. M., & Finkelhor, D. (1993). Impact of sexual abuse on children: A review and synthesis of recent empirical studies. *Psychological Bulletin, 113,* 164–180.

Khan, F. I., Welch, T. L., & Zillmer, E. A. (1993). MMPI-2 profiles of battered women in transition. *Journal of Personality Assessment, 60,* 100–111.

Klein, M. (1948). *Contributions to psychoanalysis, 1921–1945.* London: Hogarth Press.

Kolbo, J. R., Blakely, E. H., & Engleman, D. (1996). Children who witness domestic violence: A review of empirical literature. *Journal of Interpersonal Violence, 11,* 281–293.

Korchin, S. (1975). *Modern clinical psychology.* New York: Basic Books.

Kovacs, M. (1992). *Children's depression inventory.* Minneapolis: National Computer Systems.

Kunce, J., & Anderson, W. (1976). Normalizing the MMPI. *Journal of Clinical Psychology, 32,* 776–780.

Lanktree, C. B., & Briere, J. (1995). Outcome of therapy for sexually abused children: A repeated measures study. *Child Abuse and Neglect, 19,* 1145–1155.

Lawson, L., & Chaffin, M. (1992). False negatives in sexual abuse disclosure interviews. *Journal of Interpersonal Violence, 7,* 532–542.

Leavitt, F., & Labott, S. M. (1996). Authenticity of recovered sexual abuse memories: A Rorschach study. *Journal of Traumatic Stress, 9,* 483–496.

Lee, E., & Lu, F. (1989). Assessment and treatment of Asian-American survivors of mass violence. *Journal of Traumatic Stress, 2,* 93–120.

Leifer, M., Shapiro, J. P., Martone, M. W., & Kassem, L. (1991). Rorschach assessment of psychological functioning in sexually abused girls. *Journal of Personality Assessment, 56*(1), 14–28.

Levin, P. (1996, June). *Remarks on panel on efficacy of EMDR for trauma survivors as measured by the Rorschach.* Presented at the EMDR International Association Conference, Denver.

Levin, P., & Reis, B. (1997). Use of Rorschach in assessing trauma. In J. P. Wilson & T. M. Keane (Eds.), *Assessing psychological trauma and PTSD* (pp. 529–543). New York: Guilford Press.

Malamuth, N. M., Sockloskie, R. J., Koss, M. P., & Tanaka, J. S. (1991). Characteristics of aggressors against women: Testing a model using a national sample of college students. *Journal of Consulting and Clinical Psychology, 59,* 670–681.

Marsella, A. J., Friedman, M. J., & Spain, E. H. (1996). Ethnocultural aspects of PTSD: An overview of issues and research directions. In A. J. Marsella, M. J. Friedman, E. T. Gerrity, & R. M. Scurfield (Eds.), *Ethnocultural aspects of posttraumatic stress disorder: Issues, research, and clinical applications* (pp. 105–129). Washington, DC: American Psychological Association.

Masson, J. (1984). *The assault on truth: Freud's suppression of the seduction theory.* New York: Farrar, Strauss, & Giroux.

McCann, J. (1997). The MACI: Composition and clinical applications. In T. Millon (Ed.), *The Millon instruments* (pp. 363–388). New York: Guilford Press.

McCann, J. T., & Dyer, F. J. (1996). *Forensic assessment with the Millon inventories.* New York: Guilford Press.

Mikesell, R., Lusterman, D., & McDaniel, S. (1995). *Integrating family therapy: A handbook of family psychology and systems theory.* Washington, DC: American Psychological Association.

Millon, T. (1977). *Manual for the Millon multiaxial inventory (MCMI).* Minneapolis: National Computer Systems.

Millon, T. (1981). *Disorders of personality: DSM-III, Axis II.* New York: Wiley.

Millon, T. (1993). *Millon adolescent clinical inventory (MACI) manual.* Minneapolis: National Computer Systems.

Millon, T. (1994a). *Millon clinical multiaxial inventory-III manual.* Minneapolis: National Computer Systems.

Millon, T. (1994b). *Millon index of personality styles.* New York: Psychological Corporation.

Millon, T. (1996). *Disorders of personality: DSM-IV and beyond.* New York: Wiley.

Millon, T. (1997a). *Manual for the Millon multiaxial clinical inventory-III (MCMI-III).* Minneapolis: National Computer Systems.

Millon, T. (Ed.). (1997b). *The Millon instruments.* New York: Guilford Press.

Millon, T., Green, C., & Meagher, R. (1982). *Millon adolescent personality inventory manual.* Minneapolis: National Computer Systems.

Millon, T., & Klerman, G. (1986). *Contemporary directions in psychopathology: Toward the DSM-IV.* New York: Guilford Press.

Moos, R., & Moos, B. (1976). A typology of family social environments. *Family Process, 15,* 357–372.

Morey, L. C. (1991). *Personality assessment inventory: Professional manual.* Odessa, Fl: Psychological Assessment Resources.

Munley, P. H., Bains, D. S., Bloem, W. D., & Busby, R. M. (1995). Post-traumatic stress disorder and the MMPI-2. *Journal of Traumatic Stress, 8,* 171–178.

Myers, I. (1962). *Myers-Briggs type indicator.* Palo Alto: Consulting Psychologists Press.

Myers, J. E. B., Bays, J., Becker, J., Berliner, L., Corwin, D. L., & Saywitz, K. J. (1989). Expert testimony in child sexual abuse litigation. *Nebraska Law Review, 68,* 1–145.

National Computer Systems. (1997). *Catalogue.* Minneapolis: NCS.

Nichols, M. (1987). *The self in the system.* New York: Brunner/Mazel.

Norris, F. H., & Riad, J. K. (1997). Standardized self-report measures of civilian trauma and posttraumatic stress disorder. In J. P. Wilson & T. M. Keane (Eds.), *Assessing psychological trauma and PTSD* (pp. 7–42). New York: Guilford Press.

Nurse, A. R. (1993). Family psychologist as family consultant. *Family Psychologist, 9*(1), 24–45.

Nurse, A. R. (1996). The cardboard kids. *Family Psychologist, 13,* 22–23.

Nurse, A. R. (1997a). The dependent/narcissistic couple. In J. Carlson & L. Sperry (Eds.), *The disordered couple.* New York: Brunner/Mazel.

Nurse, A. R. (1997b). Using the MCMI in treating couples. In T. Millon (Ed.), *The Millon instruments.* New York: Guilford Press.

Nurse, A. R., & Thompson, P. (1997). Collaborative divorce: Oxymoron or a new process? *Family Psychologist, 13*(2), 21–25.

Nurse, A. R., Thompson, P., Wolfrum, T., & Wilde, D. (1998). *Collaborative divorce: A humane approach for an (often) inhumane process.* Presented at the American Psychological Association Annual Convention, San Francisco.

O'Dell, A. (1998, January). *Children in family violence: Caught in the crossfire.* Workshop presented at the San Diego Conference on Child Maltreatment, San Diego, CA.

Olafson, E., & Boat, B. W. (in press). Long-term management of the sexually abused child: Considerations and challenges. In R. M. Reece (Ed.), *The treatment of child abuse.* Baltimore: Johns Hopkins University Press.

Pagelow, M. D. (1992). Adult victims of domestic violence: Battered women. *Journal of Interpersonal Violence, 7,* 87–120.

Pagelow, M. D. (1993). Response to Hamberger's comments. *Journal of Interpersonal Violence, 8,* 137–139.

Perry, B. D. (1994). Neurobiological sequelae of childhood trauma: Posttraumatic stress disorder in children. In M. M. Murburg (Ed.), *Catecholamine function in posttraumatic stress disorder: Emergin concepts.* Washington, DC: American Psychiatric Press.

Perry, B. D., Pollard, R. A., Blakely, T. L., Baker, W., & Vigilante, D. (1996). Childhood trauma, the neurobiology of adaptation and "use-dependent" development of the brain: How "states" become "traits." *Infant Mental Health Journal, 16,* 271–291.

Philpot, C. (1991). Gender-sensitive couples' therapy: A systemic definition. *Journal of Family Psychotherapy, 2*(3), 19–40.

Philpot, C. (1994). A history of the division of family psychology from 1984–1994. *Family Psychologist, 10*(3), 10–17.

Philpot, C., & Brooks, G. (1995). Intergender communication and gender-sensitive family therapy. In R. Mikesell, D. Lusterman, & S. McDaniel (Eds.), *Integrating family therapy: Handbook of family psychology and systems theory* (pp. 303–325). Washington, DC: APA Books.

Philpot, C., Brooks, G., Lusterman, D., & Nutt, R. (1997). *Bridging separate gender worlds.* Washington, DC: APA Books.

Putnam, F. W. (1997a, November). *Clinical implications of longitudinal research on childhood sexual abuse.* Paper presented at the meeting of the International Society for Traumatic Stress Studies, Montreal, Canada.

Putnam, F. W. (1997b). *Dissociation in children and adolescents: A developmental perspective.* New York: Guilford Press.

Putnam, F. W., Helmers, L. A., & Trickett, P. K. (1993). Development, reliability and validity of a child dissociation scale. *Child Abuse and Neglect, 17,* 645–655.

Putnam, F. W., & Peterson, G. (1994). Further validation of the child dissociative checklist. *Dissociation, 7,* 204–211.

Putnam, F. W., & Trickett, P. K. (1993). Child sexual abuse: A model of complex trauma. *Psychiatry, 56,* 82–95.

Putnam, F. W., & Trickett, P. K. (1997). The psychobiological effects of sexual abuse: A longitudinal study. *Annals of the New York Academy of Sciences, 821,* 150–159.

Retzlaff, P. (1995). *Tactical psychotherapy of the personality disorders (An MCMI-III-based approach).* Boston: Allyn & Bacon.

Reynolds, D., & Kamphaus, F. (1992). *Manual for behavior assessment system for children* (BASC). Circle Pines, MN: American Guidance Service.

Rorschach, H. (1921/1942). *Psychodiagnostics.* Bern: Verlag Hans Huber.

Roseby, V., Erdberg, P., Bardenstein, K., & Johnston, J. R. (1995, March). *Developmental psychopathology in high-conflict families: Attachment, personality disorders and the Rorschach.* Paper presented at the Society for Research in Child Development, Kansas City, KS.

Roth, S., Newman, E., Pelcovitz, D., van der Kolk, B., & Mandel, F. S. (1997). Complex PTSD in victims exposed to sexual and physical abuse: Results from the DSM-IV field trial for posttraumatic stress disorder. *Journal of Traumatic Stress, 10,* 539–555.

Russell, M. (1995). *The 16PF fifth edition couple's counseling report user's guide.* Champaign, IL: Institute for Personality and Ability Testing.

Russell, M., & Karol, D. (1994). *16PF fifth edition administrator's manual.* Champaign, IL: Institute for Personality and Ability Testing.

Salter, A. C. (1988). *Treating child sex offenders and victims: A practical guide.* Newbury Park, CA: Sage.

Salter, A. C. (1995). *Transforming trauma: A guide to understanding and treating adult survivors of child sexual abuse.* Thousand Oaks, CA: Sage.

Satir, V. (1967). *Peoplemaking.* Palo Alto, CA: Science and Behavior Books.

Saunders, E. A. (1991). Rorschach indicators of chronic childhood abuse in female borderline patients. *Bulletin of the Menninger Clinic, 55,* 48–71.

Saunders, R. T., Gindes, M., Bray, J., Shellenberger, S., & Nurse, A. R. (1996). Should psychotherapists be concerned about the new APA child custody guidelines? *Psychotherapy, 31*(3), 28–35.

Scarf, M. (1987). *Intimate partners: Patterns in love and marriage.* New York: Ballantine Books.

Scharff, D., & Scharff, J. (1991). *Object relations family therapy.* Northvale, NJ: Jason Aronson.

Schlenger, W. E., Kulka, R. A., Fairbank, J. A., Hough, R. L., Jordan, B. K., Marmar, C., & Weiss, D. S. (1989). *The prevalence of post-traumatic stress disorder in the Vietnam generation: Findings from the National Vietnam Veterans Readjustment study.* Research Triangle Park, NC: Research Triangle Institute.

Schwartz, L., & Kaslow, F. (1997). *Painful partings: Divorce and its aftermath.* New York: Wiley.

Shapiro, F. (1995). *Eye movement desensitization and reprocessing.* New York: Guilford Press.

Slipp, S. (1984). *Object relations: A dynamic bridge between individual and family treatment.* New York: Aronson.

Slipp, S. (1991). *The technique and practice of object relations family therapy.* Northvale, NJ: Jason Aronson.

Snyder, D. (1998). *Marital satisfaction inventory–revised.* Los Angles: Western Psychological Services.

Sorenson, T., & Snow, B. (1991). How children tell: The process of disclosure in child sexual abuse. *Child Welfare, 70,* 3–15.

Spanier, G. (1976). Measuring dyadic adjustment: New scales for assessing the quality of marriage and similar dyads. *Journal of Marriage and the Family, 38,* 15–28.

Sperry, L., & Maniacci, M. (1988). The histrionic-obsessive couple. In J. Carlson & L. Sperry (Eds.), *The disordered couple*. New York: Brunner/Mazel.

Spielberger, C. (1991). *State-trait anger expression inventory, professional manual.* Odessa: Psychological Assessment Resources.

Spielberger, C. (1998). *State-trait anxiety inventory (STAI)*. Catalogue of professional testing resources. Odessa, FL: Psychological Assessment Resources.

Stahl, P. (1994). *Conducting child custody evaluations*. Thousand Oaks, CA: Sage.

Straus, M. A., & Gelles, R. J. (Eds.). (1990). *Physical violence in American families: Risk factors and adaptations to violence in 8,145 families.* New Brunswick, NJ: Transaction.

Stricker, G., & Trierweiler, S. (1995). The local clinical scientist: A bridge between science and practice. *American Psychologist, 50,* 995–1002.

Strupp, H. (1990). Preface. In J. N. Butcher (Ed.), *MMPI-2 in psychological treatment*. New York: Oxford University Press.

Summit, R. (1988). Hidden victims, hidden pain: Societal avoidance of child sexual abuse. In G. E. Wyatt & G. J. Powell (Eds.), *Lasting effects of child sexual abuse* (pp. 39–60). Newbury Park, CA: Sage.

Swann, W. B., Jr. (1983). Self-verification: Bringing social reality into harmony with the self. In J. Suls & A. G. Greenwood (Eds.), *Social psychological perspectives on the self* (Vol. 2). Hillsdale, NJ: Erlbaum.

Tellegen, A., & Ben-Porath, Y. S. (1993). Code-type comparability of the MMPI and MMPI-2: Analysis of recent findings and criticisms. *Journal of Personality Assessment, 61,* 489–500.

Thompson, L. (1975). *Kinetic family drawings of adolescents.* Unpublished doctoral dissertation, California School of Professional Psychology, San Francisco.

Tolman, R. M., & Bennett, L. W. (1990). A review of quantitative research on men who batter. *Journal of Interpersonal Violence, 5,* 87–118.

Trickett, P. K., & Putnam, F. W. (1993). Impact of child sexual abuse on females: Toward a developmental, psychobiological integration. *American Psychological Society, 4,* 81–87.

van der Kolk, B. A., & Ducey, C. (1989). The psychological processing of traumatic experience: Rorschach patterns in PTSD. *Journal of Traumatic Stress, 2,* 259–263.

Wachtel, E., & Wachtel, P. (1986). *Family dynamics in individual therapy.* New York: Guilford Press.

Weiner, I. B. (1994). The Roschach inkblot method (RIM) is not a test: Implications for theory and practice. *Journal of Personality Assessment, 62(3),* 498–504.

Weiner, I. B., & Exner, J. (1991). Rorschach changes in long-term and short-term psychotherapy. *Journal of Personality Assessment, 56,* 453–465.

Western Psychological Services. (1997–1998). *Catalogue.* Los Angles: Western Psychological Services.

Wilson, C. (1998). Are battered women responsible for protection of their children in domestic violence cases? *Journal of Interpersonal Violence, 13,* 289–293.

Wilson, J. P., & Keane, T. M. (Eds.). (1997). *Assessing psychological trauma and PTSD.* New York: Guilford Press.

Winnicott, D. (1965). *The maturational processes and the facilitating environment.* London: Hogarth Press.

Wolak, J., & Finkelhor, D. (1998). Children exposed to partner violence. In J. L. Jaskinski & L. M. Williams (Eds.), *Partner violence: A comprehensive review of 20 years of research.* Thousand Oaks, CA: Sage.

Yillo, D., & Bograd, M. (Eds.). (1988). *Feminist perspectives on wife abuse.* Newbury Park, CA: Sage.

Zinner, J., & Shapiro, R. (1972). Projective identification as a mode of perception and behavior in families of adolescents. *International Journal of Psycho-Analysis, 53,* 523–530.

Zinner, J., & Shapiro, R. (1975). Splitting in families of borderline adolescents. In J. Mack (Ed.), *Borderline states in psychiatry.* New York: Grune & Stratton.

Zlotnick, C., Zabriski, A. L., Shea, M. T., Costello, E., Begin, A., Pearlstein, T., & Simpson, E. (1996). The long-term sequelae of sexual abuse: Support for a complex posttraumatic stress disorder. *Journal of Traumatic Stress, 9,* 195–205.

# Author Index

Abel, G. G., 246, 247
Abidin, R., 293
Achenbach, T. M., 250, 251
Ackerman, M., 257, 262, 263, 266
Aiduk, R., 14
Allport, G., 102
Anderson, W., 182
Antoni, M., 177, 178, 179
Archer, R., 4, 14
Armbruster, G., 107
Armstrong, J., 238, 242, 252

Bagby, R. M., 144
Bains, D. S., 238, 239
Baker, W., 233, 236
Bardenstein, K., 271, 272, 284, 286
Bathurst, K., 199, 260, 261
Bays, J., 246
Beck, A., 292
Becker, J., 246, 247
Begin, A., 234
Bell, C. C., 235
Bengston, B. S., 252
Bennett, L. W., 247, 248
Ben-Porath, Y., 4, 13
Berliner, L., 231, 246
Berren, M., 34, 202, 205
Beutler, L., 34, 202, 205
Birchler, G. R., 14, 17, 21, 22, 25, 26, 27
Blake, S., 105
Blakely, E. H., 235, 249
Blakely, T. L., 233, 236
Bloem, W. D., 238, 239
Blum, R. W., 236
Boat, B. W., 234, 236
Bograd, M., 231
Bradshaw, E., 197
Bradwejn, J., 239
Braun, B. G., 245
Bray, J., 195

Bremner, J. D., 233
Bricklin, B., 292
Briere, J., 4, 153, 232, 233, 234, 236, 238, 239, 240, 241, 242, 243, 244, 252, 253, 255
Brooks, G., 80, 161
Brown, G., 292
Browne, A., 234
Brownstein, H. H., 249
Brunet, A., 239
Burns, R., 4, 124, 125, 126, 127
Busby, R. M., 238, 239
Butcher, J., 3, 4, 9, 10, 11, 12, 13, 14, 16, 21, 25, 30, 181, 199, 260, 261

Caldwell, A., 11, 13, 261, 262
Carlin, A. S., 239
Carlson, E. B., 232, 236, 237, 238, 239, 242, 243, 245, 252
Carlson, J., 14, 264
Carmen, E. H., 235
Cattell, A., 4, 62, 63
Cattell, H., 4, 62, 63
Cattell, R., 4, 62, 63, 65, 77, 81, 82, 83, 84, 86
Chaffin, M., 236
Chandy, J. M., 236
Charney, D. S., 233
Choca, J., 39, 59, 61
Cicchetti, D., 233
Cole, P. M., 239
Colligan, R. C., 27
Conoley, C., 196
Coons, P. M., 245
Corcoran, K., 158
Corwin, D. L., 246
Costa, P., 296
Costello, E., 234
Cotman, A., 244
Cowan, C., 43

309

# Subject Index